SEE HOW YOUR COLLEGE EXPERIENCE STUDY SKILLS EDITION CAN HELP STUDENTS...

1 ▸ PRACTICE SKILLS

2 ▸ SUCCEED

3 ▸ STAY IN COLLEGE

Designed specifically for first-year study skills courses, *Your College Experience*, Study Skills Edition, teaches students the essentials of academic success through ample in-text exercises. The newest edition in the best-selling first-year franchise by **John N. Gardner** and **Betsy O. Barefoot**, this text is designed to help students both engage in the course material and apply the skills learned to their other academic courses. This text will help students with managing time, preparing for class, developing critical textbook-reading strategies, improving note taking, and preparing for and taking tests. Look to this affordable text to guide students through the first year and beyond.

Your College Experience · Study Skills Edition
John N. Gardner · Betsy O. Barefoot
© 2013 · Paperback · 288 pages

Brief Table of Contents

A Complete Package of Instructor Support Materials, Including . . .

Instructor's Annotated Edition

The Instructor's Manual with Test Bank (available in print or online)

- Over 200 **NEW** test questions

- Over 400 total multiple-choice, true/false, short-answer, and essay questions

- **NEW** midterm and final exams

- **NEW** assessment tests

- **NEW** *Guide to Using YouTube to Teach with Your College Experience* to help you select videos for every topic

- Teaching suggestions, exercises, and activities

Computerized Test Bank

Instructor's Web Site

***PowerPoint* Slides**
Complete lecture outlines for each chapter of the book including images and figures from the text. Use as is or add your own material to make each presentation your own.

For more information

- Visit **bedfordstmartins.com/ newcollegesuccess.**

- Speak with your Bedford/St. Martin's sales rep.

1 THIS BOOK HELPS STUDENTS PRACTICE SKILLS

NEW! Guided-reading prompts and exercises help students master concepts.

Making Sure Your Schedule Works for You

Looking over your class schedule, do you see any opportunities for extra study? Do you have too many classes back-to-back or too many in one day? Does this schedule work for you and your life outside of college?

As a first-year student, you might not have had much flexibility in determining your course schedule; by the time you were allowed to register for classes, some sections of the

Focus questions begin each section of the text to reinforce learning objectives and help students with guided reading. Focus questions are a great way to reinforce the Cornell Note-Taking Method.

◄ ◄ ◄ ◄

Practice exercises follow each section of the book and provide point-of-use reinforcement of concepts. ► ► ► ►

EXERCISE 1.4
What You QUESTION Matters

Take a moment to rank the outcomes of the college experience as listed on page 13 of this section. Which ones are most important to you? Which ones are least important? Your ranking reflects your values, things that you consider essential to life. There is no right or wrong answer; the lists can be in any order, depending on your life circumstances. Also, your rankings may change as your experiences change.

Rankings—with 1 being the most important

1. _____
2. _____
3. _____

APPLY IT! What Works for YOU Matters

Think about your current academic situation, and apply some of the suggestions and strategies introduced in this chapter. Select those strategies that you think will work best for you, and then write them down in the "Your Response" column. What are YOU planning to do for YOUR college experience?

Apply It! exercises at the end of each chapter ask students to use the strategies introduced in the chapter in another academic course.

◄ ◄ ◄ ◄

QUESTIONS	SAMPLE STUDENT ANSWERS	YOUR RESPONSE
	Name: Stan Smith	
The College Experience People choose to attend college for many reasons. What are your top three reasons?	To get a degree and make money To please my parents To learn new skills	
Setting Goals for Your College Experience and Beyond Without a clear set of goals, people tend to get off track and sometimes never complete the most important tasks. What, if anything, prevents you from obtaining your goals?	I am not an early morning person, so my 8:00 a.m. class is really hard for me. Because I am working until midnight every night, I am too tired to concentrate early in the morning. I think I will try to work a different shift so I can get more rest. Also, I will not register for another 8:00 a.m. class.	
Aligning Your Sense of Purpose and Your Career What can you do to begin researching college majors and careers?	I want to know more about what I can do with a degree in biology. I am planning to meet with my academic adviser, but recently someone told me to see a career adviser too. I will make time for this next week.	
Outcomes of College College is not just about getting a degree. What else do you hope to gain from a college education? In other words, what do you value in addition to earning your diploma?	Besides the obvious (getting a good job after college), I also feel that with my college degree, people will take me more seriously. I will prove to myself that I can do this, even though I am	

2 THIS BOOK HELPS STUDENTS SUCCEED

New features throughout the text help students further engage in the course.

Assessing Your Strengths & Setting Goals boxes in each chapter ask students to identify their strengths and then set goals around their own objectives for the chapter material. This helps students stay engaged throughout the course. ▶▶▶▶

ASSESSING YOUR STRENGTHS

Time management is a challenge for almost all college students. Are you a good time manager? Now that you have read the first section of this chapter, list the strengths you have in this area.

_____

_____

_____

_____

SETTING GOALS

What are your most important objectives in learning the material in this chapter? Think about challenges you have had in the past with managing your time. List three goals that relate to time management (e.g., I will keep an hour-by-hour record this week of how I spend my time).

1. _____

_____

2. _____

---

1 COLLABORATIVE ACTIVITY

Dust off your acting skills and be prepared to demonstrate the WRONG way to act in a college classroom!

Review the list of 5 behaviors you created with your partners in Exercise 2.4. Choose one or two and demonstrate these behaviors to the class as a whole. Ask the class to identify the behavior. Your instructor is not exempt. Have him or her demonstrate the WRONG way for an instructor to behave as well.

You might wish to set some classroom guidelines for your cla[...] vested interest in your education and should advocate for th[...] possible.

Collaborative Activities at the end of each chapter provide students with strategies to use with their classmates and study groups.

TECH TIP STAY CONNECTED

Whatever your communication MO—smart phone, Facebook, or wiki—cyber etiquette is crucial. Just because you're hiding behind a computer screen doesn't mean that you should abandon your classroom manners. Failure to treat your fellow students and instructors with respect will brand you as an ignorant boor. Would you want to share a chat room with someone who writes in all caps (the digital equivalent of shouting) and belittles others' opinions? No one else does either. Emotional intelligence means being aware of your own and others' feelings. Transpose that mantra to your online world and you're good to go.

1 THE PROBLEM
There's a brave new world of ways to communicate in college, and you feel like you're from another planet.

2 THE FIX
Learn the nuts and bolts of connecting through cyberspace. If you still have questions, at least you'll have a good idea of what you're talking about.

3 HOW TO DO IT

1. E-mail: The most popular way to communicate online. If you have internet access, you can send e-mail messages galore, free of charge.

2. Texting: Just like passing notes, only it's done between smart phones or other mobile devices. Downside: You have to pay a small fee for the service.

3. Instant messaging: Also like passing notes, but via desktop computers and laptops. Upside: Like e-mail, it's free.

4. Blogs: Informal Web sites made up of journal entries, articles, and other posts. Note: Blogs can only be modified by their authors, and they can reflect biased or even uninformed viewpoints.

5. Wikis: Blogs that invite the world to weigh in on a subject. Visitors can share their knowledge by adding new entries or modifying or deleting old ones. Note: Unlike blogs, wikis often pop up through search engines like Google.

6. Online social networks: Web sites that let people share opinions, photos, music, and videos with other registered members of the group.

7. Chat rooms: Cybersites people can join to "talk" (i.e., type to one another on keyboards) in real time.

8. Web conference: An online meeting between two or more people. Participants often speak to each other via Web-camera (à la Skype) and can even work on documents or presentations together.

A FEW WORDS ABOUT TECHNOLOGY OVERLOAD

Apply extreme caution when researching an essay online and simultaneously fielding nonstop phone calls, text messages, e-mails, and Facebook updates *and* listening to your iPod: Your brain might explode. Well, not really, but even digital natives need to unplug once in a while.

Excessive multitasking raises your stress levels. It also dulls your powers of concentration, so your work suffers. Experts recommend not trying to do more than two complex tasks at once. And remember: In days of yore, students were happy to go somewhere quiet and read a book, or simply take a walk and think. For a little brain refreshment, why not step away from your gadgets and give one of these old-school, low-tech concepts a whirl?

NEW! Tech Tip features in every ▶▶▶▶ chapter introduce essential skills—such as cyber etiquette in this example—that can span the classroom and real life.

Bedford/St. Martin's is proud to offer a complete package of instructor support materials, including an Instructor's Annotated Edition with strategies and activities to help you teach this course. For more on instructor materials, see the first page.

NEW! The Instructor's Annotated Edition includes clearly marked **Retention Strategies** in every chapter: best practices from John Gardner and Betsy Barefoot for keeping students in school. ▼

> ■ RETENTION STRATEGY: Students who are easily frustrated and make impulsive decisions may give up on college. Encourage any student who expresses the wish to drop out or transfer to have a one-to-one discussion with you or a counselor before taking that step.

NEW! This 12-page insert appears at the beginning of the Instructor's Annotated Edition and includes ▶ ▶ ▶ new retention-specific **Active Learning Strategies**, as well as other chapter-specific activities that help with writing, critical thinking, working in groups, planning, reflecting, and taking action.

For more information

- Visit **bedfordstmartins.com/ newcollegesuccess.**

- Speak with your Bedford/ St. Martin's sales rep.

---

62 CHAPTER 3 Understanding Emotional Intelligence

IN CLASS: Ask students to describe the behaviors of a really successful student and one who is not successful. Keep a running tally in two columns on a blackboard or projection screen. Encourage the students to be as specific as they can be when describing each behavior, and ask them to consider behaviors both in and out of the classroom. When the list is complete, ask the class as a group to develop a list of the top eight behaviors of a successful student and those of a not-so-successful student. How do those behaviors relate to the EI competencies described on pages 54–57?

THE STANFORD MARSHMALLOW STUDY

Impulse Controlled	Impulsive
> Assertive	> Indecisive
> Cope with frustration	> Overreact to frustration
> Work better under pressure	> Overwhelmed by stress
> Self-reliant, confident	> Lower self-image
> Trustworthy	> Stubborn
> Dependable	> Impulsive
> Delay gratification	> Don't delay gratification
> Academically competent	> Poorer students
> Respond to reason	> Prone to jealousy and envy
> Concentrate	> Provoke arguments
> Eager to learn	> Sharp temper
> Follow through on plans	> Give up in face of failure
> SAT: 610 verbal, 652 math	> SAT: 524 verbal, 528 math

Source: Y. Shoda, W. Mischel, and P. K. Peake, "Predicting Adolescent Cognitive and Self-Regulatory Competencies from Preschool Delay of Gratification," *Developmental Psychology* 26, no. 6 (1990): 978–86.

had better confidence, concentration, and reliability; held better-paying jobs; and reported being more satisfied with life. The chart above details the differences between the two groups of students after fourteen years.

■ **EI skills can be enhanced in a first-year seminar.** In two separate studies, one conducted in Australia and another conducted in the United States, researchers found that college students enrolled in a first-year seminar who demonstrated good EI skills were more likely to do better in college than students who did not exhibit those behaviors. A follow-up study indicated that the students who had good EI skills also raised their scores on a measure of EI.

Without strong EI in college, it is possible to do well enough to get by,

IN CLASS: Ask the students to think about this course, its content, and its in-class activities. What have they been doing in this class—or could do more of—that might help them develop their EI skills?

■ RETENTION STRATEGY: Students who are easily frustrated and make impulsive decisions may give up on college. Encourage any student who expresses the wish to drop out

---

ACTIVE LEARNING STRATEGIES

The following exercises, which do not appear in the student edition, will help your students sharpen their critical skills for college success: writing, critical thinking, learning in groups, planning, reflecting, and taking action. Your students can also further explore the topics of each chapter by completing the exercises on this text's Web site at **bedfordstmartins.com/ycestudyskills.**

CHAPTER 1

WORKING TOGETHER The Many Reasons for College

Have your students form small groups to discuss the reasons for attending college, which were covered in this chapter. In the groups, have students share the reasons that seem most relevant to them. Each group should compile a list of the most important reasons and discuss their lists as a class with you as the leader. What did each student learn about himself or herself? What did you learn about each student's priorities?

EXERCISE 1.1 Solving a Problem

Ask your students to respond to the following questions in class or in an e-mail to you: What has

____ International fame
____ Freedom within my work setting
____ A good love relationship
____ A satisfying religious faith
____ Recognition as an attractive person
____ An understanding of the meaning of life
____ Success in my profession
____ A personal contribution to the elimination of poverty and sickness
____ A chance to direct the destiny of a nation
____ Freedom to do what I want
____ A satisfying and fulfilling marriage

(Adapted from Human Potential Seminar by James D. McHolland, Evanston, IL, 1975. Used by permission of the author.)

FOR INSTRUCTORS ONLY

ACTIVE LEARNING STRATEGIES

The following exercises, which do not appear in the student edition, will help your students sharpen their critical skills for college success: writing, critical thinking, learning in groups, planning, reflecting, and taking action. Your students can also further explore the topics of each chapter by completing the exercises on this text's Web site at **bedfordstmartins.com/ycestudyskills**.

CHAPTER 1

WORKING TOGETHER The Many Reasons for College

Have your students form small groups to discuss the reasons for attending college that were covered in this chapter. In the groups, have students share the reasons that seem most relevant to them. Each group should compile a list of the most important reasons and discuss their lists as a class with you as the leader. What did each student learn about himself or herself? What did you learn about each student's priorities?

EXERCISE 1.1 Solving a Problem

Ask your students to respond to the following questions in class or in an e-mail to you: What has been your biggest unresolved problem in college to date? What steps have you taken to solve it? Respond to students personally, and if they still have questions, invite them to meet with you during office hours.

EXERCISE 1.2 What Are Your Life Goals?

The following list includes some life goals that people set for themselves. This list can help students begin to think about the kinds of goals they might want to set. Ask students to put a check mark next to each of the goals they would like to achieve in their lives. Next, they should review the goals they have checked and circle the five they want most. Finally, students should review their list of five goals and rank them by priority on a 1-to-5 scale: 1 for most important, 5 for least important. Discuss the choices in class. Download a copy of this list at **bedfordstmartins.com/ycestudyskills**.

_____ The love and admiration of friends

_____ Good health

_____ Lifetime financial security

_____ A lovely home

_____ International fame

_____ Freedom within my work setting

_____ A good love relationship

_____ A satisfying religious faith

_____ Recognition as an attractive person

_____ An understanding of the meaning of life

_____ Success in my profession

_____ A personal contribution to the elimination of poverty and sickness

_____ A chance to direct the destiny of a nation

_____ Freedom to do what I want

_____ A satisfying and fulfilling marriage

(Adapted from Human Potential Seminar by James D. McHolland, Evanston, IL, 1975. Used by permission of the author.)

EXERCISE 1.3 With or Without

This chapter stressed the differences between a high school education and a college education. Ask students to imagine they are still trying to decide whether or not to attend college. Drawing from the material in this chapter as well as from their own ideas, have students make a list of reasons to earn a college degree and a list of reasons not to go to college. For example, pipe fitters earn impressive salaries, while librarians earn much less. How do students justify a college education on those terms?

EXERCISE 1.4 Finding Your Interests

1. Have students complete an interest inventory at the campus career center or online. One such inventory is the Holland Self-Directed Search, at **www.self-directed-search.com** (there is a fee of around $9.95 for the results). Or they can visit the _Princeton Review_ and take the Career Quiz (**http://www.princetonreview.com/careers-after-college.aspx**). Students should list their top

five occupational interests based on this instrument.

2. Have students interview a professional in one of these fields. In the interviews, students should find out as much as they can about the education that is required, skills they would need to be successful, typical career opportunities, and outlook for the future. Have them identify five key things that they learned from the interviews.

EXERCISE 1.5 Using the Occupational Outlook Handbook

Typically, students will change their minds about a major or career several times before they graduate. If you have access to a "Smart" classroom, take some class time to visit the Department of Labor's Web site (Occupational Outlook) at **www.bls.gov/ooh** to find succinct information about thousands of careers, wages in different parts of the country, training required, job outlook, and so on. Or simply introduce students to this worthwhile resource by bringing into class some data that you think will be of special interest to your particular students. Then encourage them to visit the site on their own. You might ask students with smartphones to access some data during class and share it with everyone.

EXERCISE 1.6 Focusing on the Big Picture

Have students browse the table of contents of this book. Direct them to find one or more chapters that address their most important concerns. Before you assign those chapters, encourage students to read them and try to follow the advice found in the chapters. Take a brief look at the chapters your students have chosen; you will see the topics that concern them most, and you can design your class to appeal to their interests. Suggest that your students study the tables of contents of all their textbooks to see where they are headed in each course.

RETENTION EXERCISE Smart Goal Setting

Ask students to pick a goal—either short-term or long-term—and ask them to use the SMART template below to make their goal even more attainable. Students who are skilled at setting and attaining goals are more likely to persist in college.

Write a short-term or long-term personal goal that is related to your college experience. Use the SMART method to further develop your goal.

S: How can you make this goal more **S**pecific?

M: How will you **M**easure whether you have attained this goal at a high level?

A: How do you know that there is a reasonable chance you can **A**ttain this goal?

R: How is this goal **R**elevant to your interests and broader sense of life purpose?

T: What is your **T**ime period for achieving this goal?

CHAPTER 2

WORKING TOGETHER Comparing Class Schedules

In small groups, have your students share their current class schedules with each other. Encourage them to exchange ideas on how to handle time-management problems effectively and the challenges they see in each other's schedules. Discuss together how students can arrange their schedules differently for the next term.

EXERCISE 2.1 Goal Setting

Have students complete the following lists:

A. List five goals you would like to set for yourself for the coming decade.

B. List two measurable objectives for achieving each of the goals you set.

EXERCISE 2.2 The Ideal Class Schedule

After students have participated in the Working Together exercise, use the weekly timetable (see Figure 2.2, page 35) to have students create their ideal class schedules. Then direct them to look in their campus's schedule of courses for next term and try to find courses they need that fit their ideal schedule. Have students complete this activity before meeting with advisers to talk about registration for the next term.

EXERCISE 2.3 Your Daily Plan

Have students make a to-do list for the next day. Tell them to list all appointments, noting hours of the day, plus any to-do activities. Tell students to label each item with an A, B, or C, the A's deserving the most attention and the C's deserving the least. Encourage students to compare their electronic calendar with paper calendars in their campus bookstore. Which do they think would work best for them?

To-do lists are important for class work too. Have students look at their syllabus for each course and make a list of due dates for all papers and projects and dates for all upcoming tests and quizzes. Ask them to look ahead and identify "crunch" times and slow times. In one big group or in small groups, students should discuss strategies for handling these crunch times and also brainstorm ways to maximize the times during the term that will be less stressful.

RETENTION EXERCISE Tracking "Actual Time"

Have students use a weekly timetable (see example in Figure 2.2), a planner, or a calendar on their computer or phone to keep track of how they spend time every hour for an entire week. Tell them to fill in every time slot. At the end of this week, ask students to count how many hours they spent on various activities. How many hours did they spend studying? With family? Socializing? By themselves during personal time? Exercising? Relaxing? Working? Sleeping? Doing household chores such as laundry or dishes? Watching television? Eating? Shopping? Reading for pleasure? Talking on the phone? Texting? What activities merit more time? Which activities should take less time? In what ways did students waste time?

CHAPTER 3

WORKING TOGETHER What Would You Have Done?

Share the following scenario with your students. Download a copy of this scenario at **bedfordstmartins.com/ycestudyskills**.

It's late afternoon on a Thursday, and the only thing between Josh and the weekend is a big biology test at 10:00 a.m. on Friday. There's a lot at stake with this test: It will count for one-third of his final grade. His cell phone rings. It's Susie with an invitation. "A group of us are planning to go out tonight. We thought about an early dinner and a movie. We won't be late," she says. The last time Josh went out on a night before a big test, he came home late. This time he is committed to coming home by 9:00 p.m. to review for the test. Josh goes out with Susie and her friends. He is having a wonderful time, and every time he thinks about going home, he says to himself, "Just a little longer and I will go." Before he knows it, it's 2:00 a.m., and the test is only eight hours away. Josh is exhausted and stressed. He has to decide whether he should sleep a few hours or pull an all-nighter to pass the test. He decides to sleep. He sets the alarm for 4:00 a.m., when he wakes up groggy and out of sorts. Josh starts to study, but his roommate's alarm goes off at 6:00 a.m. His roommate keeps hitting the snooze button, so the alarm goes off every 15 minutes after that. Josh is annoyed. He doesn't want to leave the room, but he has to concentrate. He complains, "I'm trying to study. Will you please be quiet!" His stress is getting worse, and now it's 8:30 a.m. His cell phone rings. It's Josh's mother reminding him about his grandmother's birthday. He snaps, "Mom. Please don't bother me now. I am studying." He quickly hangs up; he has had it. This is his worst nightmare. He is stressed, on edge, and exhausted, and he feels a big headache coming on.

Divide the class into groups of four or five. Ask the groups to spend 15 or 20 minutes discussing the following questions. Then ask each group to report its responses to the entire class for discussion. If you were in Josh's place, what would you have done? How would you evaluate Josh's emotional intelligence? What could he have done differently? What competencies does he need to improve?

EXERCISE 3.1 Are You Going to Eat That Marshmallow?

In reviewing the Stanford marshmallow study, ask students what types of results (in the chart on page 62) surprised them. Which behaviors were understandable? Discuss the concept of "delayed gratification" and how it relates to a college education. What types of things are your students doing today that are delaying gratification? Have them discuss this topic in class and if warranted extol them for their efforts!

RETENTION EXERCISE Matching Behaviors with EI Competencies

Have students match the unsuccessful student behaviors in the first column on the next page with the related EI competencies in the second column that would help the student change or overcome the behavior. (Sometimes more than one competency relates to a single behavior.) Download a copy of this table at **bedfordstmartins .com/ycestudyskills**.

CHAPTER 4

WORKING TOGETHER Multiple Intelligences

After all students have completed the Multiple Intelligences Inventory, ask them to determine

Unsuccessful Student Behavior	Related EI Competency
1. Experience stress and do not handle it well	A. Emotional self-awareness
2. Frequently feel overwhelmed	B. Self-regard
3. Don't get along with others	C. Assertiveness
4. Give up easily	D. Independence
5. Engage in destructive behaviors such as binge drinking and drugs	E. Self-actualization
6. Act very impulsively	F. Reality testing
7. Are not able to solve problems	G. Flexibility
8. Are dependent on others	H. Problem solving
9. Show unethical behavior such as stealing or cheating	I. Stress tolerance
10. Have trouble working in teams	J. Impulse control
11. Have very stereotypical views of others and are unaware of their biases and unwilling to change	K. Empathy
12. Are often sad	L. Social responsibility
13. Are not optimistic	M. Interpersonal relationship
14. Have an "I can't" attitude	
15. Blame others for their problems	
16. Think they will get a 4.0 GPA but have missed many classes	
17. Have a hard time making decisions without input from others	

their highest point scores. Then break the class into groups according to those scores. Ask group members to discuss the classes they're now taking, out-of-class activities in which they're involved, and intended majors. Each group should then describe their conversation to the whole class.

EXERCISE 4.1 Myers-Briggs Exploration

For classes using the Myers-Briggs Type Indicator, have all class members learn their own types. Form three groups of three to five students each. All members of group 1 should be extraverted/sensing types, and all members of group 2 should be introverted/intuitive types. In group 3, include as many of the different preferences represented as possible. Ask each group to outline or write a brief recruiting brochure aimed at convincing prospective students to come to your college or university. After the groups have finished, ask all three groups to share their results with the rest of the class. Ask students whether they notice any differences in the groups' approaches. Which group do they think produced the best plan for a brochure? Why?

EXERCISE 4.2 Learning Styles Models

In small groups, have students discuss the four learning styles models that are presented in this chapter. Which was the easiest to understand? Which was the most difficult? Which of the models did group members like best? Why? Each group should report its opinions to the whole class.

EXERCISE 4.3 Learning More about Learning Disabilities

Have students use the library or the Internet to find the names of three famous people not mentioned in this chapter who have learning disabilities and how they have dealt with or overcome those disabilities. Ask students to share with the class what they learned from their research.

EXERCISE 4.4 Matching Challenge

Instructors should photocopy the table on the next page and cut it along the lines into individual rectangles. Put the vocabulary words (column 1) in the first envelope and clues (columns 2 and 3) in

EXERCISE 4.4 Vocabulary Terms

Vocabulary Terms	Clues	Clues
Concrete Experience	Receptive to others	Empathizing—Kolb trait
Abstract Conceptualization	Integrate observations	Analyzing ideas systematically—Kolb trait
Reflective Observation	Remaining impartial	Different points of view—Kolb trait
Active Experimentation	Move from thinking to action	Test and solve problems—Kolb trait
Diverger	Brainstorm, imaginative, emotional	Major in humanities & social sciences
Assimilator	Think about abstract concepts	Major in math, physics, chemistry
Converger	Apply theories to real-world situations	Major in health-related field or engineering
Accommodator	Hands-on learning, rely on intuition	Major in business, marketing, sales
Extraversion	Outer world	People of action
Introversion	Inner world	Careful listeners, deep thoughts
Sensing	Enjoy facts & tradition	Practical, realistic, take care of details
Intuition	Enjoy innovative ideas	Possibilities related to concepts, future oriented, work in bursts of energy
Thinking	Prefer logic	Rational, analytical and critical, firm and fair
Feeling	Prefer affirming others	Empathetic, value harmony, dislike conflict, facilitate cooperation
Judging	Prefers organization	Planned, orderly, make decisions quickly, punctual, don't like change
Perceiving	Prefer adaptability	Wait-and-see approach, delay decisions, handle emergencies well

another. Tell students that for every vocabulary term, there are TWO clues. Their mission is to match the clues with the correct term. You may want students to use their textbook so that they learn the terms correctly from the start. Make "mission envelopes" for each group of students. Have student groups "race" to match all the clues with the terms properly.

RETENTION EXERCISE Multiple Intelligences and Success

After students take the short Multiple Intelligences Inventory, divide them into eight groups (one for each intelligence) and ask each group to think of ways that each intelligence (according to Howard Gardner) supports student success and the likelihood that someone will remain in college and graduate. Conversely, ask them to decide whether and why a specific intelligence makes it difficult for someone to be successful in college.

CHAPTER 5

WORKING TOGETHER Gathering Information for Decision Making

Divide the class into groups of four to six, and have each group choose a major problem on campus, such as binge drinking, cheating, date rape, parking, safety, class size, or lack of student participation in organizations. Between this class and the next, students should seek information about their group's problem and identify possible solutions by interviewing a campus authority on the topic, searching campus library holdings, and/ or conducting a survey of other students. During the next class, have students share their findings with other members of their group and cite their sources. Groups should try to reach a consensus on the best way to solve the problem that the group chose. If any members of the group are using emotional rather than logical arguments, point those out to them.

EXERCISE 5.1 Reflecting on Arguments

Review the list of questions on page 107 of this chapter with students. Are they the kinds of questions that students tend to ask when they read, listen to, or take part in discussions? Have students revisit the list each evening for the next week and think about whether they have asked such questions that day and tried to notice whether people were stating their assumptions or conclusions.

EXERCISE 5.2 The Challenge of Classroom Thinking

Have students think about their experiences in each of their classes so far this term and respond to the following questions:

- Have your instructors pointed out any conflicts or contradictions in the ideas they have presented? Have you noted any contradictions that they have not acknowledged?
- Have your instructors asked questions for which they sometimes don't seem to have the answers?
- Have your instructors challenged you or other members of the class to explain yourselves more fully?
- Have your instructors challenged the arguments of other experts? Have they called on students in the class to question or challenge certain ideas?
- How have you reacted to your instructors' words? Do your responses reflect critical thinking?

Ask students to write down their thoughts for possible discussion in class and to consider sharing them with their instructors.

RETENTION EXERCISE Learning about a Liberal Education

Have students choose one of their instructors whose field is in the humanities (art, literature, languages, history, government, etc.), mathematics, or the sciences (social, biological, or physical). Students should make an appointment to interview the instructor about how a liberal education and the instructor's particular field of study contribute to a fuller life, no matter what a student's major is.

CHAPTER 6

WORKING TOGETHER Comparing Notes

Have students pair up and compare class notes for this course. Students should take a few minutes to explain their note-taking systems to each other and agree on what's important. In the next class, they should use a recall column. After that class, have students share notes again and check on how each of them used the recall column. They should compare notes and what each student believed to be important. Discuss the results with the class.

EXERCISE 6.1 Using Your Five Senses to Learn

Have students refer back to page 120 in this chapter and decide which mode or modes of learning seem to work best for them: aural, visual, interactive, tactile, or kinesthetic. Ask for suggestions on how they can adapt to other styles. For example, if students are not aural learners, how can they use their preferred ways of learning to master information that is presented in lecture-style courses? Have students brainstorm ways to convert lecture material into a format that is a better match for how they best use their five senses in the learning process.

EXERCISE 6.2 What System of Note Taking Works for You?

Have students pick one of their lecture courses and try each of the methods of note taking described in this chapter over the next four or five class periods: Cornell, outline, paragraph, and list formats, or a combination. Ask students to find time within a couple of hours after a lecture to review their notes and decide which method seems to work best for them. Which method will be easiest to review when studying for tests? Are there any advantages to using a combination of methods (such as using an outline in conjunction with the Cornell format for taking notes in class, then using the recall column for testing them on the contents of the outline)?

EXERCISE 6.3 Using a Recall Column to Memorize

Have students refer to Figure 6.1 on page 128 and study the material provided in the right-hand column until they think they know it well enough to take a test on it. Then cover the right-hand column. Using the recall column, ask students to try to recite, in their own words, the main ideas from these sample notes. Allow them to uncover the right-hand column when they need to refer to it. Ask students whether this system seems to work. If not, why not?

RETENTION EXERCISE Engagement

Ask students working in small groups, either during class or out of class, to discuss the term *engagement*. What does *engagement* mean to them? Why do they think college and university educators focus so much on getting students engaged? Why do older students tend to be more engaged in learning than students just out of high school? Ask them to consider whether within their peer group it's cool to be "engaged in learning." Have groups share their ideas with the whole class.

CHAPTER 7

WORKING TOGETHER Thinking Back to High School

Ask students to write down the reading methods that worked best for them in high school. Then ask them to share these methods with others in the class to initiate a discussion about how reading in college differs from reading in high school.

EXERCISE 7.1 Previewing and Creating a Visual Map

Have students preview a chapter that is currently required reading in one of their other courses and create a visual map, noting the following information: title; introduction; key points from the introduction; any graphics (maps, charts, tables, diagrams); study questions or exercises built into or concluding the chapter; and summary paragraphs. Ask students to create either a wheel or a branching map as shown in Figure 7.1 on page 148, adding spokes or tiers as necessary. In small groups, have students compare their work. Now ask them to arrange the same information in outline form. Which seems to work better? Why?

EXERCISE 7.2 Doing What It Takes to Understand

How far must students go to understand the material in a textbook? Here is one way to find out. Have them do the following:

1. Read a brief chapter in your textbook as if you were reading for pleasure.
2. Read it a second time, but pause at the end of each section to mentally review what you just read.
3. Read it a third time, pausing at the end of each section for review. Then go back and highlight important words or sentences.
4. Read it a fourth time, and do all of the above. This time, ask a friend to read with you, and discuss each passage in the chapter before going on to the next. Stop and take notes, write in the margins, highlight, and so forth.

EXERCISE 7.3 Preparing to Read, Think, and Mark

Direct students to choose a reading assignment from one of their classes. After they preview the material as described earlier in this chapter, have students begin reading until they reach a major heading or have read at least a page or two. They should then stop and write down what they remember from the material. Next, have them go back to the same material and mark what they believe are the main ideas. Suggest that students list four main ideas from the reading so they don't fall into the trap of marking too much.

RETENTION EXERCISE Plan for Active Reading

Ask students to bring a textbook from another course to your next class. During class, ask them to consider the four-step "Plan for Active Reading" on page 147. Ask them which step is the hardest and which is the easiest. The easiest may be "marking." Ask students to check their textbooks to see if any have too much highlighting, or too many marks. The hardest stage may be "reading with concentration." Ask students to get in small groups and develop a list of ideas for "concentrating while reading." Do any of the steps seem unnecessary to your students? Discuss the importance of each step.

CHAPTER 8

WORKING TOGETHER The Name Game

Have the students sit in a circle. Each student then states his or her first name preceded by a descriptive adjective (for example, Sophisticated Susan, Tall Tom, and Jolly Jennifer). Proceed around the circle, having each student state his or her name and descriptor, followed by the names and descriptors of all preceding students. Students can help each other when someone's memory fails. After all students have had a turn, discuss what the class learned from the exercise.

EXERCISE 8.1 Getting the Big Picture

Select a concept from this book, and have students respond to the four questions under the heading "Improving Your Memory," listed on page 178. Have students share their work in small groups. Then ask one person in the group to share with the entire class.

Do this same exercise asking students to choose an example from another textbook. Any major topic shown as a heading or subheading will work to show students how applying these four questions to a major topic helps to imbed ideas in their mind, especially when working in a study group.

EXERCISE 8.2 Using Memory Strategies

Have students practice using association, visualization, and flash cards to improve their memories. Ask them to try the following strategies with a week's lessons from one of their courses:

1. Visualization. Close your eyes and "see" your notes or textbook assignments in action. Break your notes into chunks, and create a visual image for each chunk.
2. Association. Associate a chunk of information with something familiar. If you want to remember that the word *always* usually signifies a wrong answer on multiple-choice or true/false quizzes, associate *always* with a concept such as "always wrong."
3. Flash cards. Write a key word from the material on one side of a card, and put the details on the other side. An example might be as follows: Write the words "Ways to Remember" on one side; on the other side, write, "Go over it again. Use all senses. Organize it. Mnemonics. Association. Visualization. Flash cards." Review the cards often, looking at only five to nine cards at a time.

After students have tried all three methods, ask which method worked best for them.

EXERCISE 8.3 How Accurate Is Your Memory?

This exercise demonstrates how difficult it can be to remember things accurately. One student whispers the name of an object (e.g., lamp, bike, hamburger) to another student. The second student then whispers the word to a third student and adds a second word. The third student whispers both words to another student, adding still another word, and so forth. Each student who adds a word should write it down. When the final student recites the list, students whose words were left out or changed should speak up. The class should then discuss what strategies they were using to remember the list and why they forgot certain items.

RETENTION EXERCISE Creating an Acrostic

Divide the class into small groups, and have students select a list of words that someone in the group needs to remember. For instance, a group member might select the original thirteen colonies in the United States or famous composers of the Romantic period. Have each group create a sentence that everyone can remember, using the first letters of each word in the list. For instance, the composers Liszt, Chopin, Berlioz, Weber, Schumann, and Wagner could be remembered by using the sentence "Let's Call Brother While Sister Waits."

CHAPTER 9

WORKING TOGETHER Forming a Study Group

Have students form a study group for a course. Students should think about their strengths and weaknesses in a learning or studying situation. For instance, do they excel at memorizing facts but find it difficult to comprehend theories? Do they learn best by repeatedly reading the information or by applying the knowledge to a real situation? Do they prefer to learn by processing information in their heads or by participating in a hands-on demonstration? Ask students to make some notes about their learning and studying strengths and weaknesses. Then have each study group brainstorm how each strength can help others prepare for tests and exams. What helpful strengths will each student look for in another person? How can they help others? How can others help them? Students should create a study plan for their study groups. They should review the test schedule for the course and set times for future meetings. What will each member of the group do in preparation for the next meeting?

EXERCISE 9.1 Designing an Exam Plan

Use the following guidelines to have students design an exam plan for one of their courses:

1. What type of exam will be used?
2. What material will be covered? Is the exam cumulative?
3. What types of questions will the exam contain?
4. How many questions do you think there will be?
5. What approach will you use to study for the exam?
6. How many study sessions—and how much time—will you need?

Now ask students to list all material to be covered and to create a study schedule for the week before the exam, allowing as many 1-hour blocks as they will need.

Have students use this exercise to prepare for final exams. Using index cards or pages in a notebook or in a new document on their laptops—one card or page for each class—students should write down the first four questions and then the answers to these questions. If they do not know the answers, they need to meet with their instructor as soon as possible before or after class or during office hours. Once they have all the information they need, students should describe the approach they will use to study for each final, including how much time to allot.

EXERCISE 9.2 Create Your Own Peaceful Scene

Have students think about the most peaceful place they can imagine, real or imaginary. It might be a place they remember fondly from childhood, a special family vacation spot, a place where they always feel safe, a place they have always wanted to visit, or a place from a favorite book or movie. Now have them think about what they would hear, see, smell, taste, and feel if they were there right now. Do not just have them think about how relaxed they would feel; ask them to be specific about what they would experience: the warmth of a fire, a gentle breeze, the sand between their toes, rain on the roof. Have students use all five senses to take themselves to their peaceful places. Practice this technique regularly with students, and they will be able to re-create peaceful scenes with ease when they need to relax.

EXERCISE 9.3 Positive Self-Messages

Some people have a mantra, something they say to themselves to keep focused. Have students adopt a mantra of their own—a phrase or sentence to say to themselves whenever they begin to doubt their ability to succeed academically or when they start to feel anxious about a test. It can be something as simple as "I know I can do it!" or "I will succeed!" They could also quote a favorite song lyric or make the mantra special to fit their personalities.

RETENTION EXERCISE Test Taking

As you approach the midterm, ask your students to think back on the tests they've taken so far. In small groups, ask them to identify their worst and their best grade. Then ask them to discuss with each other what factors might have affected their performance, especially factors they can control (such as amount and timing of preparation, sleep, exercise, diet, self-management of distractions, etc.).

CHAPTER 10

WORKING TOGETHER Write, Pair, Write, Share

Direct your students to do this exercise in small groups of five or six. Use the following instructions:

1. Write. For about 10 minutes use the freewriting technique to write about something that is on your mind. Remember, don't stop to think; just keep writing.
2. Pair. When you are told to stop writing, pair off with another student in your group, and share what you have written by talking about it. Listen to what the other person in your minigroup has to say about what you told her or him. Take notes if you wish.
3. Write. When you are next told to write, reflect on the interaction in your minigroup, but do it individually, on paper. How has the discussion reinforced, modified, or changed your original thoughts on the subject? Write this down.
4. Share. At the given signal, return to your small group of five or six. Appoint a leader, a recorder, and a reporter. Share your thoughts with the entire group. Listen to what group members have to say. Present your report to the group at large. Reflect on what learning has taken place and what the next steps should be.

How might students apply this process to one of their other classes? Discuss how the exercise provides practice in writing, listening, note taking, and active learning.

WORKING TOGETHER Debate

Have students choose a controversial topic that relates to college life. For example, they might decide to debate about whether the campus should build more parking lots, the value of intercollegiate athletics, what constitutes cheating, or student credit card debt. After they decide on a topic, each student should select a side to research, either for or against a proposal about the issue. Give students a week to conduct their research and time in class to prepare for the debate. Decide how many minutes each side or speaker will be allotted, and ask the groups to determine who will speak for the group, who will go first, and so on. After the debate is over, call for a "division of the house," requesting that other students in the class go to one side of the room or the other to indicate whether they agree with the pro or con argument.

EXERCISE 10.1 Engage by Writing

To let students practice private writing, have them write a summary of a reading assignment they recently completed, writing down any questions the reading raised for them. Students should also write down any personal responses they might have to the material. Ask them to share their responses.

EXERCISE 10.2 The Power of Focused Observation

Remember Robert Pirsig's student, who began with the first brick of the opera house and went on to write a 5,000-word paper? Have students find a favorite spot on campus where they can sit comfortably and take a good look at the entire area. Tell them to focus on specific parts of the area. Direct them to choose something—it might be a statue, a building, a tree, or a fence. Have students look carefully at just one portion of the object they selected and start writing about it. Collect their papers, and add your remarks.

EXERCISE 10.3 Parallels

Ask students to respond to these questions: In what ways are speaking and writing similar? In what ways are they different? How do forms of electronic writing, such as e-mail and texting, differ from both speaking and writing?

EXERCISE 10.4 *PowerPoint* Presentation

Have students prepare a three- to five-slide *PowerPoint* presentation to introduce themselves to their classmates. They might create slides about their high school years, their hobbies, their jobs, their families, and so forth. Encourage them to use both visuals and text and be prepared to discuss which features of *PowerPoint* they used to make their presentation as dynamic as possible.

EXERCISE 10.5 Chiseled-in-Stone Speech

Assign students a subject for a 1-minute speech to the class. Tell them they must look like statues during the speech. They should not move their arms, legs, or heads, and they should stare at the back wall of the room without looking at their classmates. Students should note how awkward it feels not to gesture, move, or look at their listeners. Despite having stage fright, a very common reaction to public speaking, it's also natural to want to connect with the audience and get ideas across to them. Have students then give their speeches again, this time connecting with their audience.

RETENTION EXERCISE Getting Involved

Make a list of offices, centers, or activities on your campus in which students can become involved and can practice their writing and speaking skills. (Examples could include the campus radio station, a newspaper or literary magazine, student government or other leadership activity, a Greek organization, a tutoring center, a writing center, etc.) Divide students into pairs or small teams (three or four) and have each group visit one of these offices to learn more about its focus and requirements for student involvement. Have each group make a brief presentation to the class about what group members learned and especially what writing or speaking experience students could gain by becoming involved with these activities.

CHAPTER 11

WORKING TOGETHER Conducting a Group Search at the Library

Have students plan a library visit in groups of three. Before they go, one member of the group should call a librarian and ask for a brief meeting. When they arrive, they should ask the librarian to show them where to find reference books, periodicals, and abstracts. Students should also ask how to use the databases on the library computers to aid their searches. Then decide which database each student will search, and have students search for a topic of their choosing. Students should print their findings and share them with the class. What did they learn?

EXERCISE 11.1 Getting Oriented to Periodicals

To encourage students to get familiar with the periodicals in the library, have them complete the following tasks and questions:

1. Find out how your library arranges periodicals (magazines, journals, newspapers). It probably isn't obvious, so don't hesitate to ask. Why do you think the periodicals are organized in this way?
2. Select an important event that was in the news the year you were born. To find out what was

happening then, you might want to consult an almanac or ask a reference librarian to recommend a chronology. Find a contemporary (written at the time of the event) news report as well as a scholarly article that analyzes the event in a journal. Describe the event. Why was it significant? Note some of the differences you found between the news report and the scholarly article.

EXERCISE 11.2 Looking Up a Career in Information Studies

1. Have students go online and find a schedule of courses for people who are getting degrees in library or information studies at a university. Here are a few universities to check out: University of Michigan, University of Pittsburgh, University of North Carolina, University of South Carolina, University of Rhode Island, McGill University, Emporia State University, University of Arizona.
2. Direct students to examine the course titles. Would they like to study those areas and topics? Why or why not?
3. Encourage students to ask a librarian where he or she obtained the master of library science degree.
4. Have students find out whether this librarian would recommend a career in information management to them. Students should ask, "Do you like your job? Why?"

EXERCISE 11.3 Researching Careers Online

Using their new knowledge gained from Exercise 11.2—students now know how to find out about careers and explore graduate programs—and familiarity with library resources, students can research their own career interests. Have them share in class what they find out and how this either solidifies or alters their plans.

EXERCISE 11.4 Ethics

The last time a certain student (and his fifty classmates) needed an article from a print journal, he discovered that someone had torn the article from the bound periodical. So he went for his second choice. Somebody had ripped out that article, too. "The next time there's some journal article I need, I'm razoring it out," he told his classmates. Ask students why they think this student feels he must respond in this way. How could instructors help prevent such occurrences? How could librarians help students avoid these incidents?

RETENTION EXERCISE Getting Comfortable in Your Library

To encourage students to get familiar with the library, have them complete the following tasks and questions:

1. Find out where your library displays current newspapers, and discover whether the newspaper from your hometown is available.

2. Make an appointment with a librarian so you can talk about your assignment in some depth.

3. Unobtrusively observe what goes on around the information services or reference area (not the circulation desk where you check out books). Watch at least five transactions. Watch the people who ask questions, and watch the staff people who answer them. Does it appear to you that the "customers" receive friendly, competent help? Do the staff members sit and point, or are they on their feet? Do they sometimes accompany inquirers to stack areas or work with them at the computer stations? How might what you observe influence your strategy for getting help if and when you need it?

YOUR
COLLEGE
EXPERIENCE

YOUR COLLEGE EXPERIENCE

Strategies for Success

STUDY SKILLS EDITION

Instructor's Annotated Edition

John N. Gardner

President, John N. Gardner Institute for Excellence in Undergraduate Education
Brevard, North Carolina

Distinguished Professor Emeritus, Library and Information Science
Senior Fellow, National Resource Center for
   The First-Year Experience and Students in Transition
University of South Carolina, Columbia

Betsy O. Barefoot

Vice President and Senior Scholar
John N. Gardner Institute for Excellence in Undergraduate Education
Brevard, North Carolina

Bedford/St. Martin's

Boston ▪ New York

For Bedford/St. Martin's

Senior Executive Editor, College Success and Developmental Studies: Edwin Hill
Developmental Editor: Jennifer Jacobson
Senior Production Editor: Christina M. Horn
Senior Production Supervisor: Dennis J. Conroy
Senior Marketing Manager: Christina Shea
Editorial Assistant: Bethany Gordon
Production Assistant: Elise Keller
Copy Editor: Susan Zorn
Indexer: Mary White
Photo Researcher: Sue McDermott Barlow
Permissions Manager: Kalina K. Ingham
Senior Art Director: Anna Palchik
Cover Design: Billy Boardman
Cover Art: Many multicolored cogs working together. © Dimitri Vervitsiotis/Getty Images.
Text Design and Composition: Cenveo Publisher Services
Printing and Binding: RR Donnelley and Sons

President, Bedford/St. Martin's: Denise B. Wydra
Presidents, Macmillan Higher Education: Joan E. Feinberg and Tom Scotty
Editor in Chief: Karen S. Henry
Director of Marketing: Karen R. Soeltz
Production Director: Susan W. Brown
Associate Production Director: Elise S. Kaiser
Managing Editor: Elizabeth M. Schaaf

Manufactured in the United States of America.

7 6 5 4 3 2
f e d c b a

For information, write: Bedford/St. Martin's, 75 Arlington Street, Boston, MA 02116 (617-399-4000)

ISBN 978-1-4576-2574-9 (Student Edition)
ISBN 978-1-4576-3207-5 (Instructor's Annotated Edition)

Acknowledgments

Acknowledgments and copyrights appear at the back of the book on page 277, which constitutes an extension of the copyright page.

At the time of publication all Internet URLs published in this text were found to accurately link to their intended Web site. If you do find a broken link, please forward the information to collegesuccess@bedfordstmartins.com so that it can be corrected for the next printing.

Dear Student,

When we were in our first year of college, college success and study skills courses were, by and large, nonexistent. Colleges and universities just allowed new students to sink or swim. As a result, some students made it through their first year successfully, some barely survived, and some dropped out or flunked out.

Today most colleges and universities offer study skills and college success courses to provide essential help to students in navigating their way through college. You are likely reading *Your College Experience*, Study Skills Edition, because you are enrolled in a study skills or college success course. Although this book might seem different from your other textbooks, we believe it could be the most important book you read this term because it's all about improving your chances for success in college and beyond. This book will help you identify your own strengths as well as your needs for improvement. But before you start reading, you probably have some questions about the book and the course. Here are two common questions we hear from students across the country.

- **Why should I take this course?** Research conducted by colleges and universities has found that first-year students are far more likely to be successful if they participate in courses and programs designed to teach them how to succeed in college. This course is designed to help you avoid some of the academic pitfalls that trip up many beginning students.

- **What am I going to get out of this course?** This course will provide a supportive environment in which you can share your successes and your frustrations, get to know others who are beginning college, develop a lasting relationship with your instructor and some other students, and begin thinking about your plans for life after college.

As college professors, researchers, and administrators with many years of experience working with first-year students, we're well aware that starting college can be challenging. But we also know that if you apply the ideas in this book to your everyday life, you will be more likely to enjoy your time in college, graduate, and achieve your life goals. Welcome to college!

John N. Gardner
Betsy O. Barefoot

John N. Gardner brings unparalleled experience to this authoritative text for first-year seminar courses. He is the recipient of the University of South Carolina's highest award for teaching excellence. He has twenty-five years of experience directing and teaching in the most respected and most widely emulated first-year seminar in the country, the University 101 course at the University of South Carolina. He is recognized as one of the country's leading educators for his role in initiating and orchestrating an international reform movement to improve the beginning college experience. He is also the founding leader of two influential higher education centers that support campuses in their efforts to improve the learning and retention of beginning college students: the National Resource Center for The First-Year Experience and Students in Transition at the University of South Carolina (**www.sc.edu/fye**) and the John N. Gardner Institute for Excellence in Undergraduate Education (**www.jngi.org**) based in Brevard, North Carolina. The experiential basis for all of John Gardner's work is his own miserable first year of college on academic probation, an experience that he hopes to prevent for this book's readers.

Betsy O. Barefoot is a writer, researcher, and teacher whose special area of scholarship is the first year of college. During her tenure at the University of South Carolina from 1988 to 1999, she served as codirector for research and publications at the National Resource Center for The First-Year Experience and Students in Transition. She taught University 101, in addition to special-topics graduate courses on the first-year experience and the principles of college teaching. She conducts first-year seminar faculty training workshops around the United States and in other countries, and she is frequently called on to evaluate first-year seminar outcomes. She currently serves as Vice President and Senior Scholar in the Gardner Institute for Excellence in Undergraduate Education. In her Institute role she led a major national research project to identify institutions of excellence in the first college year. She currently works with both two- and four-year campuses in evaluating all components of the first year.

BRIEF CONTENTS

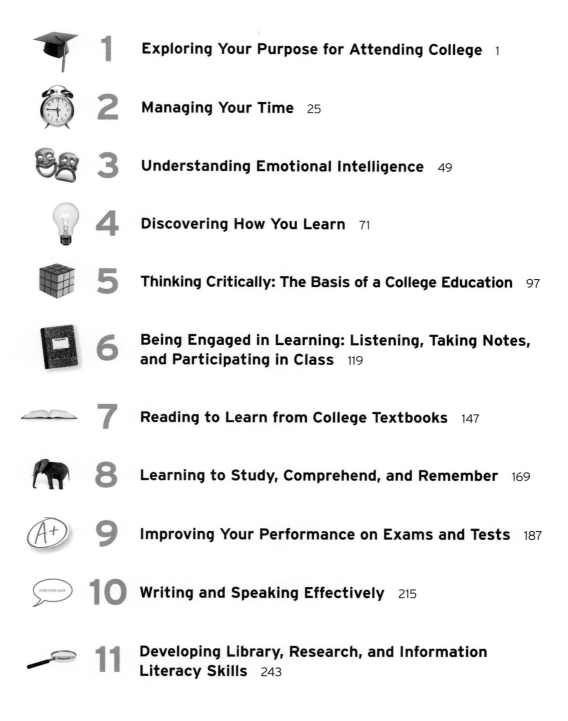

CONTENTS

6 Being Engaged in Learning: Listening, Taking Notes, and Participating in Class 119

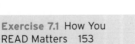

7 Reading to Learn from College Textbooks 147

10 **Writing and Speaking Effectively** 215

PREFACE

Anyone who teaches college students knows how much they have changed in recent years. Today's students are increasingly job-focused, technologically adept, and concerned about the future. We are seeing diverse students of all ages and backgrounds enrolling in both two- and four-year institutions and bringing with them the hopes and dreams that a college education can help fulfill. This textbook is designed specifically to give all students the hands-on, practical help they need to set goals, succeed, and stay in college so that those hopes and dreams can become realities.

We remain devoted to our students and their success. We have written this text for students of any age at any type of college. We aim to convey respect and admiration for our students in our writing while recognizing their continued need for challenge and support. Our text is grounded in the growing body of research on student success and retention. Simply put, we do not like to see students fail. We are confident that if students both read and heed the information found here, they will become engaged in the college experience, enjoy learning, and persist to graduation.

Designed specifically for study skills courses, the Study Skills Edition of *Your College Experience* teaches students the essential skills for academic success. With hands-on exercises and activities on nearly every page, this text will help students to engage in and practice course material and to apply the skills learned to their other academic courses. We have also paid particular attention to goal setting and strengths assessment in this text, two skills essential to starting college off right. This text will help students with the core academic skills they will need in all of their courses: skills in time management, learning styles, critical thinking, listening and taking notes, reading, studying, test taking, writing and speaking, and research and information literacy. An additional chapter on emotional intelligence helps students understand how their emotions can affect success.

Engaging and retaining today's students are challenges we know many of you face. To help you meet these challenges, we have created a complete package of support materials, including an Instructor's Annotated Edition, an Instructor's Manual, a Test Bank, a password-protected instructor Web site, and a free student Web site with video and quizzing. We have included clearly marked retention strategies and activities in the Instructor's Annotated Edition to help you engage students and keep them enrolled at your college or university. These activities, and all of the instructor support materials, will help both new and experienced instructors as they prepare to teach the course.

Whether you are considering this textbook for use in your first-year seminar or have already made a decision to adopt it, we thank you for your interest, and we trust that you will find it to be a valuable teaching aid. We also hope that this book will guide you and your campus in understanding the broad range of issues that can affect student success.

SPECIAL FEATURES OF *YOUR COLLEGE EXPERIENCE,* STUDY SKILLS EDITION

- **Guided reading prompts and exercises that help students to master concepts.**

  - **Reflection questions** that immediately follow each major heading reinforce learning objectives and help students with guided reading.
  - **Practice exercises** in every chapter follow each major section and provide hands-on, point-of-use reinforcement of concepts. Students practice skills that they can then apply to their other academic courses.
  - **Apply It! exercises** at the end of each chapter get students to apply the strategies introduced across each chapter to their college experience right away.
  - **Collaborative activities** at the end of each chapter get students interacting with classmates and provide strategies to use in all their courses.

- **A focus on self-assessment of strengths and goal setting.** The text helps students focus on purpose and motivation—and reinforces engagement in this course. A section on goal setting in Chapter 1 gets students thinking about this important topic from the get-go, and Assessing Your Strengths and Setting Goals boxes at the beginning of each chapter provide opportunity for self-assessment and goal setting.

- **A focus on technology and learning.** Tech Tip features in every chapter—such as one on learning management systems (Chapter 1)—ask students to apply many of the technology skills they may already have in an academic setting.

- **The latest research on the first-year experience.** This book represents not only the practical experience of the authors' extensive careers teaching and directing this course but also the culmination of decades of research, disseminated through two national higher education centers that they have founded and directed.

- **A streamlined Table of Contents perfect for skills-based courses** focuses on what is essential for academic success.

- **Practical tools to use in college and in life.** *Your College Experience* gives students more tools than any book of its kind for understanding themselves, making decisions, learning to think critically, and planning for the future: self-assessments for learning styles and multiple intelligences, planners for weekly to-do lists, and more.

- **Models that let students see principles in action.** Because many students learn best by example, full-size models—more than in any competing book—show realistic examples of annotating a text book, creating a mind map, multiple styles of taking notes, and other strategies for academic success.

- **Where to Go for Help boxes connect the text to student experiences.** To help students take more control of their own success, every chapter includes a quick overview of further resources for support, including fellow students, learning-assistance centers, books, and Web sites—with prompts for students to personalize the book to their own campus and college experience by writing in their own ideas, notes, and local resources they discover.

- **Critical-thinking questions and exercises in every chapter.** Features, photos, and exercises include activities to help students master concepts and think critically about the material. Checklists for Success and Did You Know features in every chapter prompt student interactivity.

RESOURCES FOR INSTRUCTORS

- **Instructor's Annotated Edition.** A valuable tool for new and experienced instructors alike, the Instructor's Annotated Edition includes the full text of the student edition with abundant marginal annotations, chapter-specific exercises, and helpful suggestions for teaching, fully updated and revised by the authors. Numerous retention exercises and collaborative learning ideas, as well as an activity in each chapter that introduces a particular strategy that students can apply to all of their academic courses, help you to help your students succeed and stay in college. ISBN: 978-1-4576-3207-5.

- **Instructor's Manual and Test Bank.** The Instructor's Manual and Test Bank includes chapter objectives, teaching suggestions, a list of common concerns of first-year students, an introduction to the first-year seminar course, a sample lesson plan for each chapter, a wealth of activities, and various case studies that are relevant to the topics covered. Look for the following:

  - More than 400 multiple-choice, true/false, short-answer, and essay questions.
  - A midterm and final exam.
  - *Using YouTube to Teach with Your College Experience* by Chris Gurrie (University of Tampa) provides tips and tricks on easily finding video to supplement each topic in the course.

  Available in print and online. ISBN: 978-1-4576-3208-20.

- **Computerized Test Bank.** The Test Bank contains more than 400 multiple-choice, true/false, short-answer, and essay questions designed to assess students' understanding of key concepts. An answer key is included. ISBN: 978-1-4576-3197-9.

- *French Fries Are Not Vegetables and Other College Lessons: A Documentary of the First Year of College.* This comprehensive instructional DVD features multiple resources for class and professional use. Also available online. ISBN: 978-0-312-65073-5.

- **Custom with Care program.** Bedford/St. Martin's Custom Publishing offers the highest-quality books and media, created in consultation with publishing professionals who are committed to the discipline. Make *Your College Experience,* Study Skills Edition, more closely fit your course and goals by integrating your own materials, the parts of the text you intend to use in your course, or both. Contact your local Bedford/St. Martin's sales representative for more information.

RESOURCES FOR STUDENTS AND PACKAGING OPTIONS

- **Free Book Companion Site for *Your College Experience:*** bedfordstmartins.com/ycestudyskills. You and your students *need* value and *want* powerful online content that you can use anywhere, anytime. The companion site for *Your College Experience*, Study Skills Edition, gives you both, with free and open resources that you can use anywhere, anytime. These resources include the following:

  - **Student Life videos** illustrate important concepts, skills, and situations that students will need to understand and master to become successful at college. Each video ends with questions to encourage further contemplation and discussion.
  - **Self Tests** help students master concepts.
  - **Downloadable podcasts** offer quick advice on note taking, money management, succeeding on tests, and many more topics.
  - **"Where to Go for Help" library of links** directs students to further online resources for support and much more. From the companion Web site, you can also access instructor materials whenever you need them.

- **VideoCentral for College Success** is a premiere collection of video content for the college success classroom. The site features the 30-minute documentary *French Fries Are Not Vegetables and Other College Lessons: A Documentary of the First Year of College*, which follows five students through the life-changing transition of the first year of college. It also includes access to the following:

  - 16 brief *Conversation Starters* that combine student and instructor interviews on the most important topics taught in first-year seminar courses.
  - 16 accompanying video glossary definitions with questions that bring these topics to life.

  Learn more at **bedfordstmartins.com/collegesuccess/catalog.**

- **Free Bedford Coursepacks.** We know it's not enough to build digital products that work in the classroom—we have to make sure that you can plug into your course-management system, whether you use Blackboard, Angel, Desire2Learn, WebCT, Moodle, or Sakai. The content of our student sites is available as downloadable coursepacks that can plug into multiple course-management systems. Learn more at **bedfordstmartins.com/aboutcoursepacks.**

- **Bedford e-Books for *Your College Experience*, Study Skills Edition.** For roughly half the cost of print books, **Bedford e-Books** offer an affordable alternative for students. For more on Bedford e-Books, visit **bedfordstmartins.com/aboutebooks.**

- **E-Book choices.** You can also find PDF versions of our books when you shop online at our publishing partners' sites: CourseSmart, Barnes & Noble NookStudy; Kno; CafeScribe; or Chegg.

- ***The Bedford/St. Martin's Planner*** includes everything that students need to plan and use their time effectively, with advice on preparing schedules and to-do lists, along with blank schedules and calendars (monthly and weekly) for planning. Integrated into the planner are tips and advice on fixing common grammar errors, note taking, and succeeding on tests; an address book; and an annotated list of useful Web sites. The planner fits easily into a backpack or purse so that students can take it anywhere. To order *The Bedford/St. Martin's Planner* packaged **free** with the text, use ISBN 978-1-4576-1441-5. To order the planner stand-alone, use ISBN 978-0-312-57447-5.

- *Bedford/St. Martin's Insider's Guides.* These concise and student-friendly booklets on topics that are critical to college success are a perfect complement to your textbook and course. Bundle one with *any* Bedford/St. Martin's textbook at no additional cost. Topics include:

  - **NEW!** *Insider's Guide to Academic Planning*
  - *Insider's Guide to Beating Test Anxiety*
  - **NEW!** *Insider's Guide to Building Confidence*
  - **NEW!** *Insider's Guide to Career Services*
  - *Insider's Guide to College Ethics and Personal Responsibility*
  - *Insider's Guide to College Etiquette*
  - *Insider's Guide to Community College*
  - *Insider's Guide to Credit Cards*
  - *Insider's Guide to Getting Involved on Campus*
  - *Insider's Guide to Global Citizenship*
  - *Insider's Guide to Time Management*

  For more information on ordering one of these guides **free** with the text, go to **bedfordstmartins.com/gardner/catalog**.

- *Journal Writing: A Beginning.* Designed to give students an opportunity to use writing as a way to explore their thoughts and feelings, this writing journal includes a generous supply of inspirational quotes placed throughout the pages, tips for journaling, and suggested journal topics. To order *Journal Writing: A Beginning* packaged **free** with the text, use ISBN 978-1-4576-1429-3. To order the journal stand-alone, use ISBN 978-0-312-59027-7.

- **TradeUp.** Bring more value and choice to your students' first-year experience by packaging *Your College Experience*, Study Skills Edition, with one of a thousand titles from Macmillan publishers at a 50 percent discount from the regular price. For more information, visit **bedfordstmartins.com/tradeup**.

ACKNOWLEDGMENTS

Special thanks to the reviewers, whose wisdom and suggestions guided the creation of this text:

Melissa Ballard, Oberlin College
Valerie Becker, University of North Dakota
Diane Fox, St. Mary College
SusAnn Key, Midwestern State University
Karlin Luedtke, University of Virginia
Pamela Moss, Midwestern State University
Pamela Price, Mercer County Community College
Jayna Spindler, Ozarks Technical Community College

As we look to the future, we are excited about the numerous improvements to all of our texts that our creative Bedford/St. Martin's team has made and will continue to make. Special thanks to Denise Wydra, President of Bedford/St. Martin's; Karen Henry, Editor in Chief; Edwin Hill, Senior Executive Editor; Jennifer Jacobson, Developmental Editor; Christina Shea, Senior Marketing Manager; Jim Camp, Senior Specialist; Bethany Gordon, Editorial Assistant; and Christina Horn, Senior Production Editor.

Most of all, we thank you, the users of our book, for you are the true inspirations for our work.

CONTRIBUTORS

Although this text speaks with the voices of its two authors, it represents contributions from many other people. We gratefully acknowledge those contributions and thank these individuals, whose special expertise has made it possible to introduce new students to their college experience through the holistic approach we deeply believe in.

 Elizabeth Huggins is the Coordinator of the Orientation/Study Skills program at Augusta State University in Augusta, Georgia. She developed the abundant and hands-on features and exercises featured throughout the Study Skills Edition.

Chris Gurrie is Assistant Professor of Speech at the University of Tampa (UT). Dr. Gurrie is an active public speaker and participates in invited lectures, workshops, and conferences in the areas of faculty development, first-year life and leadership, communicating effectively with *PowerPoint,* and communication and immediacy. Recent research in the areas of communication education, immediacy, and technology has resulted in articles published in communication and first-year outlets. Gurrie is an advocate of experiential learning and has participated in first-year activities at UT as the chairman of the First-Year Committee and as a faculty adviser. He contributed to the Tech Tip feature in each chapter of this book and wrote *Using YouTube to Teach with Your College Experience,* available online and as part of the Instructor's Manual.

We would also like to acknowledge and thank the numerous colleagues who have contributed to this book:

Chapter 1: Philip Gardner, Michigan State University
Chapters 2, 6, 7, 8, 9: Jeanne L. Higbee, University of Minnesota, Twin Cities
Chapter 3: Catherine Andersen, Gallaudet University
Chapter 4: Tom Carskadon, Mississippi State University
Chapter 7: Mary Ellen O'Leary, University of South Carolina at Columbia
Chapter 10: Constance Staley, University of Colorado at Colorado Springs
Chapter 10: R. Stephen Staley, Colorado Technical University
Chapter 11: Charles Curran, University of South Carolina at Columbia
Chapter 11: Rose Parkman Marshall, University of South Carolina at Columbia
End-of-Chapter materials: Julie Alexander-Hamilton

ALSO BY JOHN N. GARDNER AND BETSY O. BAREFOOT

 *Your College Experience*, **Tenth Edition** (ISBN: 978-1-312-60254-3; 16 chapters; 384 pages). The most comprehensive text in the series addresses the whole student, with chapters on academic skills and critical thinking as well as managing money, wellness, and choosing a career.

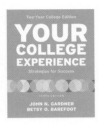 **New version!** *Your College Experience*, **Tenth Edition, Two-Year Edition** (ISBN: 978-1-4576-2804-7; 16 chapters; 384 pages). This version of *Your College Experience* covers topics relevant to students at two-year schools.

 *Your College Experience*, **Concise Tenth Edition** (ISBN: 978-1-4576-0631-1, 12 chapters, 288 pages). This less expensive, streamlined edition of *Your College Experience* presents a straightforward, realistic, and intelligent review of the skills students need to succeed in college.

 *Step by Step to College and Career Success*, **Fifth Edition** (ISBN: 978-1-4576-0634-2; 13 chapters; 208 pages). The briefest title in the Gardner/Barefoot franchise focuses on the most crucial skills and the most important choices students have to make in order to succeed in college and beyond.

For more information on these titles or to request an examination copy, visit **bedfordstmartins.com/newcollegesuccess.**

YOUR
COLLEGE
EXPERIENCE

CHAPTER 1

Exploring Your Purpose for Attending College

In 1900 fewer than 2 percent of Americans of traditional college age attended college. Today, new technologies and the information explosion are changing the workplace so drastically that in order to support themselves and their families adequately, most people will need some education beyond high school. College is so important that more than 67 percent of high school graduates (approximately 18 million students) attend. Because higher education can be essential to your future earning power and your overall well-being, we are committed to providing a set of strategies you can use to do your best. That's what this book is all about.

As you're settling into your new college routine, we want to welcome you to the world of higher education. The fact that you are reading this textbook probably means that you are enrolled in a first-year seminar or "college success" course designed to introduce you to college and help you make the most of it. In this chapter, we'll discuss how you fit into the whole idea of college. We'll consider why the United States has more colleges and universities than any other country in the world. We'll also help you explore the purposes of college—many that your college might define for you—and set goals for your college experience. But even more important, we'll help you define your purposes for being here and offer many strategies to help you succeed.

We highly recommend some activities for getting acquainted on the first day of class to lay the foundation for active learning. Ask the students to pair up and interview a classmate they do not know. The interview should take roughly 5 to 8 minutes, and topics for the interview might include name, hometown, college major, career thoughts, and/or something the individual is proud of. Have the members of each pair introduce one another to the rest of the class. Ask for anonymous feedback at the end of the first class, including thoughts on what each student hopes to learn.

IN THIS CHAPTER YOU WILL EXPLORE

What college is all about

The importance of thinking about your own purpose in attending college

How college "levels the playing field" for students from different backgrounds

The many differences between high school and college

The challenges of being an adult or returning student

The benefits of a college education

How to make sensible choices for college success

Setting goals for your college experience and beyond

IN CLASS: Ask your students what college means to them. What thoughts come to mind? The discussion might explore the expectations they had before they came to college.

The College Experience

People choose to attend college for many reasons. What are your top three reasons?

So what is the college experience? Depending on who you are, your life circumstances, and why you decided to enroll, college can mean different things. College is often portrayed in books and films as a place where young people live away from home in ivy-covered residence halls. We frequently see college depicted as a place with a major focus on big-time sports, heavy drinking, and partying. And, yes, there is some of that at some colleges. But most students today don't move away from home, don't live on campus, and don't see much ivy. College is really far more than any single image you might carry around in your head.

There are many ways to define college. For starters, college is an established process designed to further formal education so that students who attend and graduate will be prepared for certain roles in society. Today, those roles are found especially in what has become known as "the information economy." This means most college graduates are going to be earning their living by creating, managing, and using information. Because the amount of available information expands all the time, your college classes can't possibly teach you all you need to know for the future. The most important skill you will need to learn in college is how to keep learning throughout your life.

WHY COLLEGE IS IMPORTANT TO OUR SOCIETY

American society values higher education, which explains why the United States has so many colleges and universities—more than 4,400. College is the primary way in which people achieve upward social mobility, or the ability to attain a higher standard of living. In earlier centuries, a high standard of living was almost always a function of family background. Either you were born into power and money or you spent your life working for others who had power and money. But in most countries today, receiving a college degree helps to level the playing field for everyone. A college degree can minimize or eliminate differences due to background, race, ethnicity, family income level, national origin, immigration status, family lineage, and personal connections. Simply put, college participation is about ensuring that more people have the opportunity to be evaluated on the basis of merit rather than family status, money, or other forms of privilege. It makes achieving the American dream possible.

> ### DID YOU KNOW?
>
> When asked the reasons they are in college, 83% of first-year students say, "to learn more about what interests me"; 65% say, "to get training for a better job"; and 60% say, "to prepare for graduate or professional school."

◤ ASSESSING YOUR STRENGTHS ▮▮▮▮▮▮

Think about the topic of this chapter. Do you already have a good understanding of the benefits of college and some experience in setting and reaching goals? Now that you have read the first section of this chapter, list the strengths you have in this area.

_____

_____

_____

_____

◤ SETTING GOALS ▮▮▮▮▮▮

What are _your_ most important objectives in learning the material in this chapter? Think about challenges you have had in the past with understanding what college is all about or setting personal goals. List three goals that relate to chapter material (e.g., I will be able to list reasons why college is important for me).

1. _____

_____

2. _____

_____

3. _____

_____

College is also important because it is society's primary means of preparing citizens for leadership roles. Without a college degree, a person will find it difficult to be a leader in a community, company, profession, or the military.

Another purpose of a four-year college degree is to prepare students for continuing their education in a graduate or professional school. If you want to become a medical doctor, dentist, lawyer, or college professor, a four-year college degree is just the beginning.

WHY COLLEGE IS IMPORTANT FOR YOU

College is about thinking, and it will help you understand how to become a "critical thinker"—someone who doesn't believe everything he or she hears or reads but instead looks for evidence before forming an opinion. Developing critical-thinking skills will empower you to make sound decisions throughout your life.

Although college is often thought of as a time when traditional-age students become young adults, we realize that many of you are already adults. Whatever your age, college can be a time when you take some risks, learn

■ RETENTION STRATEGY: Make a positive prediction of your students' success as a result of taking this course by briefly explaining to them the pervasive research finding that students who participate in college success courses are more likely to persist in and graduate from college.

Consider staying in touch with your students electronically either by setting up a class e-mail list or by having some kind of Web presence through which students can network with their peers outside of class. Most first-year students can comfortably communicate online. At some institutions, college success classes are linked electronically with similar classes in other parts of the country. This kind of communication gives students the opportunity to develop new perspectives on beginning college successfully.

new things, and meet new and different people—all in a relatively safe environment. It's OK to experiment in college, within limits, because that's what college is designed for.

College will provide you with numerous opportunities for developing a variety of social networks, both formal and informal. These networks will help you make friends and develop alliances with faculty members and fellow students who share your interests and goals. Social networking Web sites (such as Facebook and Twitter) provide a way to enrich your real-life social networks in college.

College definitely can and should be fun, and we hope it will be for you. You will meet new people, go to athletic events and parties, build camaraderie with new friends, and feel a sense of school spirit. Many college graduates relive memories of college days throughout their lives, fanatically root for their institution's athletic teams, return for homecoming and class reunions, and encourage their own children to attend their alma mater. In fact, you might be a legacy student—someone whose parents or grandparents attended the same institution.

In addition to being fun, college is a lot of work. Being a college student means spending hours studying each week, staying up late at night, taking high-stakes exams, and possibly working harder than you ever have. For many students, college becomes much like a job, with defined duties, expectations, and obligations.

But most important, college will be a set of experiences that will help you to further define and achieve your own purpose. You might feel that you know exactly what you want to do with your life—where you want to go from here. Or, like many students, you might be struggling to find where you fit in life and work. It is possible that as you discover more about yourself and your abilities, your purpose for coming to college will change. In fact, the vast majority of college students change their academic major at least once during the college years, and some students find they need to transfer to another institution to meet their academic goals.

How would you describe your reasons for being in college and at this particular college? Perhaps you, like the vast majority of college students, see college as the pathway to a good job. Maybe you are in college to train or retrain for an occupation, or maybe you have recently experienced an upheaval in your life. Perhaps you are here to fulfill a lifelong dream of getting an education. Or maybe you are bored or in a rut and see college as a way out of it. As it happens, many students enter college without a purpose that has been clearly thought out. They have just been swept along by life's events, and now here they are.

Your college or university might require you to select a major during or before your first year, even before you have figured out your own purpose for college. Some institutions will allow you to be "undecided" or to select "no preference" for a year or two. Even if you are ready to select a major, it's a good idea to keep an open mind. There are so many avenues to pursue while you're in college—many that you might not have even considered. Or you might come to learn that the career you always dreamed of isn't what you thought it would be at all. You will learn more about choosing a major and a career later in this book, but you ought to use your first year to explore and think about your purpose for college and how that might connect with the rest of your life.

IN CLASS: Take a poll to determine how many students are "undecided" versus "have already picked a major." Assure the students that both are perfectly acceptable places to be when they first come to college. Explain that it is important for students to keep an open mind in their studies and use this time to explore their options.

■ RETENTION STRATEGY: While being undecided can have a negative correlation with retention, this is not always the case. Make sure you do not reinforce any stigma for students who are "undecided." Instead, urge them to think of themselves more positively as "exploratory." It is very important to get such students to use your career center early in the first year to influence their direction and commitment. Tell them this course will deal with major, career, and course selection.

Exercise 1.1 asks students to compare the fiction and reality of college and to discuss ideas in pairs.

EXERCISE 1.1

What You THINK Matters

How is "college life" depicted in the movies or other media? Should you believe everything you see or hear? In the left column, list *fictional* ideas about college that you held prior to attending. In the right column, record the *reality* of college—what you have personally experienced now that you are here.

Fiction? BEFORE I arrived, I thought college was . . .	Reality? NOW, I think that college is . . .

After filling in the chart with your personal examples, review them with a friend from class. Maybe it *is* just like you thought it would be . . . or maybe not!

Setting Goals for Your College Experience and Beyond

Without a clear set of goals, people tend to get off track and sometimes never complete the most important tasks. What, if anything, prevents you from obtaining your goals?

In order to achieve your purpose(s) for being in college, an important first step will be to establish goals—goals for today, this week, this year, and beyond. While some students prefer to "go with the flow" and let life happen to them, those students are less likely to achieve success in college or in a career. So instead of "going with the flow" and simply reacting to what college and life present, think instead about how you can take more control over the decisions and choices you make now that lay the foundation for the achievement of future life goals. Many of us find it easy to make vague plans for the future, but we need to determine which short-term steps are necessary if those plans are to become a reality. Researchers who study the importance of goal setting believe that you are more likely to reach goals if you have plans that are SMART: Specific, Measurable, Attainable, Relevant, and anchored to a Time period.[1]

For instance, let's assume that after you graduate you think you might want to work in an underdeveloped country, perhaps spending some time in the

[1]G. T. Doran, "There's a S.M.A.R.T. Way to Write Management's Goals and Objectives," *Management Review* 70, no. 11 (1981): 35–36.

Peace Corps. What are some short-term goals that would help you reach this long-term objective? One goal might be to take courses focused on different countries or cultures. But that goal isn't very specific, nor does it state a particular time period. A much more specific goal would be to take one course each year that would help you build a body of knowledge about other countries and cultures. An even more specific goal would be to review the course catalog and identify the courses you wanted to take and list them on a personal time line. You could also look for courses that give you the opportunity to engage in **service learning**. Course-based service activities will give you a taste of the kind of work you might be doing later in an underdeveloped country.

service learning Unpaid volunteer service that is embedded in courses across the curriculum.

You might also want to gain some actual experience before making a final decision about working in other countries. Another intermediate goal could be traveling to other countries or combining the earning of college credits with performing service abroad through an international organization such as the Partnership for Service Learning.

Before working toward any long-term goal, it's important for you to be realistic and honest with yourself. Is this your goal—one that you value and desire to pursue—or is this a goal that a parent or friend argued was "right" for you? Given your abilities and interests, is the goal realistic? Remember that dreaming up long-term goals is the easy part. You need to be very specific and systematic about the steps you will take today, this week, and throughout your college experience to reach your goals.

Exercise 1.2 allows students to practice goal setting.

EXERCISE 1.2

What You WANT Matters

Practice setting SMART goals—goals that are <u>S</u>pecific, <u>M</u>easurable, <u>A</u>ttainable, <u>R</u>elevant, and <u>T</u>imely. Using the chart below, try to set one goal in each of the areas listed: Academic, Career, Personal, and Financial. Follow the goal through time, from immediate to long term.

Goal Navigator

Types of Goals	Immediate (this week)	Short Term (this term)	Long Term (this year)
Example: Academic	I will list all of my tests and project due dates on my academic calendar.	I will make a file folder to keep my own test and exam grades in case there is a discrepancy with my final course grades.	I will search online for graduate school programs in my field to determine if I have the grades and scores to be admitted.
Academic			
Career			
Personal			
Financial			

TECH TIP PLUG IN

As you have been planning for college, you have probably heard about all the ways you'll use technology as a student. Now, for your supreme enjoyment and convenience, many colleges and universities have introduced the course-management system, or CMS. A CMS is a Web site that boosts your ability to connect with the material you're studying—as well as your instructors and classmates—both in class and out.

1 ▶ THE PROBLEM

You don't really understand what a CMS is—or have the slightest clue how to use one.

2 ▶ THE FIX

Approach this new technology with an open mind and a little patience.

3 ▶ HOW TO DO IT

- **To get motivated, think of all the advantages that a CMS offers.** It lets you keep track of your grades and assignments. It offers a digital drop box for safely submitting your work. It also makes a lot of fun things possible, like online discussion forums and interactive group projects. Some CMSs have the excellent advantage of letting you listen to recorded lectures, or even look at your instructor's lecture notes.

- **Once you learn how to log into the system, do it often.** CMS use varies from one department or instructor to another, and you want to make sure you don't miss anything. If you're having trouble logging in or figuring out your username and password, ask your instructor for help.

- **Figure how much online activity you can handle.** If you sign up for face-to-face classes, you might only use a CMS for a few things, like submitting assignments or swapping essays for peer review. If you enroll in a hybrid course, your instructor may step it up by posting outside reading material or creating online discussions on your CMS. In a fully online course, you'll probably do *everything* on the CMS, including taking exams. Before you register at college, consider which type of course suits your schedule and learning style.

PERSONAL BEST

Your college's CMS is designed to make your life easier, so don't get bogged down by issues that prevent you from taking advantage of it. Don't own your own computer? Lack basic geek skills? Ask a tech-minded friend or someone in the campus computer center for help. College is about finding solutions and learning how to make the most of the resources available to you. So go out there and embrace your CMS!

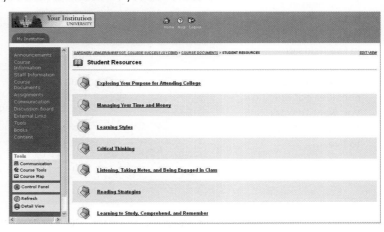

Aligning Your Sense of Purpose and Your Career

What can you do to begin researching college majors and careers?

This chapter suggests that you think very seriously about your purpose for being in college. Here are some additional questions to ask yourself as you continue thinking about why you're at this particular college or university:

- Am I here to find out who I am and to study a subject that I am truly passionate about, regardless of whether it leads to a career?
- Am I here to engage in an academic program that provides an array of possibilities when I graduate?
- Am I here to prepare myself for a graduate program or immediate employment?
- Am I here to obtain specific training in a field that I am committed to?
- Am I here to gain specific skills for a job I already have?

Remember these six simple, one-word questions. They can help you to prepare for a career and obtain that important first job:

Why? Why do you want to be a _____ ? Knowing your goals and values will help you pursue your career with passion and an understanding of what motivates you. When you speak with an interviewer, avoid clichés such as "I'm a people person" or "I like to work with people." Sooner or later, most people have to work with people. And your interviewer has heard this much too often.

RETENTION STRATEGY: The questions on this page are very important for solidifying the connection between a student's sense of purpose for being in college and his or her career choice. Purposeful students are more likely to persist in college.

What Do You Want to Be?

How do you envision your first job after graduation? Will you be working in a cubicle, behind an executive desk, or out in the fields or forests? As you plan for life after college, consider not only how you want to work, but also how you want to live.

Instead, be sure that you have crystallized your actual reasons for following your chosen career path. An interviewer will want to know why you are interested in the job, why it feels right for you at this time in your life, and whether you are committed to this career for the future.

Who? Who at your college or university or in your community can help you make career decisions? Network with people who can help you find out what work you want to do. Right now, those people might be instructors in your major, an academic adviser, and perhaps someone at your campus career center. Later, network with others who can help you attain your goal. Someone will almost always know someone else for you to talk to.

How? How will you develop the technical and communications skills required for working effectively? Don't be a technophobe. Learn how to do *PowerPoint* presentations, build Web pages, and create *Excel* spreadsheets. Take a speech course. Work on improving your writing. Even if you think your future job doesn't require these skills, you'll be more marketable with them.

What? What opportunities are available in your preferred career fields? Be aware of the range of job options an employer presents, as well as such threats as a company's decision to **outsource** certain jobs—that is, contracting with an external organization to perform particular functions at a lower cost. Clearly understand the employment requirements for the career field you have chosen. Know what training you will need if you want to remain and move up in your chosen profession.

Where? Where will your preferred career path take you? Will you be required to travel or live in a certain part of the country or the world? Or will job success require that you stay in one location? Although job requirements may change over the course of your lifetime, try to achieve a balance between your personal values and preferences and the predictable requirements of the career you are pursuing.

When? When will you need to start looking for your first job? Certain professions, such as teaching, tend to hire new employees at certain times of the year, generally spring or summer. Determine whether seasonal hiring is common for your preferred career.

IN CLASS: Have students list tasks or goals for Why, Who, How, What, Where, and When, based on their current career plan or one that might interest them. Discuss their responses.

outsource To contract out jobs to an external organization in order to lower costs.

CONNECTING YOUR MAJOR AND YOUR INTERESTS WITH YOUR CAREER

Some students are sure about their major when they enter college, but many others are at a loss. Either way, it's okay. At some point, you might ask yourself: Why am I in college? Although it sounds like an easy question to answer, it's not. Many students would immediately respond, "So I can get a good job or education for a specific career." Yet most majors do not lead to a specific career path or job. You actually can enter most career paths from any number of academic majors. Marketing, a common undergraduate business major, is a field that recruits from a wide variety of majors, including advertising,

DID YOU KNOW?

At the end of their first year, 35% of students decide to change majors and 22% remain undecided about their major.

communications, and psychology. Sociology majors find jobs in law enforcement, teaching, and public service.

Today, English majors are designing Web pages, philosophy majors are developing logic codes for operating systems, and history majors are sales representatives and business managers. You do not have to major in science to gain admittance to medical school. Of course, you do have to take the required science and math courses, but medical schools seek applicants with diverse backgrounds. Only a few technical or professional fields, such as accounting, nursing, and engineering, are tied to specific majors.

Exploring your interests is the best way to choose an academic major. If you're still not sure, take the advice of Patrick Combs, author of *Major in Success*, who recommends that you major in a subject about which you are really passionate. Most advisers would agree.

Some students will find they're not ready to select an academic major in the first year. You can use your first year and even your second year to explore your interests and find out how they might connect to various academic programs. Over time, you might make different choices than you would have during your first year.

You can major in almost anything. As this chapter emphasizes, it is how you integrate classes with extracurricular activities and work experience that prepares you for a successful transition to your career. Try a major you think you'll like, and see what develops. But keep an open mind, and don't pin your hopes on finding a career in that major alone. Your major and your career ultimately have to fit your overall life goals, purposes, values, and beliefs.

EXPLORING YOUR INTERESTS

John Holland, a psychologist at Johns Hopkins University, developed a number of tools and concepts that can help you organize the various dimensions of yourself so that you can identify potential career choices (see Table 1.1).

Holland separates people into six general categories based on differences in their interests, skills, values, and personality characteristics—in short, their preferred approaches to life. Holland's system organizes career fields into the same six categories. Career fields are grouped according to what a particular career field requires of a person (the skills and personality characteristics most commonly associated with success in those fields) and what rewards those fields provide (interests and values most commonly associated with satisfaction).

Your career choices ultimately will involve a complex assessment of the factors that are most important to you. To display the relationship between career fields and the potential conflicts people face as they consider them, Holland's model is commonly presented in a hexagonal shape (Figure 1.1). The closer the types, the closer the relationships among the career fields; the farther apart the types, the more conflict between the career fields.

Holland's model can help you address the problem of career choice in two ways. First, you can begin to identify many career fields that are consistent with what you know about yourself. Once you have identified potential fields,

TABLE 1.1   Holland Personality and Career Types

Category	Personality Characteristics	Career Fields
Realistic (R)	These people describe themselves as concrete, down-to-earth, and practical doers. They exhibit competitive/assertive behavior and show interest in activities that require action, motor coordination, skill, and physical strength. They tend to be interested in scientific or mechanical areas rather than the arts.	Environmental engineer, electrical contractor, industrial arts teacher, navy officer, fitness director, package engineer, electronics technician, Web designer
Investigative (I)	These people describe themselves as analytical, rational, and logical. They value intellectual stimulation and intellectual achievement. They usually have a strong interest in physical, biological, or social sciences.	Urban planner, chemical engineer, bacteriologist, flight engineer, marine scientist, computer programmer, environmentalist, physician, college professor
Artistic (A)	These people describe themselves as creative, innovative, and independent. They value self-expression and relating with others through artistic expression. They dislike structure, preferring tasks involving personal or physical skills.	Architect, film editor/director, actor, journalist, editor, orchestra leader, public relations specialist
Social (S)	These people describe themselves as kind, caring, helpful, understanding of others, and drawn to interpersonal relationships. They satisfy their needs in one-to-one or small-group interaction using strong speaking skills to teach, counsel, or advise.	Nurse, teacher, social worker, marriage counselor, rehabilitation counselor, school superintendent, geriatric specialist, insurance claims specialist, minister
Enterprising (E)	These people describe themselves as assertive, risk-taking, and persuasive. They value prestige, power, and status and are more inclined than other types to pursue it.	Banker, city manager, health administrator, judge, labor arbitrator, insurance salesperson, sales engineer, lawyer, marketing manager
Conventional (C)	These people describe themselves as neat, orderly, detail oriented, and persistent. They value structure, prestige, and status. They are not opposed to rules and regulations.	Accountant, statistician, hospital administrator, insurance administrator, auditor, database manager

you can use the career library at your college to get more information about those fields. Second, you can begin to identify the harmony or conflicts in your career choices. This will help you to analyze the reasons for your career decisions and be more confident as you make choices.

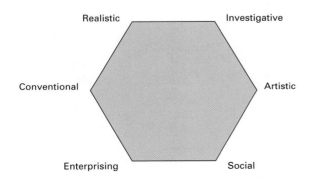

FIGURE 1.1

Holland's Hexagonal Model of Career Fields

Never feel you have to make a decision based on the results of only one assessment. Take time to talk your interests over with a career counselor or shadow an individual in the occupation that interests you to obtain a better understanding of what the occupation entails.

KEY COMPETENCIES

While employers expect skills and related work experience from today's college graduates, they also have begun to focus on additional key competencies that are critical for success in today's economy:

- **Integrity.** Your employment will depend on your being able to act in an ethical manner at work and in the community.

- **Innovation.** You should also be able to evaluate, synthesize, and create knowledge that will lead to new products and services. Employers seek individuals who are willing to take some risks and explore innovative and better ways to deliver products and services.

- **Initiative.** A great employee is able to recognize the need to take action, such as helping a team member, approaching a new client, or taking on assignments without being asked. Employers don't want employees who will wait passively for a supervisor to provide work assignments; they want people who will see what has to be done and do it.

- **Commitment.** Both employers and graduate schools look for a candidate's commitment to learning. They want you to express what you really love to study and are willing to learn on your own initiative. The best foundation for this competency is to be engaged in an academic program in which you wake up every morning eager to go to class.

EXERCISE 1.3

What You DEMONSTRATE Matters

On a scale of 1–10, with 10 being the highest, rate yourself on the following four competencies that employers and graduate schools expect. What are your strengths? Can you think of ways to improve your weaker areas? What examples from previous work settings or academic experiences might you use to communicate your strengths to a potential employer?

Integrity = Exhibit ethical behavior

Innovation = Evaluate, synthesize, and create new methods

Initiative = Recognize the need to take action

Commitment = Demonstrate effort and eagerness

| Integrity score:_____ | Innovation score: _____ | Initiative score: _____ | Commitment score:_____ |

My strongest competency: _____

My weakest competency: _____

Outcomes of College

College is not just about getting a degree. What else do you hope to gain from a college education? In other words, what do you value in addition to earning your diploma?

Although a college degree clearly will make you more professionally marketable, the college experience can enrich your life in many other ways. We hope you will take advantage of the many opportunities you'll have to learn the skills of leadership, experience diversity, explore other countries and cultures, clarify your beliefs and values, and make decisions about the rest of your life—not just what you want to do but also, more important, how you want to live.

When you made the decision to come to college, you probably didn't think about all of the positive ways in which college could affect the rest of your life. Your reasons for coming might have been more personal and more immediate. There are all sorts of reasons, circumstances, events, and pressures that bring students to college; and when you put different people with different motivations and purposes together, it creates an interesting environment for learning.

Many college graduates report that higher education changed them for the better. Read the information in the following box to learn how completing a college degree will make a positive difference for you.

We know that college will make your life different from the one you would have had if you had never been a college student. Consider the

IN CLASS: Ask your students whether they have thought about where they would like to be in the next five years. Ten years? What skills and values drive these goals? Challenge your students to write down a five- or ten-year plan and refer to the plan throughout their college years as a motivational reminder.

IN CLASS: Ask your students which is more important: education for its own sake or education for the sake of earning more money? This might lead to a lively debate.

■ RETENTION STRATEGY: Try to get students to understand the significance of these outcomes. This will aid motivation, commitment, and retention.

OUTCOMES OF THE COLLEGE EXPERIENCE

> You will learn how to accumulate knowledge.

> You will be more likely to seek appropriate information before making a decision. Such information will also help you to realize how our lives are shaped by global, local, political, social, psychological, economic, environmental, and physical forces.

> You will grow intellectually through interactions with cultures, languages, ethnic groups, religions, nationalities, and socioeconomic groups other than your own.

> You will gain self-esteem and self-confidence, which will help you realize how you might make a difference in the world.

> You will tend to be more flexible in your views, more future-oriented, more willing to appreciate differences of opinion, and more interested in political and public affairs.

> If you have children, they will be more likely to have greater learning potential, which in turn will help them to achieve more in life.

> You will be an efficient consumer, save more money, make better investments, and be more likely to spend money on your home and on intellectual and cultural interests as well as on your children.

> You will be better able to deal with bureaucracies, the legal system, tax laws, and advertising claims.

> You will be more involved in education, hobbies, and civic and community affairs.

> You will be more concerned with wellness and preventive health care. Through diet, exercise, stress management, a positive attitude, and other factors, you will live longer and suffer fewer disabilities.

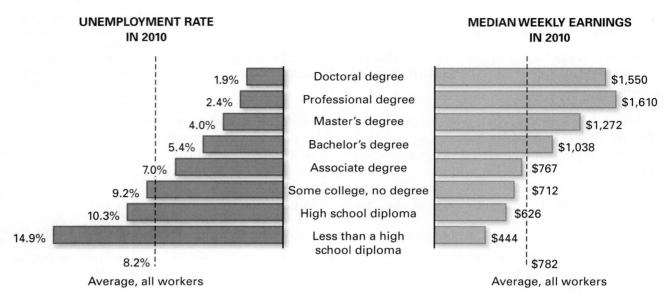

**UNEMPLOYMENT RATE
IN 2010**

1.9% — Doctoral degree
2.4% — Professional degree
4.0% — Master's degree
5.4% — Bachelor's degree
7.0% — Associate degree
9.2% — Some college, no degree
10.3% — High school diploma
14.9% — Less than a high school diploma

8.2%
Average, all workers

**MEDIAN WEEKLY EARNINGS
IN 2010**

$1,550
$1,610
$1,272
$1,038
$767
$712
$626
$444

$782
Average, all workers

FIGURE 1.2

Education Pays

Source: U.S. Department of Labor, Bureau of Labor Statistics, Current Population Survey, 2010.

following list. You will note that the first item is that college graduates earn more money. (Look at Figure 1.2 to see exactly how much more.) However, note that these differences go far beyond making more money. When compared to non-college graduates, those who graduate from college are more likely to:

- earn more money
- have a less erratic job history
- achieve more promotions
- have fewer children
- be more involved in their children's school lives
- have more discretionary time and money
- become leaders in their communities and employment settings
- stay married longer to the same person
- be elected to public office
- participate in and enjoy the arts

When compared to nongraduates, college graduates are less likely to:

- be imprisoned
- become dependent on alcohol or drugs
- be duped, conned, or swindled
- be involuntarily unemployed
- use tobacco products

Students are asked to rank outcomes of the college experience. Ask them if and how this ranking has already changed for them over time.

EXERCISE 1.4

What You QUESTION Matters

Take a moment to rank the outcomes of the college experience as listed on page 13 of this section. Which ones are most important to you? Which ones are least important? Your ranking reflects your values, things that you consider essential to life. There is no right or wrong answer; the lists can be in any order, depending on your life circumstances. Also, your rankings may change as your experiences change.

Rankings—with 1 being the most important

1. _____
2. _____
3. _____
4. _____
5. _____
6. _____
7. _____
8. _____
9. _____
10. _____

Making the Transition

College can be a lot different from high school. How will you successfully navigate the differences and handle all the freedom?

If you just graduated from high school, you will find some distinct differences between high school and college. For instance, you will probably be part of a more diverse student body, not just in terms of race but also in terms of age, religion, political opinions, and life experiences. If you attend a large college or university, you might feel like a number—not as special as you felt in high school. You will have more potential friends to choose from, but familiar assumptions about people based on where they live, where they go to church, or what high school they attend might not apply to the new people you're meeting.

You will be able to choose from many more types of courses, but managing your time is sure to be more complex because your classes will meet on various days and times, and you will have additional commitments, including work, family, activities, and sports. Your college classes might have many more students in them and meet for longer class periods. Tests are given less frequently in college—sometimes only twice a term—and you will most likely be required to do more writing in college. You will be encouraged to do original research and to investigate differing points of view on a topic. You will be expected to study outside of class, prepare assignments, do assigned reading, and be ready for in-class discussions. Your instructors might rely far less on textbooks and far more on lectures than your high school teachers did. Your

Little Fish in a Big Sea

In your first weeks in college, you may feel alone. You may not immediately meet others who look like, dress like, or feel like you. But your college will offer many ways for you to connect with other students, and soon you'll find new friends with whom you'll share much in common.

instructors will rarely monitor your progress; you're on your own. But you will have more freedom to express views that are different from those of your instructors. They will usually have private offices and keep regular office hours in order to be available for you.

CHALLENGES AND OPPORTUNITIES FOR ADULT AND RETURNING STUDENTS

If you're a "returning" student—someone who might have experienced some college before—or if you are an adult living and working off campus, you might also find that college presents new challenges and opportunities. For instance, college might feel liberating, like a new beginning or a stimulating challenge or like a path to a career. However, working full-time and attending college at night, on weekends, or both can mean extra stress, especially with a family at home.

Adult students often experience a daunting lack of freedom because of many important conflicting responsibilities. Working, caring for a family, and meeting your other commitments will compete for the time and attention it takes to do your best or even to simply stay in college. You might wonder how you will ever get through college and still manage to care for your family. You might worry that they won't understand why you have to spend time in class and studying.

In spite of your concerns, you should know that many college professors value working with adult students because, unlike eighteen-year-olds, your life experiences have shown you how important an education can be. Adult students tend to have intrinsic motivation that comes with maturity and experience, and that motivation will compensate for any initial difficulties you might have. You will bring a unique and rich perspective to what you're learning in your classes, a perspective that most eighteen-year-olds lack.

FIRST-YEAR MOTIVATION AND COMMITMENT

What attitudes and behaviors will help you to achieve your goals and be successful in college? If you are fresh out of high school, it will be important for you to learn to deal with newfound freedom. Your college professors are not going to tell you what, how, or when to study. If you live on campus, your parents won't

If you have both returning students and traditional students in class, consider a discussion in which representatives from each group share their concerns. For example, some returning students might believe they will not be able to keep up with "those kids," while the younger students might feel the class will be more difficult because of the presence of older students.

be able to wake you in the morning, see that you eat properly and get enough sleep, monitor whether or how well you do your homework, or remind you to allow enough time to get to class. In almost every aspect of your life, you will have to assume primary responsibility for your own attitudes and behaviors.

If you are an adult student, you might find yourself with less freedom: You might have a difficult daily commute and have to arrange and pay for child care. You might have to juggle work and school responsibilities and still find time for family and other duties. As you walk around campus, you might feel uncertain about your ability to keep up with academic work. You also might find it difficult to relate to younger students, some of whom don't seem to take academic work seriously.

Whatever challenges you are facing, what will motivate you to be successful? And what about the enormous investment of time and money that getting a college degree requires? Are you convinced that the investment will pay off? Have you selected a major, or is this on your list of things to do after you arrive? Do you know where to go when you need help with a personal or financial problem? If you are a minority student on your campus, are you concerned about how you will be treated?

Thoughts like these are very common. Although your classmates might not say it out loud, many of them share your concerns, doubts, and fears. This course will be a safe place for you to talk about all of these issues with people who care about you and your success in college.

IN CLASS: Ask students to name the different freedoms they have in college. Then divide the class into small groups and reach a consensus on the freedoms that pose the greatest challenges for college students. Be sure the students understand the difference between achieving group consensus by resolving their differences, and simply taking a vote, which often ignores the concerns of the minority in favor of the majority.

■ RETENTION STRATEGY: The ways that students use their collegiate freedoms will often determine whether they persist or drop out. Discuss with students the twin concepts of freedom and responsibility and how these connect with the likelihood of success in college.

Students are asked to troubleshoot common situations that hinder academic performance.

> ◣ **EXERCISE 1.5**
>
> ## What You DO Matters
>
> In this section, you read about motivation and commitment. These values have a huge impact on discovering your purpose in college. You might have all the tools you need to be successful, but occasionally, you need to work a little harder to obtain your goals.
>
> Listed below are some typical examples of situations that can hinder academic performance. What strategies can you apply to take responsibility for the problem and create a more successful outcome?
>
> | Typical Situations | Possible Strategies |
> |---|---|
> | I am always late for my 8:00 a.m. class. | |
> | The course subject is not interesting to me. | |
> | I am sitting near people who are negative and disruptive. | |
> | I have been very sick this semester. | |
> | My instructor intimidates me. | |

Grand Opening

Students attend college for many reasons, and it's a good idea to be open to all kinds of possibilities. Some students dream about opening a small business, and the future for small businesses is improving in the current economy.

OUTSIDE CLASS: Assign a campus scavenger hunt. Have the class divide into small teams, and direct each team to visit one office on campus that provides services and academic support to students. Each team is to report back to the class with information on the name, location, and services offered. Students could also bring written material to distribute in class. Another scavenger hunt might involve students visiting as many offices as possible and taking photos of themselves at each office while gathering some information. Most students have digital cameras or camera phones. It could be fun for the students to share the pictures in class or upload them to a secure Web site.

What Is Your Purpose in College?

You can set yourself up for success in many ways, not the least of which is having realistic expectations. Knowing yourself—your goals, your values, and your motivation levels—what would you say is a realistic expectation for your grade point average at the end of this term?

Consider these differences in the way a student might feel about college:

I belong in college versus *What on earth am I doing here?* Where would you fall between these opposite attitudes? You might find that your exact position shifts depending on what's going on in your academic and personal life at any given time. But no matter how you feel on a particular day, as you begin college you will need to spend time sorting out your own sense of purpose and level of motivation. The clearer you are about why you're in college, the easier it will be to stay motivated, even when times are tough.

To build a clearer sense of purpose, look around you and get to know other students who work hard to be successful. Identify students who have the same major or the same career interests, and learn about the courses they have taken, work experiences they have had, and their plans for the future. Look for courses that are relevant to your interests—but don't stop there. Seek relevance in those required general education courses that at first might seem to be a waste of time or energy. Remember that general education courses are designed to give you the kinds of knowledge and skills you need for the rest of your life. Visit your career center, your library, and the Internet to investigate your interests and learn how to develop and apply them in college and beyond. A great Web site to help you research your career interests is the U.S. Department of Labor's Bureau of Labor Statistics (**http://www.bls.gov**), which includes information about average wages for each career by region, job growth statistics, and unemployment rates.

Talk to your residence hall advisers as well as your professors, academic advisers, and campus chaplains. College is designed to give you all the tools you need to find and achieve your purpose. It's all at your fingertips—but the rest is up to you.

■ RETENTION STRATEGY: Retention and degree attainment are more likely with students who have a strongly developed sense of purpose and the ability to set short-term and long-term goals.

Students should create a visual representation of college and their future career.

EXERCISE 1.6

How You PLAN YOUR STEPS Matters

All that you are doing now—jobs you have, hobbies you pursue, organizations you join, volunteering you do, internships you take, majors you explore, careers you consider—are connected. It is important to understand how all these aspects of your life affect each other and to realize how each is an important step on your climb toward your future career. Consider the journey shown below of the student on her way to being an editor. Think about the steps that you are taking and the steps you need to take on your own journey, and map them out below.

My potential career

Editor

_____

Co-ops/internships

Last summer I worked as an intern at a textbook publisher doing assistant-type work. I made a lot of connections.

_____
_____

Majors I am exploring

English, journalism, communication, business.

_____
_____

Employment

I have a work-study job in the library.

_____
_____

Clubs/organizations

I am a reporter for my college's school paper and in a fiction-writing group.

_____
_____

Hobbies/interests

I read as often as possible—fiction and nonfiction. I submit entries to essay contests about once a month.

_____
_____

Volunteering/service learning

I tutor high school English students and help my sister's middle school with their student newspaper.

_____
_____

CHECKLIST FOR SUCCESS

GETTING OFF TO THE RIGHT START

☐ **Keep up with your weekly schedule and do your work on time.** Get a paper calendar or an electronic one, and use it consistently to keep track of assignments and appointments.

☐ **Be on time for class.** If you are frequently late, you give your instructors and fellow students the unspoken message that you don't think the class is important.

☐ **If you are a full-time student, limit the hours you work. If you must work, look for a job on campus.** Students who work a reasonable number of hours per week (about 15) and especially those who work on campus are more likely to do well in college.

☐ **Improve your study habits.** Find the most effective methods for reading textbooks, listening, taking notes, studying, and using information resources.

☐ **Use the academic skills center, library, and campus career center.** These essential services are there to help you be a better student and plan for your future.

☐ **Learn to think critically.** If you don't carefully examine and evaluate what you see, read, and hear, you're not really learning.

☐ **Strive to improve your writing and speaking.** The more you write and speak in public, the easier these skills will become now and in the future.

☐ **Speak up in class.** Research indicates that you will usually remember more about what goes on in class when you get involved.

☐ **Learn from criticism.** Criticism can be helpful to your learning. If you get a low grade, meet with your instructor to discuss how you can improve.

☐ **Study with a group.** Research shows that students who study in groups often earn the highest grades and have the fewest academic problems.

☐ **Become engaged in campus activities.** Visit the student activities office; join a club or organization that interests you; participate in community service.

☐ **Meet with your instructors out of class.** Instructors generally have office hours; successful students use them.

☐ **Find a competent and caring academic adviser or counselor.** If your personality and that of your adviser clash, ask the department office to find another adviser for you.

☐ **Take your health seriously.** How much you sleep, what you eat, whether you exercise, and how well you deal with stress will affect your college success.

☐ **Have realistic expectations.** If you are disappointed in your grades, remember that college is a new experience and your grades will probably improve if you continue to apply yourself.

APPLY IT! What Works for YOU Matters

Think about your current academic situation, and apply some of the suggestions and strategies introduced in this chapter. Select those strategies that you think will work best for you, and then write them down in the "Your Response" column. What are YOU planning to do for YOUR college experience?

QUESTIONS	SAMPLE STUDENT ANSWERS	YOUR RESPONSE
	Name: Stan Smith	
The College Experience People choose to attend college for many reasons. What are your top three reasons?	To get a degree and make money To please my parents To learn new skills	
Setting Goals for Your College Experience and Beyond Without a clear set of goals, people tend to get off track and sometimes never complete the most important tasks. What, if anything, prevents you from obtaining your goals?	I am not an early morning person, so my 8:00 a.m. class is really hard for me. Because I am working until midnight every night, I am too tired to concentrate early in the morning. I think I will try to work a different shift so I can get more rest. Also, I will not register for another 8:00 a.m. class.	
Aligning Your Sense of Purpose and Your Career What can you do to begin researching college majors and careers?	I want to know more about what I can do with a degree in biology. I am planning to meet with my academic adviser, but recently someone told me to see a career adviser too. I will make time for this next week.	
Outcomes of College College is not just about getting a degree. What else do you hope to gain from a college education? In other words, what do you value in addition to earning your diploma?	Besides the obvious (getting a good job after college), I also feel that with my college degree, people will take me more seriously. I will prove to myself that I can do this, even though I am the first in my family to attend college.	
Making the Transition College can be a lot different from high school. How will you successfully navigate the differences and handle all the freedom?	I am going to get in the habit of visiting my instructors during office hours. This will help me stay on track in my classes.	
What Is Your Purpose in College? You can set yourself up for success in many ways, not the least of which is having realistic expectations. Knowing yourself—your goals, your values, and your motivation levels— what would you say is a realistic expectation for your grade point average at the end of this term?	I started out thinking I would make straight A's. . . . but considering my work schedule and my early morning classes, I feel that my 4.0 expectation may be a little high. I need to keep a 3.0 for my scholarship, so looking at my classes, I believe I can make a 3.5.	

BUILD YOUR EXPERIENCE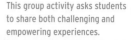

1 COLLABORATIVE ACTIVITY

Have you ever heard the saying that *good judgment comes from past bad judgment*?

TRUE STORY: One student remarked that he was afraid to ask questions out loud in class because he might appear "stupid." The student sitting next to him disagreed. She stated, "I paid for this education, so if I want to ask a stupid question, I will!" The first student realized that this attitude was exactly what he needed to adopt in order to empower himself academically.

Take a moment to discuss your responses to the Apply It! exercise with a small group of classmates. What are some situations that have interfered with your academic success? What have you learned from past mistakes that you can share with others? How has your mindset changed as a result?

2 BUILDING YOUR PORTFOLIO

What's in It for Me? Skills Matrix   How might the courses in which you are enrolled right now affect your future? Although it might be hard to imagine that there is a direct connection to your career or lifestyle after college, the classes and experiences you are now engaged in can play an important role in your future.

Developing a skills matrix will help you reflect on your college experiences and track the skills that will eventually help you land a great summer job, the hard-to-get internship, a scholarship, and, one day, a career.

1. Using Microsoft *Excel* or another spreadsheet software, develop a skills matrix to identify courses and out-of-class experiences that enhance the following skills: communications, creativity, critical thinking, leadership, research, social responsibility, and teamwork. View an example at the book Web site **bedfordstmartins.com/ycestudyskills**.

2. Add any additional skills categories or courses you would like to track.

3. Indicate what you did in your courses or activities that helped you learn one of these skills. Be specific about the assignment, project, or activity that helped you learn.

4. Save your skills matrix on your computer, flash drive, or external hard drive.

5. Update your matrix often. Add new skills categories, courses, and activities. Change the title to indicate the appropriate time period (e.g., Skills Learned in My First Two Years of College).

6. Start an electronic collection of your college work. Save papers, projects, and other relevant material in one location on your computer or on an external storage device. Be sure to back up your work to avoid digital disasters!

Chapter 1 explores how deciding to go to college, experiencing college life, and finding your own path can be a unique journey. Sometimes things that seem simple are more complex and interesting if they are given some thought. Take a minute (or several) to think about and note what you found most useful or meaningful during this class. Did anything that was covered in this chapter leave you with more questions than answers?

_____

_____

_____

_____

_____

_____

_____

_____

_____

_____

_____

_____

_____

_____

No matter how well prepared you are in your teaching, what a student hears and understands might not always be what you think you have said. The one-minute paper is a quick and easy assessment tool that will help alert you when students don't understand what was said or discussed in class. The one-minute paper will also give timid students an opportunity to ask questions and seek clarification. Ideally, you should ask for such a paper several minutes before the end of a class. The paper will also help you begin your next class, by clarifying points your students seem to be unsure of.

For more on this topic watch
French Fries Are Not Vegetables and Other College Lessons

WHERE TO GO FOR HELP . . .

ON CAMPUS

To find the college support services you need, ask your academic adviser or counselor or consult your college catalog, phone book, and college Web site. Or call or visit student services (or student affairs) offices. Most of these services are free. In subsequent chapters, we will include a Where to Go for Help feature that is specific to the chapter topic.

> **Academic Advisement Center** Help in choosing courses; information on degree requirements; help in finding a major.

> **Academic Skills Center** Tutoring; help in study and memory skills; help in studying for exams.

> **Adult Reentry Center** Programs for returning students; supportive contacts with other adult students; information about services such as child care.

> **Career Center** Career library; interest assessments; counseling; help in finding a major; job and internship listings; co-op listings; interviews with prospective employers; help with résumés and interview skills.

> **Chaplains** Worship services; fellowship; personal counseling.

> **Commuter Services** List of off-campus housing; roommate lists; orientation to community; maps; public transportation guides; child-care listings.

> **Computer Center** Minicourses; handouts on campus computer resources.

> **Counseling Center** Confidential counseling for personal concerns; stress-management programs.

> **Disabled Student Services** Assistance in overcoming physical barriers or learning disabilities.

> **Financial Aid and Scholarship Office** Information on financial aid programs, scholarships, and grants.

> **Fitness Center** Facilities and equipment for exercise and recreational sports.

> **Health Center** Help in personal nutrition, weight control, exercise, and sexuality; information on substance abuse programs and other health issues; often includes a pharmacy.

> **Housing Office** Help in locating on- or off-campus housing.

> **Legal Services** Legal aid for students; if your campus has a law school, possible assistance by senior law students.

> **Math Center** Help with math skills.

> **Writing Center** Help with writing assignments.

MY INSTITUTION'S RESOURCES

_____

_____

_____

_____

_____

_____

_____

_____

CHAPTER 2
Managing Your Time

How do you approach time? You might find that you view this important resource differently from your classmates. Some of these differences might have to do with your personality and background. And often, these differences are so automatic and ingrained that you don't even think about them. For example, if you're a natural organizer, you probably enter all due dates for assignments on your calendar, cell phone, or computer as soon as you receive each syllabus. If you take a more laid-back approach to life, you might prefer to be more flexible and go with the flow rather than following a daily or weekly schedule. You might be good at dealing with the unexpected, but you also might be a procrastinator.

Most fundamentally, how you manage time reflects what you value— what is most important to you and what consequences you are willing to accept when you make certain choices. For instance, when you value friendships above everything else, your academic work can take a back seat to social activities. What you value most and how that relates to the way you spend your time often change in college. How you manage this resource corresponds to how successful you will be in college and throughout life.

Time management involves the following:

- Knowing your goals
- Setting priorities to meet your goals
- Anticipating the unexpected
- Taking control of your time
- Making a commitment to punctuality
- Carrying out your plans

Guide students to understand that the demands of college require practical time-management plans, regardless of their previous habits, diverse backgrounds, and different personal styles.

Taking Control of Your Time

Procrastination is a *learned* behavior that sabotages your efforts to be successful in college and in life. The good news is that procrastination can be unlearned or, at the very least, reduced. Do you think you have a problem with procrastination, and if so, why do you think you should conquer this problem?

The first step to effective time management is recognizing that you can be in control. How often do you find yourself saying, "I don't have time"? Once a week? Once a day? Several times a day? The next time you find yourself saying this, stop and ask yourself whether it is really true. Do you really not have time, or have you made a choice, consciously or unconsciously, not to make time for that particular task or activity?

When we say that we don't have time, we imply that we don't have a choice. But we do have a choice. We have control over how we use our time. We have control over many of the commitments we choose to make. And we also have control over many small decisions that affect our time-management success, such as what time we get up in the morning, how much sleep we get, what we eat, how much time we spend studying, and whether we get exercise. All of these small decisions have a big impact on our success in college and in life.

Being in control means that you make your own decisions. Two of the most often cited differences between high school and college are increased **autonomy**, or independence, and greater responsibility. If you are not a recent high school graduate, you have most likely already experienced a higher level of independence, but returning to school creates responsibilities above and beyond those you already have, whether those include employment, family, community service, or other activities.

Whether you are beginning college immediately after high school or are continuing your education after a break, make sure that the way you spend your time aligns with your most important values. For instance, if you value becoming an expert in a particular academic area, you'll want to learn everything you can in that field by taking related classes and participating in internships. If you value learning about many things and postponing a specific decision about your major, you might want to spend your time exploring many different areas of interest and taking as many different types of courses as possible. To take control of your life and your time and to guide your decisions, begin by setting some goals for the future.

OVERCOMING PROCRASTINATION

Procrastination is a serious problem that trips up many otherwise capable people. There are numerous reasons why students procrastinate. In the book *Procrastination: Why You Do It, What to Do about It,* psychologists Jane Burka and Lenora Yuen summarize a number of research studies about procrastination.[1] According to these authors, even students who are highly

autonomy Self-direction or independence. College students usually have more autonomy than they did in high school.

IN CLASS: Assign students to groups of three to six, and have them compare high school and college in terms of recognizing the need for a better time-management plan. For groups of students who are not recent high school graduates, modify the activity to explore differences between being in college and the world of work or the responsibilities of being a homemaker or parent.

■ RETENTION STRATEGY: Introduce the concept of "locus of control," or the extent to which individuals believe they can control events that affect them; then relate the concept to wise choices in time management. Students who learn to take responsibility for their own choices increase their chances of persisting and graduating.

[1]Jane B. Burka and Lenora M. Yuen, *Procrastination: Why You Do It, What to Do about It* (Reading, MA: Addison-Wesley, 1983).

◤■ ASSESSING YOUR STRENGTHS ■

Time management is a challenge for almost all college students. Are you a good time manager? Now that you have read the first section of this chapter, list the strengths you have in this area.

_____

_____

_____

_____

◤■ SETTING GOALS ■

What are your most important objectives in learning the material in this chapter? Think about challenges you have had in the past with managing your time. List three goals that relate to time management (e.g., I will keep an hour-by-hour record this week of how I spend my time).

1. _____

_____

2. _____

_____

3. _____

_____

motivated often fear failure, and some students even fear success (although that might seem counterintuitive). Some students procrastinate because they are perfectionists; not doing a task might be easier than having to live up to your own very high expectations—or those of your parents, teachers, or peers. Others procrastinate because they find an assigned task boring or irrelevant or consider it "busy work," believing that they can learn the material just as effectively without doing the homework.

Simply not enjoying an assignment is not a good reason to put it off; it's an *excuse*, not a valid *reason*. Throughout life you'll be faced with tasks that you don't find interesting, and in many cases you won't have the option not to do them. For instance, when you work in an entry-level job, you might find that you are assigned tedious tasks that are generally reserved for new employees. On a more personal level, you might occasionally put off cleaning your house or your room until the day comes when you can't find an important file or document. At that point, cleaning your personal space becomes an essential task, not an optional one.

When you're in college, procrastinating can signal that it's time to reassess your goals and objectives; maybe you are not ready to make a commitment to academic priorities at this point in your life. Only you can decide, but a counselor or academic adviser can help you sort it out.

■ RETENTION STRATEGY: Ask students to discuss times when they have succeeded or struggled with time management. Successful students often report that their number one success strategy is time management, and conversely students who leave college often do so because they could not manage their time.

IN CLASS: Ask students to think about times when they have procrastinated in completing an assignment or a project. Why do they think they procrastinated? Why is procrastination a problem in managing time? Are there psychological reasons why people procrastinate?

IN CLASS: Ask students to share how they deal with distractions and procrastination. To stimulate discussion, ask students to brainstorm ideas, make a list on the board, and vote on what strategies would work best for them.

Nine More Minutes

Are you ever tempted to hit the snooze button repeatedly when you shouldn't? In the morning, get up in time to eat breakfast and make it to class without feeling frazzled. Think of your alarm clock as an important tool for college success.

OUTSIDE CLASS: Assign a short paper on how students experience the results of procrastination. They should describe the situation, revealing the cause of procrastination and the consequences. The paper should also explain how the student could have handled the situation better.

IN CLASS: Discuss ways to avoid procrastination. What works for you? Give examples from your experience.

■ RETENTION STRATEGY: Procrastination can be related to poor academic performance and hence attrition.

Here are some strategies for beating procrastination:

■ Remind yourself of the possible consequences if you do not get down to work, and then get started.

■ Create a to-do list. Check off things as you get them done. Use the list to focus on the things that aren't getting done. Move them to the top of the next day's list, and make up your mind to do them. Working from a list will give you a feeling of accomplishment.

■ Break big jobs into smaller steps. Tackle short, easy-to-accomplish tasks first.

■ Promise yourself a reward for finishing the task, such as watching your favorite TV show or going out with friends. For more substantial tasks, give yourself bigger and better rewards.

■ Find a place to study that's comfortable and doesn't allow for distractions and interruptions. Say "no" to friends and family members who want your attention; agree to spend time with them later.

■ Don't talk on the phone, send e-mail or text messages, or surf the Web during planned study sessions. If you study in your room, close your door.

If these ideas don't sufficiently motivate you to get to work, you might want to reexamine your purposes, values, and priorities. Keep coming back to some basic questions: Why am I in college here and now? Why am I in this course? What is really important to me? Are these values important enough to forgo some short-term fun or laziness in order to get down to work? Are my academic goals really my own, or were they imposed on me by family members, my employer, or societal expectations? If you are not willing to stop procrastinating and get to work on the tasks at hand, perhaps you should reconsider why you are in college and if this is the right time to pursue higher education.

Researchers at Carleton University in Canada have found that college students who procrastinate in their studies also avoid confronting other tasks and problems and are more likely to develop unhealthy habits, such as higher levels of alcohol consumption, smoking, insomnia, a poor diet, or lack of exercise.[2] If you cannot get procrastination under control, it is in your best interest to seek help at your campus counseling service before you begin to feel as though you are also losing control over other aspects of your life.

SETTING PRIORITIES

To help combat the urge to procrastinate, you should think about how to prioritize your tasks, goals, and values. Which goals and objectives are most important to you and most consistent with your values? Which are the most urgent? For example, studying in order to get a good grade on tomorrow's test might have to take priority over attending a job fair today. However, don't ignore long-term goals in order to meet short-term goals. With good time management you can study during the week prior to the test so that you can attend the job fair the day before. Skilled time managers often establish priorities by maintaining a to-do list (discussed in more detail later in this chapter), ranking the items on the list to determine schedules and deadlines for each task.

Another aspect of setting priorities while in college is finding an appropriate way to balance your academic schedule with the rest of your life. Social activities are an important part of the college experience. Time alone and time to think are also essential to your overall well-being.

IN CLASS: Ask students whether they need to relinquish any commitments. What are the ramifications of giving up these commitments? What commitments are realistic to maintain while attending school full-time? Part-time?

Work Study

Did you know that the majority of college students have jobs? If you need to work, try to find a job that is flexible and allows you to study during your off-time. Use every available minute to stay up to date with your classwork.

[2]Timothy A. Pychyl and Fuschia M. Sirois, "Procrastination: Costs to Health and Well-being" (presentation at the APA Convention, August 22, 2002, Chicago).

For many students, the greatest challenge of prioritizing will be balancing school with work and family obligations that are equally important and are not optional. Good advance planning will help you meet these challenges. But you will also need to talk with your family members and your employer to make sure that they understand your academic responsibilities. Most professors will work with you when conflicts arise, but if you have problems that can't be resolved easily, be sure to seek support from the professionals in your college's counseling center. They will understand your challenges and help you manage and prioritize your many responsibilities.

STAYING FOCUSED

Many of the decisions you make today are reversible. You can change your major, your career, and even your life goals. But it is important to take control of your life by establishing your own goals for the future, setting your priorities, and managing your time accordingly. Many first-year students, especially recent high school graduates, might temporarily forget their primary purposes for coming to college, lose sight of their goals, and spend their first term of college engaging in a wide array of new experiences. This is okay to do within limits, but some students spend the next four or five years trying to make up for poor decisions they made early in their college careers, such as skipping class and not taking their assignments seriously. Such decisions can lead to plummeting grade point averages (GPAs) and the threat of academic probation or, worse, academic dismissal. Staying focused means always keeping your eyes on your most important purposes for being in college. Ask yourself whether what you are doing at any moment contributes to, or detracts from, those purposes.

Many students of all ages question their decision to attend college and might sometimes feel overwhelmed by the additional responsibilities it brings. Prioritizing, rethinking some commitments, letting some things go, and weighing the advantages and disadvantages of attending school part-time versus full-time can help you work through this adjustment period. Again, keep your long-term goals in mind and find ways to manage your stress rather than reacting to it. While this book is full of suggestions for enhancing academic success, the bottom line is to stay focused and take control of your time and your life. Make a plan that begins with your priorities: attending classes, studying, working, and spending time with the people who are important to you. Then think about the necessities of life: sleeping, eating, exercising, and relaxing. Leave time for fun things such as talking with friends, checking out Facebook, watching TV, and going out. But finish what *needs* to be done before you move from work to pleasure. And don't forget about personal time. If you live in a residence hall or share an apartment with other students, talk with your roommates about how you can coordinate your class schedules so that each of you has some privacy. If you live with your family, particularly if you are a parent, work together to create special family times as well as quiet study times.

> ## DID YOU KNOW?
> 35% of first-year students find it difficult to adjust to the academic demands of college.

IN CLASS: Time management often requires the use of the word *no*. Ask students to discuss how saying *no* relates to the way they manage their time.

IN CLASS: Have pairs of students discuss their "perfect life" ten years from now. What goals do they need to set now to achieve their dreams?

IN CLASS: Brainstorm skills and experiences that students might like to have on their résumés when they complete their education that will make them stand out from the pack and impress future employers. Encourage students to write down ideas they could set for themselves as short-term goals.

This exercise asks students to calculate their procrastination quotients.

What You DON'T DO Matters

PROCRASTINATION QUOTIENT

For each item, indicate the column that most applies to you.

	Statement	Strongly Agree	Mildly Agree	Mildly Disagree	Strongly Disagree
1.	I usually find reasons for not beginning a difficult assignment immediately.				
2.	I know what I am supposed to be doing, but frequently I get distracted and do other things instead.				
3.	I carry my books/work assignments with me to various places but do not open them.				
4.	I work best at the last minute when the pressure is really on.				
5.	There are too many interruptions that interfere with my accomplishing my top priorities.				
6.	I avoid straightforward, honest answers when pressed for an unpleasant decision.				
7.	I frequently use stall tactics to avoid taking unpleasant or difficult actions.				
8.	I have been too tired, nervous, or upset to do a difficult task that faces me.				
9.	I like to get my room in good order before starting a difficult task.				
10.	I find myself waiting for inspiration before becoming involved in most important study/work tasks.				
	TOTAL RESPONSES				
	WEIGHT	× 4	× 3	× 2	× 1
	SCORE				

TOTAL SCORE _____

Multiply the TOTAL RESPONSES row by the corresponding WEIGHT to get the SCORE for each column. Add up the SCORE row to determine your total score: This number is your Procrastination Quotient. (This rating system is by H. E. Florey of the University of Alabama Counseling Center.)

Procrastination Quotient, below 20: Occasional Procrastinator

Procrastination Quotient, 21–30: Chronic Procrastinator

Procrastination Quotient, above 30: Severe Procrastinator

Finally: Can you think of the number of times you may have been late (one of the symptoms of procrastination) this week alone? Think back. Take the quiz on the next page.

(continued)

Situation	Number of Times This Week
How many times were you late to class?	_____
How many times were you late for appointments/dates?	_____
How many times were you late for work, a carpool, or another job and/or responsibility?	_____
How many times were you late returning an e-mail, phone call, or text such that a problem resulted from this lateness?	_____
How many times were you late paying a bill or mailing any important document?	_____
How many times were you late getting to bed or waking up?	_____
TOTAL	_____

Did the total number of times you were late surprise you? Two to five incidences of being late in a week is fairly normal. Everyone is late sometimes. Being late more than eight times this week might indicate that you are avoiding situations and tasks that are unpleasant for you. Or maybe you find it difficult to wait for other people, and so you would rather have others wait for you. Try and think of lateness from the other person's perspective. Getting more organized might help if you find that you don't have enough hours in the day to get everything done in the way you think it should be done. Position yourself for success and develop the reputation for being dependable!

IN CLASS: Caution students to be specific when filling in their planners. For instance, "Read Chapter 8 in history" is preferable to "study history," which is still better than simply "study." Remind them to use the time between classes to review material from the previous class and prepare for the next class.

Getting Organized

Having a plan of action is especially important while attending college. What kinds of calendars or planners do you currently use? Which ones would you consider adopting in the future?

In college, as in life, you will quickly learn that managing time is important to success. Almost all successful people use some sort of calendar or planner, either paper or electronic, to help them keep up with their appointments, assignments or tasks, and other important activities and commitments.

DID YOU KNOW?

48% of first-year students find it difficult to manage their time effectively.

USE A PLANNER

Your college might design and sell a calendar in the campus bookstore designed specifically for your school, with important dates and deadlines already provided. Or you might prefer to use an online calendar or the calendar that comes on your computer or cell phone. Regardless of the format you prefer (electronic or hard copy), it's a good idea to begin the term by completing a term assignment preview (Figure 2.1). This is a template you can use to map your schedule for an entire term.

To create a term assignment preview, begin by entering all of your commitments for each week: classes, assignment due dates, work hours, family commitments, and so on. Examine your toughest weeks during the term. If paper deadlines and test dates fall during the same week, find time to finish some assignments early to free up study and writing time. Note this on your cell phone or

OUTSIDE CLASS: Have students try different daily plans for a week, and then have them discuss what works best for them.

	Monday	Tuesday	Wednesday	Thursday	Friday
Week 1	╳	╳	First day of <u>Classes!</u>	Read Ch. 1–2 English	Discuss Ch. 1–2 History in Class Work 2–5
Week 2	English Quiz Ch. 1–2 Work 4–7	Psych Quiz Ch. 1	English Essay #1 Due Work 4–7	History Quiz Ch. 1–2	English Quiz Ch. 1–2 Work 2–5
Week 3	English Quiz Ch. 3–4 Work 4–7	Psych Quiz Ch. 2 Read Bio Ch. 1–2	English Essay Due Work 4–7	Be Ready for Bio Lab Experiment	Discuss English pp. 151–214 Work 2–5
Week 4	Work 4–7	Read English pp. 214–275	English Essay Due Work 4–7 Discuss pp. 214–275	Read English pp. 276–311	Discuss English pp. 276–311 Work 2–5

	Monday	Tuesday	Wednesday	Thursday	Friday
Week 5	Work 4–7	Psych Quiz Ch. 3–4	English Essay Due Work 4–7	Bio Lab Experiment	Prepare Psych Experiment Work 2–5
Week 6	Work 4–7	Present Psych Experiment	English Essay Due Work 4–7	Bio Lab Experiment	Work 2–5
Week 7	Work 4–7	Study for English Mid-Term	English Mid-Term!! Work 4–7	Bio Lab Experiment	Study Psych Mid-Term Work 2–5
Week 8	Study for Psych Mid-Term Work 4–7	Psych Mid-Term!!	Study for History Mid-Term Work 4–7	Bio Lab Experiment Study for History Mid-Term	History Mid-Term!! Work 2–5

FIGURE 2.1

Term Assignment Preview

Using the course syllabi provided by your instructors, create your own term calendar. You can find blank templates on the book's Web site at **bedfordstmartins.com/ycestudyskills.** Remember, for longer assignments, such as term papers, divide the task into smaller parts and establish your own deadline for each part of the assignment, such as deadlines for choosing a topic, completing your library research, developing an outline of the paper, writing a first draft, and so on.

calendar. If you use an electronic calendar, set a reminder for these important deadlines and dates. Break large assignments (term papers, for example) into smaller steps, such as choosing a topic, doing research, creating an outline, learning necessary computer skills, writing a first draft, and so on. Add deadlines in your term assignment preview for each of the smaller portions of the project. Breaking a large project into smaller steps is something you will probably have to do for yourself. Most professors won't provide this level of detailed assistance.

After you complete your term assignment preview, enter important dates and notes from the preview sheets into your calendar or planner and continue to enter all due dates as soon as you know them. Write down meeting times and locations, scheduled social events (including phone numbers in case you need to cancel), study time for each class you're taking, and so forth. It's best not to rely solely on an electronic calendar. Keep a backup copy on paper in case you lose your phone, you can't access the Internet, or your computer crashes. It's also a good idea to carry your calendar or planner with you in a place where you're not likely to lose it. Your first term of college is the time to get into the habit of using a planner to help you keep track of commitments and maintain control of your schedule. This practice will become invaluable to you in your career. Check your notes daily at the same time of day for the current week as well as the coming week. It takes just a moment to be certain that you aren't forgetting something important, and it helps to relieve stress.

CHART A WEEKLY TIMETABLE

Now that you have created a term preview, the weekly timetable model in Figure 2.2 can help you tentatively plan how to spend your hours in a typical week. Here are some tips for creating a weekly schedule:

- As you create your schedule, try to reserve at least 2 hours of study time for each hour spent in class. This universally accepted "2-for-1" rule reflects faculty members' expectations for how much work you should be doing to earn a good grade in their classes. This means that if you take a typical full-time class load of fifteen credits, for example, you should plan to study an additional 30 hours per week. Think of this 45-hour-per-week commitment as comparable to a full-time job. If you are also working, reconsider how many hours per week it will be reasonable for you to be employed above and beyond this commitment, or consider reducing your credit load.

biorhythms The internal mechanisms that drive our daily patterns of physical, emotional, and mental activity.

- Depending on your **biorhythms**, obligations, and potential distractions, decide whether you study more effectively in the day or in the evening, or a combination of both. Determine whether you are capable of getting up very early in the morning to study or how late you can stay up at night and still wake up for morning classes.

- Not all assignments are equal. Estimate how much time you will need for each one, and begin your work early. A good time manager frequently finishes assignments before actual due dates to allow for emergencies.

Keep track of how much time it takes you to complete different kinds of tasks. For example, depending on your skills and interests, it might take longer to read a chapter in a biology text than to read one in a literature text.

	Sunday	Monday	Tuesday	Wednesday	Thursday	Friday	Saturday
6:00							
7:00							
8:00			BREAKFAST	⟶			
9:00	SLEEP IN!	Review English	PSYCH 101	Review English	PSYCH 101	Review English	
10:00		English 101	Review PSYCH	English 101	Review PSYCH	English 101	ENJOY!
11:00		LUNCH		LUNCH			
12:00		HISTORY 101	LUNCH	HISTORY 101	LUNCH	HISTORY 101	
1:00							
2:00		BIO 101		BIO 101	BIO 101 LAB	WORK	BE LAZY!
3:00					↓	↓	
4:00		WORK		WORK			
5:00		↓		↓			GO
6:00	STUDY ENGLISH	DINNER	DINNER	DINNER	DINNER	DINNER	OUT
7:00	STUDY HISTORY		STUDY ENGLISH		STUDY ENGLISH		WITH
8:00			STUDY HISTORY		STUDY HISTORY		FRIENDS
9:00		STUDY PSYCH	STUDY BIO	STUDY PSYCH			
10:00							
11:00							

FIGURE 2.2

Weekly Timetable

Using your term calendar, create your own weekly timetable. You can find blank templates on the book's Web site at **bedfordstmartins.com/ycestudyskills.** As you complete your timetable, keep in mind the suggestions in this chapter. Do you want your classes back-to-back or with breaks in between? How early in the morning are you willing to start classes? Do you prefer—or do work or family commitments require you—to take evening classes? Are there times of day when you are more alert? Less alert? How many days per week do you want to attend classes? At some institutions you can go to school full-time by attending classes exclusively on Saturday. Plan how you will spend your time for the coming week. Track all of your activities for a full week by entering into your schedule everything you do and how much time each task requires. Use this record to help you estimate the time you will need for similar activities in the future.

Keeping track of your time will help you estimate how much time to allocate for similar tasks in the future. How long does it really take you to solve a set of twenty math problems or to write up a chemistry lab? Use your weekly timetable to track how you actually spend your time for an entire week.

MAINTAIN A TO-DO LIST

Once you have plotted your future commitments with a term planner and decided how your time will be spent each week, you can stay on top of your obligations with a to-do list, which is especially handy for last-minute reminders. It can help you keep track of errands you need to run, appointments you need to make, e-mail messages you need to send, and so on—anything you're prone to forget. You can keep this list on your cell phone or in your notebook, or you can post it on your bulletin board. Some people start a new list every day or once a week. Others keep a running list, and throw a page away only when everything on the list is done. Whichever method you prefer, use your to-do list to keep track of all the tasks you need to remember, not just academics. You might want to develop a system for prioritizing the items on your list: highlight; different colors of ink; one, two, or three stars; or lettered tasks with A, B, C (see Figure 2.3). As you complete each task, cross it off your list. You might be surprised by how much you have accomplished—and how good you feel about it.

FIGURE 2.3

Daily and Weekly To-Do Lists

Almost all successful people keep a daily to-do list. The list may be in paper or electronic form. Get in the habit of creating and maintaining your own daily list of appointments, obligations, and activities.

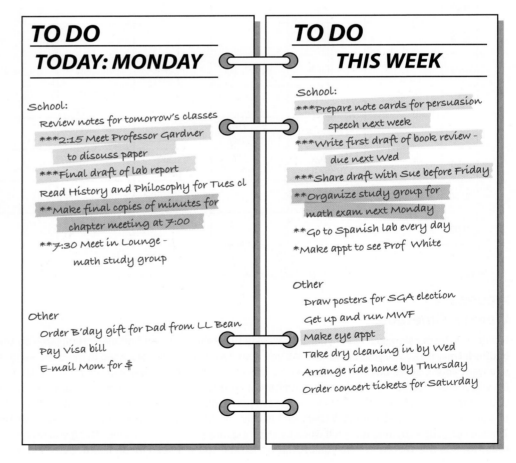

Exercise 2.2 asks students to consider the many distractions in their lives.

What You ANTICIPATE Matters

Planning your time is closely associated with planning your goals (see Chapter 1). What you do on a daily basis affects your outcomes for that week, for that month, for that year, and so on. However, things may distract you and push you off course and away from your intended goals. In this chapter, you will find a weekly timetable to plan your schedule for the week ahead, but what happens when *life happens*? Take control of distractions you know are difficult for you. When you allow distractions to take control of your life, you feel anxiety about the areas of your life you have ignored.

Here are some situations that may or may not distract you. Choose Yes (a problem) or No (not a problem) for each one. Are the problems you identify controllable? If so, as a responsible student, what solutions will help you take control of your time?

Situations	Yes (Y) No (N)	Controllable (C) Uncontrollable (U)	Solutions?
Cell phone			
Internet/Facebook			
Gaming/Videos/Music			
Sports/Hobbies			
Television			
Lack of sleep			
Relationship problems			
Meals/Snacking			
Daydreaming			
Perfectionism			
Errands/Shopping			
Lost items			
Worries/Stress			
Children/Siblings			
Socializing/ Friends			
Multitasking			
Illness, self or others			
Work schedule			
Pleasure reading			
Family			

Making Sure Your Schedule Works for You

Looking over your class schedule, do you see any opportunities for extra study? Do you have too many classes back-to-back or too many in one day? Does this schedule work for you and your life outside of college?

As a first-year student, you might not have had much flexibility in determining your course schedule; by the time you were allowed to register for classes, some sections of the courses you needed might already have been closed. You also might not have known whether you would prefer taking classes back-to-back or giving yourself a break between classes.

How might you wisely use time between classes? This might have been your first opportunity to take classes that do not meet five days a week. Do you prefer spreading your classes over five or six days of the week, or would you like to go to class just two or three days a week or even once a week for a longer class period? Your attention span and other commitments should influence your decision. In the future, you might have more control over how you schedule your classes. Before you register, think about how to make your class schedule work for you—in other words, how you can create a schedule that allows you to use your time more efficiently. Also consider your own biorhythms and recognize the part of the day or evening in which you are most alert and engaged.

OUTSIDE CLASS: Ask students to read this box, and assign a short paper on three points they find most valuable and why. Students can meet in groups to discuss their answers. Each group can present their most valuable points and defend their choices. Make a summary of the points the students find most valuable when organizing their days.

ORGANIZE YOUR DAYS

Being a good student does not necessarily mean studying day and night and doing little else. Notice that the Daily Planner (Figure 2.4) includes time for classes and studying as well as time for other activities. Keep the following points in mind as you organize your day:

> Set realistic goals for your study time. Assess how long it takes to read a chapter in different types of textbooks and how long it takes you to review your notes from different instructors, and schedule your time accordingly. Give yourself adequate time to review and then test your knowledge when preparing for exams.

> Use waiting time to review (on the bus, before class, before appointments). Prevent forgetting what you have learned by allowing time to review as soon as is reasonable after class. (Reviewing immediately after class might be possible but not reasonable if you are too burned out to concentrate!)

> Know your best times of day to study. Schedule other activities, such as laundry, e-mail, or spending time with friends, for times when it will be difficult to concentrate.

> Restrict repetitive, distracting, and time-consuming tasks such as checking your e-mail, Facebook, or text messages to a certain time, not every hour.

> Avoid multitasking. Even though you might actually be quite good at it, or at least think that you are, the reality is (and research shows) that you will be able to study most effectively and retain the most information if you concentrate on one task at a time.

> Be flexible. You cannot anticipate every disruption to your plans. Build extra time into your schedule so that unexpected interruptions do not prevent you from meeting your goals.

Month(s) October

Monday the _____ 3 _____

Time	Activity	Time	Activity
7 AM		2	Review for stats Quiz—Wed!
8		3	Do English reading assignment
9		4	
10	Stats	5	
11	English 101	6	Gym
NOON		7	
1 PM	Lunch w/Jenn	8	

Tuesday the _____ 4 _____

Time	Activity	Time	Activity
7 AM		2	
8		3	History (3:30)
9	Gym	4	
10		5	Review for stats Quiz
11	Volunteer @ MSPCA	6	Work 6–11
NOON		7	
1 PM	Biology (1:30)	8	

Wednesday the _____ 5 _____

Time	Activity	Time	Activity
7 AM		2	Do English Reading Assignment
8	Review for stats Quiz	3	
9		4	
10	Stats (Quiz Today!)	5	Meet w/Bio Study Group
11	English 101	6	
NOON		7	
1 PM		8	Volleyball

FIGURE 2.4
Daily Planner
On your daily planner, be sure to enter times for exercise, obligations, and classes. Also add your personal activities, and block out time to study.

CREATE A WORKABLE CLASS SCHEDULE

If you live on campus, you might want to create a schedule that situates you near a dining hall at mealtimes or allows you to spend breaks between classes at the library. Or you might need breaks in your schedule for relaxation, catching up with friends, or spending time in a student lounge, college union, or campus center. You might want to avoid returning to your residence hall room to take a nap between classes if the result is you feel lethargic or oversleep and miss later classes. Also, if you attend a large university, be sure that you allow adequate time to get from one class to another.

If you're a commuter student or if you must carry a heavy workload to afford going to school, you might prefer to schedule your classes in blocks without breaks. However, while taking back-to-back classes allows you to cut travel time by attending school one or two days a week and might provide for more flexible scheduling of a job or family commitments, it can also have significant drawbacks.

When all your classes are scheduled in a block of time, you run several risks. If you become ill on a class day, you could fall behind in all of your classes. You might also become fatigued from sitting in class after class. When one class immediately follows another, it will be difficult for you to have a last-minute study period immediately before a test because you will be attending another class and are likely to have no more than a 15-minute break. Finally, remember that for back-to-back classes, several exams might be held on the same day. Scheduling classes in blocks might work better if you have the option of attending lectures at alternative times in case you are absent, if you alternate classes with free periods, and if you seek out instructors who are flexible with due dates for assignments.

DON'T OVEREXTEND YOURSELF

Being overextended is a primary source of stress for college students. Determine what a realistic workload is for you, but note that this can vary significantly from one person to another. Although being involved in campus life is very important, don't allow your academic work to take a backseat to extracurricular activities or other time commitments. Do not take on more than you can handle. Learn to say "no." Do not feel obligated to provide a reason; you have the right to decline requests that will prevent you from getting your own work done.

Even with the best intentions, some students who use a time-management plan overextend themselves. If there is not enough time to carry your course load and meet your commitments, drop a course before the drop deadline so that you won't have a low grade on your permanent record. If you receive financial aid, keep in mind that you must be registered for a minimum number of credit hours to be considered a full-time student and thereby maintain your current level of financial aid.

If dropping a course is not feasible or if other activities are lower on your list of priorities, which is likely for most college students, assess your other time commitments and let go of one or more. Doing so can be very difficult, especially if you think that you are letting other people down. However, it is far preferable to excuse yourself from an activity in a way that is respectful to others than to fail to come through at the last minute because you have committed to more than you can possibly achieve.

IN CLASS: Ask students to think about distractions and report the kinds of distractions they have in their environments. How are distractions a problem?

Better Late Than Never?

Be on time to class, but if you have an emergency situation that causes you to run late, talk to your instructor. He or she will understand a real emergency and help you make up work you missed.

REDUCE DISTRACTIONS

Where should you study? Some students find that it's best not to study in places associated with leisure, such as the kitchen table, the living room, or in front of the TV, because these places lend themselves to interruptions and other distractions. Similarly, it might be unwise to study on your bed because you might drift off to sleep when you need to study or learn to associate your bed with studying and not be able to go to sleep when you need to. Instead, find quiet places, both on campus and at home, where you can concentrate and develop a study mind-set each time you sit down to do your work.

Try to stick to a routine as you study. The more firmly you have established a specific time and a quiet place to study, the more effective you will be in keeping up with your schedule. If you have larger blocks of time available on the weekend, for example, take advantage of that time to review or catch up on major projects, such as term papers, that can't be completed effectively in 50-minute blocks. Break down large tasks and take one thing at a time; you will make more progress toward your ultimate academic goals.

Here are some more tips to help you deal with distractions:

- Turn off the computer, TV, CD or DVD player, iPod, or radio unless the background noise or music really helps you concentrate on your studies or drowns out more distracting noises (people laughing or talking in other rooms or hallways, for instance). Consider silencing your cell phone so that you aren't distracted by incoming calls or text messages.

TECH TIP GET ORGANIZED

Mapping out your schedule needn't be a chore. Think of a well-appointed calendar as a compass for a college student. It's a guide for navigating your current term and will also keep you pointed toward your long-term goals.

 1 ▶ THE PROBLEM

You haven't planned the semester on your calendar yet.

 2 ▶ THE FIX

Map out this term's assignments and make a running to-do list on paper. Then take it digital.

 3 ▶ HOW TO DO IT

- **Find out if your college sells a special planner** in the campus bookstore with important dates or deadlines already marked. If not, grab a sheet of paper or download a blank calendar page from the Internet.

- **Draw up a term plan,** entering your commitments for each week: classes, work hours, assignment deadlines, study groups (including contact numbers), and exam and vacation dates.

- **Transfer all the information** into *Outlook*, *iCal*, or a similar *ShareWare* program. When you open *Outlook* or *iCal*, you can view by day, week, or month. Simply click on a date or time slot, follow instructions on the toolbar to create a new entry, and start typing.

- **A useful trick** is to highlight the most important items. As you type in each new entry, you'll have the option to set color-code items by category (e.g., school, work, family). Set reminder alarms to keep yourself on track.

- **Use the to-do list** on the side of the screen to jot down and prioritize tasks. Start a new to-do list every day or once a week. Every time you complete a task, cross it off the list.

- **Sync your calendar and to-do list** to your computer, phone, or BlackBerry. If you need help, visit your college's computer lab or IT department. Alternately, turn to a hyperorganized friend for advice, or click to an *Outlook* tutorial on the Internet.

- **Back up everything,** and file your original paper calendar away for safekeeping in case you experience technical difficulties down the road.

DON'T HAVE *OUTLOOK*?

No problem. You'll find lots of free time-management tools online, like Google Calendar (**www.google.com**), Yahoo Calendar (**www.calendar.yahoo .com**).

PERSONAL BEST

Set up a calendar with all of your classes for the term, and create specific to-do lists for your first three assignments.

EXTRA CREDIT

While you're at it, write up a tentative four-year plan, including required classes in your major and the types of internships or volunteer work you'll need to build your résumé. The exercise will help to demystify the college process—even if you change your major many times down the road.

- Stay away from the computer if you're going to be tempted to check e-mail or Facebook.

- Try not to let personal concerns interfere with studying. If necessary, call a friend or write in a journal before you start to study, and then put your worries away.

- Develop an agreement with your roommate(s) or family about quiet hours. If that's not possible, find a quiet place where you can go to concentrate.

This exercise asks students to determine their circadian rhythms and use the information in building their schedules.

EXERCISE 2.3

What You KNOW Matters

Have you heard of a *circadian rhythm*? This is an internal body clock that determines our personal sleeping and wakeful patterns within a 24-hour day. Certain times of day are naturally better for taking on more difficult cognitive tasks—such as studying math, history, or science—and certain times of day are beneficial for relaxing, doing laundry, or catching up on some sleep. Understanding your internal body clock is helpful in creating successful class and study schedules. Take the test at the following link to determine your circadian rhythm: **http://webenhanced.lbcc.edu/learnka/learn11ka/otherhandouts/timeschedules/BodyClock_Quiz .pdf.** Then plan to carry a heavier workload during those times of day when you are most alert.

Respecting Others' Time

Some students consistently come into class late, create distractions with personal conversations, or leave early before class is finished. Not only do these behaviors show a lack of respect, but they can detract from your instructor's message and create problems for you on your next exam! What can be done about these situations that would help everyone involved?

IN CLASS: Facilitate a discussion of behaviors that students consider rude or disrespectful. What role can students play in enhancing respect for others in the classroom?

How does time management relate to respect? Think of the last time you made an appointment with someone who either forgot the appointment entirely or was very late. Were you upset or disappointed by the person for wasting your time? Most of us have experienced the frustration of having someone else disrespect our time. In college, if you repeatedly arrive late for class or leave before class periods have officially ended, you are breaking the basic rules of politeness, and you are intentionally or unintentionally showing a lack of respect for your instructors and your classmates.

IN CLASS: Discuss how time management relates to respect. Why might a faculty member and other students be irritated if a student arrives late to class? What might tardy students miss?

At times, instructors might perceive certain behaviors to be inappropriate or disrespectful. In college, punctuality is a virtue. This might be a difficult adjustment for some students, but you need to be aware of faculty members' expectations at your college or university.

Be in class on time. Arrive early enough to shed your coat, shuffle through your backpack, and have your assignments, notebooks, and writing utensils ready to go. Likewise, be on time for scheduled appointments. Avoid behaviors that show a lack of respect for both the instructor and other students, such as leaving class to feed a parking meter or answer your cell phone, returning 5 or 10 minutes later, thus disrupting class twice. Similarly, text messaging, sending instant messages, doing homework for another class, falling asleep, or talking (even whispering) disrupts the class. Make adequate transportation plans in advance, get enough sleep at night, wake up early enough to be on time for class, and complete assignments prior to class.

Time management is a lifelong skill. Securing a good job after college will likely mean managing your own time and possibly that of other people you supervise. If you decide to go to graduate or professional school, time management will continue to be essential to your success. But not only is time management important for you, it is also a way in which you show respect for others: your friends, family, and your college instructors.

Exercise 2.4 gets students discussing civility and politeness on campus.

EXERCISE 2.4

What You DEMONSTRATE Matters

Civility is a heated topic on many college campuses today. The term *civility* refers to behavior between persons and groups that conforms to some agreed-upon social norm. When college students (or, for that matter, college professors) are late to class, it demonstrates an unspoken sense of disrespect for others. In our culture, punctuality is not only a virtue; it is expected.

So what other behaviors are considered uncivilized for a college classroom? Take a moment to discuss this with a few of your classmates, and write down a list of behaviors that break the rules of politeness. We will use these later.

5 Things NOT to Do in a College Classroom

1. _____

2. _____

3. _____

4. _____

5. _____

CHECKLIST FOR SUCCESS

TIME MANAGEMENT

☐ **Make sure the way you use your time supports your goals for being in college.** All your time doesn't have to be spent studying, but remember the "2 hours out of class for each hour in class" rule.

☐ **Work to overcome procrastination in your academic work and your life.** If procrastination is a serious problem, seek help from your campus counseling center.

☐ **Get organized by using a planner.** Choose either an electronic format or a paper calendar. Your campus bookstore will have a campus-specific version.

☐ **Devise a weekly timetable of activities, and then stick to it.** Be sure to include special events or responsibilities in addition to recurring activities such as classes, athletic practice, or work hours.

☐ **Create and use day-by-day paper or electronic to-do lists.** Crossing off those tasks you have completed will give you a real sense of satisfaction.

☐ **Identify the things that distract you, and work on reducing those distractions.** Distractions can include people who want your time and attention, loud music, or the chirp of your cell phone letting you know that you have a text message.

☐ **Practice punctuality so you don't miss important activities and unintentionally offend others who are expecting you to be on time.** When you are unavoidably late, apologize to others who were expecting you to be on time.

APPLY IT! What Works for YOU Matters

Think about your current academic situation, and apply some of the suggestions and strategies introduced in this chapter. Select those strategies that you think will work best for you, and then write them down in the "Your Response" column. What are YOU planning to do for YOUR college experience?

QUESTIONS	SAMPLE STUDENT ANSWERS	YOUR RESPONSE
	Name: Demetrius Wilson	
Taking Control of Your Time Procrastination is a *learned* behavior that sabotages your efforts to be successful in college and in life. The good news is that procrastination can be unlearned or, at the very least, reduced. Do you think you have a problem with procrastination, and if so, why do you think you should conquer this problem?	I know I have a problem with procrastination. It seems like I have the hardest time getting started on big tasks, like research papers—they overwhelm me. But, honestly, when I sit down and start researching it really isn't as bad as I thought it would be—especially when I use the library. The librarian's advice usually saves me a lot of time. I guess my motivation to stop procrastinating would be getting a good grade, without the anxiety and fear of turning in a late paper.	
Getting Organized Having a plan of action is especially important while attending college. What kinds of calendars or planners do you currently use? Which ones would you consider adopting in the future?	The college gave me a free annual calendar, so I use this for tests and paper deadlines. What I really want to do is try out the calendar on my phone. That way, it is always with me. I'm not sure how to create it, but someone told me that IT services in my college could help.	
Making Sure Your Schedule Works for You Looking over your class schedule, do you see any opportunities for extra study? Do you have too many classes back-to-back or too many in one day? Does this schedule work for you and your life outside of college?	I have a great schedule: two classes on T/TH and three on M, W, and F. But my three classes are back-to-back with no breaks. By the time I get to my last class, I zone out and can't focus. I won't do that again. On the day I have two classes, I have an hour break in between. I have not been using this to study, but it might help reduce my stress at night if I could knock out a little homework during the day.	
Respecting Others' Time Some students consistently come into class late, create distractions with personal conversations, or leave early before class is finished. Not only do these behaviors show a lack of respect, but they can detract from your instructor's message and create problems for you on your next exam! What can be done about these situations that would help everyone involved?	I admit, I am one of those students. I am always late to my 8:00 class. I know now that I am not a morning person, so I will avoid early classes next term, but for now, I need to set two alarms to get up on time. I didn't think about how my lateness affected other students . . . I only thought that it hurt my own chances on the test. Now that I know, I guess I will try harder to be more considerate. As for the students in my class who talk all the time, I will let them know I am having trouble concentrating because of their personal discussions—maybe they will hold it down if I ask them after class and not in front of everyone.	

BUILD YOUR EXPERIENCE

This group activity calls on instructors and students to demonstrate wrong ways to behave.

1 COLLABORATIVE ACTIVITY

Dust off your acting skills and be prepared to demonstrate the WRONG way to act in a college classroom!

Review the list of 5 behaviors you created with your partners in Exercise 2.4. Choose one or two and demonstrate these behaviors to the class as a whole. Ask the class to identify the behavior. Your instructor is not exempt. Have him or her demonstrate the WRONG way for an instructor to behave as well.

You might wish to set some classroom guidelines for your class. Remember, you have a vested interest in your education and should advocate for the best learning environment possible.

2 BUILDING YOUR PORTFOLIO

Time Is of the Essence   This chapter includes many great tips for effectively managing your time. Those skills are necessary for reducing the stress of everyday life, but have you thought about managing your time over the long term? What are your long-term goals? Preparing yourself for a particular career is probably high on your list, and it's not too early to begin thinking about what kind of preparation is necessary for the career (or careers) you are considering.

First, to help you determine the careers you're most interested in pursuing, schedule an appointment with the career center on your campus and ask for information on career assessments to help you identify your preferences and interests. This portfolio assignment will help you realize that it is important to plan ahead and consider what implications your long-term goals have for managing your time right now.

1. In a *Word* document or *Excel* spreadsheet, create a table. See an example on the book's Web site at **bedfordstmartins.com/ycestudyskills**.

2. Choose a career or careers in which you're most interested. In the example on the Web site, a student needs to plan ahead for activities that will help to prepare for a future as a certified public accountant. It is okay if you have not decided on just one major or career; this is a process that you can repeat as your interests change. An "action step" is something that you need to do within a certain time frame.

3. Talk with someone in the career center, a professor, an upperclass student in your desired major, or a professional in your chosen career to get an idea of what you need to be considering, even now.

4. Fill in the action steps, to-dos, time line, and notes sections of your own chart, and update the chart as you learn more about the career you are exploring.

5. Save your work in your portfolio.

ONE-MINUTE PAPER

Chapter 2 gives you a lot of tips for managing your time. It can be frustrating to realize that you have to spend time organizing yourself in order to manage your time effectively. Did any of the time-management tips in this chapter really appeal to you? If so, which ones and why? Did anything in this chapter leave you with more questions than answers? If so, what are your questions?

_____

_____

_____

_____

_____

_____

_____

_____

_____

_____

_____

_____

_____

_____

No matter how well prepared you are in your teaching, what a student hears and understands might not always be what you think you have said. The one-minute paper is a quick and easy assessment tool that will help alert you when students don't understand what was said or discussed in class. The one-minute paper will also give timid students an opportunity to ask questions and seek clarification. Ideally, you should ask for such a paper several minutes before the end of a class. The paper will also help you begin your next class by clarifying points your students seem to be unsure of.

For more on this topic watch
French Fries Are Not Vegetables and Other College Lessons

WHERE TO GO FOR HELP...

ON CAMPUS

> **Academic Skills Center** Along with assistance in studying for exams, reading textbooks, and taking notes, your campus academic skills center has specialists in time management who can offer advice for your specific problems.

> **Counseling Center** If your problems with time management involve emotional issues you are unable to resolve, consider visiting your school's counseling office.

> **Your Academic Adviser/Counselor** If you have a good relationship with this person, he or she might be able to offer advice or to refer you to another person on campus, including those in the offices mentioned above.

> **A Fellow Student** A friend who is a good student and willing to help you with time management can be one of your most valuable resources.

MY INSTITUTION'S RESOURCES

_____

_____

_____

_____

_____

_____

_____

_____

CHAPTER 3

Understanding Emotional Intelligence

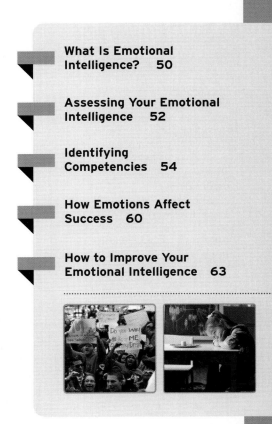

It has been said that many successful businesspeople and politicians were C students who spent more time in college socializing than studying. That's not necessarily true, but the popular belief embodies a key aspect of education that is often overlooked.

The ability to understand and get along with people is vital for success in school, work, and life. Another element of success is the ability to manage time well and get things done. Why do some individuals handle stressful situations with ease while others struggle? Although we tend to think of these abilities as inborn personality traits that can't be changed, the fact is that social skills and stress-management skills can be learned and improved.

Particularly in the first year of college, many students who are intellectually capable of succeeding have difficulty establishing positive relationships with others, dealing with pressure, or making wise decisions. Other students exude optimism and happiness and seem to adapt to their new environment without any trouble. The difference lies not in academic talent but in emotional intelligence (EI), or the ability to recognize and manage moods, feelings, and attitudes. A growing body of evidence shows a clear connection between students' EI and whether or not they stay in college.

As you read this chapter, you will develop an understanding of emotional intelligence, and you will learn how to use it to become a more successful student and person. You will begin to look at yourself and others through an EI lens, observe the behaviors that help people do well, get to know yourself better, and take the time to examine why you are feeling the way that you do before you act. Then, as you read each subsequent chapter in this book, try to apply what you have learned about EI and think about how it might relate to the behaviors of successful college students. You can't always control the challenges and frustrations of life, but with practice you *can* control how you respond to them.

There are many competing theories and assessment tools for EI—just look online. Four basic models are the most widely used because of their reliability and validity: the MSCEIT (Mayer-Salovey-Caruso Emotional Intelligence Test) developed by John Mayer, Peter Salovey, and David Caruso; Daniel Goleman and Richard Boyatzis's Emotional Competence Inventory; Esther Orioli and Robert Cooper's EQ Map; and the EQ-i (Emotional Quotient Inventory) and the EQ 360, developed by Reuven Bar-On. Because the EQ-i was the first validated tool for college-age students and because most of the research in college has been done using this instrument, this is the tool and model we use as the focus of this chapter.

emotional intelligence
The ability to recognize, understand, use, and manage moods, feelings, and attitudes.

What Is Emotional Intelligence?

How aware are you of your emotions and those of others?

Emotional intelligence is the ability to identify, use, understand, and manage emotions. Emotions are a big part of who you are; you should not ignore them. The better the emotional read you have on a situation, the more appropriately you can respond to it. Being aware of your own and others' feelings helps you to gather accurate information about the world around you and allows you to respond in appropriate ways.

There are many competing theories about EI, some of them very complex. While experts vary in their definitions and models, all agree that emotions are real, can be changed for the better, and have a profound impact on whether or not a person is successful.

In the simplest terms, emotional intelligence consists of two general abilities:[1]

- **Understanding emotions** involves the capacity to monitor and label feelings accurately (nervous, happy, angry, relieved, and so forth) and to determine why you feel the way you do. It also involves predicting how others might feel in a given situation. Emotions contain information, and the ability to understand and think about that information plays an important role in behavior.

Anger Management

Since the 1960s, college students have used their anger about political, social, and campus-specific issues (like tuition increases) in positive ways through organized demonstrations. Such demonstrations have influenced major actions in American history, such as the decision of a former U.S. president to resign and the end of the Vietnam War. Are there any issues that would "bring students to the barricades" today?

[1]Adapted from *BarON EQ-i Technical Manual*. Copyright © 1997, 1999, 2000 by Multi-Health Systems, Toronto, Canada. Reproduced by permission of Multi-Health Systems.

◤ ▰ ASSESSING YOUR STRENGTHS ▰

How well you understand and manage your emotions will affect your success in college. Now that you have read the first section of this chapter, list what you believe are your current strengths in the area of emotional intelligence.

_____

_____

_____

_____

◤ ▰ SETTING GOALS ▰

What are your most important objectives in learning the material in this chapter? Think about challenges you have had in the past with understanding your emotions and managing your reactions to frustrating circumstances. List three goals that relate to emotional intelligence (e.g., This week I will keep a list of interactions with other people that frustrate me and how I react).

1. _____

_____

2. _____

_____

3. _____

_____

■ RETENTION STRATEGY: Emotions can be distractions and disruptions or they can be supporters and enablers of college success and retention. Ask students to discuss how their emotions help them engage in their coursework.

■ **Managing emotions** builds on the belief that feelings can be modified, even improved. At times, you need to stay open to your feelings, learn from them, and use them to take appropriate action. Other times, it is better to disengage from an emotion and return to it later. Anger, for example, can blind you and lead you to act in negative or antisocial ways; used positively, however, the same emotion can help you overcome adversity, bias, and injustice.

Identifying and using emotions can help you know which moods are best for different situations and learn how to put yourself in the "right" mood. Developing an awareness of emotions allows you to use your feelings to enhance your thinking. If you are feeling sad, for instance, you might view the world in a certain way, while if you feel happy, you are likely to interpret the same events differently. Once you start paying attention to emotions, you can learn not only how to cope with life's pressures and demands but also how to harness your knowledge of the way you feel for more effective problem solving, reasoning, decision making, and creative endeavors.

Emotional intelligence is not a new concept, although it was made popular by Daniel Goleman's best-selling book *Emotional Intelligence: Why It Can Matter More Than IQ* (1995). The concept of intelligence having more than the cognitive or academic component has been discussed for decades. As early as the 1970s, experts who studied intelligence began to believe that looking only at the cognitive part did not give a full picture of individuals' potential. In the next chapter of this book, students will learn about Howard Gardner's theory of multiple intelligences, learning styles (Kolb and VARK), and the Myers-Briggs Type Indicator as tools they can use to help define their strengths and challenges.

Students can work on their own to identify people they know with strong EI skills and what makes them so.

What You THINK Matters

Some people are just naturally good at understanding the emotions of others. These are the people you go to for personal counseling or crisis management. Maybe all of your friends say this about you! Then there are those people who, when you try to tell them something, interrupt you, don't listen to you, or act too busy to care.

Below, list a few people whom you trust—people you know you can talk to. (Use names of family and friends or initials only if you prefer.) Then rate each person on a scale of 1 to 5 (the higher the rating, the better the person is at understanding his or her own emotions and those of others). Finally, identify why the people on your list are trusted friends. Are they good at *understanding emotions* or *managing emotions*?

Trusted Listeners and Friends	Rating (Scale of 1–5)	What makes them emotionally intelligent?

NOW: In comparison to these trusted friends and family members, how do you rate *yourself* in understanding your own emotions and those of others? Scale of 1–5 _____

What makes you emotionally intelligent (or not)? _____

Assessing Your Emotional Intelligence

Have you ever taken "quizzes" in magazines and books that give insight into your personality? Why do people find these tests so interesting?

A number of sophisticated tools can be used to assess emotional intelligence. Some first-year seminars and many campus counseling centers offer the opportunity to complete a professionally administered questionnaire, such as the Emotional Quotient Inventory (EQ-i), which provides a detailed assessment of your emotional skills and a graphic representation of where you stand in comparison with other students. But even without a formal test, you can take a number of steps to get in touch with your own EI (see the box on page 53). You'll have to dig deep inside yourself and be willing to be honest about how you really think and how you really behave. This can take time, and that's fine. Think of your EI as a work in progress.

EMOTIONAL INTELLIGENCE QUESTIONNAIRE

Your daily life gives you many opportunities to take a hard look at how you handle emotions. Here are some questions that can help you begin thinking about your own EI.

1. What do you do when you are under stress?

☐ A. I tend to deal with it calmly and rationally.

☐ B. I get upset, but it usually blows over quickly.

☐ C. I get upset but keep it to myself.

2. My friends would say that:

☐ A. I will play, but only after I get my work done.

☐ B. I am ready for fun anytime.

☐ C. I hardly ever go out.

3. When something changes at the last minute:

☐ A. I easily adapt.

☐ B. I get frustrated.

☐ C. It doesn't matter, since I don't really expect things to happen as I plan.

4. My friends would say that:

☐ A. I am sensitive to their concerns.

☐ B. I spend too much time worrying about other people's needs.

☐ C. I don't like to deal with other people's petty problems.

5. When I have a problem to solve, such as too many things due at the end of the week:

☐ A. I write down a list of the tasks I must complete, come up with a plan indicating specifically what I can accomplish and what I cannot, and follow my plan.

☐ B. I am very optimistic about getting things done and just dig right in and get to work.

☐ C. I get a little frazzled. Usually I get a number of things done and then push aside the things that I can't do.

Review your responses. A responses indicate that you probably have a good basis for strong emotional intelligence. **B** responses indicate you may have some strengths and some challenges in your EI. **C** responses indicate that your success in life and school could be negatively affected by your EI.

In this partner exercise students can exchange thoughts on a choice they would make differently if they could get a "do-over."

EXERCISE 3.2

Who You ARE Matters

Think back to a time when you made a poor choice. This may have been last week, last month, or even this morning before class! The expression "Hindsight is 20/20" means that if you knew then what you know now, you would have made different decisions. Life gives you many opportunities to make decisions, but rarely do we have the chance for a "do-over." If you could go back in time, what would you change to make your life simpler today? Be willing to share with someone else in class.

Fill in the blanks:

Back when I was _____, I decided I was going to _____

because I was too _____. So then, I _____ and as a result, this happened:

_____

_____

_____.

(continued)

Now, knowing myself and the situation better, I would tell myself NEVER to

_____ .

I would instead _____ .

Note to my future self: As a stronger, more emotionally intelligent being, I have decided to make the following changes to be a more successful student, friend, employee, and/or citizen.

I will _____

_____ .

IN CLASS: This chapter lays out EI "competencies" and describes them on the next several pages. Ask the students to think about the contexts within the college experience, as they are coming to know it, in which they could practice developing these competencies. The basic idea is for the students to see how college is an environment that can develop them more fully. For example, one of the competencies describes "interpersonal skills." In what kinds of college activities, settings, and circumstances could students hope to develop these skills?

Identifying Competencies

Why do you think that understanding yourself is the key to success in college and in life?

Emotional intelligence includes many capabilities and skills that influence a person's ability to cope with life's pressures and demands. Reuven Bar-On, a professor at the University of Texas, Austin, and world-renowned EI expert, developed a model that demonstrates how these categories of emotional intelligence directly affect general mood and lead to effective performance (see Figure 3.1).

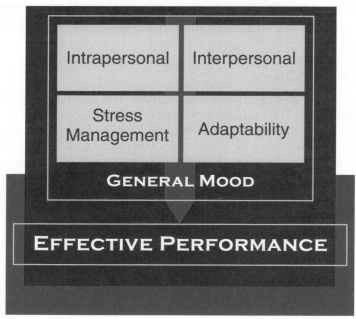

FIGURE 3.1
Bar-On Model of Emotional Intelligence

Help Yourself

Do you depend on other people to raise your own level of self-esteem? It is easy to allow comments from others to affect how we feel about ourselves. If you have a strong level of emotional intelligence, you will be less vulnerable to insult or empty flattery.

Let's take a closer look at the specific skills and competencies that Bar-On has identified as the pieces that make up a person's emotional intelligence.[2] It's something like a jigsaw puzzle, and when you have put all of the pieces together, you will begin to see yourself and others more clearly.

INTRAPERSONAL SKILLS

The first category, intrapersonal, relates to how well you know and like yourself, as well as how effectively you can do the things you need to do to stay happy. This category is made up of five specific competencies:

- **Emotional self-awareness.** Knowing how and why you feel the way you do.
- **Assertiveness.** Standing up for yourself when you need to without being too aggressive.
- **Independence.** Making important decisions on your own without having to get everyone's opinion.
- **Self-regard.** Liking yourself in spite of your flaws (and we all have them).
- **Self-actualization.** Being satisfied and comfortable with what you have achieved in school, work, and your personal life.

Understanding yourself and why you think and act as you do is the glue that holds all of the EI competencies together. Knowledge of self is strongly connected to respect for others and their way of life. If you don't understand yourself and why you do the things you do, it can be difficult for you to understand others. What's more, if you don't like yourself, you can hardly expect others to like you.

IN CLASS: At the beginning of class, ask your students to review the fifteen EI competencies, select their strongest and their weakest competency, and write those anonymously on slips of paper, identifying each as a strength or a weakness. Ask another student or a peer leader to tally the results to see which weaknesses and strengths are most common in your class. Facilitate a class discussion to generate ideas for addressing the most common weaknesses students identify.

[2]Adapted from R. Bar-On, "The Bar-On Model of Emotional-Social Intelligence (ESI)," *Psicothema,* 18 (2006, suppl. 13–25): 21, http://www.eiconsortium.org/pdf/baron_model_of_emotional_social_intelligence.pdf.

INTERPERSONAL SKILLS

Recent studies have shown that people with extensive support networks are generally happier and tend to enjoy longer, healthier lives. Forging relationships and getting along with other people depend on the competencies that form the basis for the interpersonal category:

- **Empathy.** Making an effort to understand another person's situation or point of view.
- **Social responsibility.** Establishing a personal link with a group or community and cooperating with other members in working toward shared goals.
- **Interpersonal relationships.** Seeking out healthy and mutually beneficial relationships—such as friendships, professional networks, family connections, mentoring, and romantic partnerships—and making a persistent effort to maintain them.

ADAPTABILITY

Things change. Adaptability, the ability to adjust your thinking and behavior when faced with new or unexpected situations, helps you cope and ensures that you'll do well in life, no matter what the challenges. This category includes three key competencies:

- **Reality testing.** Ensuring that your feelings are appropriate by checking them against external, objective criteria.
- **Flexibility.** Adapting and adjusting your emotions, viewpoints, and actions as situations change.
- **Problem solving.** Approaching challenges step-by-step and not giving up in the face of obstacles.

Think Outside the Bowl

Good problem solvers sometimes have to work alone and be persistent. Help is not always readily available. Harness your own creativity to solve your problems in college. That way you won't feel like a fish out of water.

"The key to stress management is knowing how to vent your frustration."

Don't Blow Your Top
There are good ways and bad ways to vent frustration. Having it out with another person and eating a gallon of ice cream are poor strategies. But going for a walk or a run, doing yoga, or "talking it out" with someone you trust will help you deal with the frustrations that are common to college life without making things worse.

STRESS MANAGEMENT

In college, at work, and at home, now and in the future, you'll be faced with what can seem like never-ending pressures and demands. Managing the inevitable resulting stress depends on two skills:

- **Stress tolerance.** Recognizing the causes of stress and responding in appropriate ways; staying strong under pressure.
- **Impulse control.** Thinking carefully about potential consequences before you act and delaying gratification for the sake of achieving long-term goals.

DID YOU KNOW?

40% of college students feel overwhelmed by all they have to do in their first year of college.

GENERAL MOOD AND EFFECTIVE PERFORMANCE

It might sound sappy, but having a positive attitude really does improve your chances of doing well. Bar-On emphasizes the importance of two emotions in particular:

- **Optimism.** Looking for the "bright side" of any problem or difficulty and being confident that things will work out for the best.
- **Happiness.** Being satisfied with yourself, with others, and with your situation in general.

It makes sense: If you feel good about yourself and manage your emotions, you can expect to get along with others and enjoy a happy, successful life.

IN CLASS: Ask students to role-play stressful or difficult situations in college. You can use, for example, the two case studies in Chapter 3 of the Instructor's Manual or you can create your own scenario. Ask students to react to and discuss the situations.

TECH TIP STAY CONNECTED

Whatever your communication MO—smart phone, Facebook, or wiki—cyber etiquette is crucial. Just because you're hiding behind a computer screen doesn't mean that you should abandon your classroom manners. Failure to treat your fellow students and instructors with respect will brand you as an ignorant boor. Would you want to share a chat room with someone who writes in all caps (the digital equivalent of shouting) and belittles others' opinions? No one else does either. Emotional intelligence means being aware of your own and others' feelings. Transpose that mantra to your online world and you're good to go.

1 ▸ THE PROBLEM

There's a brave new world of ways to communicate in college, and you feel like you're from another planet.

2 ▸ THE FIX

Learn the nuts and bolts of connecting through cyberspace. If you still have questions, at least you'll have a good idea of what you're talking about.

3 ▸ HOW TO DO IT

1. E-mail: The most popular way to communicate online. If you have Internet access, you can send e-mail messages galore, free of charge.

2. Texting: Just like passing notes, only it's done between smart phones or other mobile devices. Downside: You have to pay a small fee for the service.

3. Instant messaging: Also like passing notes, but via desktop computers and laptops. Upside: Like e-mail, it's free.

4. Blogs: Informal Web sites made up of journal entries, articles, and other posts. Note: Blogs can only be modified by their authors, and they can reflect biased or even uninformed viewpoints.

5. Wikis: Blogs that invite the world to weigh in on a subject. Visitors can share their knowledge by adding new entries or modifying or deleting old ones. Note: Unlike blogs, wikis often pop up through search engines like Google.

6. Online social networks: Web sites that let people share opinions, photos, music, and videos with other registered members of the group.

7. Chat rooms: Cybersites people can join to "talk" (i.e., type to one another on keyboards) in real time.

8. Web conference: An online meeting between two or more people. Participants often speak to each other via Web-camera (à la *Skype*) and can even work on documents or presentations together.

A FEW WORDS ABOUT TECHNOLOGY OVERLOAD

Apply extreme caution when researching an essay online and simultaneously fielding nonstop phone calls, text messages, e-mails, and Facebook updates *and* listening to your iPod: Your brain might explode. Well, not really, but even digital natives need to unplug once in a while.

Excessive multitasking raises your stress levels. It also dulls your powers of concentration, so your work suffers. Experts recommend not trying to do more than two complex tasks at once. And remember: In days of yore, students were happy to go somewhere quiet and read a book, or simply take a walk and think. For a little brain refreshment, why not step away from your gadgets and give one of these old-school, low-tech concepts a whirl?

Exercise 3.3 asks students to chart their intrapersonal skills.

EXERCISE 3.3

What You DEMONSTRATE Matters

The chart below represents how a student, Aida, views her own intrapersonal skills in the five categories listed in the book. She determines that her independence is her greatest strength but her self-actualization is a little weak.

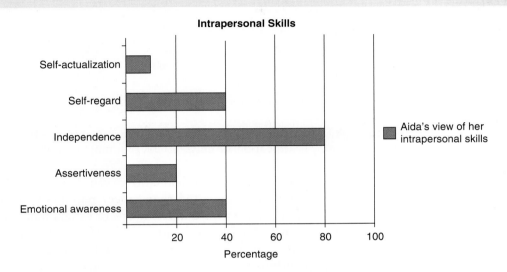

Aida seems to know herself fairly well. What are *your* strengths? Can you think of ways to improve on your weaker areas? What might be the best way to determine what areas are stronger for you or weaker? Below are some blank charts you can use to identify your strong and weak areas. Understanding yourself and why you think and act as you do is strongly connected to your personal happiness and understanding of others.

The charts below are for you to graphically demonstrate your skills and their relative strengths. Shade in the following skills to the percentage you believe you currently possess.

Intrapersonal Skills	0	20	40	60	80	100
Self-actualization						
Self-regard						
Independence						
Assertiveness						
Emotional self-awareness						

Intrapersonal Skills	0	20	40	60	80	100
Empathy						
Social responsibility						
Interpersonal relationships						

Adaptability	0	20	40	60	80	100
Reality testing						
Flexibility						
Problem solving						

(continued)

Stress Management	0	20	40	60	80	100
Stress tolerance						
Impulse control						

General Mood and Effective Performance	0	20	40	60	80	100
Optimism						
Happiness						

Ask the students to keep a chart or notes and record how frequently they notice fellow students who strike them as being "together" emotionally and who are also doing well in college academically. Ask them to consider what at least might be the correlation, if not some elements of causation.

How Emotions Affect Success

Do you think that people can change their behaviors as they mature, such as by learning to delay gratification, or do you think that most people resist change?

Emotions are strongly tied to physical and psychological well-being. For example, some studies have suggested that cancer patients who have strong EI live longer. People who are aware of the needs of others tend to be happier than people who are not. A large study done at the University of Pennsylvania found that the best athletes do well in part because they're extremely optimistic. In light of tremendous obstacles and with the odds stacked against them, emotionally intelligent people nonetheless go on to succeed.

A number of studies link strong EI skills to college success in particular. Here are a few highlights:

- **Emotionally intelligent students get higher grades.** Researchers looked at students' grade point averages at the end of the first year of college. Students who had tested high for intrapersonal skills, stress tolerance,

Accentuate the Positive

You probably know people who always find the negative in any situation. Constantly focusing on what's missing or what's not perfect will likely make you the kind of person whom others avoid. Practice looking on the bright side.

Patience Is a Virtue

Delaying gratification when you really want something is tough for people of all ages. But sometimes postponing your desires is the right thing to do. Delaying things you can't afford or don't have time for will help you reach your long-term goals.

and adaptability when they entered in the fall did better academically than those who had lower overall EI test scores.

- **Students who can't manage their emotions struggle academically.** Some students have experienced full-blown panic attacks before tests. Others who are depressed can't concentrate on coursework. And far too many turn to risky behaviors (drug and alcohol abuse, eating disorders, and worse) in an effort to cope. Dr. Richard Kadison, chief of Mental Health Service at Harvard University, notes that "the emotional well-being of students goes hand-in-hand with their academic development. If they're not doing well emotionally, they are not going to reach their academic potential."[3] Even students who manage to succeed academically in spite of emotional difficulties can be at risk if unhealthy behavior patterns follow them after college.

- **Students who can delay gratification tend to do better overall.** Impulse control leads to achievement. In the famous "Marshmallow Study" performed at Stanford University, researchers examined the long-term behaviors of individuals who, as four-year-olds, did or did not practice delayed gratification. The children were given one marshmallow and told that if they didn't eat it right away, they could have another. Fourteen years later, the children who ate their marshmallow immediately were more likely to experience significant stress, irritability, and inability to focus on goals. The children who waited scored an average of 210 points higher on the SAT;

DID YOU KNOW?

11% of first-year students feel depressed.

IN CLASS: A component of "impulse control" is "delaying gratification." Divide the class into small groups and ask them to discuss this concept and how it relates to today's society—children, college students, and adults. When is it okay for us to get what we want immediately, and when are we better off practicing delayed gratification?

[3]Richard Kadison and Theresa Foy DiGeronimo, *College of the Overwhelmed: The Campus Mental Health Crisis and What to Do About It* (San Francisco: Jossey-Bass, 2004), 156.

IN CLASS: Ask students to describe the behaviors of a really successful student and one who is not successful. Keep a running tally in two columns on a blackboard or projection screen. Encourage the students to be as specific as they can be when describing each behavior, and ask them to consider behaviors both in and out of the classroom. When the list is complete, ask the class as a group to develop a list of the top eight behaviors of a successful student and those of a not-so-successful student. How do those behaviors relate to the EI competencies described on pages 54–57?

THE STANFORD MARSHMALLOW STUDY

Impulse Controlled	Impulsive
> Assertive	> Indecisive
> Cope with frustration	> Overreact to frustration
> Work better under pressure	> Overwhelmed by stress
> Self-reliant, confident	> Lower self-image
> Trustworthy	> Stubborn
> Dependable	> Impulsive
> Delay gratification	> Don't delay gratification
> Academically competent	> Poorer students
> Respond to reason	> Prone to jealousy and envy
> Concentrate	> Provoke arguments
> Eager to learn	> Sharp temper
> Follow through on plans	> Give up in face of failure
> SAT: 610 verbal, 652 math	> SAT: 524 verbal, 528 math

Source: Y. Shoda, W. Mischel, and P. K. Peake, "Predicting Adolescent Cognitive and Self-Regulatory Competencies from Preschool Delay of Gratification," *Developmental Psychology* 26, no. 6 (1990): 978–86.

had better confidence, concentration, and reliability; held better-paying jobs; and reported being more satisfied with life. The chart above details the differences between the two groups of students after fourteen years.

- **EI skills can be enhanced in a first-year seminar.** In two separate studies, one conducted in Australia and another conducted in the United States, researchers found that college students enrolled in a first-year seminar who demonstrated good EI skills were more likely to do better in college than students who did not exhibit those behaviors. A follow-up study indicated that the students who had good EI skills also raised their scores on a measure of EI.

Without strong EI in college, it is possible to do well enough to get by, but you might miss out on the full range and depth of competencies and skills that can help you to succeed in your chosen field and have a fulfilling and meaningful life.

■ IN CLASS: Ask the students to think about this course, its content, and its in-class activities. What have they been doing in this class—or could do more of—that might help them develop their EI skills?

■ RETENTION STRATEGY: Students who are easily frustrated and make impulsive decisions may give up on college. Encourage any student who expresses the wish to drop out or transfer to have a one-to-one discussion with you or a counselor before taking that step.

Exercise 3.4 uses going to college as an example of delaying gratification.

EXERCISE 3.4

What You GIVE UP Matters

When you read the Stanford University "Marshmallow Study," did you immediately identify with one group of the children? Which one? Are you more likely to delay gratification or seize the moment?

If you don't know for sure, then think about the last time you ate an Oreo cookie. Imagine one in your hand right now—hmmm, don't get too hungry! Now, in your mind, take the cookie and twist it, opening the cookie so that you have the frosted side in one hand and the hard cookie in the other. Which side do you eat first? If you (knowing that you love frosting) eat the hard cookie first, then you are delaying gratification. College is like this. You are eating your hard cookie right now, this morning, sitting in class.

> What kinds of things could you be doing besides attending class? List below things you have "given up" just to go to college (such as work, friends, or sleep).
>
> 1. _____
> 2. _____
> 3. _____
> 4. _____
>
> Knowing that you have given up so much in order to obtain your future "frosting" (your college degree and a great career), don't do anything that might jeopardize this opportunity. Eat your hard cookies first, *every day*. Study first, and then go out. Read your history, and then go shopping. Do your math homework, and then take off on that road trip. Delaying gratification will only make your frosting that much sweeter in the end! BUT, only you can make these choices, and this takes emotional intelligence.

How to Improve Your Emotional Intelligence

How does the process of creating goals and sticking to them relate to your emotional intelligence?

Developing your EI is an important step toward getting the full benefit of a college education. Think about it. Do you often give up because something is just too hard or you can't figure it out? Do you take responsibility for what you do, or do you blame others if you fail? Can you really be successful in life if you don't handle change well or if you are not open to diverse groups and their opinions? How can you communicate effectively if you are not assertive or if you are overly aggressive? If you're inflexible, how can you solve problems, get along with coworkers and family members, or learn from other people's points of view?

The good news is you can improve your EI. It might not be easy—old habits are hard to change—but it can definitely be done. Here are some suggestions:

1. **Identify your strengths and weaknesses.** Take a hard look at yourself, and consider how you respond to situations. Most people have trouble assessing their own behaviors realistically, so ask someone you trust and respect

for insight. And if you have an opportunity to take a formal emotional intelligence test or to meet with a behavioral counselor, by all means, do.

2. **Set realistic goals.** As you identify areas of emotional intelligence that you would like to improve, be as specific as possible. Instead of deciding to be more assertive, for example, focus on a particular issue that is giving you trouble, such as nagging resentment toward a friend who always orders the most expensive thing on the menu and then expects to split the whole check evenly.

3. **Formulate a plan.** With a particular goal in mind, identify a series of steps you could take to achieve the goal, and define the results that would indicate success. As you contemplate your plan, consider all of the emotional competencies discussed on pages 54–57 of this chapter: You might find that to be more assertive with your friend about the restaurant situation, for instance, you need to figure out why you're frustrated (emotional self-awareness), identify possible causes for your friend's behavior (empathy), and consider what you might be doing to encourage it (reality testing).

4. **Check your progress on a regular basis.** Continually reassess whether or not you have met your goals, and adjust your strategy as needed.

Suppose you know that you don't handle stress well. When things get tough—too many things are due at once, your roommate leaves clothes and leftover food all over the place, and your significant other seems a bit distant—you begin to fall apart. Here is a model you might use for improving the way you handle stress.

EI competency: Stress tolerance

Specific goal: To get control of the things that are causing stress this week

Plan: Identify each stressor, and select a strategy for addressing it

- List everything that needs to be done this week. Allot time for each item on the list, and stick to a schedule. Reassess the schedule many times during the week.

- Ask yourself whether your roommate is bothering you only because you are stressed. Do you do some of the same things your roommate does? Ask yourself what the next step should be: Talking to your roommate? Looking for another place to study?

- Ask yourself whether your significant other is acting differently for any reason. Is he or she under stress? Are you overreacting because you feel insecure in the relationship? After answering these questions, decide what the next step will be: Talking to your significant other and sharing your feelings with him or her? Reassessing the situation in another week when things calm down?

- Identify what reduces stress for you and still allows you to stay on target to get things done. Exercising? Working in small chunks with rewards when you finish something? Playing a musical instrument?

Success indicator: You are feeling less stressed, and you have accomplished many of the things on your list. You are working out three times a week. Your significant other seems just fine, and your place is still a mess but it's not bothering you. You leave your room and decide to study in the library.

IN CLASS: Now that your students have been thinking and talking about EI, ask them to write their own personal definition of EI. Have them share it with another student and receive feedback.

It's important not to try to improve everything at once. Instead, identify specific EI competencies that you can define, describe, and identify, and then set measurable goals for change. Don't expect success overnight. Remember that it took you a while to develop your specific approach to life, and it will take commitment and practice to change it.

Exercise 3.5 proposes a situation students are likely to encounter in college so they can come up with strategies to handle it using EI competencies.

EXERCISE 3.5

How You REACT Matters

In the last section, you read about emotional intelligence. What are some practical ways to improve yours? Below is an example of a situation you might encounter in college. Take a few moments to assess your EI and come up with some strategies to deal with the problem. These strategies might be the key to improving your own emotional intelligence.

Typical Situation:

I am assigned to work with a partner in my biology class. He is always late and is never prepared. While he's a really nice guy and seems really smart, I am afraid that my grade might suffer because of his behavior!

Competencies	Your Answer
Emotional self-awareness: How do you feel about this situation?	
Empathy: What might be making your partner late/unprepared?	
Reality testing: What might YOU be doing to encourage this behavior?	
Stress tolerance: What can you do to decrease your own stress level and still respond in appropriate ways?	
Optimism: Is there a bright side to this situation? How will this turn out?	

CHECKLIST FOR SUCCESS

EVALUATING YOUR EMOTIONAL INTELLIGENCE

☐ **Using the questionnaire in this chapter, assess your emotional intelligence.** Note areas in which your EI is strong and areas that need improvement.

☐ **Be aware of how your emotions affect the way you react to difficult or frustrating situations.** Use your awareness ahead of time to try to control your negative reactions.

☐ **Learn and then practice EI improvement strategies such as:**

- Identifying your strengths and weaknesses
- Setting realistic goals
- Formulating a plan
- Checking your progress on a regular basis

☐ **If you aren't satisfied with your emotional reactions, make an appointment in the campus counseling center to discuss your feelings and get help.** Counselors can help you monitor and understand your emotional responses in a confidential setting.

APPLY IT! What Works for YOU Matters

Think about your current academic situation, and apply some of the suggestions and strategies introduced in this chapter. Select those strategies that you think will work best for you, and then write them down in the "Your Response" column. What are YOU planning to do for YOUR college experience?

QUESTIONS	SAMPLE STUDENT ANSWERS	YOUR RESPONSE
	Name: Aida Kanto	
What Is Emotional Intelligence? How aware are you of your emotions and those of others?	People always tell me that I am easy to talk to, that I am like their personal psychiatrist. That's fine, but sometimes this makes me feel frustrated, especially when I don't have anyone I can totally trust.	
Assessing Your Emotional Intelligence Have you ever taken "quizzes" in magazines and books that give insight into your personality? Why do people find these tests so interesting?	I have taken many of those quizzes in magazines, but they seem really one-sided or narrowly focused. I am really looking forward to this class because we take the Myers-Briggs next week. This test will tell me more about my preferences, not just my personality.	
Identifying Competencies Why do you think that understanding yourself is the key to success in college and in life?	I know it may sound silly, but I really don't know who I am. I don't know what I want to do or what career I need to pursue. I have an easier time telling other people how to plan their lives than planning my own. If I don't find a pathway soon, I might have to stay in college longer!	
How Emotions Affect Success Do you think that people can change their behaviors as they mature, such as by learning to delay gratification, or do you think that most people resist change?	I think that people can change if they decide that it is important, but most people get into this comfort zone where they just don't want to try new things. I am going to try reviewing my history notes right after class, just to see if it helps. This is huge for me because I usually wait until the night before the test.	
How to Improve Your Emotional Intelligence How does the process of creating goals and sticking to them relate to your emotional intelligence?	Well, I am guessing that making a goal, like changing my note-reviewing strategy for history class, is related to my EI. It means that I have to think positively, to be willing to try new things, to be more assertive with my own academics, and to do some reality testing in the end.	

BUILD YOUR EXPERIENCE ■■■

1 COLLABORATIVE ACTIVITY

This is a group exercise.

Two Truths and a Lie

One way to improve your EI is to learn to "read people." Determining when people are comfortable with a situation and when they are not is a helpful skill!

Using *study skills* as the overall topic, list two *truths* about you, such as "I love group work" and "I prefer reading charts and graphs," and one *lie*, such as "I love making *Excel* spreadsheets."

Now it's your turn.
Truths:

1. _____

2. _____

Lie:

1. _____

Read these out loud, mixing them up, and then ask the group which one is the "lie." The group needs to see your face and read your nonverbal communication to determine the answer. For a change of pace, you can use topics other than study skills, like sports, books, travel, or food.

2 BUILDING YOUR PORTFOLIO

Know Thyself   Understanding your own behavior can sometimes be more difficult than understanding someone else's. Review the questionnaire on page 53 of this chapter. Were you honest in your assessment of yourself?

1. In a *Word* document, list the questions from page 53 that you answered with a B or a C. For example, did you rate yourself with a B or a C on a question such as "I am okay when things change at the last minute"?

2. Next, note the EI competencies that relate to each question. For the example above, the key competency is adaptability, as evidenced in reality testing, flexibility, and problem solving.

3. For each question that you have listed, describe your strategy for improving your response to certain situations. For example, when things change suddenly, you might say, "I am going to take a few minutes to think about what I need to do next. I will remind myself that I am still in control of my actions."

4. Save your responses in your portfolio. Revisit your responses to the questions listed above as you experience similar situations.

Pay special attention to how your emotional intelligence affects your daily life. As you become more aware of your emotions and actions, you will begin to see how you can improve in the areas that are most difficult for you.

Emotional intelligence might be a term that you were not familiar with before reading this chapter. What did you find to be the most interesting information in this chapter? Make a note of any information that was hard to understand or apply to your own life. What kinds of questions do you still have for your instructor?

_____

_____

_____

_____

_____

_____

_____

_____

_____

_____

_____

_____

_____

_____

No matter how well prepared you are in your teaching, what a student hears and understands might not always be what you think you have said. The one-minute paper is a quick and easy assessment tool that will help alert you when students don't understand what was said or discussed in class. The one-minute paper will also give timid students an opportunity to ask questions and seek clarification. Ideally, you should ask for such a paper several minutes before the end of a class. The paper will also help you begin your next class by clarifying points your students seem to be unsure of.

For more on this topic watch
French Fries Are Not Vegetables and Other College Lessons

WHERE TO GO FOR HELP . . .

If you think that you might need some help developing some of these EI skills, especially if you feel that you are not happy or optimistic or you're not handling stress well, do something about it. Although you can look online and get some tips about being an optimistic person, for example, there is nothing like getting some help from a professional. Consider visiting your academic adviser or a wellness or counseling center on campus. Look for any related workshops that are offered on campus or nearby. Remember that the good news about EI is that with persistence it can be improved.

MY INSTITUTION'S RESOURCES

_____

_____

_____

_____

_____

_____

_____

_____

CHAPTER 4

Discovering How You Learn

Have you ever thought about how you learn? People learn differently. This is hardly a novel idea, but if you are to do well in college, it is important that you become aware of your preferred way, or style, of learning. Experts agree that there is no one best way to learn.

Maybe you have trouble paying attention to a long lecture, or maybe listening is the way you learn best. You might love classroom discussion, or you might consider hearing what other students have to say in class a big waste of time.

Perhaps you have not thought about how college instructors, and even particular courses, have their own inherent styles, which can be different from your preferred style of learning. Many instructors rely almost solely on lecturing; others use lots of visual aids, such as *PowerPoint* outlines, charts, graphs, and pictures. In science courses, you will conduct experiments or go on field trips where you can observe or touch what you are studying. In dance, theater, or physical education courses, learning takes place in both your body and your mind. And in almost all courses, you'll learn by reading both textbooks and other materials. Some instructors are friendly and warm; others seem to want little interaction with students. It's safe to say that in at least some of your college courses, you won't find a close match between the way you learn most effectively and the way you're being taught. This chapter will help you first to understand how you learn best and then to think of ways in which you can create a link between your style of learning and the expectations of each course and instructor.

There are many ways of thinking about and describing **learning styles**. Some of these will make a lot of sense to you; others might initially seem confusing or counterintuitive. Some learning style theories are very simple, and

IN CLASS: Ask students to discuss why it is important for new college students to understand how they learn best. Do they understand what is meant by "learning style"?

IN CLASS: Ask students to think about the ways that faculty members approach teaching. Are there different styles of teaching? What is the relationship between teaching and learning?

learning styles Particular ways of learning, unique to each individual. For example, one person prefers reading to understand how something works, whereas another prefers using a "hands-on" approach.

IN THIS CHAPTER YOU WILL EXPLORE

Many approaches to understanding your learning styles or preferences

....

How learning styles and teaching styles often differ

....

How to optimize your learning style in any classroom setting

....

How to understand and recognize a learning disability

learning disabilities Disorders, such as dyslexia, that affect people's ability to either interpret what they see and hear or connect information across different areas of the brain.

some are complex. You will notice some overlap between the different theories, but using several of them might help you do a more precise job of discovering your learning style. If you are interested in reading more about learning styles, the library and campus learning center will have many resources.

In addition to its focus on learning styles, this chapter will also explore **learning disabilities**, which are very common among college students. You might know someone who has been diagnosed with a learning disability, such as dyslexia or attention deficit disorder. It is also possible that you have a special learning need and are not aware of it. This chapter seeks to increase your self-awareness and your knowledge about such challenges to learning. In reading this chapter, you will learn more about common types of learning disabilities, how to recognize them, and what to do if you or someone you know has a learning disability.

■ RETENTION STRATEGY: One aspect of retention is giving students the tools they will need for successful academic learning. At the beginning of the chapter, ask students to brainstorm ways that each style supports student success.

ASSESSING YOUR STRENGTHS

Understanding your own preferred style of learning will help you study and earn good grades. Do you know how you learn best? Now that you have read the first section of this chapter, list your insights about your own learning styles.

_____

_____

_____

_____

SETTING GOALS

What are your most important objectives in learning the material in this chapter? Think about challenges you have had with relating to the way some instructors teach and expect you to learn. List three goals that relate to understanding learning styles (e.g., I will make a list of my favorite and least favorite classes and think about how my preferences might relate to my preferred style of learning).

1. _____

_____

2. _____

_____

3. _____

_____

The VARK Learning Styles Inventory

Do you think there is a relationship between the teaching styles of instructors and the learning styles of students? What teaching style do you prefer—Visual, Aural, Read/Write, or Kinesthetic?

The VARK Inventory focuses on how learners prefer to use their senses (hearing, seeing, writing, reading, or experiencing) to learn. The acronym VARK stands for "Visual," "Aural," "Read/Write," and "Kinesthetic." Visual learners prefer to learn information through charts, graphs, symbols, and other visual means. Aural learners prefer to hear information. Read/Write learners prefer to learn information that is displayed as words. Kinesthetic learners prefer to learn through experience and practice, whether simulated or real. To determine your learning style according to the VARK Inventory, respond to the following questionnaire.

THE VARK QUESTIONNAIRE, VERSION 7.0

This questionnaire is designed to tell you something about your preferences for the way you work with information. Choose answers that explain your preference. Check the box next to those items. Please select as many boxes as apply to you. If none of the response options apply to you, leave the item blank.

1. You are helping someone who wants to go to your airport, town center, or railway station. You would:
   - ☐ A. go with her.
   - ☐ B. tell her the directions.
   - ☐ C. write down the directions (without a map).
   - ☐ D. draw, or give her a map.

2. You are not sure whether a word should be spelled "dependent" or "dependant." You would:
   - ☐ A. see the words in your mind and choose by the way they look.
   - ☐ B. think about how each word sounds and choose one.
   - ☐ C. find it in a dictionary.
   - ☐ D. write both words on paper and choose one.

3. You are planning a holiday for a group. You want some feedback from them about the plan. You would:
   - ☐ A. describe some of the highlights.
   - ☐ B. use a map or Web site to show them the places.
   - ☐ C. give them a copy of the printed itinerary.
   - ☐ D. phone, text, or e-mail them.

4. You are going to cook something as a special treat for your family. You would:
   - ☐ A. cook something you know without the need for instructions.
   - ☐ B. ask friends for suggestions.
   - ☐ C. look through a cookbook for ideas from the pictures.
   - ☐ D. use a cookbook where you know there is a good recipe.

5. A group of tourists want to learn about the parks or wildlife reserves in your area. You would:
   - ☐ A. talk about, or arrange a talk for them, about parks or wildlife reserves.
   - ☐ B. show them Internet pictures, photographs, or picture books.
   - ☐ C. take them to a park or wildlife reserve and walk with them.
   - ☐ D. give them a book or pamphlets about the parks or wildlife reserves.

6. You are about to purchase a digital camera or mobile phone. Other than price, what would most influence your decision?
   - ☐ A. Trying or testing it.
   - ☐ B. Reading the details about its features.
   - ☐ C. Thinking that it is a modern design and looks good.
   - ☐ D. Hearing about its features from the salesperson.

(continued)

7. Remember a time when you learned how to do something new. Try to avoid choosing a physical skill (e.g., riding a bike). You learned best by:

- ☐ A. watching a demonstration.
- ☐ B. listening to somebody explaining it and asking questions.
- ☐ C. diagrams and charts— visual clues.
- ☐ D. written instructions—e.g., a manual or textbook.

8. You have a problem with your knee. You would prefer that the doctor:

- ☐ A. give you an online source or written materials to read about your problem.
- ☐ B. use a plastic model of a knee to show what was wrong.
- ☐ C. describe what was wrong.
- ☐ D. show you a diagram of what was wrong.

9. You want to learn a new program, skill, or game on a computer. You would:

- ☐ A. read the written instructions that came with the program.
- ☐ B. talk with people who know about the program.
- ☐ C. use the controls or keyboard.
- ☐ D. follow the diagrams in the book that came with it.

10. You like Web sites that have:

- ☐ A. things you can click on, shift, or try.
- ☐ B. interesting design and visual features.
- ☐ C. interesting written descriptions, lists, and explanations.

- ☐ D. audio channels where you can hear music, radio programs, or interviews.

11. Other than price, what would most influence your decision to buy a new nonfiction book?

- ☐ A. Thinking it looks appealing.
- ☐ B. Quickly reading parts of it.
- ☐ C. Hearing a friend talk about it and recommend it.
- ☐ D. Its real-life stories, experiences, and examples.

12. You are using a book, CD, or Web site to learn how to take photos with your new digital camera. You would like to have:

- ☐ A. a chance to ask questions and talk about the camera and its features.
- ☐ B. clear written instructions with lists and bullet points about what to do.
- ☐ C. diagrams showing the camera and what each part does.
- ☐ D. many examples of good and poor photos and how to improve them.

13. You prefer a teacher or a presenter who uses:

- ☐ A. demonstrations, models, or practical sessions.
- ☐ B. question and answer, talk, group discussion, or guest speakers.
- ☐ C. handouts, books, or readings.
- ☐ D. diagrams, charts, or graphs.

14. You have finished a competition or test and would like some feedback:

- ☐ A. using examples from what you have done.
- ☐ B. using a written description of your results.
- ☐ C. from somebody who talks it through with you.
- ☐ D. using graphs showing what you had achieved.

15. You are going to choose food at a restaurant or café. You would:

- ☐ A. choose something that you have had there before.
- ☐ B. listen to the waiter or ask friends to recommend choices.
- ☐ C. choose from the descriptions in the menu.
- ☐ D. look at what others are eating or look at pictures of each dish.

16. You have to make an important speech at a conference or special occasion. You would:

- ☐ A. make diagrams or get graphs to help explain things.
- ☐ B. write a few key words and practice saying your speech over and over.
- ☐ C. write out your speech and learn from reading it over several times.
- ☐ D. gather many examples and stories to make the talk real and practical.

SCORING THE VARK

Use the following scoring chart to find the VARK category to which each of your answers belongs. Circle the letters that correspond to your answers. For example, if you answered b and c for question 3, circle V and R in the 3 row.

Question	A Category	B Category	C Category	D Category
3	K	(V)	(R)	A

Count the number of each of the VARK letters you have circled to get your score for each VARK category.

SCORING CHART

Question	A Category	B Category	C Category	D Category
1	K	A	R	V
2	V	A	R	K
3	K	V	R	A
4	K	A	V	R
5	A	V	K	R
6	K	R	V	A
7	K	A	V	R
8	R	K	A	V
9	R	A	K	V
10	K	V	R	A
11	V	R	A	K
12	A	R	V	K
13	K	A	R	V
14	K	R	A	V
15	K	A	R	V
16	V	A	R	K

Total number of **V**s circled = _____

Total number of **A**s circled = _____

Total number of **R**s circled = _____

Total number of **K**s circled = _____

Because you could choose more than one answer for each question, the scoring is not just a simple matter of counting. It is like four stepping stones across some water. Enter your scores **from highest to lowest** on the stones in the figure, with their V, A, R, and K labels.

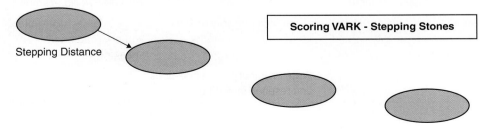

Stepping Distance

Scoring VARK - Stepping Stones

Your stepping distance comes from this table:

The total of my four VARK scores is	My stepping distance is
16-21	1
22-27	2
28-32	3
More than 32	4

Follow these steps to establish your preferences.

1. Your first preference is always your highest score. Check that first stone as one of your preferences.
2. Now subtract your second highest score from your first. If that figure is larger than your stepping distance, you have a single preference. Otherwise, check this stone as another preference and continue with step 3.
3. Subtract your third score from your second one. If that figure is larger than your stepping distance, you have a bimodal preference. If not, check your third stone as a preference and continue with step 4.
4. Last, subtract your fourth score from your third one. If that figure is larger than your stepping distance, you have a trimodal preference. Otherwise, check your fourth stone as a preference, and you have all four modes as your preferences!

Note: If you are bimodal or trimodal or you have checked all four modes as your preferences, you can be described as *multimodal* in your VARK preferences.

USING VARK RESULTS TO STUDY MORE EFFECTIVELY

How can knowing your VARK score help you do better in your college classes? The following table offers suggestions for using learning styles to develop your own study strategies.

IN CLASS: After the students have completed the inventory, discuss the model. Take a poll to determine the variety of learning styles among the class. What does this mean for the dynamics of the class?

OUTSIDE CLASS: Ask students to write a short paper on what they learned after completing and scoring the VARK.

Study Strategies by Learning Style

Visual	Aural	Read/Write	Kinesthetic
Underline or highlight your notes.	Talk with others to verify the accuracy of your lecture notes.	Write and rewrite your notes.	Use all your senses in learning: sight, touch, taste, smell, and hearing.
Use symbols, charts, or graphs to display your notes.	Put your notes on tape and listen or tape class lectures.	Read your notes silently.	Supplement your notes with real-world examples.
Use different arrangements of words on the page.	Read your notes out loud; ask yourself questions and speak your answers.	Organize diagrams or flow charts into statements.	Move and gesture while you are reading or speaking your notes.
Redraw your pages from memory.		Write imaginary exam questions and respond in writing.	

How You ADAPT Matters

Try to use the VARK to figure out how your instructors teach their classes.

List your classes, your instructor's teaching styles, and then your learning style. Do they match? If not, list a strategy you can use to adapt.

My Classes	Teaching Style	My Learning Style	Match: Yes or No?
Example: Psychology	Loves PowerPoints with her lecture so: Visual and Auditory	I am Kinesthetic and visual.	No, but I can ride a stationary bike while looking over my notes.

Exercise 4.1 asks students to compare the teaching styles of their instructors to their own learning style.

The Kolb Inventory of Learning Styles

You may find yourself in a class that is not compatible with your normal learning style. What other learning style might you adopt to be successful in a class you are struggling with right now?

A learning model that is more complex than the VARK Inventory is the widely used and referenced Kolb Inventory of Learning Styles. While the VARK Inventory investigates how learners prefer to use their senses in learning, the Kolb Inventory focuses on abilities we need to develop in order to learn. This inventory, developed in the 1980s by David Kolb, is based on a four-stage cycle of learning (see Figure 4.1).

According to Kolb, effective learners need four kinds of abilities:

- *Concrete experience* abilities, which allow them to be receptive to others and open to other people's feelings and specific experiences. An example of this type of ability is learning from and empathizing with others.
- *Reflective observation* abilities, which help learners to reflect on their experiences from many perspectives. An example of this type of ability is remaining impartial while considering a situation from a number of different points of view.
- *Abstract conceptualization* abilities, which help learners to integrate observations into logically sound theories. An example of this type of ability is analyzing ideas intellectually and systematically.
- *Active experimentation* abilities, which enable learners to make decisions, solve problems, and test what they have learned in new situations. An example of this type of ability is being ready to move quickly from thinking to action.

IN CLASS: After a short explanation of the Four-Stage Cycle of Learning, group the students to discuss their understandings of this model. What questions do they have? Do they consider this model useful? Why or why not?

FIGURE 4.1

Kolb's Four-Stage Cycle of Learning

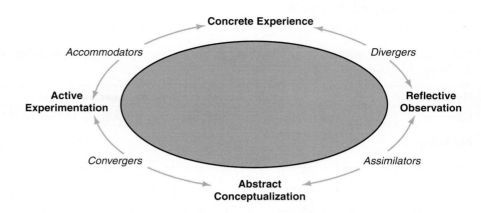

If you are interested in using the Kolb Inventory of Learning Styles, the twelve-item questionnaire and workbook are available online. For information about costs of single or multiple copies, go to http://www.haygroup.com/tl/Questionnaires_Workbooks/Kolb_Learning_Style_Inventory.aspx.

Kolb's Inventory of Learning Styles measures differences along two basic dimensions that represent opposite styles of learning. The first dimension is *abstract-concrete*; the second is *active-reflective*. See Figure 4.1 to visualize how these polar-opposite characteristics link together to create four discrete groups of learners: *divergers*, *assimilators*, *convergers*, and *accommodators*.

Doing well in college will require you to adopt some behaviors that are characteristic of each of these four learning styles. Some of them might be uncomfortable for you, but that discomfort will indicate that you're growing, stretching, and not relying on the learning style that might be easiest or most natural.

If you are a diverger, you are adept at reflecting on situations from many viewpoints. You excel at brainstorming, and you're imaginative, people oriented, and sometimes emotional. On the downside, you sometimes have difficulty making decisions. Divergers tend to major in the humanities or social sciences.

If you are an assimilator, you like to think about abstract concepts. You are comfortable in classes where the instructor lectures about theoretical ideas without relating the lectures to real-world situations. Assimilators often major in math, physics, or chemistry.

If you are a converger, you like the world of ideas and theories, but you also are good at thinking about how to apply those theories to real-world, practical situations. You differ from divergers in your preference for tasks and problems rather than social and interpersonal issues. Convergers tend to choose health-related and engineering majors.

IN CLASS: Ask students to discuss the following statement: "Doing well in college will require you to adopt some behaviors that are characteristic of each of the four styles."

If you are an accommodator, you prefer hands-on learning. You are skilled at making things happen, and you rely on your intuition. You like people, but you can be pushy and impatient at times, and you might use trial and error, rather than logic, to solve problems. Accommodators often major in business, especially in marketing or sales.[1]

In all your classes, but especially in liberal arts and social science courses, you will need to develop the strengths of divergers: imagination, brainstorming, and listening with an open mind. The abilities that are characteristic of assimilators, developing theories and concepts, are valuable for all students, especially those in the sciences. If you major in the health sciences or in engineering, you will routinely practice the skills of convergers: experimenting with new ideas and choosing the best solution. Finally, whatever your major and ultimate career, you'll need to get things done, take some risks, and become a leader—skills that are characteristic of accommodators.

[1]Adapted from David A. Kolb, "Learning Styles and Disciplinary Differences," in *The Modern American College*, ed. Arthur W. Chickering (San Francisco: Jossey Bass, 1981), 232–35.

Exercise 4.2 asks students to reflect on their preferred learning style and to share ideas with a classmate on how to adapt to each of their classes.

EXERCISE 4.2

What You DEVELOP Matters

As this section explains, the Kolb Inventory of Learning Styles measures differences along two basic dimensions that represent opposite styles of learning: abstract-concrete and active-reflective. While you may be more comfortable with one style or another, we all have components of *all* styles within our capabilities; it is just that sometimes we have to practice a less comfortable style in a particular class.

Let's consider how you write your name.

Sign your name with your hand that is dominant: _____

Now sign your name with your nondominant hand: _____

What do you notice about the two signatures? The same can be said for your learning styles that you do not often use.

Take a moment to determine which one of the four groups of learners best reflects your typical behavior: diverger, assimilator, converger, or accommodator (see descriptions of each on page 78).

Typically, I am a _____.

Now think about your current class schedule and the type of learner that best matches the instructor:

	Class:	Type of Learner:
1.	_____	_____
2.	_____	_____
3.	_____	_____
4.	_____	_____

How can you use this information to overcome challenges to your comfortable learning style? For example, if you are an accommodator but find yourself in a science class that is heavy on theories that are not directly applied to real-world situations, can you create a study group that might focus on discussing what you need to learn in a pragmatic way? Take a moment to share some ideas with a partner in class who might have a solution you can use!

The Myers-Briggs Type Indicator

How does your "type" affect the way you learn? In what way does your MBTI affect your significant relationships?

One of the best-known and most widely used personality inventories that can also be used to describe learning styles is the Myers-Briggs Type Indicator, or MBTI.[2] While the VARK measures your preferences for using your senses to learn and the Kolb Inventory focuses on learning abilities, the MBTI investigates basic personality characteristics and how those relate to human interaction and learning. Created by Isabel Briggs Myers and her mother, Katharine Cook Briggs, the MBTI identifies and measures psychological type as developed in the personality theory of Carl Gustav Jung, the great twentieth-century psychoanalyst. The MBTI is given to several million people around the world each year. Employers often use this test to give employees insight into how they perceive

An online bibliography listing almost 8,000 known studies on the MBTI is available at **www.capt.org**. Volume 60 of the *Journal of Psychological Type* contains abstracts of over 400 studies that have appeared in that publication, available through the Mississippi State University Psychology Department.

[2]Isabel Briggs Myers, *Introduction to Type*, 6th ed. (Palo Alto, CA: CPP, 1998).

the world, go about making decisions, and get along with other people. Many first-year seminar or college success courses also include a focus on the MBTI because it provides a good way to begin a dialogue about human interaction and how personality type affects learning.

All the psychological types described by the MBTI are normal and healthy; there is no good or bad or right or wrong—people are simply different. When you complete the Myers-Briggs survey instrument, your score represents your "psychological type"—the combination of your preferences on four different scales. These scales measure how you take in information and how you then make decisions or come to conclusions about that information. Each preference has a one-letter abbreviation. The four letters together make up your type. Although this book doesn't include the actual survey, you will find a description of the basic MBTI types below. In each case, which sounds more like you?

EXTRAVERSION (E) VERSUS INTROVERSION (I): THE INNER OR OUTER WORLD

The E-I preference indicates whether you direct your energy and attention primarily toward the outer world of people, events, and things or the inner world of thoughts, feelings, and reflections. Personality characteristics of extraverts and introverts are summarized here:

For instructors in any academic specialty, workshops (including online workshops) to train and qualify you to give the MBTI are available from several reputable organizations listed on the Myers & Briggs Foundation Web site (www.myersbriggs.org).

Extraverts	Introverts
Outgoing, gregarious, talkative (may talk too much)	Shy, reflective; careful listeners
People of action (may act before they think)	Consider actions deeply (may think too long before acting or neglect to act at all)
Energized by people and activity	Refreshed by quiet and privacy
Good communicators and leaders	Less likely to voice their opinions; often viewed as unaware of people and situations around them

Take a Time-out

Do you find that you need some occasional time by yourself? Although introverts are more likely to enjoy time alone, even extraverts can benefit from private time to relax or escape from the hustle and bustle of daily life.

SENSING (S) VERSUS INTUITION (N): FACTS OR IDEAS

The S-N preference indicates how you perceive the world and take in information: directly, through your five senses, or indirectly, using your intuition. Personality characteristics of sensing and intuitive types are summarized here:

IN CLASS: Ask students their thoughts about an inventory that claims to measure types. Ask for student volunteers to do an Internet search on the Myers-Briggs Type Inventory and share their findings in class.

Sensing Types	Intuitive Types
Interested above all in the facts, what they can be sure of; dislike unnecessary complication; prefer practicing skills they already know	Fascinated by concepts and big ideas; prefer learning new skills over those already mastered
Relatively traditional and conventional	Original, creative, and nontraditional
Practical, factual, realistic, and down-to-earth	Innovative but sometimes impractical; need inspiration and meaning; prefer to look to the future rather than at the present
Accurate, precise, and effective with routine and details; sometimes miss the "forest" for the "trees"	May exaggerate facts unknowingly; dislike routine and details; work in bursts of energy

THINKING (T) VERSUS FEELING (F): LOGIC OR VALUES

The T-F preference indicates how you prefer to make your decisions: through logical, rational analysis or through your subjective values, likes, and dislikes. Personality characteristics of thinking types and feeling types are summarized here:

IN CLASS: Develop a lesson on the Myers-Briggs types. Explain how the letters are used and make up a type. Ask someone on campus who has experience with the Myers-Briggs to assist you or to come to class. Usually career counselors and student development staff have worked with the Myers-Briggs.

Thinking Types	Feeling Types
Logical, rational, analytical, and critical	Warm, empathetic, and sympathetic
Relatively impersonal and objective in making decisions, less swayed by feelings and emotions; sometimes surprised and puzzled by others' feelings	Need and value harmony; often distressed or distracted by argument and conflict; reluctant to tackle unpleasant interpersonal tasks
Need and value fairness; can deal with interpersonal disharmony	Need and value kindness and harmony
Fair, logical, and just; firm and assertive	Facilitate cooperation and goodwill in others; sometimes unable to be assertive when appropriate
May seem cold, insensitive, and overly blunt and hurtful in their criticisms	Occasionally illogical, emotionally demanding, and unaffected by objective reason and evidence

JUDGING (J) VERSUS PERCEIVING (P): ORGANIZATION OR ADAPTABILITY

The J-P preference indicates how you characteristically approach the outside world: by making decisions and judgments or by observing and perceiving. Personality characteristics of judging and perceiving types are summarized here:

There is fierce academic debate as to whether the four MBTI preferences are simply additive or truly interactive. Type theory posits that feeling, for instance, will be manifested differently in an ISFP than, say, in an ENFP. This matter is too complicated for a brief introduction to students, but in the exercises and resources they will find more detailed descriptions of their complete four-letter types than they can get by simply compiling the descriptions of the four scales.

Judging Types	Perceiving Types
Orderly, organized, punctual, and tidy	Spontaneous and flexible
In control of their own world and sphere of influence	Adapt to their world rather than try to control it; comfortable dealing with changes and unexpected developments
Quick decision makers; like to make and follow plans	Slow to make decisions; prefer a wait-and-see approach
Sometimes judgmental and prone to jump to conclusions or make decisions without enough information; have trouble changing plans	Tendency toward serious procrastination and juggling too many things at once without finishing anything; sometimes messy and disorganized

Estimates of the relative frequencies of each four-letter psychological type for men and women in the general population can be found in the 1998 edition of the *MBTI® Manual* and in Volume 37 of the *Journal of Psychological Type.*

It is inappropriate, unethical, and illegal to use the MBTI as a screening device to decide whether or not to hire an applicant for a job (or admit someone to an educational program). The proper use of the MBTI is to help people identify satisfying career specialties for themselves.

IN CLASS: If your students have taken the MBTI, try this: Arrange the chairs or desks in a circle or square, beginning with the most sensing students and progressing to the most intuitive students as you circuit around the group. Arrange students by MBTI type, as much as possible so that students are next to people with whom they feel naturally comfortable and can quickly make friends. Note that they are sitting opposite, and are thus most likely to speak and listen to, people whose viewpoints are quite different from theirs. It might sound odd, but it really works!

Myers's *Introduction to Type* (see note 2) is the only full-length book on psychological type. It is richly informative and requires no prior training in psychology. Our favorite brief discussion is *Introduction to Type in Organizations* by Sandra Hirsh, Consulting Psychologists Press, 1998.

HOW TO USE YOUR STRONGEST— AND WEAKEST—PREFERENCES

Because each of four different preferences has two possible choices, sixteen psychological types are possible. No matter what your Myers-Briggs type, all components of personality have value in the learning process. The key to success in college, therefore, is to use all of the attitudes and functions (E, I, S, N, T, F, J, and P) in their most positive sense. As you go about your studies, we recommend this system:

1. *Extraversion:* Take action. Now that you have a plan, act on it. Do whatever it takes. Create note cards, study outlines, study groups, and so on. If you are working on a paper, now is the time to start writing.

2. *Introversion:* Think it through. Before you take any action, carefully review everything you have encountered so far.

3. *Sensing:* Get the facts. Use sensing to find and learn the facts. How do we know facts when we see them? What is the evidence for what is being said?

4. *Intuition:* Get the ideas. Now use intuition to consider what those facts mean. Why are those facts being presented? What concepts and ideas are being supported by those facts? What are the implications? What is the big picture?

5. *Thinking:* Critically analyze. Use thinking to analyze the pros and cons of what is being presented. Are there gaps in the evidence? What more do we need to know? Do the facts really support the conclusions? Are there alternative explanations? How well does what is presented hang together logically? How could our knowledge of it be improved?

6. *Feeling:* Make informed value judgments. Why is this material important? What does it contribute to people's good? Why might it be important to you personally? What is your personal opinion about it?

7. *Judging:* Organize and plan. Don't just dive in! Now is the time to organize and plan your studying so you will learn and remember everything you need to. Don't just plan in your head either; write your plan down, in detail.

8. *Perceiving:* Change your plan as needed. Be flexible enough to change something that isn't working. Expect the unexpected, and deal with the unforeseen. Don't give up the whole effort the minute your original plan stops working. Figure out what's wrong, and come up with another, better plan and start following that.[3]

[3]Myers, *Introduction to Type.*

Exercise 4.3 sets up a scenario to give students practice in understanding how Myers-Briggs types affect relationships, as well as how two people with alternate Myers-Briggs characteristics might handle the same situation differently.

EXERCISE 4.3

What You UNDERSTAND about Others Matters

Do you remember when you suddenly realized that not everyone is like you? Maybe you came to this conclusion in middle school or maybe more recently. When you recognize the differences in people, it is easier to appreciate another person's position, even when he or she disagrees with you. Now, think about someone who looks at life differently from the way that you do. Maybe it is a friend, your boss, or your significant other. When you disagree, it may be because your Myers-Briggs types differ.

Scenario: You are planning a trip to visit some far-off country. You have decided to bring along a person with whom you do not always agree. Thinking about the potential issues ahead of time can reduce the friction that your differences might create during the trip. Take just one pair of the MBTI preferences—judging vs. perceiving—and think about how this might affect the following:

Situation	Judging Person Might:	Perceiving Person Might:
Booking the hotels		
Financing the trip		
Planning meals		

Try this with another preference—extravert vs. introvert. You are on your trip and having a wonderful time, but you get terribly lost! You have no map and cannot speak the language very well. How might an extravert handle this situation? What about an introvert? Answer the following questions:

As an extravert who is talkative and wants to "take action," here is how I would solve this problem:

_____

_____

_____

_____

As an introvert who is reflective and wants to "think it through first," I would solve this problem in this way:

_____

_____

_____

_____

What would be a good compromise between the two approaches?

_____

_____

_____

_____

A number of daily decisions and dilemmas can lead to conflict with the people you know and care about. Understanding yourself and anticipating the preferences of others will help you to avoid these conflicts and learn to create harmony in relationships.

Multiple Intelligences

Have you ever considered that you have several types of intelligences? After you read this section, what do you think are your strongest intelligences, and how can knowing these help you in college?

IN CLASS: Ask students to discuss the meaning of the term *intelligence*. Why is Howard Gardner's work controversial?

Another way of measuring how we learn is the theory of *multiple intelligences*, developed in 1983 by Dr. Howard Gardner, a professor of education at Harvard University. Gardner's theory is based on the premise that the traditional notion of human intelligence is very limited. He proposes eight different intelligences to describe how humans learn.

As you might imagine, Gardner's work is controversial because it questions our long-standing definitions of intelligence. Gardner argues that students should be encouraged to develop the abilities they have and that evaluation should measure all forms of intelligence, not just linguistic and logical-mathematical intelligence.

As you think of yourself and your friends, what kinds of intelligences do you have? Do college courses measure all the ways in which you are intelligent? Here is a short inventory that will help you recognize your multiple intelligences.

MULTIPLE INTELLIGENCES INVENTORY

According to Gardner, all human beings have at least eight different types of intelligence. Depending on your background and age, some intelligences are likely to be more developed than others. This activity will help you find out what your intelligences are. Knowing this, you can work to strengthen the other intelligences that you do not use as often. Put a check mark next to the items that apply to you.

Verbal/Linguistic Intelligence

_____ I enjoy telling stories and jokes.

_____ I enjoy word games (for example, Scrabble and puzzles).

_____ I am a good speller (most of the time).

_____ I like talking and writing about my ideas.

_____ If something breaks and won't work, I read the instruction book before I try to fix it.

_____ When I work with others in a group presentation, I prefer to do the writing and library research.

Logical/Mathematical Intelligence

_____ I really enjoy my math class.

_____ I like to find out how things work.

_____ I enjoy computer and math games.

_____ I love playing chess, checkers, or Monopoly.

_____ If something breaks and won't work, I look at the pieces and try to figure out how it works.

Visual/Spatial Intelligence

_____ I prefer a map to written directions.

_____ I enjoy hobbies such as photography.

_____ I like to doodle on paper whenever I can.

_____ In a magazine, I prefer looking at the pictures rather than reading the text.

_____ If something breaks and won't work, I tend to study the diagram of how it works.

Bodily/Kinesthetic Intelligence

_____ My favorite class is gym because I like sports.

_____ When looking at things, I like touching them.

_____ I use a lot of body movements when talking.

_____ I tend to tap my fingers or play with my pencil during class.

_____ If something breaks and won't work, I tend to play with the pieces to try to fit them together.

Musical/Rhythmic Intelligence

_____ I enjoy listening to CDs and the radio.

_____ I like to sing.

_____ I like to have music playing when doing homework or studying.

_____ I can remember the melodies of many songs.

_____ If something breaks and won't work, I tend to tap my fingers to a beat while I figure it out.

Interpersonal Intelligence

_____ I get along well with others.

_____ I have several very close friends.

_____ I like working with others in groups.

_____ Friends ask my advice because I seem to be a natural leader.

_____ If something breaks and won't work, I try to find someone who can help me.

Intrapersonal Intelligence

_____ I like to work alone without anyone bothering me.

_____ I don't like crowds.

_____ I know my own strengths and weaknesses.

_____ I find that I am strong-willed, independent, and don't follow the crowd.

_____ If something breaks and won't work, I wonder whether it's worth fixing.

Naturalist Intelligence

_____ I am keenly aware of my surroundings and of what goes on around me.

_____ I like to collect things like rocks, sports cards, and stamps.

_____ I like to get away from the city and enjoy nature.

_____ I enjoy learning the names of living things in the environment, such as flowers and trees.

_____ If something breaks down, I look around me to try and see what I can find to fix the problem.

A **verbal/linguistic learner** likes to read, write, and tell stories and is good at memorizing information. A **logical/mathematical** learner likes to work with numbers and is good at problem solving and logical processes. A **visual/spatial** learner likes to draw and play with machines and is good at puzzles and reading maps and charts. A **bodily/kinesthetic** learner likes to move around and is good at sports, dance, and acting. A **musical/rhythmic** learner likes to sing and play an instrument and is good at remembering melodies and noticing pitches and rhythms. An **interpersonal** learner likes to have many friends and is good at understanding people, leading others, and mediating conflicts. **Intrapersonal** learners like to work alone, understand themselves well, and are original thinkers. A **naturalistic** learner likes to be outside and is good at preservation, conservation, and organizing a living area.

You can use your intelligences to help you make decisions about a major, choose activities, and investigate career options. Which of these eight intelligences best describes you?

TOTAL SCORE

_____ Verbal/Linguistic

_____ Logical/Mathematical

_____ Visual/Spatial

_____ Bodily/Kinesthetic

_____ Musical/Rhythmic

_____ Interpersonal

_____ Intrapersonal

_____ Naturalist

Add the number of check marks you made in each section. Your score for each intelligence will be a number between 1 and 6. Your high scores of 3 or more will help you to get a sense of your own multiple intelligences.

Source: Greg Gay and Gary Hams, "Multiple Intelligences Inventory." Copyright © Learning Disabilities Resource Community, www.ldrc.ca. Reprinted by permission of the authors.

This exercise gets students thinking about how types of intelligences and career types match up.

EXERCISE 4.4

What You CHOOSE Matters

It is good to know that of the many forms of intelligence, individuals will have different levels of each one. None of us is a genius at everything. Certain careers and skills seem to fit with certain intelligences. Brainstorm careers that match the different types of intelligences in the chart below. Examples are provided to get you started. Add at least two more careers to each row. Which careers in particular interest you? Rate your interest level for each career you add and for the example provided.

Type of Intelligence	Associated Careers (brainstorm with class/partners)	Your Interest Level in These Careers (1 = not interested; 2 = no opinion; 3 = interested)
Verbal/Linguistic	(Journalist)	
Logical/Mathematical	(Computer Programmer)	
Visual/Spatial	(Designer)	
Bodily/Kinesthetic	(Athlete, Neurosurgeon)	
Musical/Rhythmic	(Performer)	
Interpersonal	(Politician)	
Intrapersonal	(Self-Help Writer)	
Naturalistic	(Meteorologist)	

When Learning Styles and Teaching Styles Conflict

Consider your learning style(s), and remember a time when your preferred style of learning was in direct conflict with an instructor's teaching style. How did you handle this situation? As a college student, how can you create a positive learning outcome, even when your learning style conflicts with the way you are being taught?

■ RETENTION STRATEGY: Retention is connected to how well students can engage with faculty. A good predictor of first-year persistence is out-of-class interaction between students and faculty.

Educators who study learning styles maintain that instructors tend to teach in ways that conform to their own particular styles of learning. So an introverted instructor who prefers abstract concepts and reflection (an assimilator, according to Kolb) and learns best in a read/write mode or aural mode will probably structure the course in a lecture format with little opportunity for either interaction or visual and kinesthetic learning. Conversely, an instructor who needs a more interactive, hands-on environment will likely involve students in discussion and learning through experience.

Do you enjoy listening to lectures, or do you find yourself gazing out the window or dozing? When your instructor assigns a group discussion, what is your immediate reaction? Do you dislike talking with other students, or is that the way you learn best? How do you react to lab sessions when you have to conduct an actual experiment? Is this an activity you look forward to or one that you dread? Each of these learning situations appeals to some students

TECH TIP BRANCH OUT

If the thought of a 2-hour lecture in an auditorium crammed with two hundred students fills you with a warm glow, chances are you're an auditory learner. But what if you're a visual learner who needs charts, graphs, and videos? Or a hands-on, group type who thrives best when immersed in a project?

1 ▶ THE PROBLEM

Course-management systems (CMSs) require that you learn material in a whole new way.

2 ▶ THE FIX

Figure out your learning style (by taking an online survey or test like Myers-Briggs), and look for classes that complement your strengths. At the same time, find ways to adapt to teaching techniques that lie outside your comfort zone.

3 ▶ HOW TO DO IT

The basic ingredients of a CMS — video, audio, and text — appeal to different learning styles.

1. If you're an auditory learner, you'll love audio recordings.

To get the most from text, read your notes and textbook passages aloud as you study. (You can even record them to play back to yourself.) While you're at it, listen to books on tape and join a study group for discussions.

To get the most from video clips, listen to them once, and then play them back with your eyes closed.

2. If you're a visual learner, you'll love videos, pictures, maps, and graphs.

To get the most from audio recordings and text, take notes and illustrate them, playing up key points with colored highlighters, pictures, or symbols. Or create a graph or chart to display important concepts.

3. If you're a hands-on learner, you'll love labs, group projects, and any kind of fieldwork.

To get the most from audio, video, and text, sit in the front row of your classroom, take notes, and read things aloud as you study. Build models or spreadsheets. Take field trips to gather experience. In other words, get creative.

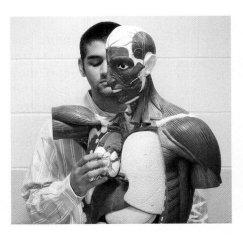

KNOW THIS

A CMS offers lots of other ways to help you connect with your instructors, your classmates, and the material. Not only can you tune in to helpful video or audio recordings, but you can also submit assignments online, keep track of your grades, sketch ideas on whiteboards that other students can view, or even collaborate on written assignments in real time.

PERSONAL BEST

Need help navigating your course or school's CMS? Turn to your favorite type-A classmate, your instructor or TA, or the campus computer lab or student success center.

Learn to Adapt

Do you know your personal learning style? In college you will find that some instructors may have teaching styles that are challenging for you. Seek out the kinds of classes that conform to the way you like to learn, but also develop your adaptive strategies to make the most of any classroom setting.

"As we start a new school year, Mr. Smith, I just want you to know that I'm an Abstract-Sequential learner and trust that you'll conduct yourself accordingly!"

more than others, but each is inevitably going to be part of your college experience. Your college or university has intentionally designed courses for you to have the opportunity to listen to professors who are experts in their field, interact with other students in structured groups, and learn through doing. Because these are all important components of your college education, it's important for you to make the most of each situation.

When you recognize a mismatch between how you best learn and how you are being taught, it is important that you take control of your learning process. Don't depend on the instructor or the classroom environment to give you everything you need to maximize your learning. Employ your own preferences, talents, and abilities to develop many different ways to study and retain information. Look back through this chapter to remind yourself of the ways in which you can use your own learning styles to be more successful in any class you take.

IN CLASS: Ask the students to share the learning styles that they discovered in this chapter and how they plan to apply them to be successful in any class.

This exercise calls on students to recall times when their learning style was in conflict with their instructor's teaching style with either a successful or frustrating conclusion.

EXERCISE 4.5

How You REACT Matters

This chapter discusses differences in the way that people think, view life, and react to change and, of course, differences in abilities. There will be times when you will take a class from an instructor whose teaching style does not match your learning style. Maybe you want structure, and she wants you to learn through trial and error. Maybe your instructor is a subject matter expert and wants you to learn through lecture and listening, while you learn best with hands-on exercises. Regardless, the goal is to be successful as a student, no matter what the class environment. How you handle conflicting situations is a reflection of your maturity as a student.

Think back to a time when you struggled in a class and yet were successful in the end. What methods did you use to persevere?

_____

_____

(continued)

Think back to a time when you may have been overly challenged by an instructor's style and simply gave up trying. Knowing yourself better today, what would you do differently to obtain a more successful outcome?

_____

_____

Take a moment to turn to a partner in class and share your experiences with him or her. Sometimes you can learn from someone else's mistakes!

Learning with a Learning Disability

Whether you have personal experience with any of the challenges discussed in this section, you may know someone who does. What have you learned from this person that you can apply to your own college survival?

While everyone has a learning style, a portion of the population has what is characterized as a learning disability. Learning disabilities are usually recognized and diagnosed in grade school, but some students can successfully compensate for a learning problem, perhaps without realizing that's what it is, and reach college without having been properly diagnosed or assisted.

IN CLASS: Ask students to discuss what, if any, direct experience they have had with learning disabilities.

Learning disabilities affect people's ability to interpret what they see and hear or to link information across different parts of the brain. These limitations can show up as specific difficulties with spoken and written language, coordination, self-control, or attention. Such difficulties can impede learning to read, write, or do math. The term *learning disability* covers a broad range of possible causes, symptoms, treatments, and outcomes. Because of this, it is difficult to diagnose a learning disability or pinpoint the causes. The types of learning disabilities that most commonly affect college students are attention disorders and disorders that affect the development of academic skills, including reading, writing, and mathematics.

> **DID YOU KNOW?**
>
> 3.3% of first-year students report suffering from a learning disability.

ATTENTION DISORDERS

Attention disorders are common in children, adolescents, and adults. Some students who have attention disorders appear to daydream excessively, and once you get their attention, they can be easily distracted. Individuals with attention deficit disorder (ADD) or attention deficit hyperactivity disorder (ADHD) often have trouble organizing tasks or completing their work. They don't seem to listen to or follow directions, and their work might be messy or appear careless. Although they are not strictly classified as learning disabilities, ADD and ADHD can seriously interfere with academic performance, leading some educators to classify them along with other learning disabilities.

If you have trouble paying attention or getting organized, you won't really know whether you have ADD or ADHD until you are evaluated. Check out resources on campus or in the community. After you have been evaluated, follow the advice you get, which might or might not mean taking medication. If you do receive a prescription for medication, be sure to take it according to the physician's directions. In the meantime, if you're having trouble getting and staying organized, whether or not you have an attention disorder, you can improve your focus through your own behavioral choices. The National Institute of Mental Health offer the following suggestions (found on their Web site) for adults with attention disorders:

> Adults with ADD or ADHD can learn how to organize their lives by using "props," such as a large calendar posted where it will be seen in the morning, date books, lists, and reminder notes. They can have a special place for keys, bills, and the paperwork of everyday life. Tasks can be organized into sections so that completion of each part can give a sense of accomplishment. Above all, adults who have ADD or ADHD should learn as much as they can about their disorder (**http://www.nimh.nih.gov/health/publications/attention-deficit-hyperactivity-disorder/can-adults-have-adhd.shtml**).

COGNITIVE LEARNING DISABILITIES

Other learning disabilities are related to cognitive skills. Dyslexia, for example, is a common developmental reading disorder. A person can have problems with any of the tasks involved in reading. However, scientists have found that a significant number of people with dyslexia share an inability to distinguish or separate the sounds in spoken words. For instance, dyslexic individuals sometimes have difficulty assigning the appropriate sounds to letters, either individually or when letters combine to form words. However, there is more to reading than recognizing words. If the brain is unable to form images or relate new ideas to those stored in memory, the reader can't understand or remember the new concepts. So other types of reading disabilities can appear when the focus of reading shifts from word identification to comprehension.

Writing, too, involves several brain areas and functions. The brain networks for vocabulary, grammar, hand movement, and memory must all be in good working order. So a developmental writing disorder might result from problems in any of these areas. Someone who can't distinguish the sequence of sounds in a word will often have problems with spelling. People with writing disabilities, particularly expressive language disorders (the inability to express oneself using accurate language or sentence structure), are often unable to compose complete, grammatical sentences.

A student with a developmental arithmetic disorder will have difficulty recognizing numbers and symbols, memorizing facts such as the multiplication table, aligning numbers, and understanding abstract concepts such as place value and fractions.

Anyone who is diagnosed with a learning disability is in good company. The pop star Jewel; Michael Phelps, the Olympic gold medal swimmer; and actors Keira Knightley, Orlando Bloom, Patrick Dempsey, and Vince Vaughn are just a few of the famous and successful people who have diagnosed learning

IN CLASS: Share information on where students should go for help on campus if they think they might have a learning disability.

disabilities. A final important message: A learning disability is a learning difference but is in no way related to intelligence. Having a learning disability is not a sign that you are stupid. In fact, some of the most intelligent individuals in human history have had a learning disability.

The following questions may help you determine whether you or someone you know should seek further screening for a possible learning disability:

- Do you perform poorly on tests even when you feel you have studied and are capable of performing better?
- Do you have trouble spelling words?
- Do you work harder than your classmates at basic reading and writing?
- Do your instructors tell you that your performance in class is inconsistent, such as answering questions correctly in class but incorrectly on a written test?
- Do you have a really short attention span, or do your family members or instructors say that you do things without thinking?

Although responding "yes" to any of these questions does not mean that you have a disability, the resources of your campus learning center or the office for student disability services can help you address any potential problems and devise ways to learn more effectively.

This exercise asks students to reflect on challenges related to learning disabilities and disorders that face some college students.

EXERCISE 4.6

What You DO to Help Others Matters

In this section we learned about a few, although certainly not all, of the challenges facing typical college students with learning disabilities and disorders. Most of us know people who face these challenges every day. What information in this section surprised you? What information did you not know before?

_____

_____

_____

_____

_____

Where can you go on your campus for assistance or counseling to determine if you or someone you know should seek screening for a possible learning disability or disorder?

_____

_____

_____

_____

_____

CHECKLIST FOR SUCCESS

USE YOUR LEARNING STYLE TO HELP YOU SUCCEED

☐ **Take a learning styles inventory, either in this chapter or at your campus learning or counseling center(s).** See if the results might explain, at least in part, your level of performance in each class you are taking this term.

☐ **Learn about and accept your unique learning preferences.** Especially make note of your strengths in terms of those things you learn well and easily. See if those skills could be applied to other learning situations.

☐ **Adapt your learning style to the teaching styles of your professors.** Consider talking to your professors about how you might best be able to adapt to their teaching strategies.

☐ **Use your learning style to develop study strategies that work best for you.** You can walk, talk, read, listen, or even dance while you are learning.

☐ **If you need help with making the best use of your learning style, visit your learning center.** Consider taking some courses in the social and behavioral sciences that would help you better understand how humans learn.

☐ **If you think you might have a learning disability, go to your campus learning center and ask for a diagnostic assessment so you can develop successful coping strategies.** Make sure you ask for a personal interpretation and follow-up counseling or tutoring.

APPLY IT! What Works for YOU Matters

Think about your current academic situation, and apply some of the suggestions and strategies introduced in this chapter. Select strategies that you think will work best for you, and then write them down in the "Your Response" column. What are YOU planning to do for YOUR college experience?

QUESTIONS	SAMPLE STUDENT ANSWERS	YOUR RESPONSE
The VARK Learning Styles Inventory Do you think there is a relationship between the teaching styles of instructors and the learning styles of students? What teaching style do you prefer—Visual, Aural, Read/Write, or Kinesthetic?	**Name: Peyton Moss** There definitely is a relationship between my learning style and whether I understand the professor. As an athlete, I need to see a practical, hands-on approach to learning. Years of looking at game plans makes me a visual learner too. If my professor just lectures, then I zone out.	

QUESTIONS	SAMPLE STUDENT ANSWERS	YOUR RESPONSE
The Kolb Inventory of Learning Styles You may find yourself in a class that is not compatible with your normal learning style. What other learning style might you adopt to be successful in a class you are struggling with right now?	I guess I am a converger. I like to see real-world applications for what I am learning. That is why I was struggling in Chemistry—until last week. When we started our Labs, I suddenly understood the theories we had been talking about. It actually came to life. To be successful, I need to see it or experience it to believe it.	
The Myers-Briggs Type Indicator How does your "type" affect the way you learn? In what way does your MBTI affect your significant relationships?	After taking the MBTI in class, I discovered I was an ESFP. This is great for my athletic program but will affect my academics if I don't work on getting my assignments in on time. I am really great socially but have to remember not to overshadow my more introverted friends.	
Multiple Intelligences Have you ever considered that you have several types of intelligences? After you read this section, what do you think are your strongest intelligences, and how can knowing these help you in college?	I was relieved to know I wasn't being measured on verbal and math alone. I am strong in bodily kinesthetic and have a fairly strong intrapersonal and verbal strength skill set, too. This will help me when I try to get people together for study groups and group projects. I can be a leader in the classroom as well as on the field.	
When Learning Styles and Teaching Styles Conflict Consider your learning style(s), and remember a time when your preferred style of learning was in direct conflict with an instructor's teaching style. How did you handle this situation? As a college student, how can you create a positive learning outcome, even when your learning style conflicts with the way you are being taught?	I remember in high school I had this one class that really did not fit well with my learning style. It was a math class. The teacher just lectured and I couldn't read the board from the back of the classroom. If I had to do this again, I would move to the front so I would stay more focused and maybe get some help in the tutoring lab, where I could talk about the lesson with other students. I need to take a more active role in these classes so that I can be successful.	
Learning with a Learning Disability Whether you have personal experience with any of the challenges discussed in this section, you may know someone who does. What have you learned from this person that you can apply to your own college survival?	I have lots of friends with disabilities. I think I may actually have ADD myself, but I have never been tested. It might be good to do that, just so I would know and could make adjustments to my own study strategies. My friends who have ADD are generally successful in college because they make the effort. I could learn from them—practice is key to success.	

BUILD YOUR EXPERIENCE

Place the name of each of the eight multiple intelligences on a poster or paper that you distribute. You may choose to give one example for each of the intelligences to help get students started in sharing strategies. Students should walk away with new ideas that match their strengths and intelligences.

1 COLLABORATIVE ACTIVITY

Each of the eight multiple intelligences has been written on a poster or a piece of paper in the classroom. With colorful markers in hand (which visual learners will especially like), walk around the room, and on the posters for the intelligences that are your strongest, list study strategies that have been useful for you in learning, studying, or listening in class. For example, a bodily/kinesthetic learner might use a stationary bike while reading a chapter in a textbook.

When you're finished, take the sheets of paper off the wall and read the strategies out loud to your classmates. Discuss the different strategies and strive to find at least one new one to try.

2 BUILDING YOUR PORTFOLIO

Are We on the Same Page?   After reading about the Myers-Briggs Type Indicator in this chapter, can you guess what type you are?

1. Create a *Word* document, and note each type that you think best fits your personality.

   - Extravert or Introvert
   - Sensing or Intuition
   - Thinking or Feeling
   - Judging or Perceiving

2. Note what you think your four MBTI letters would be (for example, ESTP).

3. Using your favorite Internet search engine, search for "suggested careers for MBTI types." You will find several Web sites that suggest specific careers based on specific personality types.

4. Visit one site, and list at least two careers that are recommended for the MBTI type that you identify. Have you thought about these careers before? Do you think they would be a good fit for you? Why or why not?

   (Example: Careers recommended for ESTP: sales representatives, marketers, police, detectives, paramedics, medical technicians, computer technicians, computer technical support, entrepreneurs. Suggestions found at **www.knowyourtype.com**.)

5. Save your findings in your portfolio. Revisit this document as you continue to explore different majors and careers.

ONE-MINUTE PAPER

Recognizing that people have different ways of learning can be a relief. After reading this chapter, do you have a better understanding of your own learning style? What did you find to be the most interesting point in this chapter? What would you like to learn more about?

_____

_____

_____

_____

_____

_____

_____

_____

_____

_____

_____

_____

_____

_____

_____

No matter how well prepared you are in your teaching, what a student hears and understands might not always be what you think you have said. The one-minute paper is a quick and easy assessment tool that will help alert you when students don't understand what was said or discussed in class. The one-minute paper will also give timid students an opportunity to ask questions and seek clarification. Ideally, you should ask for such a paper several minutes before the end of a class. The paper will also help you begin your next class, by clarifying points your students seem to be unsure of.

For more on this topic watch
French Fries Are Not Vegetables and Other College Lessons

WHERE TO GO FOR HELP . . .

ON CAMPUS

To learn more about learning styles and learning disabilities, talk to your first-year seminar instructor about campus resources. Most campuses have a learning center or a center for students with disabilities. You might also find that instructors in the areas of education or psychology have a strong interest in the processes of learning. Finally, don't forget your library or the Internet. A great deal of published information is available to describe how we learn.

BOOKS

> **Learning Outside the Lines** Edward M. Hallowell (Foreword), Jonathan Mooney, and David Cole, *Two Ivy League Students with Learning Disabilities and ADHD Give You the Tools for Academic Success and Educational Revolution* (New York: Fireside, 2000).

> Kathleen G. Nadeau, *Survival Guide for College Students with ADD or LD* (Washington, DC: Magination Press, 1994).

> **ADD and the College Student** Patricia O. Quinn, MD, ed., *A Guide for High School and College Students with Attention Deficit Disorder* (Washington, DC: Magination Press, 2001).

ONLINE

> **LD Pride www.ldpride.net/learningstyles .MI.htm.** This site was developed in 1998 by Liz Bogod, an adult with learning disabilities. It provides general information about learning styles and learning disabilities and offers an interactive diagnostic tool to determine your learning style.

> **National Center for Learning Disabilities www.ncld.org.** This is the official Web site of the National Center for Learning Disabilities. The site provides a variety of resources on diagnosing and understanding learning disabilities.

> **Facebook www.facebook.com.** There are groups on Facebook that were created by students who have learning disabilities or ADHD. These groups are a great way to connect with other students with learning disabilities at your college or university or at other institutions. If you have been diagnosed with a disability, the members of these groups can offer support and help you seek out appropriate resources in order to be successful in college.

MY INSTITUTION'S RESOURCES

_____

_____

_____

_____

_____

_____

_____

_____

_____

_____

Thinking Critically: The Basis of a College Education

Arguably the most important skill you'll acquire in college is the ability and confidence to think for yourself. Courses in every discipline will encourage you to ask questions, to sort through competing information and ideas, to form well-reasoned opinions, and to defend them. A liberal college education teaches you to investigate all sides of an issue and all possible solutions to a problem before you reach a conclusion or decide on a plan of action. Indeed, the word *liberal* (from the Latin *libero*, meaning "to free") has no political connotation in this context but represents the purpose of a college education: to liberate your mind from biases, superstitions, prejudices, and lack of knowledge so that you'll be in a better position to seek answers to difficult questions.

If you have just completed high school, you might be experiencing an awakening as you adjust to college. If you're an older returning student, discovering that your instructors trust you to find valid answers could be both surprising and stressful. If a high school teacher asked, "What are the three branches of the U.S. government?" there was only one acceptable answer: "legislative, executive, and judicial." A college instructor, on the other hand, might ask, "Under what circumstances might conflicts arise among the three branches of government, and what does this reveal about the democratic process?" There is no simple—or single—answer, and that's the point of higher education. Questions that suggest complex answers engage you in the process of critical thinking.

Most important questions don't have simple answers, and satisfying answers can be elusive. To reach them, you will have to discover numerous ways to view important issues. You will need to become comfortable with uncertainty. And you must be willing to challenge assumptions and conclusions, even those presented by so-called experts. It is natural to find critical thinking difficult and to feel frustrated by answers that are seldom entirely wrong or right. Yet the complicated questions are usually the ones that are most worthy of study, and working out the answers can be both intellectually

Critical thinking is one of the most important concepts in this book. Point out the relationship between this concept and your institution's mission statement in the campus bulletin or catalog. Discuss the campus mission statement to help your students understand your institution's educational goals; tie in the meaning of a liberal education as appropriate. You might want to point out that most employers value critical-thinking skills above the particular information or knowledge students may have gleaned from their classes.

IN CLASS: Ask students for their definition of critical thinking. As each student responds, ask the next student to refine what the previous student said.

IN CLASS: Ask several students what it means to impose intellectual standards.

IN CLASS: Ask students why some people do not think for themselves but rely on others to think for them.

■ RETENTION STRATEGY: One factor that motivates students to persist is having a clear employment goal after college. Point out to them that critical thinking is a skill in high demand by employers.

exciting and personally rewarding. In this chapter, we will explain how developing and applying your critical-thinking skills can make the search for truth a worthwhile and stimulating adventure.

What Is Critical Thinking, and Why Is It Important?

Why is it dangerous to rely on others to think or make decisions for you?

Let's start with what critical thinking is *not*. By "critical," we do not mean "negative" or "harsh." Rather, the term refers to thoughtful consideration of the information, ideas, and arguments that you encounter. Critical thinking is the ability to think for yourself and to reliably and responsibly make the decisions that affect your life.

As Richard Paul and Linda Elder of the National Council for Excellence in Critical Thinking explain it, "critical thinking is that mode of thinking about any subject, content, or problem in which the thinker improves the quality of his or her thinking by skillfully . . . imposing intellectual standards upon [his or her thoughts]."[1] They believe that much of our thinking, left to itself, is biased, distorted, partial, uninformed, or downright prejudiced. Yet the quality of our life and the quality of what we produce, make, or build depend precisely on the quality of our thoughts.

Paul and Elder also caution that shoddy thinking is costly. How so? You probably know people who simply follow authority. They do not question, are not curious, and do not challenge people or groups who claim special knowledge or insight. These people do not usually think for themselves but rely on others to think for them. They might indulge in wishful, hopeful, and emotional thinking, assuming that what they believe is true simply because they wish it, hope it, or feel it to be true. As you might have noticed, such people tend not to have much control over their circumstances or to possess any real power in business or society.

Critical thinkers, in contrast, investigate problems, ask questions, pose new answers that challenge the status quo, discover new information, question authorities and traditional beliefs, challenge received dogmas and doctrines, make independent judgments, and develop creative solutions. When employers say they want workers who can find reliable information, analyze it, organize it, draw conclusions from it, and present it convincingly to others, they are seeking individuals who are critical thinkers.

Whatever else you do in college, make it a point to develop and sharpen your critical-thinking skills. You won't become an accomplished critical thinker overnight. But with practice, you can learn how to tell whether information is truthful and accurate. You can make better decisions, come up with fresh solutions to difficult problems, and communicate your ideas strategically and persuasively.[2]

[1]Richard Paul and Linda Elder, *The Miniature Guide to Critical Thinking Concepts and Tools* (Dillon Beach, CA: Foundation for Critical Thinking Press, 2008).
[2]Liz Brown, *Critical Thinking* (New York: Weigl Publishers, 2008), 4.

◤ ASSESSING YOUR STRENGTHS ▮▮▮▮▮▮▮▮

Critical thinking is one of the most valuable skills you can practice for success in college and in the workplace. Are you a good critical thinker? Now that you have read the first section of this chapter, list specific examples of your strengths in critical thinking.

_____

_____

_____

_____

◤ SETTING GOALS ▮▮▮▮▮▮▮▮

What are your most important objectives in learning the material in this chapter? Do you know the difference between critical thinking and "being critical"? List three goals that relate to developing and practicing critical-thinking skills (e.g., This week I will watch one TV news show, such as *Meet the Press*, *The O'Reilly Factor*, or *The Daily Show*, and make a list of "facts" I question and why).

1. _____

_____

2. _____

_____

3. _____

_____

■ RETENTION STRATEGY: Critical thinking is one of the most difficult concepts to teach and learn in college, yet it is the foundation for college success and retention. Have your students interview one of their instructors about how critical thinking and a liberal education contribute to a fuller life. This exercise will also help them become more engaged in the campus.

This exercise asks students to rate their own critical thinking. You might use this assessment a few times during the semester and ask students how their results change.

EXERCISE 5.1

How You THINK Matters

Now that you have read about critical thinking, it would be beneficial to rate yourself as a critical thinker. Perhaps at this point in the term, critical thinking may seem unnecessary to you; however, it will be interesting to see how you will change in the next few weeks and months.

Circle the number that best fits you in each of the critical situations described below.

Critical Situations	Never				Sometimes				Always	
In class, I ask lots of questions when I don't understand.	1	2	3	4	5	6	7	8	9	10
If I don't agree with what the group decides is the correct answer, I challenge the group opinion.	1	2	3	4	5	6	7	8	9	10
I believe there are many solutions to a problem.	1	2	3	4	5	6	7	8	9	10

(continued)

Critical Situations	Never				Sometimes				Always	
I admire those people in history who challenged what was believed at the time, such as "the earth is flat."	1	2	3	4	5	6	7	8	9	10
I make an effort to listen to both sides of an argument before deciding which way I will go.	1	2	3	4	5	6	7	8	9	10
I ask lots of people's opinions about a political candidate before making up my mind.	1	2	3	4	5	6	7	8	9	10
I am not afraid to change my belief system if I learn something new.	1	2	3	4	5	6	7	8	9	10
Authority figures do not intimidate me.	1	2	3	4	5	6	7	8	9	10

The more 7–10 scores you have circled, the more likely it is that you use your critical-thinking skills often. The lower scores indicate that you may not be using critical-thinking skills very often or use them only during certain activities, such as an educational class.

Becoming a Critical Thinker

Often in a college class you are confronted with ideas or thoughts that are different from your own. Under what circumstances would it make sense to consider changing your opinion?

In essence, critical thinking is a search for truth. In college and in life, you'll be confronted by a mass of information and ideas. Much of what you read and hear will seem suspect, and a lot of it will be contradictory. (If you have ever talked back to a television commercial or doubted a politician's campaign promises, you know this already.) How do you decide what to believe?

Paul and Elder remind us that there may be more than one right answer to any given question. The task is to determine which of the "truths" you read or hear are the most plausible and then draw on them to develop ideas of your own. Difficult problems practically demand that you weigh options and think through consequences before you can reach an informed decision. Critical thinking also involves improving the way you think about a subject, statement, or idea. To do that, you'll need to ask questions, consider several different points of view, and draw your own conclusions.

ASK QUESTIONS

The first step of thinking critically is to engage your curiosity. Instead of accepting statements and assertions at face value, question them. When you come across an idea or a "fact" that strikes you as interesting, confusing, or suspicious, ask yourself first what it means. Do you fully understand what is being said, or do you need to pause and think to make sense of the idea? Do you agree with the statement? Why or why not? Can the material be interpreted in more than one way?

DID YOU KNOW?

54% of first-year students say they "frequently evaluate the quality or reliability of information they receive."

Don't stop there. Ask whether you can trust the person or institution making a particular claim, and ask whether they have provided enough evidence to back up an assertion (more on this later). Ask who might be likely to agree or disagree and why. Ask how a new concept relates to what you already know, where you might find more information about the subject, and what you could do with what you learn. Finally, ask yourself about the implications and consequences of accepting something as truth. Will you have to change your perspective or give up a long-held belief? Will it require you to do something differently? Will it be necessary to investigate the issue further? Do you anticipate having to try to bring other people around to a new way of thinking?

CONSIDER MULTIPLE POINTS OF VIEW

Once you start asking questions, you'll typically discover a slew of different possible answers competing for your attention. Don't be too quick to latch onto one and move on. To be a critical thinker, you need to be fair and open-minded, even if you don't agree with certain ideas at first. Give them all a fair hearing, because your goal is to find the truth or the best action, not to confirm what you already believe.

Often, you will recognize the existence of competing points of view on your own, perhaps because they're held by people you know personally. You might discover them in what you read, watch, or listen to for pleasure. Reading assignments might deliberately expose you to conflicting arguments and theories about a subject, or you might encounter differences of opinion as you do research for a project.

In class discussions, also, your instructors might often insist that more than one valid point of view exists: "So, for some types of students, you agree that bilingual education might be best? What types of students might not benefit?" Your instructors will expect you to explain in concrete terms any point you reject: "You think this essay is flawed. Well, what are your reasons?" They might challenge the authority of experts: "Dr. Fleming's theory sounds impressive. But here are some facts he doesn't account for. . . ." Your instructors will also sometimes reinforce your personal views and experiences: "So something like this happened to you once, and you felt exactly the same way. Can you tell us why?"

The more ideas you entertain, the more sophisticated your own thinking will become. Ultimately, you will discover not only that it is okay to change your mind, but that a willingness to do so is the mark of a reasonable, educated person.

DRAW CONCLUSIONS

Once you have considered different points of view, it's up to you to reach your own conclusions, to craft a new idea based on what you've learned, or to make a decision about what you'll do with the information you have.

This process isn't necessarily a matter of figuring out the best idea. Depending on the goals of the activity, it might be simply the one that you think is the most fun or the most practical, or it might be a new idea of your own creation. For a business decision, it might involve additional cost-benefit

IN CLASS: Critical thinking and information literacy are related concepts. If students have difficulty knowing what to do with information they read or find, consider incorporating the goals of information literacy (see pages 244–248 of Chapter 11, Developing Library, Research, and Information Literacy Skills) into your discussion of critical thinking.

IN CLASS: Ask whether students have been told that once they make up their minds, they have to stick with their decisions. If so, who told them that? Under what circumstances? Why does it make more sense to be able to change your mind if you believe you have a better solution?

analysis to decide which computer equipment to purchase for your office. In a chemistry lab, it might be a matter of interpreting the results of an experiment. In a creative writing workshop, students might collaborate to select the most workable plot for a classmate's short story. Or a social worker might conduct multiple interviews before recommending a counseling plan for a struggling family.

Drawing conclusions involves looking at the outcome of your inquiry in a more demanding, critical way. If you are looking for solutions to a problem, which ones really seem most promising after you have conducted an exhaustive search for materials? Do some answers conflict with others? Which ones can be achieved? If you have found new evidence, what does that new evidence show? Do your original beliefs hold up? Do they need to be modified? Which notions should be abandoned? Most important, consider what you would need to do or say to persuade someone else that your ideas are valid. Thoughtful conclusions aren't very useful if you can't share them with others.

This exercise asks students to use a "pro-con" diagram to create a visual that helps reveal the complexity of an issue and the importance of appreciating multiple points of view.

EXERCISE 5.2

What You CONSIDER Matters

Life is full of controversies. Many issues have been debated for years with no resolution. Even within your own college or university, instructors are likely struggling with "hot topics" that seemingly have no right or wrong answer. Sometimes it is helpful to consider multiple points of view before drawing conclusions, which is a great exercise for any serious inquiry that demands looking at a topic critically. Every argument has pros and cons as well as some components that everyone can agree on. For example, with an issue such as whether to open a campus health care center, there will be pros and cons, but everyone will probably agree to take students' best interests into consideration.

Choose a topic with two opposing views, and write the pros and cons in the ovals of the diagram below—include also the views that both sides share. You can even attempt this with a partner in class who has a differing opinion. It is beneficial to try to put yourself in "another person's shoes" in an effort to understand a different point of view. Here are some ideas for topics: increasing student fees for a new or improved student activity center; changing core courses to include a class on global economics; requiring students to attend a certain number of activities before graduation so that they are well-rounded.

How does working with this diagram help you to see both sides of the argument?

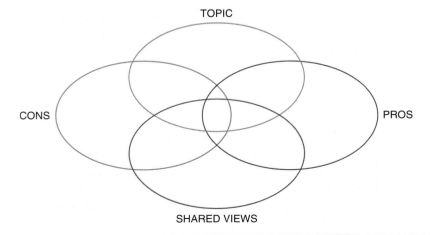

Get a Second Opinion

One way to become a better critical thinker is to practice with other people. By getting feedback from another person, you can see the possible flaws in your own position. You will also learn that there are few black-and-white answers to any question.

How Collaboration Fosters Critical Thinking

Educational researchers report that teamwork improves the ability to think critically, but what if working in a group intimidates you? How can you overcome this fear in order to create a positive collaborative experience?

A 1995 study by Professor Anuradha A. Gokhale at Western Illinois University, published in the *Journal of Technology Education*, found that students who participated in collaborative learning performed significantly better on a test requiring critical thinking than did students who studied individually. The study also found that the two groups did equally well on a test that required only memorization.[3]

Having more than one student involved in the learning process generates a greater number of ideas. People think more clearly when they are talking as well as listening (a very good reason to participate actively in your classes). Creative brainstorming and group discussion encourage original thought. These habits also teach participants to consider alternative points of view carefully and to express and defend their own ideas clearly. As a group negotiates ideas and learns to agree on the most reliable thoughts, it moves closer to a surer solution.

IN CLASS: Discuss the value of collaborative thinking as it applies to critical thinking, especially in the area of creative brainstorming.

[3]Anuradha Gokhale, "Collaborative Learning Enhances Critical Thinking," *Journal of Technology Education* 7, no. 1 (1995).

Collaboration occurs not only face-to-face but also over the Internet. Christopher P. Sessums, creator of an award-winning blog, writes:

> Weblogs offer several key features that I believe can support a constructive, collaborative, reflective environment. For one, it's convenient. The medium supports self-expression and "voice." Collaboration and connectivity can be conducted efficiently, especially in terms of participants' time or place. Publishing your thoughts online forces you to concretize your thoughts.

"Collaborative weblogs," Sessums concludes, "promote the idea of learners as creators of knowledge, not merely consumers of information."[4] So do online discussion groups, wikis (which allow users to add, update, and otherwise improve material that others have posted), and, of course, face-to-face collaboration.

Whether in person or through electronic communication, teamwork improves your ability to think critically. As you leave college and enter the world of work, you will find that collaboration is essential in almost any career you pursue, not only with people in your work setting, but also with others around the globe.

This exercise asks students to perform a similar task twice—first on their own and then in a group—and then compare the experiences.

[4]Christopher Sessums, Eduspaces Web log, November 9, 2005, http://eduspaces.net/csessums/weblog/archive/2005/11.

EXERCISE 5.3

How You WORK with Others Matters

While working with others is not always easy or ideal (schedule conflicts, personality conflicts), it is good to have this ability as part of your skill set going forward. Practice makes perfect, so the more you work in groups, the easier it will become for you.

INDIVIDUAL WORK:

Take about 2 minutes and try to memorize the following list of items:

> blue, seven, block, coin, duck, street, caribou, football, politician, slippers, math, chair, crackers, gate, association, poem, jump

On a sheet of paper and (without looking at the list), try to recall as many items as you can in 30 seconds.

Number remembered: _____

--(hide information below here)--

GROUP WORK:

Now, with a group or partner, take a look at this list and discuss it, creating associations within the word list—maybe a story or something personal—and talk about it for about 2 minutes.

> buffalo, stick, helicopter, two, nurse, science, volleyball, dime, swing, green, swan, highway, ice, sandals, run, essay, corporation

On a sheet of paper (and without looking at the list), try to recall as many items as you can in 30 seconds. You can work together as a group.

(continued)

Number remembered: _____

Is there a difference in the number of items recalled? Was it more difficult to memorize a list alone or to recall a list with others? Generally speaking, discussing information, such as what might be on an upcoming test, not only creates associations but also activates your auditory memory. This example uses a memorized list of information. How much more powerful this might be if the information were more complex, requiring brainstorming and critical thinking!

Thinking Critically about Arguments

Critical arguments are not yelling matches but rather an effort to push or pull someone in your direction using sound reason or evidence. When was the last time you witnessed a civilized debate of ideas—a critical argument—in the media, whether on TV, in a blog, online, on Facebook, or in a movie?

What does the word *argument* mean to you? If you're like most people, the first image it conjures up might be an ugly fight you had with a friend, a yelling match you witnessed on the street, or a heated disagreement between family members. True, such unpleasant confrontations are arguments. But the word also refers to a calm, reasoned effort to persuade someone of the value of an idea.

When you think of it this way, you'll quickly recognize that arguments are central to academic study, work, and life in general. Scholarly articles, business memos, and requests for spending money all have something in common: The effective ones make a general claim, provide reasons to support it, and back up those reasons with evidence. That's what argument is.

As we have already seen, it's important to consider multiple points of view, or arguments, in tackling new ideas and complex questions. But arguments are not all equally valid. Good critical thinking involves thinking creatively about the assumptions that might have been left out and scrutinizing the quality of the evidence that is used to support a claim. Whether examining an argument or communicating one, a good critical thinker is careful to ensure that ideas are presented in an understandable, logical way.

CHALLENGE ASSUMPTIONS

All too often, our beliefs are based on gut feelings or on blind acceptance of something we've heard or read. To some extent, that's unavoidable. If we made a habit of questioning absolutely everything, we would have trouble making it through the day. Yet some assumptions should be examined more thoughtfully, especially if they will influence an important decision or serve as the foundation for an argument.

For an example, imagine that the mayor of the city where your school is located has announced that he wants to make a bid to host the Olympic Games. Many people on campus are excited at the prospect, but your friend Richard is less than thrilled.

"The Olympic Games just about ruined my hometown," Richard tells you. "Road signs all over Atlanta had to be changed so that visitors could find the game sites easily. Because the city couldn't supply enough workers to

■ RETENTION STRATEGY: You may find that some students believe that the "grass is greener" somewhere else and may be tempted to transfer to a different institution. Help them challenge these assumptions before making a snap decision to transfer.

IN CLASS: Ask what is the importance of seeking the truth and how this relates to Richard's opening remarks.

complete the task on time, the organizers brought thousands of immigrants to town to help with the task, and some of them were illegal aliens.

"The Games are intended to foster national and international pride, but these immigrants could care less about that. They were there to earn money for their families. The Hispanic population nearly doubled once the Games were over. And if people understood how much political corruption went on behind the scenes, they would understand why the Olympic Games are not healthy for a host city."

Another friend, Sally, overhears your conversation, and she's not buying Richard's conclusions. "How do you know all of that is accurate?" she asks. "I just know it," says Richard.

Eager to get at the truth of the matter, Sally decides to look into other points of view. She does a quick Web search and finds an article about the Atlanta Olympics in the *American Historical Review*, the journal of record for the history profession in the United States. Its author notes that "the Games provided an enormous engine for growth" and comments that the city's "surging population is the most obvious marker of Atlanta's post-Olympic transformation." The article continues: "By the 1996 Games the metro population had reached three million, and today [is] 4,458,253. Winning the Olympic bid marked a turning point that put Atlanta on the world's radar screen."[5]

Although Sally has found good information from a reputable source, you should be uncomfortable with the totally upbeat tone of the article. If you and Sally dig a little further, you might land on the Web site of the Utah Office of Tourism, which includes a report that was prepared when that state was investigating the potential impacts of hosting the 2002 Winter Games in Salt Lake City. According to the report, "Among the key legacies of the Atlanta Olympics was the regeneration of certain downtown districts that had fallen into urban decay." The authors also note that "the Olympic-spurred development in [Atlanta] has provided a much-needed stimulus for revitalization."[6]

Finding a second positive analysis would give you a compelling reason to believe that the Olympic Games are good for a city, but Richard might easily discover a report from the European Tour Operators Association, which concludes that visitors are likely to stay away from host countries during and following the Games, causing a significant long-term decline in revenue for hotels and other businesses that depend on tourism.[7]

Unfortunately, simply learning more about the benefits and costs of hosting the Olympics doesn't yield any concrete answers. Even so, you, Richard, and Sally have uncovered assumptions and have developed a better understanding of the issue. That's an important first step.

EXAMINE THE EVIDENCE

The evidence that is offered as support for an argument can vary in quality. While Richard started with no proof other than his convictions ("I just know it"),

IN CLASS: How many of your students have justified the accuracy of what they have said by giving an answer like Richard's ("I just know it")? Encourage them to tell you what they mean by such an answer.

IN CLASS: Point out that Sally's research contains specifics—numbers, facts, and so forth—that Richard had ignored. Without specifics, truth can be very elusive!

IN CLASS: Ask your students why they should be uncomfortable with the upbeat tone of the material Sally found, even though it comes from a scholarly source. They might need some prodding to understand that an overly positive spin on a subject can suggest bias or, in the case of this piece (taken from the schedule for the American Historical Association's 2006 conference in Atlanta), a purpose that is out of sync with the reader's inquiry.

---

[5]Mary G. Rolinson, visiting lecturer in the Georgia State University History Department, "Atlanta Before and After the Olympics." Copyright © American Historical Association, http://www .historians.org/perspectives/issues/2006/0611/0611ann6.cfm.

[6]Utah Office of Tourism, *Observations from Past Olympic Host Communities: Executive Summary*, http://travel.utah.gov/research_and_planning/2002_olympics.

[7]"Olympics Have Negative Effect on Tourism," July 10, 2008, http://www.travelbite.co.uk.

Sally looked to expert opinion and research studies for answers to her question. Even so, one of her sources sounded overly positive, prompting a need to confirm the author's claims with additional evidence from other sources.

Like Sally, critical thinkers are careful to check that the evidence supporting an argument—whether someone else's or their own—is of the highest possible quality. To do that, simply ask a few questions about the arguments as you consider them:

- What general idea am I being asked to accept?
- Are good and sufficient reasons given to support the overall claim?
- Are those reasons backed up with evidence in the form of facts, statistics, and quotations?
- Does the evidence support the conclusions?
- Is the argument based on logical reasoning, or does it appeal mainly to the emotions?
- Do I recognize any questionable assumptions?
- Can I think of any counterarguments? What facts can I muster as proof?
- What do I know about the person or organization making the argument?

IN CLASS: Ask why emotional decisions sometimes stray from the truth. When might an emotional decision be appropriate (falling in love, praising a movie, etc.)? When might it be inappropriate?

If, after you have evaluated the evidence used in support of a claim, you're still not certain of its quality, it's best to keep looking. Drawing on questionable evidence for an argument has a tendency to backfire. In most cases, a little persistence will help you find something better. (You can find tips on how to find and evaluate sources in Chapter 11, Developing Library, Research, and Information Literacy Skills.)

Facebook Causes Lung Cancer

Do you believe everything you read? The Internet and other forms of media are filled with outlandish claims that are often totally false. Use your own critical-thinking abilities to practice healthy skepticism about anything you see in print that seems far-fetched. Check it out by using other credible sources.

TECH TIP RESEARCH WISELY

Don't assume that any information you find on the Internet is accurate or unbiased. Thanks to the First Amendment, people can publish whatever they want online. It's up to you to filter out what's valuable, objective, and up-to-date.

 THE PROBLEM

You're not sure how to evaluate the types of information found on the Web.

 THE FIX

Get some context.

3 **HOW TO DO IT**

- **Portals:** One-stop shops that serve up a full range of cyber services. Expect to find search engines; news, weather, and news updates; stock quotes; reference tools; even movie reviews. (Bonus: Most services are free.) Prime examples: **Google.com** and **Yahoo.com**.

- **News:** Sites that offer news and analysis of current events, politics, business trends, sports, entertainment, and so on. They're often sponsored by magazines, newspapers, and radio stations and include special online extras. Prime examples: **NYTimes.com**, Harvard Business Review (**hbr.org**), and **CNN.com**.

- **Corporate and marketing:** Promotional sites for businesses. Some company Web sites let you order their products or services online; others even list job openings. Prime examples: **Ford.com** and **BenJerry.com**.

- **Informational:** Fact-based sites, often created by government agencies. Click to these for information on everything from passports to city bus schedules to census data. Prime examples: **NYCsubway.org** and **Travel.State.gov**.

- **Blogs:** Informal Web sites where people can air their views and opinions. Some businesses create blogs to connect with their customers; other blogs are strictly personal, designed to share with family and friends. Prime examples: **Gawker.com** and **thelawsonspilltheirguts.blogspot.com**.

- **Wikis:** Informational Web sites that allow for open editing by registered users or, in some cases, by the general public. Prime examples: **Wikipedia.com** and **TechCrunch.com**.

 social change through simple living

Getting Lost in the Twitterverse and other Misadventures
by TAMMY on JUNE 6, 2011

Editor's Note: This is a guest post by Dusti Arab. Dusti is a writer and the author of The Minimalist Mom and The Digital Dominatrix. You can find her most recent work at Undefinable You.

In late January, I had a meltdown. Pretty much an epic episode which involved my entire life going down the proverbial tube in a matter of days. My relationship was broken and lying on the ground in a million pieces. I couldn't write. I couldn't function.

How had I gotten here?

Well, it was longer series of events. Having become fully indoctrinated as a blogger and writer, I found myself plugged in much more often. In September, I finally got a smart phone. The perceived pressure was to respond to requests and comments immediately.

Couldn't miss an opportunity. Had to post frequently. Oh, can't forget the networking. I had to be skyping at least twice a week in order to maintain and develop an ever growing group of acquaintances and friends.

Keep in mind that there's a big difference between the *Journal of the American Medical Association* and a journal written by Fred from Pomona. And no, you can't use an ad for Shake Weight as a source for a fitness article: It's an ad. Be discerning. To make sure that the research you use is unbiased and current, look for tip-offs. Most reputable Web sites are easy to navigate, contain little advertising, and list author names and credentials.

PERSONAL BEST

Should you trust the information on a wiki? In a word, no. Wikis are useful, but not academically viable research sources. (Do not list **Wikipedia.com** in the bibliography of a college essay. Ever.) *Wiki-wiki* means "quick" in Hawaiian, and different people can manipulate Wikipedia that fast.

BEWARE OF LOGICAL FALLACIES

A critical thinker has an attitude—an attitude of wanting to avoid nonsense, to find the truth and to discover the best action. It's an attitude that rejects intuiting what is right in favor of requiring reasons. Instead of being defensive or emotional, critical thinkers aim to be logical.

Although logical reasoning is essential to solving any problem, whether simple or complex, you need to go one step further to make sure that an argument hasn't been compromised by faulty reasoning. Here are some of the most common missteps people make in their use of logic:

- **Attacking the person.** It's perfectly acceptable to argue against other people's positions or to attack their arguments. It is not okay, however, to go after their personalities. Any argument that resorts to personal attack ("Why should we believe a cheater?") is unworthy of consideration.

- **Begging.** "Please, officer, don't give me a ticket because if you do, I'll lose my license, and I have five little children to feed and won't be able to feed them if I can't drive my truck." None of the driver's statements offer any evidence, in any legal sense, as to why she shouldn't be given a ticket. Pleading *might* work, if the officer is feeling generous, but an appeal to facts and reason would be more effective: "I fed the meter, but it didn't register the coins. Since the machine is broken, I'm sure you'll agree that I don't deserve a ticket."

LUSTRE-CREME is the favorite beauty shampoo of 4 out of 5 top Hollywood stars... and you'll love it in its new Lotion Form, too!

Marilyn Monroe
starring in
"GENTLEMEN PREFER BLONDES"
A 20th Century-Fox Production
Color by Technicolor

False Advertising

Advertisers know that the public can be easily influenced to buy a product if a famous actor, musician, or sports star promotes it. But good critical thinkers will evaluate the product on its own merits. Don't fall victim to false claims, even if they come out of the mouth of a star.

- **Appealing to false authority.** Citing authorities, such as experts in a field or the opinions of qualified researchers, can offer valuable support for an argument. But a claim based on the authority of someone whose expertise is questionable relies on the appearance of authority rather than real evidence. We see this all the time in advertising: Sports stars who are not doctors, dieticians, or nutritionists urge us to eat a certain brand of food, or famous actors and singers who are not dermatologists extol the medical benefits of a pricey remedy for acne.

- **Jumping on a bandwagon.** Sometimes we are more likely to believe something if a lot of other people believe it. Even the most widely accepted truths, however, can turn out to be wrong. There was a time when nearly everyone believed that the world was flat—until someone came up with evidence to the contrary.

- **Assuming that something is true because it hasn't been proven false.** Go to a bookstore, and you'll find dozens of books detailing close encounters with flying saucers and extraterrestrial beings. These books describe the person who had the close encounter as beyond reproach in integrity and sanity. Because critics could not disprove the claims of the witnesses, the events are said to have really occurred. Even in science, few things are ever proved completely false, but evidence can be discredited.

- **Falling victim to false cause.** Frequently, we make the assumption that just because one event followed another, the first event must have caused the second. This reasoning is the basis for many superstitions. The ancient Chinese once believed that they could make the sun reappear after an eclipse by striking a large gong, because they knew that the sun reappeared after a large gong had been struck on one such occasion. Most effects, however, are usually the result of a complex web of causes. Don't be satisfied with easy before-and-after claims; they are rarely correct.

- **Making hasty generalizations.** If someone selected one green marble from a barrel containing a hundred marbles, you wouldn't assume that the next marble would be green. After all, there are still ninety-nine marbles in the barrel, and you know nothing about the colors of those marbles. However, given fifty draws from the barrel, each of which produced a green marble after the barrel had been shaken thoroughly, you would be more willing to conclude that the next marble drawn would be green, too. Reaching a conclusion based on the opinion of one source is like figuring that all the marbles in the barrel are green after pulling out only one.

Fallacies like these can slip into even the most careful reasoning. One false claim can derail an entire argument, so be on the lookout for weak logic in what you read and write. Never forget that accurate reasoning is a key factor for success in college and in life.

What You SAY Matters

Sometimes the best way to learn a new skill is to see an old behavior for what it is—ineffective. Have some fun with logical fallacies by reviewing how Anna responds to her professor.

Scenario: *Anna is a college freshman who just received a D on her English paper. Up to this point, she has earned A's or B's on all her other papers. She can't figure out what went wrong. After talking with her classmates, she discovers that almost everyone in her class also received a poor grade. She intends to speak with her instructor after class to discuss what happened. However, in her attempt to dispute her grade, she uses weak arguments that are based on four types of logical fallacies. See if you can guess what these weak arguments are, and write them in the chart below.*

Type of logical fallacy	Example of what Anna might have said in making a weak and ineffective argument
Attacking the Person (going after the person in charge)	
Begging (pleading for generosity using emotionality)	
Jumping on a Bandwagon (using other people as reasoning why something is wrong)	
Assuming Something Is True	

Knowing that using calm and reasoned language is more persuasive, think about what Anna could have said to convince the instructor that she is a critical thinker—a logical, nonemotional person who uses evidence, not attitude. Discuss Anna's critical-thinking strategy with your classmates. Then ask your instructor how Anna's effective argument would have changed the situation.

Think of a similar situation you have faced. Describe what happened.

_____

_____

_____

_____

_____

Exercise 5.4 asks students to work independently to develop a list of nonsense arguments. Students share their nonsense arguments with others in a small group, and the group members work together to write a reasoned argument and present it to the class. Offer your opinion about which groups used good critical-thinking skills to develop the most convincing arguments and why.

Critical Thinking in College and Everyday Life

> Critical thinking takes practice. As you continue to be open to new ideas and ways of thinking in college, at some point you will develop a level of comfort with your ability to discern fact from fiction, truth from fallacy. What classes are you currently taking that stretch your critical-thinking skills?

As you practice the skills of critical thinking in college, they start to become a natural part of your life. Eventually, you will be able to think your way through many everyday situations, such as these:

- You try to reach a classmate on the phone to ask a question about tomorrow's quiz. When you can't reach her, you become so anxious that you can't study or sleep.
- On the day an important paper is due, a heavy snowstorm rolls in. You brave the cold to get to class. When you arrive, no one—including the teacher—is there. You take a seat and wait.

Now let's transform you into a critical thinker and examine the possible outcomes:

- When you can't reach a classmate on the phone to ask a question about tomorrow's quiz, you review the material once more, then call one or more other classmates. Then you consider their views and those of your textbook and class. Instead of deciding on one point of view for each important topic, you decide to keep in mind all of those that make sense, leaving your final decision until you have the quiz in your hand.
- Before heading out to class in a big snowstorm, you check the college Web site and discover that classes have been canceled. You stay at home.

If you hang on to the guidelines in this chapter, we can't promise your classes will be easier, but they will certainly be more interesting. You will now know how to use critical thinking to figure things out instead of depending purely on how you feel or what you've heard. As you listen to a lecture, try to predict where it is heading and why. When other students raise issues, ask yourself whether they have enough information to justify what they have said. And when you raise your hand, remember that asking a sensible question can be more important than trying to find the elusive—and often nonexistent—"right answer."

Imagine a world in which physicians tried a new procedure on a patient before it had been tested, your history course was taught by someone who never studied history, and you put your total faith in a hair restorer just because the advertising said it would grow hair in two weeks.

As a critical thinker, you would know better.

IN CLASS: Now that your students have reviewed the entire chapter, ask for their thoughts on the meaning and significance of critical thinking.

This exercise gives students the chance to create their own study tool to use in mastering the chapter content.

EXERCISE 5.5

How You PLAN AHEAD Matters

You have learned about the importance of critical thinking, what it means, its value in society, and its meaning for you as a college student. You have also learned about some of the pitfalls of not using critical thinking. Take a moment to review the material in Chapter 5, either individually or with partners (which we have learned is the most effective way to learn), and map out what you have learned in the diagram below using main topics from the chapter to guide you. This is a great way to prepare for your test. Use this kind of tool to study other subjects as well.

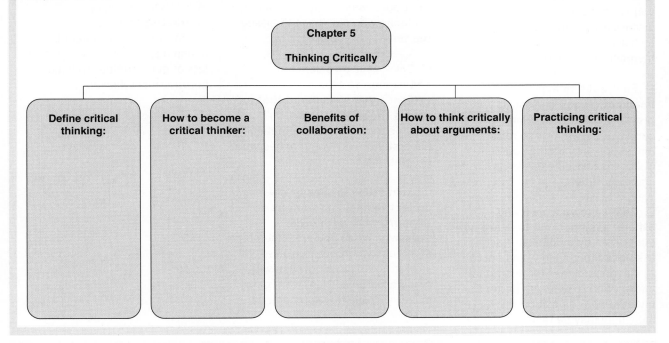

CHECKLIST FOR SUCCESS

CRITICAL THINKING

☐ **Make sure you understand what *critical thinking* means.** If you are not clear about this term, discuss it with another student, the instructor of this course, or a staff member in the learning center.

☐ **Find ways to express your imagination and curiosity; practice asking questions.** If you have the impulse to raise a question, don't stifle yourself. College is for self-expression and exploration.

☐ **Challenge your own and others' assumptions that are not supported by evidence.** Practice asking politely, calmly, and not in a rejecting manner for additional information to help you better understand the position the individual may be taking.

☐ **During class lectures, presentations, and discussions, practice thinking about the subjects being discussed from multiple points of view.** Start with the view you would most naturally take toward the matter at hand. Then force yourself to imagine what questions might be raised by someone who didn't see the issue the same way you do.

☐ **Draw your own conclusions, and explain to others what evidence you considered that led you to these positions.** Don't assume that anyone automatically understands why you reached your conclusions.

☐ **Join study groups or class project teams, and work as a team member with other students.** When you are a member of a team, volunteer for roles that stretch you. This is how you will really experience significant gains in learning and development.

☐ **Learn to identify false claims in commercials and in political arguments.** Then look for the same faulty reasoning in people you encounter each day.

☐ **Practice critical thinking not only in your academic work but also in your everyday interactions with friends and family.** Your environment both in and out of college will give you lots of opportunities to become a better critical thinker.

APPLY IT! What Works for YOU Matters

Think about your current academic situation, and apply some of the suggestions and strategies introduced in this chapter. Select strategies that you think will work best for you, and then write them down in the "Your Response" column. What are YOU planning to do for YOUR college experience?

QUESTIONS	SAMPLE STUDENT ANSWERS	YOUR RESPONSE
	Name: Brittany Jones	
What Is Critical Thinking, and Why Is It Important? Why is it dangerous to rely on others to think or make decisions for you?	I'm impressionable. I can change my mind, just by listening to one friend or another. I guess the danger would be that I don't have an opinion of my own and that people can use me to justify their own personal agendas.	
Becoming a Critical Thinker Often in a college class you are confronted with ideas or thoughts that are different from your own. Under what circumstances would it make sense to consider changing your opinion?	This term, I have a political science class that goes against what I have been taught. My parents wouldn't approve of what the professor says, and it stresses me out. Because some of his ideas are supported by evidence that seems logical, I am going to keep an open mind—for now.	
How Collaboration Fosters Critical Thinking Educational researchers report that teamwork improves the ability to think critically, but what if working in a group intimidates you? How can you overcome this fear in order to create a positive collaborative experience?	I'd rather work in groups only with people I know. Strangers keep asking me to study. I'm intimidated and uncertain about it. I think what's best is to jump right in and get everyone to share ideas right away. I am pretty good at facilitating.	
Thinking Critically about Arguments Critical arguments are not yelling matches but rather an effort to push or pull someone in your direction using sound reason or evidence. When was the last time you witnessed a civilized debate of ideas—a critical argument—in the media, whether on TV, in a blog, online, on Facebook, or in a movie?	I see mostly UNcivil arguments on TV. I suppose that's because all that violence sells. The only place I see real debates of ideas are on news channels—a commentator and a couple of key speakers. Often times these are really biased, but at least they present their ideas without yelling. Actually, that's what my political science teacher was asking us to do last week during a class debate. I didn't realize it was all part of critical thinking.	
Critical Thinking in College and Everyday Life Critical thinking takes practice. As you continue to be open to new ideas and ways of thinking in college, at some point you will develop a level of comfort with your ability to discern fact from fiction, truth from fallacy. What classes are you currently taking that stretch your critical-thinking skills?	My poli sci class keeps pushing my comfort zone. But most of my professors are asking me to back up my ideas with some kind of proof—totally different from high school. I am on the fence about having to prove my ideas right or wrong, but I see the value of having my professors do it as well. I feel more like an adult now and more responsible for my education.	

BUILD YOUR EXPERIENCE

This exercise sets up in-class debates.

1 COLLABORATIVE ACTIVITY

THE GREAT DEBATE

Now is the time to use all the skills you have acquired as a critical thinker and put them to the test. In teams you will debate each other, using controversial topics. Of course, you and your group should avoid using the logical fallacies described in this chapter. In the end, a neutral party will determine the winner of each debate. Here's how this will work:

1. The class is divided randomly into four groups: A, B, C, and D.

2. Groups A and B choose a topic or are assigned one. Each group is randomly assigned to either a PRO or CON position and then takes about 3–5 minutes to write down three of the most compelling reasons for its side to "win." Groups A and B debate each other. Groups C and D determine the winner and explain their decision by discussing which team proved to be better at thinking critically and arguing persuasively.

3. Then the groups switch roles. Groups C and D choose a topic or are assigned one. Each group is randomly assigned to either a PRO or CON position and then takes about 3–5 minutes to write down three of the most compelling reasons for its side to "win." Groups C and D debate each other. Groups A and B determine the winner and explain their decision by discussing which team proved to be better at thinking critically and arguing persuasively.

Possible topics to debate (or brainstorm topics that reflect issues from your school):

1. Laptops in the classroom
2. Guns on campus
3. Online classes
4. College football teams
5. Required core classes
6. Campus health center funded by student fees

2 BUILDING YOUR PORTFOLIO

My Influences Our past experiences have shaped the way in which we think about and perceive the world around us. Sometimes it is easy to interpret things without stopping to think about why we feel the way we do. How have other people shaped the way you see the world today?

1. In your personal portfolio, create a *Word* document and
   - Describe at least three people (such as family, friends, celebrities, national leaders) who you feel have most influenced the way you think.
   - Describe how these individuals' values, actions, expectations, and words have shaped the way you think about yourself and the world.

2. Describe an experience you have had since coming to college that has challenged you to think about an issue in a new and different way.

3. Save your work in your portfolio.

One major shift from being a high school student to being a college student involves the level of critical thinking your college instructors expect of you. After reading this chapter, how would you describe critical thinking to a high school student?

_____

_____

_____

_____

_____

_____

_____

_____

_____

_____

_____

_____

_____

_____

_____

_____

No matter how well prepared you are in your teaching, what a student hears and understands might not always be what you think you have said. The one-minute paper is a quick and easy assessment tool that will help alert you when students don't understand what was said or discussed in class. The one-minute paper will also give timid students an opportunity to ask questions and seek clarification. Ideally, you should ask for such a paper several minutes before the end of a class. The paper will also help you begin your next class by clarifying points your students seem to be unsure of.

For more on this topic watch
French Fries Are Not Vegetables and Other College Lessons

WHERE TO GO FOR HELP . . .

ON CAMPUS

> **Logic Courses** Check out your philosophy department's introductory course in logic. This might be the single best course designed to teach you critical-thinking skills. Nearly every college offers such a course.

> **Argument Courses and Critical-Thinking Courses** These are usually offered in the English department. They will help you develop the ability to formulate logical arguments and avoid such pitfalls as logical fallacies.

> **Debating Skills** Some of the very best critical thinkers developed debating skills during college. Go to either your student activities office or your department of speech/drama, and find out whether your campus has a debate club or team. Debating can be fun, and chances are you will meet some interesting student thinkers that way.

LITERATURE

> *12 Angry Men* **by Reginald Rose (New York: Penguin Classics, 2006)** This is a reprint of the original teleplay, which was written in 1954 and made into a film in 1958. It is also available on DVD. The stirring courtroom drama pits twelve jurors against one another as they argue the outcome of a murder trial in which the defendant is a teenage boy. While critical thinking is needed to arrive at the truth, all the jurors except one use noncritical arguments to arrive at a guilty verdict. However, the analysis of that one holdout produces a remarkable change in their attitudes.

ONLINE

> Check the following Web site for a critical review of *The Encyclopedia of Stupidity:* **http:// metapsychology.mentalhelp.net/poc/view_doc .php?type=book&id=2558.**

> *A Guide to Critical Thinking About What You See on the Web:* **http://www.ithaca.edu/library/ training/think.html.**

MY INSTITUTION'S RESOURCES

CHAPTER 6

Being Engaged in Learning: Listening, Taking Notes, and Participating in Class

In virtually every college class you take, you'll need to master certain skills to earn high grades, such as listening, taking notes, and being engaged in learning. Engagement in learning means that you take an active role in your classes by listening critically, asking questions, contributing to discussions, and providing answers. These active learning behaviors will enhance your ability to understand abstract ideas, find new possibilities, organize those ideas, and recall the material once the class is over.

Your academic success relies on practicing the habits of active engagement both in and out of class. In the classroom, engagement starts with the basics: listening, taking notes, and participating in class discussions. Many of the questions on college exams will be drawn from class lectures and discussions. Therefore you need to attend each class and be actively involved. In addition to taking notes, you might consider recording the lecture and discussion if you have the instructor's permission. If there are points you don't understand, take the time to meet with the instructor after class or during office hours. Another strategy to increase your engagement and your learning is to meet with a study group to compare your understanding of course material with that of your classmates.

This chapter reviews several note-taking methods. Choose the one that works best for you. Because writing down everything the instructor says is probably not possible and you might not be sure what is most important, ask questions in class. This will ensure that you clearly understand your notes. Reviewing your

IN CLASS: This chapter is one of many that contains information critical to success in the classroom. Emphasize the importance of effective listening, note taking, and engagement in class. Let students know that many test questions on college exams are drawn from class lectures, not textbooks. Ask how many of their current courses are lecture-based and how many are discussion-based.

IN THIS CHAPTER YOU WILL EXPLORE

How to use your senses in learning and remembering

How to prepare before class

Why you should participate in class by speaking up

How to listen critically

How to assess and improve your note-taking skills

Why it is important to review your notes and textbook materials soon after class

How being engaged in the classroom improves your learning

IN CLASS: Ask students to try to determine which of their senses they use most when they are trying to sort and remember material for class. You might have them form groups by preferred sense. If some individuals are standing alone, put them in another group and have them explain their method and listen to other students explain theirs.

IN CLASS: Review with your students how the VARK Learning Styles Inventory (Chapter 4) focuses on learners' sensory preferences for learning. Visual learners prefer to learn information through charts, graphs, symbols, and other visual means. Aural learners prefer to hear information. Read/Write learners prefer to learn information displayed as words. Kinesthetic learners prefer to learn through experience and practice.

notes with a tutor, someone from your campus learning center, or a friend from class can also help you clarify your understanding of the most important points.

Most of all, be sure to speak up. When you have a question to ask or a comment to share, don't let embarrassment or shyness stop you. You will be more likely to remember what happens in class if you are an active participant.

Using Your Senses in the Learning Process

> What sensory mode seems to describe your preferred learning style? How can you use your sensory preferences to learn most effectively?

You can enhance your memory by using as many of your senses as possible while learning. How do you believe you learn most effectively?

1. **Aural:** Are you an auditory learner? Do you learn by listening to other people talk, or does your mind begin to wander when you listen passively for more than a few minutes?

2. **Visual:** Do you like reading? Do you learn best when you can see the words on the printed page? During a test, can you actually visualize where the information appears in your text? Can you remember data best when it's presented in the form of a picture, graph, chart, map, or video?

3. **Interactive:** Do you enjoy discussing coursework with friends, classmates, or the instructor? Does talking about information from the lecture or the text help you remember it?

4. **Tactile:** Do you learn through your sense of touch? Does typing your notes help you remember them?

5. **Kinesthetic:** Can you learn better when your body is in motion? When you are participating in sports, dancing, or working out, do you know immediately if a movement feels right? Do you learn more effectively by doing something than by listening or reading about it?

6. **Olfactory:** Does your sense of taste or smell contribute to your learning process? Do you cook using a recipe or by tasting and adding ingredients? Are you sensitive to odors?

Two or three of these modes probably describe your preferred ways of learning better than the others. At the college level, faculty members tend to share information primarily via lecture and the textbook. However, many students like to learn through visual and interactive means. This creates a mismatch between learning and teaching styles. Is this a problem? Not necessarily. It is a problem only if you do not learn how to adapt lecture material and the text to your preferred modes of learning.

◤ ASSESSING YOUR STRENGTHS

Students who are engaged in college life practice the behaviors that are reviewed in this chapter. What about you—how would you rate your level of engagement? Now that you have read the first section of this chapter, list specific examples of your strengths in the area of engagement.

_____

_____

_____

_____

◤ SETTING GOALS

What are *your* most important objectives in learning the material in this chapter? Do you have a good method of note taking? Do you devote time and energy to academic work by attending class and studying out of class? List three goals that relate to engagement in learning (e.g., I will schedule a visit with one of my professors to show him or her my notes from the last class to make sure I'm writing down the most important points).

1. _____

_____

2. _____

_____

3. _____

_____

■ RETENTION STRATEGY: This chapter contains a number of strategies for different types of learners. Be sure students identify the strategies that work best for them and help them stay engaged. Research finds that students who exhibit high levels of engagement are retained at a higher level than unengaged students.

EXERCISE 6.1

What You BRING Matters

One way to prepare for class is to approach it like getting ready for bed at night or cooking a meal—routines or rituals that involve a distinct set of steps that work for you. Your preparation might depend on how you use your senses for learning and remembering. For example, kinesthetic learners might take notes on a laptop or tap their feet. Auditory learners might want to tape the lecture (with the instructor's permission).

Based on your preferred mode(s) of learning (you can have more than one), list things that you will do or items to bring to class to help you prepare mentally. Some examples have been provided; now fill in the rest of the chart to make it applicable to *you*.

Items to Bring/Things to Do	Applicable Mode of Learning
Bring printout of instructor's PowerPoint	Visual
Sip coffee	Kinesthetic
Use tape recorder (with permission!)	Auditory

This exercise gets students to think about ways to prepare for class that make sense based on how they learn.

Preparing for Class

What do you do to get mentally ready for class? What could you be doing differently to improve your chances for success?

OUTSIDE CLASS: Give students a reading assignment either on the topic of college success or from your own discipline.

IN CLASS: Follow up with a related lecture in class. Then give students a quiz the next day, drawing about half of the questions from the reading and the rest from your lecture. Lead a discussion on the questions that students missed most, asking them to consider why they missed these questions.

Have you ever noticed how easy it is to learn the words of a song? We remember songs more easily than other kinds of information because songs follow a tune and have a beat and because they often have a personal meaning for us: We often relate songs to something in our everyday lives. We remember prose less easily unless we make an effort to relate it to what we already know. In your first-year classes, you'll be listening to and reading material that might seem hard to understand. Beginning on the first day of class, you will be more likely to remember what you hear and read if you try to link it to something you have already learned or experienced.

Because some lectures are hard to follow and understand, you need to be prepared before class begins. You would not want to be unprepared to give a speech, interview for a job, plead a case in court, or compete in a sport. For each of these situations, you would prepare in some way. For the same reasons, you should begin listening, learning, and remembering before the lecture.

Even if lectures don't allow for active participation, you can do a number of things to become more engaged and to make your listening and note taking more efficient. You will then learn and remember more, understand what the instructor considers important, and ultimately earn better grades.

This exercise gets students to give previewing a try so that they see how simple and effective a strategy it is.

What You PREVIEW Matters

Previewing information before class is important. Previewing creates an organized mental outline for the lecture ahead of time. Take a moment to write down in your notebook or type on your laptop the *title* and *headings* of this chapter:

Being Engaged in Learning: Listening, Taking Notes, and Participating in Class

Using Your Senses in the Learning Process

Preparing for Class

Participating in Class

Taking Effective Notes

Reviewing Your Notes

Becoming Engaged in Learning

Leave significant space between the headings for any notes, anecdotes, or ideas that the professor might mention in the class lecture. *Hint:* The more information the instructor provides under a particular heading, the more likely that information will be emphasized on a test.

You can use this previewing technique for all lecture classes that use a textbook as the main required reading, and it *only takes 5 minutes to set up before class.*

Participating in Class

Do you find it difficult to speak up in class even when you know your classmates and the instructor? What might make participation easier for you?

Learning is not a spectator sport. To really learn, you must listen critically, talk about what you are learning, write about it, relate it to past experiences, and make what you learn part of yourself. Participation is the heart of **active learning.** When we say something in class, we are more likely to remember it than we will when someone else says something. So when a teacher tosses a question your way or you have a question to ask, you're actually making it easier to remember the day's lesson.

active learning Learning by participation, such as listening critically, discussing what you are learning, and writing about it.

LISTENING CRITICALLY AND WITH AN OPEN MIND

Listening in class is not like listening to a TV show, listening to a friend, or even listening to a speaker at a meeting. Knowing how to listen in class can help you get more out of what you hear, understand better what you have heard, and save time.

BEFORE-CLASS TIPS

1. Do the assigned reading. Otherwise, you might find the lecturer's comments disjointed, and you might not understand some terms that your instructor will use. Some instructors refer to assigned readings for each class session; others might distribute a **syllabus** (course outline) and assume you are keeping up with the assigned readings. Completing assigned reading on time will help you listen better and pick out the most important information when taking notes in class. As you read, take good notes. In books that you own, **annotate** (add critical or explanatory margin notes), highlight, or underline the text. In books that you do not own, such as library books, make a photocopy of the pages and then annotate or highlight.

2. Pay careful attention to your course syllabus. Syllabi are formal statements of course expectations, requirements, and procedures. Instructors assume that students will understand and follow course requirements with few or no reminders once they have received a syllabus.

3. Make use of additional materials provided by the instructors. Many instructors post lecture outlines or notes on a Web site before class. Download and print these materials for easy reference during class. They often provide hints about the topics that the instructor considers most important; they also can create an organizational structure for taking notes.

4. Warm up for class by reviewing chapter introductions and summaries, referring to related sections in your text, and scanning your notes from the previous class period. This prepares you to pay attention, understand, and remember.

5. Get organized. Decide what type of notebook will work best for you. Many study skills experts suggest using three-ring binders because you can punch holes in syllabi and other course handouts and keep them with class notes. You might want to buy notebook paper with a larger left-hand margin (sometimes called "legal-ruled"), which will help you to easily annotate your lecture notes. If you take notes on your laptop, keep your files organized in separate folders for each of your classes, and make sure that the file name of each document reflects the date and topic of the class.

---

syllabus A formal statement of course requirements and procedures or a course outline provided by instructors to all students on the first day of class.

annotate To add critical or explanatory margin notes on a page as you read.

Here are some suggestions:

1. **Be ready for the message.** Prepare yourself to hear, to listen, and to receive the message. If you have done the assigned reading, you will already know details from the text, so you can focus your notes on key concepts during the lecture. You will also be able to notice information that the text does not cover, and you will be prepared to pay closer attention when the instructor is presenting unfamiliar material.

2. **Listen to the main concepts and central ideas, not just to fragmented facts and figures.** Although facts are important, they will be easier to remember and will make more sense when you can place them in a context of concepts, themes, and ideas.

3. **Listen for new ideas.** Even if you are an expert on a topic, you can still learn something new. Do not assume that college instructors will present the same information you learned in a similar course in high school. Even if you're listening to the lecture again (perhaps because you recorded your lectures), you will pick out and learn new information. As a critical thinker, make a note of questions that arise in your mind as you listen, but save the judgments for later.

4. **Repeat mentally.** Words can go in one ear and out the other unless you make an effort to retain them. Think about what you hear, and restate it silently in your own words. If you cannot translate the information into your own words, ask the instructor for further clarification.

5. **Decide whether what you have heard is not important, somewhat important, or very important.** If it's really not important, let it go. If it's very important, make it a major point in your notes by highlighting or underscoring it, or use it as a major topic in your outline if that's the method you use for taking notes. If it's somewhat important, try to relate it to a very important topic by writing it down as a subset of that topic.

6. **Keep an open mind.** Every class holds the promise of letting you discover new ideas and uncover different perspectives. Some teachers might intentionally present information that challenges your value system. One of the purposes of college is to teach you to think in new and different ways and to learn to provide support for your own beliefs. Instructors want you to think for yourself; they don't necessarily expect you to agree with everything they or your classmates say. However, if you want people to respect your values and ideas, you must show respect for theirs as well by listening to what they have to say with an open mind.

7. **Ask questions.** Early in the term, determine whether the instructor is open to responding to questions during the lecture. Some teachers prefer to save questions for the end or want students to ask questions during separate discussion sections or office hours. To some extent, this might depend on the nature and size of the class, such as a large lecture versus a small seminar. If your teacher answers questions as they arise, do not hesitate to ask if you did not hear or understand what was said. It is best to clarify things immediately, if possible, and other students are likely to have the same questions. If you can't hear another student's question or response, ask that it be repeated.

8. **Sort, organize, and categorize.** When you listen, try to match what you are hearing with what you already know. Take an active role in deciding how best to recall what you are learning.

SPEAKING UP

Naturally, you will be more likely to participate in a class in which the teacher emphasizes interactive discussion, calls on students by name, shows signs of approval and interest, and avoids criticizing students for an incorrect answer. Often, answers you and others offer that are not quite correct can lead to new perspectives on a topic.

DID YOU KNOW?

42% of first-year students say they frequently contribute to class discussions.

IN CLASS: As an experiment, tell your students not to take notes but to listen for the main points as you give a 5-minute lecture. Next, ask them to write down those main points and, working in small groups, compare their notes with those of other students. Finally, ask each group to report to the class. To encourage and model active listening, ask students to paraphrase the previous speaker's main points before presenting their own reports. How many groups remembered all of the main points? Why did some forget?

IN CLASS: Participation in class is an essential element of active learning and engagement. Speaking in public is one of the most common human fears. Ask students to brainstorm with each other ways to overcome this fear.

Speak Up

Participating in class not only helps you learn but also shows your instructor that you're interested and engaged. Like anything else, the first time you raise your hand might make you anxious. But after that first time, you'll likely find that contributing to class raises your interest and enjoyment.

In large classes instructors often use the lecture method, and large classes can be intimidating. If you ask a question in a class of 100 and think you have made a fool of yourself, you also believe that 99 other people already know the answer. That's somewhat unrealistic, since you have probably asked a question that others were too timid to ask, and they'll silently thank you for doing so. If you're lucky, you might even find that the instructor takes time out to ask or answer questions. To take full advantage of these opportunities, try using the following techniques:

1. **Take a seat as close to the front as possible.** If students are seated by name and your name begins with Z, visit your instructor during office hours and request to be moved up front.

2. **Keep your eyes trained on the instructor.** Sitting up front will make this easier to do.

3. **Focus on the lecture.** Do not let yourself be distracted. It might be wise not to sit near friends who can distract you.

4. **Raise your hand when you don't understand something.** The instructor might answer you immediately, ask you to wait until later in the class, or throw your question to the rest of the class. In each case, you benefit in several ways. The instructor will get to know you, other students will get to know you, and you will learn from both the instructor and your classmates. But don't overdo it. The instructor and your peers will tire of too many questions that disrupt the flow of the class.

IN CLASS: Take time in class to ask and answer questions. Discuss how to take notes in question-and-answer sessions. Point out the value to the entire class of students' questions. Try putting up overhead transparencies or *PowerPoint* slides that show only part of the material at a time, in comparison to showing the entire message in advance. Discuss how this affects students' attention to the topic.

5. **Speak up in class.** Ask a question or volunteer to answer a question or make a comment. This becomes easier every time you do it.

6. **Never feel that you're asking a stupid question.** If you don't understand something, you have a right to ask for an explanation.

7. **When the instructor calls on you to answer a question, don't bluff.** If you know the answer, give it. If you're not certain, begin with, "I think . . . , but I'm not sure I have it all correct." If you don't know, just say so.

8. **If you have recently read a book or article that is relevant to the class topic, bring it in.** Use it either to ask questions about the topic or to provide information that was not covered in class.

Point out this exercise to your students to give them a chance to submit these question cards at the beginning of the class period when you present the material in Chapter 6. Students will appreciate your attention to their questions and ideas.

EXERCISE 6.3

What You QUESTION Matters

Using a couple of blank note cards, create *question cards* with questions you have about this chapter that you would like answered, or write down a new idea from the chapter that you had never considered before. Here are some examples:

> Q: I didn't realize that there were different note-taking methods. Is there one that is better for my history class?

> Q: I'm not sure about our institution's tutoring resources. Can you tell me more?

Turn in these cards to your instructor before the next class so that he or she will be aware of key points that need more attention. This method of submitting questions and ideas allows you to participate without feeling intimidated, and you can listen to your instructor's answers and comments with an open mind. You'll likely discover that other students had the same question(s) as you, and you may grow comfortable enough to ask your questions in class.

Taking Effective Notes

Why might the note-taking techniques you used in high school not work as well in college? What new techniques are you willing to try?

What are "effective notes"? They are notes that cover all the important points of the lecture or reading material without being too detailed or too limited. Most important, effective notes prepare you to do well on quizzes or exams. Becoming an effective note-taker takes time and practice, but this skill will help you improve your learning and your grades in the first year and beyond.

NOTE-TAKING FORMATS

You can make class time more productive by using your listening skills to take effective lecture notes, but first you have to decide on a system. Any system can work as long as you use it consistently.

Cornell Format.   Using the Cornell format, one of the best-known methods for organizing notes, you create a "recall" column on each page of your notebook by drawing a vertical line about two to three inches from the left border (see Figure 6.1). As you take notes during lecture—whether writing down ideas, making lists, or using an outline or paragraph format—write only in the wider column on the right; leave the recall column on the left blank. (If you have large handwriting and this method seems unwieldy, consider using the back of the previous notebook page for your recall column.) The recall column is the place where you write down the main ideas and important details for tests and examinations as you sift through your notes as

■ RETENTION STRATEGY: Although there is no direct research linking note taking and retention, this is one of the critical skills that can determine academic success and therefore the likelihood that students will persist. Note taking is a skill that few students learn in high school because there is less lecturing in high school classes.

IN CLASS: Discuss the kinds of courses and topics that might be difficult to outline. Ask students how they might supplement regular note taking in these situations.

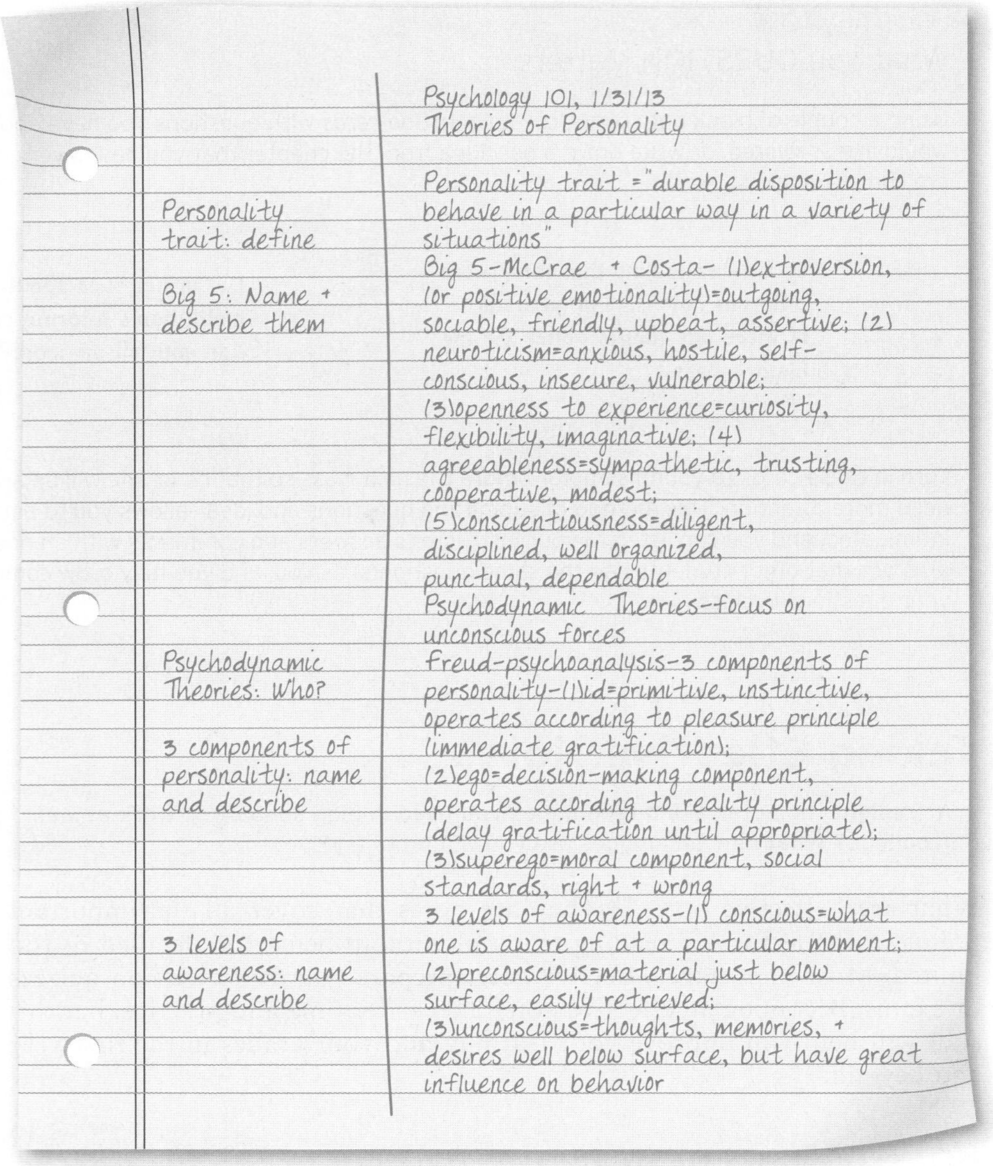

> Psychology 101, 1/31/13
> Theories of Personality
>
> Personality trait: define — Personality trait ="durable disposition to behave in a particular way in a variety of situations"
>
> Big 5: Name + describe them — Big 5-McCrae + Costa- (1)extroversion, (or positive emotionality)=outgoing, sociable, friendly, upbeat, assertive; (2) neuroticism=anxious, hostile, self-conscious, insecure, vulnerable; (3)openness to experience=curiosity, flexibility, imaginative; (4) agreeableness=sympathetic, trusting, cooperative, modest; (5)conscientiousness=diligent, disciplined, well organized, punctual, dependable
>
> Psychodynamic Theories: Who? — Psychodynamic Theories-focus on unconscious forces Freud-psychoanalysis-3 components of personality-(1)id=primitive, instinctive, operates according to pleasure principle (immediate gratification);
>
> 3 components of personality: name and describe — (2)ego=decision-making component, operates according to reality principle (delay gratification until appropriate); (3)superego=moral component, social standards, right + wrong
>
> 3 levels of awareness: name and describe — 3 levels of awareness-(1) conscious=what one is aware of at a particular moment; (2)preconscious=material just below surface, easily retrieved; (3)unconscious=thoughts, memories, + desires well below surface, but have great influence on behavior

FIGURE 6.1
Note Taking in the Cornell Format

soon after class as is feasible, preferably within an hour or two. Many students have found the recall column to be a critical part of effective note taking, one that becomes an important study device for tests and exams.

Outline Format.   Some students find that an outline is the best way for them to organize their notes. You probably already know what a formal outline looks like, with key ideas represented by Roman numerals and other ideas relating to each key idea represented in order by uppercase letters, numbers, and lowercase letters. If you use this approach, try to determine the instructor's outline and recreate it in your notes. Add details, definitions, examples, applications, and explanations (see Figures 6.2 and 6.5).

IN CLASS: With students taking notes, lecture for about 20 minutes. Assign different students to use the Cornell format, outline format, paragraph format, and list format. Have students work in groups to compare the formats. Discuss the strengths of each.

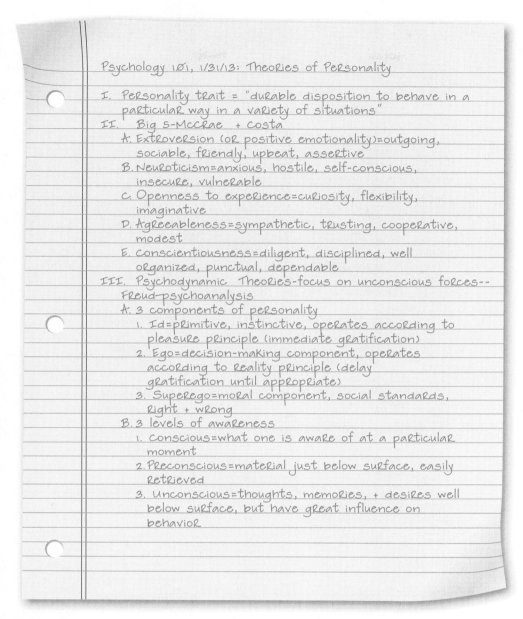

Psychology 101, 1/31/13: Theories of Personality

I. Personality trait = "durable disposition to behave in a particular way in a variety of situations"
II. Big 5-McCrae + Costa
   A. Extroversion (or positive emotionality)=outgoing, sociable, friendly, upbeat, assertive
   B. Neuroticism=anxious, hostile, self-conscious, insecure, vulnerable
   C. Openness to experience=curiosity, flexibility, imaginative
   D. Agreeableness=sympathetic, trusting, cooperative, modest
   E. Conscientiousness=diligent, disciplined, well organized, punctual, dependable
III. Psychodynamic Theories-focus on unconscious forces-- Freud-psychoanalysis
   A. 3 components of personality
      1. Id=primitive, instinctive, operates according to pleasure principle (immediate gratification)
      2. Ego=decision-making component, operates according to reality principle (delay gratification until appropriate)
      3. Superego=moral component, social standards, right + wrong
   B. 3 levels of awareness
      1. Conscious=what one is aware of at a particular moment
      2. Preconscious=material just below surface, easily retrieved
      3. Unconscious=thoughts, memories, + desires well below surface, but have great influence on behavior

FIGURE 6.2
Note Taking in the Outline Format

Paragraph Format. You might decide to write summary paragraphs when you are taking notes on what you are reading. This method might not work as well for class notes because it's difficult to summarize a topic until your instructor has covered it completely. By the end of the lecture, you might have forgotten critical information (see Figure 6.3).

List Format. This format can be effective in taking notes on lists of terms and definitions, facts, or sequences, such as the body's pulmonary system. It is easy to use lists in combination with the Cornell format, with

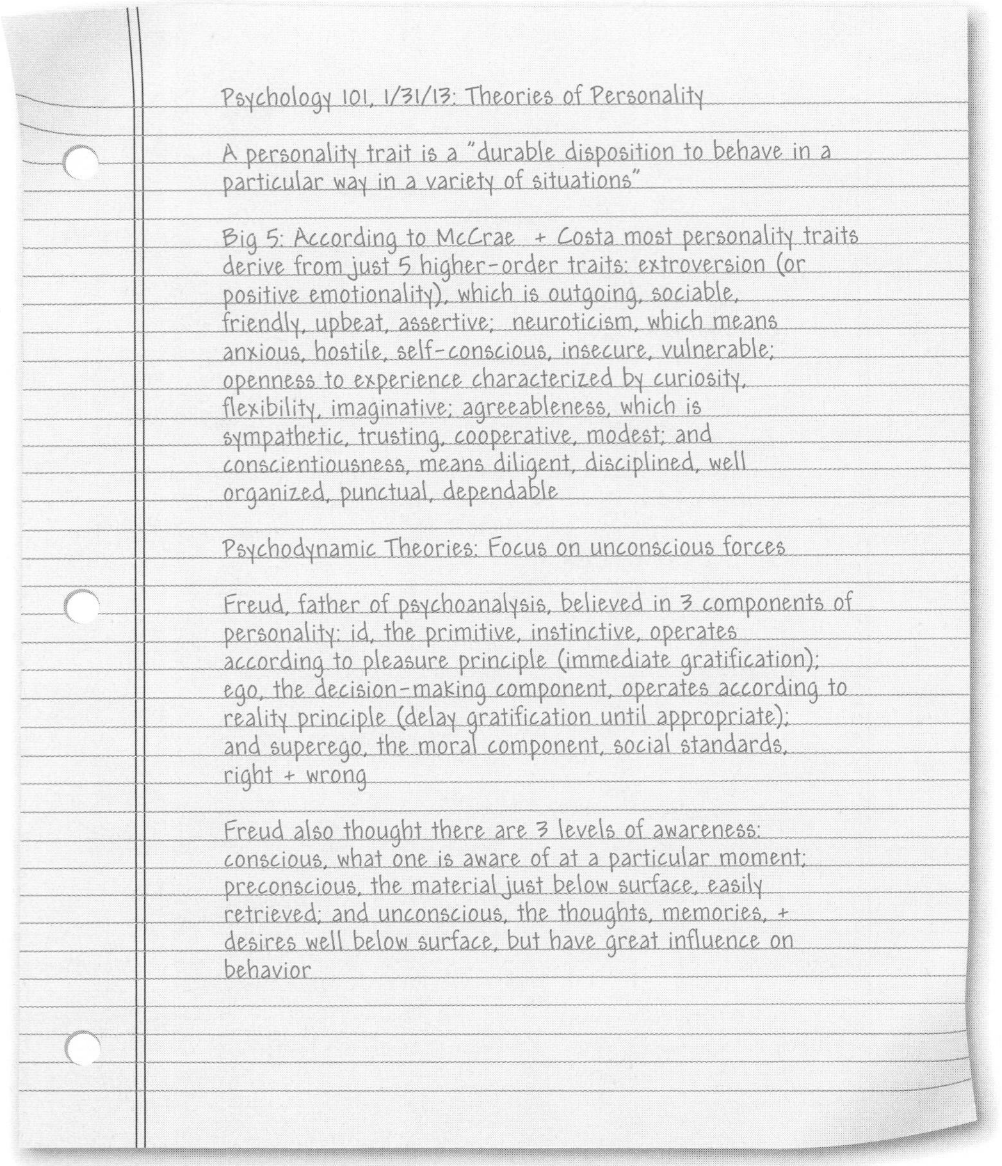

Psychology 101, 1/31/13: Theories of Personality
A personality trait is a "durable disposition to behave in a particular way in a variety of situations"
Big 5: According to McCrae + Costa most personality traits derive from just 5 higher-order traits: extroversion (or positive emotionality), which is outgoing, sociable, friendly, upbeat, assertive; neuroticism, which means anxious, hostile, self-conscious, insecure, vulnerable; openness to experience characterized by curiosity, flexibility, imaginative; agreeableness, which is sympathetic, trusting, cooperative, modest; and conscientiousness, means diligent, disciplined, well organized, punctual, dependable
Psychodynamic Theories: Focus on unconscious forces
Freud, father of psychoanalysis, believed in 3 components of personality: id, the primitive, instinctive, operates according to pleasure principle (immediate gratification); ego, the decision-making component, operates according to reality principle (delay gratification until appropriate); and superego, the moral component, social standards, right + wrong
Freud also thought there are 3 levels of awareness: conscious, what one is aware of at a particular moment; preconscious, the material just below surface, easily retrieved; and unconscious, the thoughts, memories, + desires well below surface, but have great influence on behavior

FIGURE 6.3
Note Taking in the Paragraph Format

key terms on the left and their definitions and explanations on the right (see Figure 6.4).

Once you have decided on a format for taking notes, you might also want to develop your own system of abbreviations. For example, you might write "inst" instead of "institution" or "eval" instead of "evaluation." Just make sure you will be able to understand your abbreviations when it's time to review.

IN CLASS: Lecture to the class, and ask students to take notes. Give them an additional 5 minutes to revise and complete their notes. Collect and review their notes, or prepare a handout in which you have taken notes and used a recall column. Discuss the differences and similarities between their notes and yours. You might use overhead transparencies or *PowerPoint* slides to show how you made notes in the assigned reading materials.

NOTE-TAKING TECHNIQUES

Whatever note-taking system you choose, follow these important steps:

1. **Identify the main ideas.** Well-organized lectures always contain key points. The first principle of effective note taking is to identify and write down the

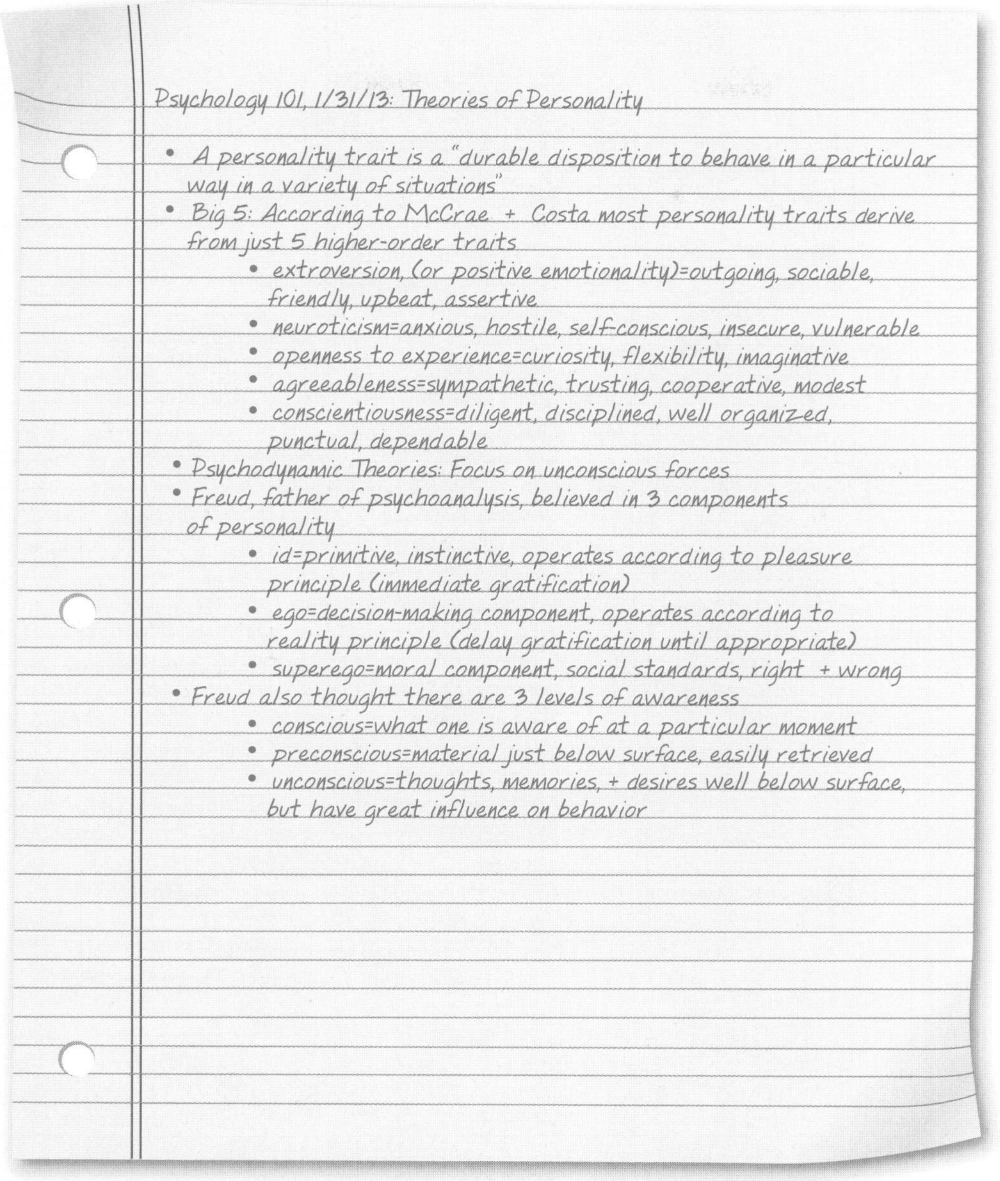

Psychology 101, 1/31/13: Theories of Personality

- A personality trait is a "durable disposition to behave in a particular way in a variety of situations"
- Big 5: According to McCrae + Costa most personality traits derive from just 5 higher-order traits
  - extroversion, (or positive emotionality)=outgoing, sociable, friendly, upbeat, assertive
  - neuroticism=anxious, hostile, self-conscious, insecure, vulnerable
  - openness to experience=curiosity, flexibility, imaginative
  - agreeableness=sympathetic, trusting, cooperative, modest
  - conscientiousness=diligent, disciplined, well organized, punctual, dependable
- Psychodynamic Theories: Focus on unconscious forces
- Freud, father of psychoanalysis, believed in 3 components of personality
  - id=primitive, instinctive, operates according to pleasure principle (immediate gratification)
  - ego=decision-making component, operates according to reality principle (delay gratification until appropriate)
  - superego=moral component, social standards, right + wrong
- Freud also thought there are 3 levels of awareness
  - conscious=what one is aware of at a particular moment
  - preconscious=material just below surface, easily retrieved
  - unconscious=thoughts, memories, + desires well below surface, but have great influence on behavior

FIGURE 6.4
Note Taking in the List Format

most important ideas around which the lecture is built. Although supporting details are important as well, focus your note taking on the main ideas. Such ideas can be buried in details, statistics, anecdotes, or problems, but you will need to identify and record them for further study.

Some instructors announce the purpose of a lecture or offer an outline, thus providing you with the skeleton of main ideas, followed by the details. Other instructors develop *PowerPoint* presentations. If they make these materials available on a class Web site before the lecture, you can print them and take notes on the teacher's outline or next to the *PowerPoint* slides.

Some lecturers change their tone of voice or repeat themselves for each key idea. Some ask questions or promote discussion. If a lecturer

Personality trait	I. Personality trait = "durable disposition to behave in a particular way in a variety of situations"
	II. Big 5-McCrae + Costa
Big 5: Who? Name + describe them	A. Extroversion (or positive emotionality)=outgoing, sociable, friendly, upbeat, assertive
	B. Neuroticism=anxious, hostile, self-conscious, insecure, vulnerable
	C. Openness to experience=curiosity, flexibility, imaginative
	D. Agreeableness=sympathetic, trusting, cooperative, modest
	E. Conscientiousness=diligent, disciplined, well organized, punctual, dependable
	III. Psychodynamic Theories-focus on unconscious forces-- Freud-psychoanalysis
Psychodynamic Theories: Who? 3 components. Name, define, relate each to a principle	A. 3 components of personality
	1. Id=primitive, instinctive, operates according to pleasure principle (immediate gratification)
	2. Ego=decision-making component, operates according to reality principle (delay gratification until appropriate)
	3. Superego=moral component, social standards, right + wrong
	B. 3 levels of awareness
3 levels of awareness: name and describe	1. conscious=what one is aware of at a particular moment
	2. preconscious=material just below surface, easily retrieved
	3. unconscious=thoughts, memories, + desires well below surface, but have great influence on behavior

FIGURE 6.5

Cornell Format Combined with Outline Format

says something more than once, chances are it is important. Ask yourself, "What does my instructor want me to know at the end of today's class?"

2. **Don't try to write down everything.** Some first-year students try to do just that. They stop being thinkers and become stenographers. As you take notes, leave spaces so that you can fill in additional details that you might have missed during class but remember later. Take the time to review and complete your notes as soon after class as possible.

3. **Don't be thrown by a disorganized lecturer.** When a lecture is disorganized, it's your job to try to organize what is said into general and specific frameworks. When the order is not apparent, you will need to indicate in your notes where the gaps lie. After the lecture, consult the reading material or classmates to fill in these gaps, or ask your instructor.

Most instructors have regular office hours for student appointments, yet it is amazing how few students use these opportunities for one-on-one instruction. Asking questions can help your instructor find out which parts of the lecture need more attention and clarification.

4. **Keep your notes and supplementary materials for each course in a separate three-ring binder.** Label the binder with the course number and name. If the binders are too bulky to carry in your backpack, create a separate folder for each class, stocked with loose-leaf notebook paper. Before class, label and date the paper you will be using for taking notes. Then, as soon after class as possible, move your notes from the folder to the binder.

5. **Download any notes, outlines, or diagrams, charts, graphs, and other visuals** from the instructor's Web site before class and bring them with you. You might be able to save yourself considerable time during the lecture if you do not have to try to copy complicated graphs and diagrams while the instructor is talking. Instead, you can focus on the ideas being presented while adding your own labels and notes to the visual images.

6. **Organize your notes chronologically in your binder.** Then create separate tabbed sections for homework, lab assignments, returned tests, and other materials.

7. **If handouts are distributed in class, label them and place them in your binder** near the notes for that day. Buy a portable three-ring hole-punch that can be kept in your binder. Do not let handouts accumulate in your folders; add any handouts to your binders as you review your notes each day.

Taking Notes in Nonlecture Courses.

Always be ready to adapt your note-taking methods to match the situation. Group discussion is becoming a popular way to teach in college because it engages students in active participation. On your campus you might also have **Supplemental Instruction (SI)** classes that provide further opportunity to discuss the information presented in lectures. How do you keep a record of what's happening in such classes? Assume you are taking notes in a problem-solving group assignment. You would begin your notes by asking yourself, "What is the problem?" and writing down the answer. As the discussion progresses, you would list the solutions that are offered. These would be your main ideas. The important details might include the positive and negative aspects of each view or solution. The important thing to remember when taking notes in nonlecture courses is that you need to record the information presented by your classmates as well as by the instructor and to consider all reasonable ideas, even though they might differ from your own.

When a course has separate lecture and discussion sessions, you will need to understand how the discussion sessions relate to and augment the lectures. If different material is covered in lecture or discussion, you might need to ask for guidance in organizing your notes. When similar topics are covered, you can combine your notes so that you have comprehensive, unified coverage of each topic.

How to organize the notes you take in a class discussion depends on the purpose or form of the discussion. It usually makes good sense to begin with the list of issues or topics that the discussion leader announces. Another approach is to list the questions that participants raise for discussion. If the discussion explores reasons for and against a particular argument, divide your notes into columns or sections for pros and cons. When conflicting views are presented in discussion, record different perspectives and the

IN CLASS: Ask students whether an organized note-taking system is more, or less, essential in nonlecture courses. Remind students that many of their best instructors will use a combination of lectures and other teaching modes and that other students' comments might help clarify the material.

Supplemental Instruction (SI) Classes that provide further opportunity to discuss the information presented in lectures.

TECH TIP TAKE NOTES LIKE A ROCK STAR

Studies have shown that people remember only half of what they hear, which is a major reason you need to take lecture notes. Solid note taking will also help you distill key concepts and make it easier to study for tests. So why not take your note-taking skills up a notch?

1 ▶ THE PROBLEM

You don't know how to make your digital lecture notes leap off the screen and engrave themselves on your brain.

2 ▶ THE FIX

Clue into the many ways you can use basic programs like *Word*, *Excel*, and *PowerPoint* to sharpen your note-taking skill set.

3 ▶ HOW TO DO IT

1. *Word* is great for taking notes in most classes. To highlight main ideas, you can bold or underline text. You can change the font size and color, highlight whole swaths of text, or insert text boxes or charts. You can make bullet points or properly formatted outlines and insert comment bubbles for emphasis. You can cut and paste material as you review your notes to make things more coherent. You can also create different folders for each of your classes so you can find everything you need with one click. (Note: It's worth playing around on the toolbar until you get it all down pat.)

2. *Excel* is especially good for economics and accounting courses, or any class that involves making scientific calculations or financial statements. You can embed messages inside the cells of a spreadsheet to explain calculations. The notes will magically appear whenever you use your cursor to hover over that cell.

3. *PowerPoint* can be an invaluable tool for visual learners. Instead of keeping your notes in one giant, potentially confusing *Word* document, you can open up a *PowerPoint* slideshow and type right into it. That way, every time your professor changes gears, you can open a new slide. It's a nice way to break up the material. *Good to know*: Some instructors post the *PowerPoint* slides that they plan to use in class a few hours in advance. Print them out and take them with you as note-taking tools; you can even write notes on the slides themselves.

CLEVER TRICKS

Date your notes. Focus on writing down the main points (the material your professor emphasizes or repeats), using phrases or key words instead of long sentences. Keep all of your notes in order and in one place. Back up *everything*. If you're not a tech whiz, keep a pen and paper handy for sketching graphs and diagrams. Label your notes clearly to make it easy to look things up. And if you find yourself struggling to keep up, practice your listening and typing skills.

PERSONAL BEST

What concrete steps could you take to create an organized note-taking system for the semester? Start by picking a note-taking style that appeals to you. If you love a chart or spreadsheet, *Excel* is your kind of program. If you're an old-school type who loves nothing better than a spiral notebook and a ballpoint pen, that's okay, too.

rationales behind them. Your teacher might ask you to defend your own opinions in comparison to those of other students.

Taking Notes in Science and Mathematics Courses.   Many mathematics and science courses build on each other from term to term and from year to year. When you take notes in these courses, you will likely need to refer to them in the future. For example, when taking organic chemistry, you might need to refer to notes taken in earlier chemistry courses. This can be particularly important when time has passed since your last related course, such as after a summer break. Taking notes in math and science courses can be different from taking notes in other types of classes. The box below offers tips to keep in mind specifically when taking notes in quantitative and science classes.

Using Technology to Take Notes.   While some students use laptops for note taking, others prefer taking notes by hand so they can easily circle important items or copy complex equations or diagrams while these are

---

TIPS FOR NOTE TAKING IN QUANTITATIVE AND SCIENCE CLASSES

> Write down any equations, formulas, diagrams, charts, graphs, and definitions that the instructor puts on the board or screen.

> Quote the instructor's words as precisely as possible. Technical terms often have exact meanings and cannot be paraphrased.

> Use standard symbols, abbreviations, and scientific notation.

> Write down all worked problems and examples, step-by-step. They often provide the template for exam questions. Actively engage in solving the problem yourself as it is being solved at the front of the class. Be sure that you can follow the logic and understand the sequence of steps. If you have questions you cannot ask during lecture, write them down in your notes so that you can ask them in discussion, in the lab, or during the instructor's office hours.

> Consider taking your notes in pencil or erasable pen. You might need to make changes if you are copying long equations while also trying to pay attention to the instructor. You want to keep your notes as neat as possible. Later, you can use colored ink to add other details.

> Listen carefully to other students' questions and the instructor's answers. Take notes on the discussion and during question-and-answer periods.

> Use asterisks, exclamation points, question marks, or symbols of your own to highlight important points in your notes or questions that you need to come back to when you review.

> Refer back to the textbook after class; the text might contain more accurate diagrams and other visual representations than you can draw while taking notes in class. If they are not provided in handouts or on the instructor's Web site, you might even want to scan or photocopy diagrams from the text and include them with your notes in your binder.

> Keep your binders for math and science courses until you graduate (or even longer if there is any chance that you will attend graduate school at some point in the future). They will serve as beneficial review materials for later classes in math and science and for preparing for standardized tests such as the Graduate Record Exam (GRE) or Medical College Admission Test (MCAT). In some cases, these notes can also prove helpful in the workplace.

being presented. If you handwrite your notes, entering them on a computer after class for review purposes might be helpful, especially if you are a kinesthetic learner. After class you can also cut and paste diagrams and other visual representations into your notes and print a copy that might be easier to read than notes you wrote by hand.

Some students, especially aural learners, find it is advantageous to record lectures. But if you record, resist the temptation to become passive in class instead of actively listening. Students with specific types of disabilities might be urged to record lectures or use the services of note-takers who type on a laptop while the student views the notes on a separate screen.

This activity takes students to the Bedford/St. Martin's Web site to listen to a podcast about note taking and to try out one of the note-taking methods described in the chapter.

EXERCISE 6.4

What You HEAR Matters

Part of learning is practicing. Note taking does not come naturally to some people. But the more you practice, the better you'll be as a note-taker. Research has shown a relationship between good note taking and good grades, so here's one way to practice using fun technology.

Go to this textbook's Web site and listen to the podcast on note taking by "Get It Done Guy" at **bedfordstmartins.com/ycestudyskills.**

Take notes on the information in this podcast using one of the methods described in the text: the Cornell format, the outline format, the paragraph format, or the list format. Which method appeals to you and why?

_____

Reviewing Your Notes

How will you avoid the "forgetting curve" and remember what you have learned?

Most forgetting takes place within the first 24 hours of encountering the information, a phenomenon known as the "forgetting curve." So if you do not review your notes almost immediately after class, it can be difficult to retrieve the material later. In two weeks, you will have forgotten up to 70 percent of it! Forgetting can be a serious problem when you are expected to learn and remember many different facts, figures, concepts, and relationships for a number of classes. Once you understand how to improve your ability to remember, you will retain information more easily and completely. Retaining information will help your overall understanding as well as your ability to recall important details during exams.

Don't let the forgetting curve take its toll on you. As soon after class as possible, review your notes and fill in the details you still remember but missed writing down. One way to remember is to recite important data to yourself every few minutes. If you are an aural learner, you might want to repeat your notes out loud. Another idea is to tie one idea to another idea, concept, or name so that thinking of one will prompt recall of the other. Or you might want to create your own poem, song, or slogan using the information.

For interactive learners, the best way to learn something might be to teach it to someone else. You will understand something better and remember it

IN CLASS: Ask how many students take class notes on laptops. Have these students discuss the advantages and drawbacks of taking notes this way. Ask how they use their notes to study for exams.

IN CLASS: To demonstrate how easy it is to forget information, ask students to think back to a lecture from the previous day and write down as many main ideas and supporting details as they can remember.

OUTSIDE CLASS: For homework, ask students to compare these lists to the notes they took while the class was in session.

KEYS TO REMEMBERING

1. Write down the main ideas. For 5 or 10 minutes, quickly review your notes and select key words or phrases that will act as labels or tags for main ideas and key information in your notes.

2. Recite your ideas out loud. Recite a brief version of what you understand from the class. If you don't have a few minutes after class when you can concentrate on reviewing your notes, find some other time during that same day to review what you have written. You might also want to ask your instructor to glance at your notes to determine whether you have identified the major ideas.

3. Review your notes from the previous class just before the next class session. As you sit in class the next time it meets, waiting for the lecture to begin, use the time to quickly review your notes from the previous class session. This will put you in tune with the lecture that is about to begin and prompt you to ask questions about material from the previous lecture that might not have been clear to you.

longer if you try to explain it. This helps you discover your own reactions and uncover gaps in your comprehension of the material. (Asking and answering questions in class can also provide you with the feedback you need to make certain your understanding is accurate.) Now you're ready to embed the major points from your notes in your memory. Use the three important steps in the box above for remembering the key points from the lecture. These three ways to engage with the material will pay off later, when you begin to study for your exams.

What if you have three classes in a row and no time for studying between them? Recall and recite as soon after class as possible. Review the most recent class first. Never delay recall and recitation longer than one day; if you do, it will take you longer to review, select main ideas, and recite. With practice, you can complete the review of your main ideas from your notes quickly, perhaps between classes, during lunch, or while riding the bus.

COMPARING NOTES

You might be able to improve your notes by comparing notes with another student or in a study group, Supplemental Instruction session, or a learning community, if one is available to you. Knowing that your notes will be seen by someone else will prompt you to make your notes well organized, clear, and accurate. Compare your notes: Are they as clear and concise as those of other students? Do you agree on the most important points? Share with each other how you take and organize your notes. You might get new ideas for using abbreviations. Take turns testing each other on what you have learned. This will help you predict exam questions and determine whether you can answer them. Comparing notes is not the same as copying another student's notes. You simply cannot learn as well from someone else's notes, no matter how good they are, if you have not attended class.

If your campus has a note-taking service, check with your instructor about making use of this for-pay service, but keep in mind that such notes are intended to supplement the ones you take, not to substitute for them. Some students choose to copy their own notes as a means of review or

IN CLASS: Talk about comparing notes for the purpose of learning versus plagiarism and cheating. Show how sharing notes can be a good practice to compare what each person thought was important. Show how sharing notes can be counterproductive when students use someone else's notes because they missed class or failed to take good notes themselves.

because they think their notes are messy and that they will not be able to understand them later. Unless you are a tactile learner, copying or typing your notes might not help you learn the material. A more profitable approach might be to summarize your notes in your own words.

Finally, have a backup plan in case you need to be absent because of illness or a family emergency. Exchange phone numbers and e-mail addresses with other students so that you can contact one of them to learn what you missed and get a copy of his or her notes. Also contact your instructor to explain your absence and set up an appointment during office hours to make sure you understand the work you missed.

CLASS NOTES AND HOMEWORK

OUTSIDE CLASS: After students read the suggestions under Class Notes and Homework, ask them to practice these steps and report the results.

Good class notes can help you complete homework assignments. Follow these steps:

1. **Take 10 minutes to review your notes.** Skim the notes, and put a question mark next to anything you do not understand at first reading. Draw stars next to topics that warrant special emphasis. Try to place the material in context: What has been going on in the course for the past few weeks? How does today's class fit in?

2. **Do a warm-up for your homework.** Before doing the assignment, look through your notes again. Use a separate sheet of paper to rework examples, problems, or exercises. If there is related assigned material in the textbook, review it. Go back to the examples. Cover the solution, and attempt to answer each question or complete each problem. Look at the author's work only after you have made a serious effort to remember it. Keep in mind that it can help to go back through your course notes, reorganize them, highlight the essential items, and thus create new notes that let you connect with the material one more time and could be better than the originals.

3. **Do any assigned problems, and answer any assigned questions.** When you start doing your homework, read each question or problem and ask: What am I supposed to find or find out? What is essential and what is extraneous? Read each problem several times, and state it in your own words. Work the problem without referring to your notes or the text, as though you were taking a test. In this way, you will test your knowledge and know when you are prepared for exams.

4. **Persevere.** Don't give up too soon. When you encounter a problem or question that you cannot readily handle, move on only after a reasonable effort. After you have completed the entire assignment, come back to any items that stumped you. Try once more, and then take a break. You might need to mull over a particularly difficult problem for several days. Let your unconscious mind have a chance. Inspiration might come when you are waiting at a stoplight or just before you fall asleep.

5. **Complete your work.** When you finish an assignment, talk to yourself about what you learned from it. Think about how the problems and questions were different from one another, which strategies were successful, and what form the answers took. Be sure to review any material you have not mastered. Seek assistance from the instructor, a classmate, a study group, the campus learning center, or a tutor to learn how to answer questions that stumped you.

This is a group activity in which students should work with two or three other students.

EXERCISE 6.5

What You WRITE Matters

In high school, you may have heard your teachers tell you not to compare notes—in other words, not to cheat! But this exercise is asking you to compare your notes. Because people learn in different ways, it is helpful to compare what you learned in class with what someone else heard or experienced. They may have picked up different information.

Get together with two or three other students, and exchange notes from the podcast in Exercise 6.4. As you look at your classmates' notes, answer each of the questions below. Take into consideration that everyone's note taking will be slightly different depending on his or her preferred note-taking method. What have you learned about your own notes by looking at your partners' notes?

Note-Taking Assessment Form

Your Name   _____

Your Partners' Names   _____   _____   _____

Date   _____

Topic/Chapter   _____

Questions about your partners' notes:

1. Are the notes legible (clearly written)?   Y or N
2. Are the key points clearly defined (either underlined or boldfaced)?   Y or N
3. Are there sufficient details under each heading?   Y or N
4. Are there any extraneous details that do not reflect the main topic?   Y or N
5. Which formats did your partners use?   _____
    Which one did you choose?   _____
6. Did you emphasize the same information?   Y or N

Name one thing you might do differently now that you have compared your notes.

_____

_____

_____

OUTSIDE CLASS: The literature on the advantages of active learning is extensive. Consider asking students to do a search on the topic, using library and Internet resources. Ask each student to bring in just one benefit of active learning from their search.

Becoming Engaged in Learning

What subjects naturally engage you? In subjects where you struggle to stay focused, how can you become more engaged?

No matter how good your listening and note-taking techniques are, you will not get the most out of college unless you become an engaged learner. Engaged students devote the time and the energy necessary to develop a real love of learning, both in and out of class.

Although you might acquire knowledge by listening to a lecture, you might not be motivated to think about what that knowledge means to you. When you are actively engaged in learning, you will learn not only the material in your notes and textbooks, but also how to:

- Work with others
- Improve your critical thinking, listening, writing, and speaking skills
- Function independently and teach yourself
- Manage your time
- Gain sensitivity to cultural differences

IN CLASS: In the Hawaiian language, the words for *teaching* and *learning* are the same. Ask students how they would explain this. How can one be teaching and learning at the same time? Why is it okay to collaborate with another student? What makes that different from cheating?

Engagement in learning requires that you be a full and active participant in the learning process. Your instructors will set the stage and provide valuable information, but it's up to you to do the rest. Your college experience will be most rewarding if you take advantage of the resources your college offers, including the library, cultural events, the faculty, and other students. This approach to learning has the potential to make you well rounded in all aspects of life.

OTHER TIPS FOR ENGAGEMENT

> Before choosing a class, ask friends which instructors encourage active learning.

> Go beyond the required reading. Investigate other information sources in the library or on the Internet.

> If you disagree with what your instructor says, politely offer your opinion. Most instructors will listen. They might still disagree with you, but they might also think more of you for showing you can think independently.

> Interact with professors, staff members, and other students. One easy way is through e-mail. Some professors offer first-year students the opportunity to collaborate in research projects and service activities. You will also find many opportunities to become involved in campus organizations. Getting involved in out-of-class opportunities will help you develop relationships with others on campus.

> Use Facebook to connect with other students and with campus activities and groups. Join in discussions that are happening in those groups.

This exercise asks students to do a self-assessment on seven aspects of development and then strategize on how to improve their weaker areas.

EXERCISE 6.6

What You DO Matters

The seven aspects of student development are listed in the table below: intellectual, social, spiritual, emotional, vocational, physical, and cultural. Optimal development depends on each area supporting every other area. Rate yourself on these aspects using a scale of 1–10. Be honest—not all of them will be high or low.

After rating yourself, consider your strengths in each aspect of development. Where do you excel? Add these strengths to the chart below. Next, think about areas in which you would like to improve. What are some ways to do this in a classroom setting? For example, if you want to work on your social development, you might arrive to class early to chat with students who sit near you.

Put these ideas on paper in the form of goals for improvement, and then list strategies you might use to meet these goals. The key is becoming engaged in your own learning, taking ownership of your future, and making this happen for you.

Development Aspect	Rating (1–10)	Strengths	Goals for Improvement	Self-Management Strategies
(Example) *Intellectual*	*6*	*Taking clear notes* *Online research*	*Overcoming test anxiety*	*Go see my academic adviser for ideas.* *Take more "practice" tests online.*
Intellectual (active learning, study skills, writing, speaking, critical thinking)				
Social (relationships with instructors, students, family, friends)				
Spiritual (ethics, values, knowing yourself)				
Emotional (sexuality, stress)				
Vocational (careers and majors)				
Physical (exercise, diet, alcohol and drugs)				
Cultural (diversity, liberal arts)				

CHECKLIST FOR SUCCESS

BECOME MORE ENGAGED

☐ **Practice the behaviors of engagement.** These behaviors include listening attentively, taking notes, and contributing to class discussion. But engagement also means participating in out-of-class activities without being "required" to do so.

☐ **Be aware of all the "senses" you have to aid your learning.** Which ones do you use the most? Try to increase your use of the other senses.

☐ **Prepare for class before class; it is one of the simplest and most important things you can do.** Read your notes from the previous class and do the assigned readings.

☐ **Go to class.** Ninety-five percent of success is simply showing up. You have no chance of becoming engaged in learning if you're not there.

☐ **Identify the different types of note taking covered in this chapter and decide which one(s) might work best for you.** Compare your notes with those of another good student to make sure you are covering the most important points.

☐ **As you review your notes before each class starts, make a list of any questions you have, and ask both fellow students and your professor for help.** Don't wait until just before the exam to try to find answers to your questions.

☐ **Seek professors who practice "active" teaching.** Ask other students, your seminar instructor, and your adviser to suggest the most engaging professors.

APPLY IT! What Works for YOU Matters

Choose another class that you are taking right now and apply some of the suggestions and strategies introduced in this chapter to that class. Select those strategies that you feel will work best for you, and then write them down in the "Your Response" column. What are YOU planning to do for YOUR course?

QUESTIONS	SAMPLE STUDENT ANSWERS	YOUR RESPONSE
	Name: Becky Han	
Using Your Senses in the Learning Process What sensory mode seems to describe your preferred learning style? How can you use your sensory preferences to learn most effectively?	I'm an aural learner, so I'll grab lunch with a friend after our next class so we can talk over the main points of the lecture. I'd like to try to improve my visual strategies, so comparing my notes with a friend might help.	
Preparing for Class What do you do to get mentally ready for class? What could you be doing differently to improve your chances for success?	Yesterday, I read the textbook chapter on Motivation before attending class and the lecture seemed less confusing. Tomorrow, I might try to put the chapter's headings and subheadings down on paper to outline my notes and then bring these to class.	
Participating in Class Do you find it difficult to speak up in class even when you know your classmates and the instructor? What might make participation easier for you?	Our class is really large, so I am hesitant to speak up in front of so many people. But my professor encouraged us to attend a small-group study session and this will make it easier to ask questions.	
Taking Effective Notes Why might the note-taking techniques you used in high school not work as well in college? What new techniques are you willing to try?	I never used anything but the list method in high school, but this isn't working for my psychology class. Next time I will try the Cornell method and the recall column to remember all of the psychodynamic theories.	
Reviewing Your Notes How will you avoid the "forgetting curve" and remember what you have learned?	Right after class I will "clean up" my notes. My handwriting can sometimes be illegible and I won't be able to read them in 2 weeks if I don't review them now! My study partner and I will get together once a week to organize and compare our notes.	
Becoming Engaged in Learning What subjects naturally engage you? In subjects where you struggle to stay focused, how can you become more engaged?	My professor is an expert on health psychology, which really interests me, so I'll go to office hours to ask him more about it. On the other hand, I really struggle with history—memorizing dates is difficult for me. But maybe watching a historic movie will help me get more involved in the class.	

BUILD YOUR EXPERIENCE

Two options are provided for students to work collaboratively. The first gets students to debate active learning, and the second encourages students to anticipate what content from this chapter their instructor is likely to put on the exam.

1 COLLABORATIVE ACTIVITY

ACTIVITY A

After reading this chapter, you know how to get engaged in your learning. You know that taking notes is important and that listening critically and participating in class discussions are keys to success.

Now, it's time to defend this position.

Your instructor will divide the class into two groups. One side takes the position that it is imperative to get engaged in learning. The other side is to reject this idea and argue that learning should be passive—no discussion, no questioning the professor. Take turns sharing ideas—pro, con, pro, con. See what happens when you have to debate one of the oldest educational controversies: Should students be responsible for their own education?

ACTIVITY B

What will be on the test? Take a few minutes to think about what main points in Chapter 6 will be important to know for the upcoming exam. Then brainstorm as a class and write ideas on the board so that everyone can see and make a note of the ideas you develop. Get into the mind-set of your professor and create a "practice test" for the class!

2 BUILDING YOUR PORTFOLIO

MAKING MEANING   Chapter 6 includes several examples of note-taking strategies, but did you catch the emphasis on what you should do with your notes after class? Sometimes it is helpful to associate a concept with an interest you have. And preparing to teach someone else how to do something or explaining a complex idea to others can help you to understand the information more fully. Test this idea for yourself.

1. Choose a set of current class notes (it doesn't matter which class they are from), and specifically look for connections between the subject matter and your personal interests and goals (future career, social issue, sports, hobbies, etc.).

2. Next, develop a 5-minute presentation using *PowerPoint* that both outlines your class notes and shows the connection to your interests. Develop the presentation as though you were going to teach a group of students about the concept. Use a combination of graphics, photos, music, and video clips to help your imaginary audience to connect with the material in a new and interesting way.

3. Save the *PowerPoint* in your portfolio. Use your *PowerPoint* presentation as one way to study for your next exam in that course.

You probably won't be creating *PowerPoint* presentations for all of your class notes, but making a habit of connecting class content to your life is an easy way to help yourself remember information. When it is time to prepare for a test, try pulling your notes into a presentation that you would feel comfortable giving to your classmates.

3 ONE-MINUTE PAPER

This chapter explores multiple strategies for being an effective listener and being engaged in class. What new strategies did you learn that you had never thought about or used before? What questions about effective note taking do you still have?

_____

_____

_____

_____

_____

_____

_____

_____

_____

_____

_____

_____

_____

_____

_____

No matter how well prepared you are in your teaching, what a student hears and understands might not always be what you think you have said. The one-minute paper is a quick and easy assessment tool that will help alert you when students don't understand what was said or discussed in class. The one-minute paper will also give timid students an opportunity to ask questions and seek clarification. Ideally, you should ask for such a paper several minutes before the end of a class. The paper will also help you begin your next class by clarifying points your students seem to be unsure of.

For more on this topic watch
French Fries Are Not Vegetables and Other College Lessons

WHERE TO GO FOR HELP . . .

ON CAMPUS

> **Learning Assistance Center** Almost every campus has one of these, and this chapter's topic is one of their specialties. More and more, the best students—and good students who want to be better students—use learning centers as much as students who are having academic difficulties. Services at learning centers are offered by both full-time professionals and highly skilled student tutors.

> **Fellow College Students** Often, the best help we can get comes from those who are closest to us: fellow students. Keep an eye out in your classes, residence hall, co-curricular groups, and other places for the most serious, purposeful, and directed students. Those are the ones to seek out. Find a tutor. Join a study group. Students who do these things are most likely to stay in college and be successful. It does not diminish you in any way to seek assistance from your peers.

ONLINE

> Toastmasters International offers public-speaking tips at **http://www.toastmasters.org.**

> See guidelines for speaking in class at **http://www.school-for-champions.com/grades/speaking.htm.**

MY INSTITUTION'S RESOURCES

_____

_____

_____

_____

_____

_____

_____

CHAPTER 7

Reading to Learn from College Textbooks

Why is reading college textbooks more challenging than reading high school texts or reading for pleasure? College texts are loaded with concepts, terms, and complex information that you are expected to learn on your own in a short period of time. Although many students think that the only reason for studying is to do well on exams, a far more important reason is to learn and understand course information. If you study to increase your understanding, you are more likely to remember and apply what you learn not only to tests but also to future courses and to life beyond college. To accomplish all this, you will find it helpful to learn and use the active reading strategies in this chapter. They are intended to help you get the most out of your college reading.

A Plan for Active Reading

Active reading occurs when you put forth extra effort to understand and store information. What strategies have been the most useful for you in creating review tools?

The following plan for active reading is designed to help you read college textbooks. When you read actively, you use strategies that help you stay focused. Active reading is different from reading novels or magazines for pleasure. Pleasure reading doesn't require you to annotate, highlight, or take notes. But as you read college textbooks, you'll use all these strategies and more. This plan will increase your focus and concentration, promote greater understanding of what you read, and prepare you to study for tests and exams. The four steps in active reading:

1. Previewing
2. Marking Your Textbook
3. Reading with Concentration
4. Reviewing

IN CLASS: Ask students to practice previewing with one of their texts for another class by talking their way through it with a study partner.

IN CLASS: In response to the inevitable argument that a systematic reading method takes too much time, emphasize that students will understand more of the chapter using this method and will therefore spend less time rereading.

IN THIS CHAPTER YOU WILL EXPLORE

How to prepare to read

How to preview reading material

How to read your textbooks efficiently

How to mark your textbooks

How to review your reading

How to adjust your reading style to the material

How to develop a more extensive vocabulary

PREVIEWING

The purpose of previewing is to get the big picture, that is, to understand how what you are about to read connects with what you already know and to the material the instructor covers in class. Begin by reading the title of the chapter. Ask yourself: What do I already know about this subject? Next, quickly read through the introductory paragraphs. Then read the summary at the beginning or end of the chapter if there is one. Finally, take a few minutes to skim the chapter, looking at the headings and subheadings. Note any study exercises at the end of the chapter.

As part of your preview, note how many pages the chapter contains. It's a good idea to decide in advance how many pages you can reasonably expect to cover in your first study period. This can help build your concentration as you work toward your goal of reading a specific number of pages. Before long, you'll know how many pages are practical for you.

Keep in mind that different types of textbooks can require more or less time to read. For example, depending on your interests and previous knowledge, you might be able to read a psychology text more quickly than a logic text that presents a whole new symbol system.

mapping A preview strategy of drawing a wheel or branching structure to show relationships between main ideas and secondary ideas and how different concepts and terms fit together and help you make connections to what you already know about the subject.

Mapping. Mapping the chapter as you preview it provides a visual guide for how different chapter ideas fit together. Because many students identify

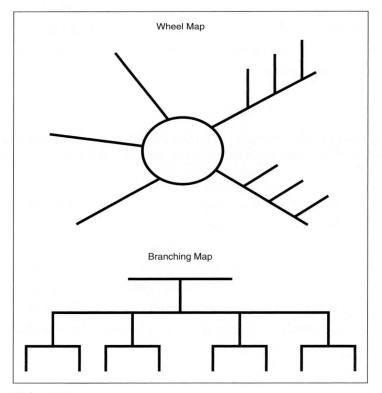

FIGURE 7.1
Wheel and Branching Maps

■ ASSESSING YOUR STRENGTHS

Are you a good reader? Do you make it a practice to do all the assigned reading for each of your classes? Now that you have read the first section of this chapter, list specific examples of your strengths in the area of reading college textbooks and supplementary academic material.

_____

_____

_____

_____

■ SETTING GOALS

What are _your_ most important objectives in learning the material in this chapter? How can you improve your reading abilities and strategies? List three goals that relate to improving your reading of college texts (e.g., I will go back to all my course syllabi to make sure I'm up-to-date with my assigned reading. If not, I will catch up this week).

1. _____

_____

2. _____

_____

3. _____

_____

■ RETENTION STRATEGY: The inability to read and comprehend college textbooks is one of the most significant academic problems of new college students today and therefore is a factor in student dropout. Be on the lookout for students who do not read at a college level and help them seek assistance at your institution.

themselves as visual learners, visual mapping is an excellent learning tool for test preparation, as well as reading (see Chapter 4, Discovering How You Learn). To map a chapter, use either a wheel structure or a branching structure as you preview the chapter (see Figure 7.1). In the wheel structure, place the central idea of the chapter in the circle. The central idea should be in the introduction to the chapter and might be apparent in the chapter title. Place secondary ideas on the spokes emanating from the circle, and place offshoots of those ideas on the lines attached to the spokes. In the branching map, the main idea goes at the top, followed by supporting ideas on the second tier and so forth. Fill in the title first. Then, as you skim the chapter, use the headings and subheadings to fill in the key ideas.

OUTSIDE CLASS: After discussing how to map a chapter, have students map a chapter from a textbook they are using in another course.

IN CLASS: Have students bring the maps to class for sharing.

Alternatives to Mapping. Perhaps you prefer a more linear visual image. If so, consider making an outline of the headings and subheadings in the chapter. You can fill in the outline after you read. Alternatively, make a list. A list can be particularly effective when you are dealing with a text that introduces many new terms and their definitions. Set up the list with the

chunking A previewing method that involves making a list of terms and definitions from the reading and then dividing the terms into smaller clusters of five, seven, or nine to more effectively learn the material.

terms in the left column, and fill in definitions, descriptions, and examples on the right after you read. Divide the terms on your list into groups of five, seven, or nine, and leave white space between the clusters so that you can visualize each group in your mind. This practice is known as **chunking**. Research indicates that we learn material best when it is in chunks of five, seven, or nine.

If you are an interactive learner, make lists or create a flash card for each heading and subheading. Then fill in the back of each card after reading each section in the text. Use the lists or flash cards to review with a partner, or recite the material to yourself.

Previewing, combined with mapping, outlining, or flash cards, might require more time up front, but it will save you time later because you will have created an excellent review tool for quizzes and tests. You will be using your visual learning skills as you create advanced organizers to help you associate details of the chapter with the larger ideas. Such associations will come in handy later. As you preview the text material, look for connections between the text and the related lecture material. Call to mind the related terms and concepts that you recorded in the lecture. Use these strategies to warm up. Ask yourself: Why am I reading this? What do I want to know?

IN CLASS: Students might complain that a marked book won't get a high buyback price when the course is over. As an exercise in values, ask them to consider which they value more: the cash or the better grade. Ask them to check buyback policies at local bookstores to find out how much of the book's value they will lose by marking in their books.

marking An active reading strategy of making marks in the text by underlining, highlighting, and writing margin notes or annotations.

MARKING YOUR TEXTBOOK

After completing your preview, you are ready to read the text actively. With your skeleton map or outline, you should be able to read more quickly and with greater comprehension. To avoid marking too much or marking the wrong information, first read without using your pencil or highlighter.

Think a moment about your goals for making marks in your own texts. Some students report that **marking** is an active reading strategy that helps them to focus and concentrate on the material as they read. In addition, most students expect to use their text notations when they study for tests. To meet these goals, some students like to underline, some prefer to highlight, and others use margin notes or annotations. Figure 7.2 provides an example of each method. No matter what method you prefer, remember these two important guidelines:

1. **Read before you mark.** Finish reading a section before you decide which are the most important ideas and concepts. Mark only those particular ideas, using your preferred methods (highlighting, underlining, circling key terms, annotating).

2. **Think before you mark.** When you read a text for the first time, everything can seem important. Only after you have completed a section and have reflected on it will you be ready to identify the key ideas. Ask yourself: What are the most important ideas? What will I see on the test? This can help you avoid marking too much material.

Sometimes highlighting or underlining can provide you with a false sense of security. You might have determined what is most important, but you have not necessarily tested yourself on your understanding of the material. When you force yourself to put something in your own words while taking notes, you are not only predicting exam questions but also assessing whether you

WHAT IS STRESS?   **481**

CULTURE AND HUMAN BEHAVIOR 12.1

The Stress of Adapting to a New Culture

[margin note: differences affecting cultural stress]

Refugees and immigrants are often unprepared for the dramatically different values, language, food, customs, and climate that await them in their new land. Coping with a new culture can be extremely stress-producing (Johnson & others, 1995). The process of changing one's values and customs as a result of contact with another culture is referred to as *acculturation*. Thus, the term **acculturative stress** describes the stress that results from the pressure of adapting to a new culture (Berry, 1994, 2003).

[margin note: acceptance of new culture reduces stress also speaking new language, education, & social support]

Many factors can influence the degree of acculturative stress that a person experiences. For example, when the new society is one that accepts ethnic and cultural diversity, acculturative stress is reduced (Shuval, 1993). The ease of transition is also enhanced when the person has some familiarity with the new language and customs, advanced education, and social support from friends, family members, and cultural associations (Finch & Vega, 2003).

[margin note: how attitudes affect stress]

Cross-cultural psychologist John Berry has found that a person's *attitudes* are important in determining how much acculturative stress is experienced. When people encounter a new cultural environment, they are faced with two fundamental questions: (1) Should I seek positive relations with the dominant society? (2) Is my original cultural identity of value to me, and should I try to maintain it?

[margin note: 4 patterns of acculturation]

The answers to these questions result in one of four possible patterns of acculturation: integration, assimilation, separation, or marginalization (see the diagram). Each pattern represents a different way of cop-

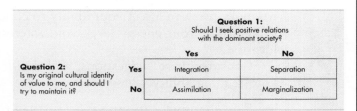

Question 1:
Should I seek positive relations with the dominant society?

		Yes	No
Question 2: Is my original cultural identity of value to me, and should I try to maintain it?	**Yes**	Integration	Separation
	No	Assimilation	Marginalization

Patterns of Adapting to a New Culture According to cross-cultural psychologist John Berry (1994, 2003), there are four basic patterns of adapting to a new culture. Which pattern is followed depends on how the person responds to the two key questions shown.

ing with the stress of adapting to a new culture (Berry, 1994, 2003).

1* *Integrated* individuals continue to value their original cultural customs but also seek to become part of the dominant society. Ideally, the integrated individual feels *comfortable* in both her culture of origin and the culture of the dominant society, moving easily from one to the other (LaFromboise, Coleman, & Gerton, 1993). The successfully integrated individual's level of acculturative stress will be low (Ward & Rana-Deuba, 1999).

2* *Assimilated* individuals give up their old cultural identity and try to become part of the new society. They may adopt the new clothing, religion, and social values of the new environment and *abandon* their old customs and language.

Assimilation usually involves a moderate level of stress, partly because it involves a psychological loss—one's previous cultural identity. People who follow this pattern also

[margin note: possible rejection by both cultures]

face the possibility of being rejected either by members of the majority culture or by members of their original culture (LaFromboise & others, 1993). The process of learning new behaviors and suppressing old behaviors can also be moderately stressful.

3* Individuals who follow the pattern of *separation* maintain their cultural identity and avoid contact with the new culture. They may refuse to learn the new language, live in a neighborhood that is primarily populated by others of the same ethnic background, and socialize only with members of their own ethnic group.

*[margin note: *separation may be self-imposed or discriminating]*

In some instances, such withdrawal from the larger society is self-imposed. However, separation can also be the result of discrimination by the dominant society, as when people of a particular ethnic group are discouraged from fully participating in the dominant society. Not surprisingly, the level of acculturative stress associated with separation is likely to be very high.

[margin note: higher stress with separation]

4* Finally, the *marginalized* person lacks cultural and psychological contact with *both* his traditional cultural group and the culture of his new society. By taking the path of marginalization, he has lost the important features of his traditional culture but has not replaced them with a new cultural identity.

*[margin note: *marginalized = higher level of stress]*

Marginalized individuals are likely to experience the greatest degree of acculturative stress, feeling as if they don't really belong anywhere. Essentially, they are stuck in an unresolved conflict between the traditional culture and the new social environment. They are also likely to experience feelings of alienation and a loss of identity (Berry & Kim, 1988).

Acculturative Stress As this Sikh family crossing a busy street in Chicago has discovered, adapting to a new culture can be a stressful process. What factors can make the transition less stressful? How can the acculturation process be eased?

FIGURE 7.2

Examples of Marking

Using a combination of highlighting, lines, and margin notes, the reader has boiled down the content of this page for easy review. Without reading the text, note the highlighted words and phrases and the margin notes, and see how much information you can gather from them. Then read the text itself. Does the markup serve as a study aid? Does it cover the essential points? Would you have marked this page any differently? Why or why not?

Source: "The Stress of Adapting to a New Culture," from *Discovering Psychology*, 4th ed., p. 481, by D. H. Hockenbury and S. E. Hockenbury. Copyright © 2007 by Worth Publishers. Used with permission of the publisher.

can answer them. Although these active reading strategies take more time initially, they can save you time in the long run because they promote concentration and also make it easy to review. If you can use these strategies effectively, you probably won't have to pull an all-nighter before an exam.

READING WITH CONCENTRATION

Many factors can affect your ability to concentrate and understand texts: the time of day, your energy level, your interest in the material, and your study location.

Consider these suggestions, and decide which would help you improve your reading ability:

- Find a study location that is removed from traffic and distracting noises, such as the campus library. Turn off your cell phone's ringer, and store the phone in your purse or book bag (someplace where you can't easily feel it vibrating). If you are reading an electronic document on your computer, download the information that you need and disconnect from the network to keep you from easily going online and chatting, e-mailing, or checking Facebook or Twitter.

- Read in blocks of time, with short breaks in between. Some students can read for 50 minutes; others find that a 50-minute reading period is too long. By reading for small blocks of time throughout the day instead of cramming in all your reading at the end of the day, you should be able to process material more easily.

- Set goals for your study period, such as "I will read twenty pages of my psychology text in the next 50 minutes." Reward yourself with a 10-minute break after each 50-minute study period.

- If you have trouble concentrating or staying awake, take a quick walk around the library or down the hall. Stretch or take some deep breaths, and think positively about your study goals. Then resume studying.

- Jot study questions in the margins, take notes, or recite key ideas. Reread confusing parts of the text, and make a note to ask your instructor for clarification.

- Focus on the important portions of the text. Pay attention to the first and last sentences of paragraphs and to words in italics or bold print.

- Use the glossary in the text or a dictionary to define unfamiliar terms.

REVIEWING

The final step in active textbook reading is reviewing. Many students expect to read through their text material once and be able to remember the ideas four, six, or even twelve weeks later at test time. More realistically, you will need to include regular reviews in your study process. Here is where your notes, study questions, annotations, flash cards, visual maps, or outlines will be most useful. Your study goal should be to review the material from each chapter every week.

Consider ways to use your many senses to review. Recite aloud. Tick off each item in a list on each of your fingertips. Post diagrams, maps, or outlines around your living space so that you will see them often and will likely be able to visualize them while taking the test.

OUTSIDE CLASS: Divide the class into groups of four students. In each group, ask students to choose two or more of the tips for building concentration and understanding. Ask them to practice during the next few days and report on what worked, what did not work, and why.

OUTSIDE CLASS: Encourage students to use the learning center's reading resources to improve their reading rate and to master various methods of remembering material.

This exercise asks students to practice marking a section of their textbook.

How You READ Matters

How many times have you been reading a textbook or an article and at the end of the page you suddenly stop and ask yourself, "What did I just read?" You were reading on *auto pilot*. Reading isn't necessarily active unless you put some effort into it. Active reading requires thought and planning on your part. The information you are taking in won't actually enter your memory unless you work with it. There are several ways to be active in your reading; in fact, the more you work with the information, the better you will retain it.

After reading a section of your textbook, take a pen or highlighter and underline or highlight the most important information, but avoid marking too much. Most experts agree that marking about 40 percent of any paragraph is about the right amount—much more than that and you are simply rereading the entire text when you go back. Remember to finish reading the section before you mark, and think before you mark. Also, refer to Figure 7.2 on page 151 for a great example of the different marking methods.

Now you try it:

1. Underline the complete topic sentence and important details, facts, or statistics.

2. Circle vocabulary words to make them stand out.

3. Make margin notes (try using shorthand or texting language) on the side of a paragraph to summarize what you just read. Make a picture or visual graphic if necessary.

See the list below, and put a check mark beside the notations you have used. What other notations, not shown here, do you use? _____

Notation	Meaning	Yes/No	Notation (✓)	Meaning	Yes/No (✓)	Notation	Meaning	Yes/No (✓)
#	number		w/o	without		RE:	regarding	
%	percentage		Sol.	solution		Sum.	summary	
&	and		Ex.	example		+/−	positive/ negative	
@	at		Imp.	important		=	equals	
!	surprising		Def.	definition		>	greater than	
→	leads to		Diff.	differences		<	less than	
↑	increases		??	test question		b/c	because	

When you studied the section you chose for this exercise, how did the marking help you identify the most important information? _____

Strategies for Reading Textbooks

Reading a textbook is like working on a puzzle. Different textbooks have different ways to put the puzzle together. Of all your current textbooks, which is your favorite and why? How does it help you understand the material?

IN CLASS: Ask students how they usually read a textbook chapter. Do they just read? Do they highlight or take notes as they go? Use the discussion to introduce this section on reading from a textbook.

As you begin reading, be sure to learn more about the textbook and its author by reading the frontmatter in the book, such as the preface, foreword, introduction, and author's biographical sketch. The preface is usually written by the author (or authors) and will tell you why they wrote the book and what material it covers. Textbooks often have a preface written to the instructor and a separate preface for the students. The foreword is often an endorsement of the book written by someone other than the author, which can add to your understanding of the book and its purpose. Some books have an additional introduction that reviews the book's overall organization and its contents chapter by chapter. Frontmatter might also include biographical information about the authors that will give you important details about their background.

Some textbooks include questions at the end of each chapter that you can use as a study guide or as a quick check on your understanding of the chapter's main points. Take time to read and respond to these questions, whether or not your instructor requires you to do so.

Textbooks must try to cover a lot of material in a fairly limited space. Although many textbooks seem detailed, they won't necessarily provide all the things you want to know about a topic—the things that can make your reading more interesting. If you find yourself fascinated by a particular topic, go to the **primary sources**—the original research or document. You'll find those referenced in many textbooks, either at the end of the chapters or in the back of the book. You can read more information about primary and supplementary sources on page 158.

primary sources The original research or documentation on a topic, usually referenced either at the end of a chapter or at the back of the book.

You might also go to other related sources that are credible—whatever makes the text more interesting and informative for you. Remember that most texts are not designed to treat topics in depth. Your textbook reading will be much more interesting if you dig a bit further in related sources. Because some textbooks are sold with test banks that are available to instructors, your instructors might draw their examinations directly from the text, or they might use the textbook only to supplement the lectures. Ask your instructors, if they have not made it clear, what the tests will cover and the types of questions that will be used. In addition, you might try to find a student who has taken a course with your instructor so that you can get a better idea of how that instructor designs tests. Some instructors expect that you will learn the kinds of detail that you can get only through the textbook. Other instructors are much more concerned that you be able to understand broad concepts that come from lectures in addition to texts and other readings.

Finally, not all textbooks are equal. Some are simply better designed and written than others. If your textbook is exceptionally hard to understand or seems disorganized, let your instructor know your opinion. On the basis of what you say, your instructor might focus on explaining the text and how it is organized or might decide to use a different text for future classes.

MATH TEXTS

While the previous suggestions about textbook reading apply across the board, mathematics textbooks present some special challenges because they tend to have lots of symbols and very few words. Each statement and every line in the solution of a problem need to be considered and digested slowly. Typically, the author presents the material through definitions, theorems, and sample problems. As you read, pay special attention to definitions. Learning all the terms that relate to a new topic is the first step toward understanding.

Math texts usually include derivations of formulas and proofs of theorems. You must understand and be able to apply the formulas and theorems, but unless your course has a particularly theoretical emphasis, you are less likely to be responsible for all the proofs. So if you get lost in the proof of a theorem, go on to the next item in the section. When you come to a sample problem, it's time to get busy. Pick up pencil and paper, and work through the problem in the book. Then cover the solution and think through the problem on your own. Of course, the exercises that follow each text section form the heart of any math book. A large portion of the time you devote to the course will be spent completing assigned textbook exercises. It is absolutely vital that you do this homework in a timely manner, whether or not your instructor collects it. Success in mathematics requires regular practice, and students who keep up with math homework, either alone or in groups, perform better than students who don't.

After you complete the assignment, skim through the other exercises in the problem set. Reading the unassigned problems will deepen your understanding of the topic and its scope. Finally, talk the material through to yourself, and be sure your focus is on understanding the problem and its solution, not on memorization. Memorizing something might help you remember how to work through one problem, but it does not help you understand the steps involved so that you can employ them for other problems.

SCIENCE TEXTS

Your approach to your science textbook will depend somewhat on whether you are studying a math-based science, such as physics, or a text-based science, such as biology. In either case, you need to become acquainted with the overall format of the book. Review the table of contents and the glossary, and check the material in the appendices. There, you will find lists of physical constants, unit conversions, and various charts and tables. Many physics and chemistry books also include a minireview of the math you will need in science courses.

IN CLASS: Ask a reading specialist from your campus developmental skills or learning center to come to class to provide tips on how to approach a science textbook.

Notice the organization of each chapter, and pay special attention to graphs, charts, and boxes. The amount of technical detail might seem overwhelming, but—believe it or not—the authors have sincerely tried to present the material in an easy-to-follow format. Each chapter might begin with chapter objectives and conclude with a short summary, sections that can be useful to study both before and after reading the chapter. You will usually find answers to selected problems in the back of the book. Use the answer key or the student solutions manual to promote your mastery of each chapter.

As you begin an assigned section in a science text, skim the material quickly to gain a general idea of the topic. Begin to absorb the new vocabulary and technical symbols. Then skim the end-of-chapter problems so you'll know what to look for in your detailed reading of the chapter. State a specific goal: "I'm going to learn about recent developments in plate tectonics," or "I'm going to distinguish between mitosis and meiosis," or "Tonight I'm going to focus on the topics in this chapter that were stressed in class."

Should you underline and highlight, or should you outline the material in your science textbooks? You might decide to underline or highlight for a subject such as anatomy, which involves a lot of memorization. But use restraint

All Textbooks Are Not Created Equal

Science texts are filled with graphs and figures that you will need to understand in order to grasp the content and the classroom presentations. If you have trouble reading and understanding your science textbooks, get help from your instructor or your learning center.

IN CLASS: Explain that a large percentage of students have difficulty with introductory or "gateway" science and mathematics courses such as calculus, physics, or organic chemistry. Discuss why doing well in these courses is especially critical for some majors.

with a highlighter; it should pull your eye only to important terms and facts. If highlighting is actually a form of procrastination for you (you are reading through the material but planning to learn it at a later date) or if you are highlighting nearly everything you read, your highlighting might be doing you more harm than good. You won't be able to identify important concepts quickly if they're lost in a sea of color. Ask yourself whether the frequency of your highlighting is helping you be more active in your learning process. If not, you might want to highlight less or try a different technique such as margin notes or annotations.

In most sciences, it is best to outline the text chapters. You can usually identify main topics, subtopics, and specific terms under each subtopic in your text by the size of the print. For instance, in each chapter of this textbook, the main topics (or level-1 headings) are in large orange letters. Following each major topic heading, you will find subtopics, or level-2 headings, printed in smaller, capital orange letters. The level-3 headings, which tell more about the subtopics, are in bold, orange letters, but are much smaller than the level-1 headings.

To save time when you are outlining, you won't write full sentences, but you will include clear explanations of new technical terms and symbols. Pay special attention to topics that the instructor covered in class. If you aren't sure whether your outlines contain too much or too little detail, compare them with the outlines members of your study group have made. You could also consult with your instructor during office hours. In preparing for a test, it's a good idea to make condensed versions of your chapter outlines so that you can see how everything fits together.

TECH TIP EMBRACE THE E-BOOK

1 ▸ THE PROBLEM

You're getting a hunchback from carrying twenty books around all day.

2 ▸ THE FIX

Discover how a digital reader differs from (and can even be better than) reading traditional ink-on-paper books.

3 ▸ HOW TO DO IT

THE PROS

- Digital reading devices are eminently portable—most weigh about a pound—and can carry thousands of books. (They're fantastic for those transatlantic flights when you don't want to pack the entire Sookie Stackhouse series.)
- They can hold a range of media, from books to newspapers to magazines.
- They save trees: no shipping costs, low carbon footprint.
- They let you buy books online from anywhere; you can start reading within minutes.
- They let you shop internationally. Even if you're in a remote Chinese village, you can easily find plenty of cyber books in English.
- You can type notes in an e-book, highlight passages, or copy and paste sections.
- You can print out pages simply by hooking the device up to your printer.
- Many of the books you can access are free: You can download books from the public library; you can even click to the British Library's Online Gallery to peruse some of the oldest and rarest books on record.
- Some e-books come with bonus audio, video, or animation features.
- Many digital reading devices even accept audio books and can read to you aloud.
- The backlit screen means you can read in bed with the light off, without keeping your roommate awake.
- You can adjust the size of the text, making it easier to read.
- E-books are searchable, and even sharable.

THE CONS

- Digital reading devices are expensive.
- Unlike books, they can break if you drop them.
- It's harder to flip through pages of an e-book.
- Textbooks are not yet widely available for digital reading devices.
- You miss out on the romantic sensation of opening, smelling, and carrying a real book.

GOOD TO KNOW

The most popular electronic e-readers include the iPad, Amazon's Kindle, Barnes & Noble's Nook, and Spring Design's Alex. The Kindle is the most popular basic model; others offer touch color screens, Web browsers, calculators, and even music.

PERSONAL BEST

Do you use an e-reader? How does using an e-book differ when reading a textbook versus reading a trade book?

_____

_____

_____

_____

_____

_____

_____

_____

_____

SOCIAL SCIENCE AND HUMANITIES TEXTS

Many of the suggestions that apply to science textbooks also apply to reading in the social sciences (sociology, psychology, anthropology, economics, political science, and history). Social science texts are filled with special terms or jargon that is unique to the particular field of study. These texts also describe research and theory building and contain references to many primary sources. Your social science texts might also describe differences in opinions or perspectives. Social scientists do not all agree on any one issue, and you might be introduced to a number of ongoing debates about particular issues. In fact, your reading can become more interesting if you seek out different opinions about a common issue. You might have to go beyond your particular textbook, but your library will be a good source of various viewpoints about ongoing controversies.

Textbooks in the **humanities** (philosophy, religion, literature, music, and art) provide facts, examples, opinions, and original material, such as stories or essays. You will often be asked to react to your reading by identifying central themes or characters.

Some instructors believe that the way in which colleges and universities structure courses and majors artificially divides human knowledge and experience. For instance, they argue that subjects such as history, political science, and philosophy are closely linked and that studying each subject separately results in only partial understanding. By stressing the links between courses, these instructors encourage students to think in an **interdisciplinary** manner. You might be asked to consider how the book or story you're reading or the music you're studying reflects the political atmosphere or the culture of the period. Your art history instructor might direct you to think about how a particular painting gives you a window on the painter's psychological makeup or religious beliefs.

SUPPLEMENTARY MATERIAL

Whether or not your instructor requires you to read material in addition to the textbook, your understanding will be enriched if you go to some of the primary and supplementary sources that are referenced in each chapter of your text. These sources can take the form of journal articles, research papers, dissertations (the major research papers that students write to earn a doctoral degree), or original essays, and they can be found in your library and on the Internet. Reading source material will give you a depth of detail that few textbooks accomplish.

Many sources were originally written for other instructors or researchers. Therefore they often use language and refer to concepts that are familiar to other scholars but not necessarily to first-year college students. If you are reading a journal article that describes a theory or research study, one technique for easier understanding is to read from the end to the beginning. Read the article's conclusion and discussion sections. Then go back to see how the author performed the experiment or formulated the ideas. If you aren't concerned about the specific method used to collect the data, you can skip over the "methodology" section. In almost all scholarly journals, articles are introduced by an abstract, a paragraph-length summary of the methods and major findings. Reading the **abstract** is a quick way to get the gist of a research article before you dive in. As you're reading research articles, always ask yourself: So what? Was the research important to what we know about the topic, or, in your opinion, was it unnecessary?

humanities Branches of knowledge that investigate human beings, their culture, and their self-expression. They include the study of philosophy, religion, literature, music, and art.

interdisciplinary Linking two or more academic fields of study, such as history and religion. Encouraging an interdisciplinary approach to teaching can offer a better understanding of modern society.

abstract A paragraph-length summary of the methods and major findings of an article in a scholarly journal.

This exercise walks students through building a set of flash cards.

How You STUDY Matters

No matter what kind of textbook you are reading, if you don't work with the material, it won't stay with you very long. To retain the information, try making some study tools. Create a map or an outline. Make some flash cards, or use the Cornell format with its recall column. Summarize the information out loud and develop your own podcast. Make drawings of what is being said within the paragraphs. All of these tools are great for reviewing right before a test.

Let's try flash cards. There's a new way to create flash cards that will help you remember the words better. (This is a great tool for visual and kinesthetic learners.) Try making two types of cards: Heading Cards (like a cover page) and Vocabulary Cards (under each heading).

For Heading Cards

Put the chapter heading on the FRONT and the subheadings on the BACK:

A Plan for Active Reading

Previewing

Marking Your Textbook

Reading with Concentration

Reviewing

For Vocabulary Cards

Then take the subheadings listed on the back of each heading card and create Vocabulary Cards.

The term to define will be on the FRONT:

And a three-part definition will be on the BACK: 1) the heading the term falls under; 2) the actual definition; 3) a cue or detail to help you remember

Previewing

1) Active Reading Strategy

2) Overview reading to get the big picture

3) Look at headings/summary

When you have finished making flash cards for the entire chapter, stack them in order by placing vocabulary under each corresponding heading. This is one way to learn the information in small chunks and create a strong mental file folder in your memory. Many test questions come from headings and subheadings. Professors will often try to trick you by mixing up the vocabulary with the wrong heading, as you see in this example:

True or False:

1. Mapping is a powerful strategy for Monitoring Your Reading.

Answer: False—It falls under the "Active Reading" heading. By studying the vocabulary words under specific headings, you will avoid falling into this trap!

Monitoring Your Reading

One way to maintain your concentration level while reading is to get inside the head of the instructor and try to determine what is "test-worthy." How often do you stop to monitor your comprehension? After each paragraph? Each page? Each section? Or do you forget about it until the end of the chapter?

An important step in textbook reading is to monitor your comprehension. As you read, ask yourself: Do I understand this? If not, stop and reread the material. Look up words that are not clear. Try to clarify the main points and how they relate to one another.

Another way to check comprehension is to try to recite the material aloud, either to yourself or to your study partner. Using a study group to monitor your comprehension gives you immediate feedback and is highly motivating. After you have read and marked or taken notes on key ideas from the first section of the chapter, proceed to each subsequent section until you have finished the chapter.

After you have completed each section and before you move on to the next section, ask again: What are the key ideas? What will I see on the test? At the end of each section, try to guess what information the author will present in the next section.

This exercise asks students to examine headings and subheadings and anticipate how their instructors use these for test questions.

EXERCISE 7.3

How You UNLOCK the Meaning Matters

One way to stay focused on your reading is to get into the mind-set of the instructor and ask yourself, "What would be a good test question from this paragraph?" Below are the headings and subheadings from this chapter. Turn them into probable questions you might see on your next test. Then answer them as you read each section. You can do this for any textbook.

Headings/Subheadings	Your Own Test Question	Your Answer
A Plan for Active Reading	What is active reading?	Reading for the big picture, briefly looking at headings, subheadings, and the summary in the back of chapter material
Previewing		
Marking Your Textbook		
Reading with Concentration		
Reviewing		

(continued)

Strategies for Reading Textbooks		
Math Texts		
Science Texts		
Social Science and Humanities Texts		
Supplementary Material		
Monitoring Your Reading		
Improving Your Reading		
Developing Your Vocabulary		
If English Is Not Your First Language		

Improving Your Reading

Making connections is part of critical thinking. Some classes are foundational in that everything you read today is based on what you have read or learned in the past. Everything you will learn tomorrow assumes you have mastered the information today. What classes like this are you taking now?

With effort, you can improve your reading dramatically, but remember to be flexible. How you read should depend on the material. Assess the relative importance and difficulty of the assigned readings, and adjust your reading style and the time you allot accordingly. Connect one important idea to another by asking yourself: Why am I reading this? Where does this fit in? When the textbook material is virtually identical to the lecture material, you can save time by concentrating mainly on one or the other. It takes a planned approach to read textbook materials and other assigned readings with good understanding and recall.

DEVELOPING YOUR VOCABULARY

Textbooks are full of new terminology. In fact, one could argue that learning chemistry is largely a matter of learning the language of chemists and that mastering philosophy, history, or sociology requires a mastery of the terminology of each particular **discipline**.

discipline An area of academic study, such as sociology, anthropology, or engineering.

VOCABULARY-BUILDING STRATEGIES

> During your overview of the chapter, notice and jot down unfamiliar terms. Consider making a flash card for each term or making a list of terms.

> When you encounter challenging words, consider the context. See whether you can predict the meaning of an unfamiliar term by using the surrounding words.

> If context by itself is not enough, try analyzing the term to discover the root, or base part, or other meaningful parts of the word. For example, *emissary* has the root "to emit" or "to send forth," so we can guess that an emissary is someone who is sent forth with a message. Similarly, note prefixes and suffixes. For example, *anti* means "against," and *pro* means "for." Use the glossary of the text, a dictionary, or the online **Merriam-Webster Dictionary (http://www .merriam-webster.com)** to locate the definition. Note any multiple definitions, and search for the meaning that fits this usage.

> Take every opportunity to use these new terms in your writing and speaking. If you use a new term a few times, you'll soon know it. In addition, studying new terms on flash cards or study sheets can be handy at exam time.

If words are such a basic and essential component of our knowledge, what is the best way to learn them? Follow the basic vocabulary-building strategies outlined in the box at the top of the page.

IF ENGLISH IS NOT YOUR FIRST LANGUAGE

■ RETENTION STRATEGY: Non-native English speakers are at risk for poor academic performance and loss of self-confidence. Although many such students are highly intelligent and motivated to persist and may have been successful in school in another country, they will likely experience barriers to their academic progress. Make sure that these students and their families understand the policies and procedures of higher education and that ESL students are given the help they need to improve their English-language skills.

The English language is one of the most difficult languages to learn. Words are often spelled differently from the way they sound, and the language is full of idioms—phrases that are peculiar and cannot be understood from the individual meanings of the words. If you are learning English and are having trouble reading your texts, don't give up. Reading slowly and reading more than once can help you improve your comprehension. Make sure that you have two good dictionaries—one in English and one that links English with your primary language—and look up every word that you don't know. Be sure to practice thinking, writing, and speaking in English, and take advantage of your college's helping services. Your campus might have ESL (English as a Second Language) tutoring and workshops. Ask your adviser or your first-year seminar instructor to help you locate those services.

Listening, note taking, and reading are the essentials for success in each of your classes. You can perform these tasks without a plan, or you can practice some of the ideas presented in this chapter. If your notes are already working, great. If not, now you know what to do.

This exercise stresses the importance of building vocabulary and gives students fun ideas to get started.

EXERCISE 7.4

What You UNDERSTAND Matters

Mastering new words, understanding them, and using them correctly in the right context are outward signs of a learned person. If you can speak using words that are considered college level, your future employers will take you more seriously. Most of us, however, don't associate with people whose use of language is superior to our own. In fact, most of us do a lot of "horizontal" modeling of behavior, not "vertical," meaning we hang out with friends, not older and wiser people. So, how do we incorporate new words into our vocabulary? Try an experiment!

Listed below are some Web sites that are known to have vocabulary words that "every college student should know."

WEB SITES

www.drkenhunt.com/100words.html

www.justcolleges.com/college/coll_sat_top100.htm

quizlet.com/1022309/college-board-top-100-common-satact-vocabulary-words-flash-cards/

Visit one of these sites, choose ONE word, and learn its definition. Begin using it in everyday language around your friends and coworkers, and then *see how long it takes before one of them starts using it back to you*! It's a great way to share your positive influence and do a little experimenting at the same time!

Here are some ideas taken from "100 Words Every College Graduate Should Know," compiled by Dr. Ken Hunt and found at **www.drkenhunt.com/100words.html:**

New Vocabulary	Definition
1. capricious	whimsical, changeable
2. ameliorate	to make or grow better
3. caveat	a warning or caution
4. loquacious	very talkative
5. reticent	inclined to keep quiet

CHECKLIST FOR SUCCESS

READING IN COLLEGE

☐ **Be sure to practice the four steps of active reading: previewing, marking, concentrating while you read, and then reviewing.** If you practice these steps, you will understand and retain more of what you read.

☐ **Take your course textbooks seriously.** They contain essential information you'll be expected to learn and understand. Never try to "get by" without the text.

☐ **Remember that not all textbooks are the same.** They vary by subject area and style of writing. Some may be easier to comprehend than others, but don't give up if the reading level is challenging.

☐ **Learn and practice the different techniques suggested in this chapter for reading and understanding texts on different subjects.** Which texts come easiest for you? Which are the hardest? Why?

☐ **In addition to the textbook, be sure to read all supplemental assigned reading material.** Also, try to find additional materials to take your reading beyond just what is required. The more you read, the more you will understand, and the better your performance will be.

☐ **As you read, be sure to take notes on the material.** Indicate in your notes what specific ideas you need help in understanding.

☐ **Get help with difficult material before much time elapses.** College courses use sequential material that builds on previous material. You will need to master the material as you go along.

☐ **Discuss difficult readings in study groups.** Explain to each other what you do and don't understand.

☐ **Find out what kind of assistance your campus offers to increase reading comprehension and speed.** Check out your learning and counseling centers for free workshops. Even faculty and staff sometimes take advantage of these. Most everyone wants to improve reading speed and comprehension.

☐ **Use reading as a means to build your vocabulary.** Learning new words is a critical learning skill and outcome of college. The more words you know, the more you'll understand, and your grades will show it.

APPLY IT! What Works for YOU Matters

Think about your current academic situations, and apply some of the suggestions and strategies introduced in this chapter. Select strategies that you think will work best for you, and then write them down in the "Your Response" column. What are YOU planning to do for YOUR college experience?

QUESTIONS	SAMPLE STUDENT ANSWERS	YOUR RESPONSE
	Name: Thomas Sinclair	
A Plan for Active Reading Active reading occurs when you put forth extra effort to understand and store information. What strategies have been the most useful for you in creating review tools?	I have no problem reading when it comes to comic books or magazines, but reading a textbook makes me zone out. I learned recently to read twice. Once for the "Big Picture" and then I take a short break before I go back and reread, highlighting or taking notes on the passages for all of the details and vocabulary.	
Strategies for Reading Textbooks Reading a textbook is like working on a puzzle. Different textbooks have different ways to put the puzzle together. Of all your current textbooks, which is your favorite and why? How does it help you understand the material?	I really like my psychology textbook. For a visual learner, it contains appealing charts and graphs and even some cartoons to describe an idea. It also has a summary of the material at the end of the chapter. If I read the summary first, then read the chapter, I know what the key points are and can then understand the material better.	
Monitoring Your Reading One way to maintain your concentration level while reading is to get inside the head of the instructor and try to determine what is "test-worthy." How often do you stop to monitor your comprehension? After each paragraph? Each page? Each section? Or do you forget about it until the end of the chapter?	For some of my classes, the textbook isn't that difficult, so I can stop after each section. But for my biology class, I have to stop after each paragraph to make sure I really "got" the material. That information can be so dense with vocabulary that I have to read much more slowly and take a lot of notes. Flash cards have been a huge help with this class. Many of my test questions assume I already know the vocabulary words so I have to know them well enough to use them to figure out complicated problems.	
Improving Your Reading Making connections is part of critical thinking. Some classes are foundational in that everything you read today is based on what you have read or learned in the past. Everything you will learn tomorrow assumes you have mastered the information today. What classes like this are you taking now?	My Biology class is definitely foundational. We are studying microorganisms and it is assumed that we retained the information from the previous chapters. My math class is also foundational. If I don't understand the concepts this week, I will be lost next week. The key is getting tutoring help now and not waiting until the end of the term.	

BUILD YOUR EXPERIENCE

This group exercise allows students to experiment with mapping and to compare the different types of maps.

1 COLLABORATIVE ACTIVITY

The class will be divided into small groups. Each group will be given a large sheet of paper and asked to draw a map, either wheel or branching, for Chapter 7. Use at least three levels of information: the chapter title, the headings, and the subheadings, as well as any vocabulary words that seem important.

Then compare ALL of the mappings.

Was anything left out?

Were they relatively easy to read or too jumbled?

Would this be a tool you could use for review before a test? Why or why not?

What kinds of learners benefit most from this type of strategy?

2 BUILDING YOUR PORTFOLIO

The Big Picture   This chapter introduces a reading strategy called **mapping** as a visual tool for getting the "big picture" of what you are preparing to read. Mapping a textbook chapter can help you quickly recognize how different concepts and terms fit together and make connections to what you already know about the subject. A number of ways of mapping, including wheel maps and branching maps, are described in this chapter. You might also use other types of maps, such as *matrixes* to compare and contrast ideas or show cause and effect, a *spider web* to connect themes, or *sketches* to illustrate images, relationships, or descriptions.

1. Look through your course syllabi, and identify a reading assignment that you need to complete in the next week.

2. Begin by previewing the first chapter of the reading assignment.

3. Practice mapping the chapter by creating your own map using the drawing toolbar in *Microsoft Word*.

4. Save your map in your portfolio.

For an example of this exercise, go to the book's Web site at **bedfordstmartins.com/ ycestudyskills.**

Reading a textbook efficiently and effectively requires that you develop reading strategies that will help you to make the most of your study time. Mapping can help you to organize and retain what you have read, making it a good reading and study tool. Writing, reciting, and organizing the main points, supporting ideas, and key details of the chapter will help you to recall the information on test day.

CHAPTER 8

Learning to Study, Comprehend, and Remember

Y ou might have learned to study effectively while you were in high school, or you might be finding that you need to learn more about how to study. In college you will need to spend time out of class reviewing course material, doing assigned reading, and keeping up with your homework. Occasionally, you will also want to go the extra mile by doing additional (unassigned) reading and investigating particular topics that interest you.

Studying, comprehending, and remembering are essential to getting the most out of your college experience. Although many students think that the only reason for studying is to do well on exams, a far more important reason is to learn and understand course information. If you study to increase your understanding, you are more likely to remember and apply what you learn not only to tests, but also to future courses and to life beyond college.

This chapter offers you a number of strategies for making the best use of your study time. It also addresses the important topic of memory. There's no getting around it: If you can't remember what you have read or heard, you won't do well on course exams.

Studying to Understand and Remember

> If you can't remember what you just read or heard in class, you can't expect to do well on the next exam. How can you improve your level of concentration in class? How can you stay more focused while reading?

Studying will help you accomplish two goals: understanding and remembering. While memory is a necessary tool for learning, what's most important is that you study to develop a deep understanding of course information. When you truly comprehend what you are learning, you will be able to place names, dates, and specific facts in context. You will also be able to exercise your critical-thinking abilities.

■ RETENTION STRATEGY: One of the reasons that first-year seminars are correlated with retention is that these courses focus on study skills essential for college success. Even if your students tell you they have heard all of this before, do not neglect this important component of your seminar class. Also remind them that college-level study skills are, in fact, different skills. If you don't feel comfortable teaching study skills, find someone on your campus who can be a resource person for you.

IN CLASS: Divide the class into groups, and ask students to brainstorm the pros and cons of study groups. Have the groups report back to the class. Ask the class to offer suggestions on how to create and maintain effective study groups.

The human mind has discovered ingenious ways to understand and remember information. Here are some methods that might be useful to you as you're trying to nail down the causes of World War I, remember the steps in a chemistry problem, or absorb a mathematical formula:

1. **Pay attention to what you're hearing or reading.** This suggestion is perhaps the most basic and the most important. If you're sitting in class thinking about everything except what the professor is saying or if you're reading and you find that your mind is wandering, you're wasting your time. Force yourself to focus.

2. **"Overlearn" the material.** After you know and think you understand the material you're studying, go over it again to make sure that you'll retain it for a long time. Test yourself, or ask someone else to test you. Recite aloud, in your own words, what you're trying to remember.

3. **Check the Internet.** If you're having trouble remembering what you have learned, Google a key word, and try to find interesting details that will engage you in learning more, not less, about the subject. Many first-year courses cover such a large amount of material that you'll miss the more interesting details unless you seek them out for yourself. As your interest increases, so will your memory for the topic.

4. **Be sure you have the big picture.** Whenever you begin a course, make sure that you're clear on what the course will cover. You can talk with someone who has already taken the course, or you can take a brief look at all the reading assignments. Having the big picture will help you understand and remember the details of what you're learning.

5. **Look for connections between your life and what's going on in your courses.** College courses might seem irrelevant to you, but if you look more

Work Together

One way to enhance your memory is through working collaboratively with others. Each of you can share your own memory strategies such as mnemonics or acrostics. You can also check specific facts and details through group consensus.

◼ ASSESSING YOUR STRENGTHS ◼

What study skills have you learned and practiced, and how do you need to improve? Now that you have read the first section of this chapter, list specific examples of your strengths in studying and remembering course material.

_____

_____

_____

_____

◼ SETTING GOALS ◼

What are *your* most important objectives in learning the material in this chapter? How do you need to improve your study skills and your memory? List three goals in this area (e.g., I will make sure that I am not distracted when I am studying; I will find a space where I can be alone, either the library or a study lounge; and I will turn off my cell phone during study time).

1. _____

_____

2. _____

_____

3. _____

_____

carefully, you'll find many connections between course material and your daily life. Seeing those connections will make your courses more interesting and will help you remember what you're learning. For example, if you're taking a music theory course and studying chord patterns, listen for those patterns in contemporary music.

6. **Get organized.** If your desk or your computer is organized, you'll spend less time trying to remember a file name or where you put a particular document. And as you rewrite your notes, putting them in a logical order (either chronological or thematic) that makes sense to you will help you learn and remember them.

7. **Reduce stressors in your life.** Although there's no way to determine the extent to which worry or stress causes you to be unable to focus or to forget, most people will agree that stress can be a distraction. Healthy, stress-reducing behaviors, such as meditation, exercise, and sleep, are especially important for college students. Many campuses have counseling

IN CLASS: Advise students that it is important to be conscious of times when their minds wander. They can bring themselves back if they are aware that their focus is not on the material.

IN CLASS: Have students discuss how stress can affect memory. What experiences have they had when stress caused memory problems?

DID YOU KNOW?

92% of students study with others in their first year.

TECH TIP   DON'T BE A VIRTUAL WALLFLOWER

1 ▶ THE PROBLEM

How do you create community in an online course?

2 ▶ THE FIX

Jump out of your cyber box and make some connections.

3 ▶ HOW TO DO IT

Studies show that you'll retain more of what you learn online if you like your school, your teacher, and your fellow classmates. Who says that taking a class remotely means you have to feel like a lonely hermit?

1. Don't pass up online discussion forums or Web casts that let you interact with your instructor and other students.

2. As in a traditional course, your instructor may ask students to say a few things about themselves. To foster conversation, give people something to work with. Don't just say, "I'm John from Fresno" and leave it at that. You need a lure. Try questions like "What's the worst boss you've ever worked for and why?" Then everyone can chime in with a shared experience.

3. Go ahead and e-mail three or four students privately: "Hi, I'm John in the online leadership course. I wondered if you're really getting our latest assignment. I noticed last night that you had a question, too." Students like to sympathize with each other.

4. Reach out to your instructor with thoughtful questions, too: "Are there any conferences that have to do with leadership that students can attend?"

5. Extra credit: To enrich your learning experience, find out if you can create a class wiki page or Facebook account so students can share articles, offer feedback, and have more of a presence.

PERSONAL BEST

How can you apply some of these skills to a traditional course? Get to class early and talk to some other students or your professor, for starters. If you have a group assignment, write down the e-mail addresses and phone numbers of the people on your team. (If you get sick, at least you'll be able to find out what you missed.) Single out the biggest brains in your class and form a study group. And remember: A college class is a safe zone for exploring opposing views. Be prepared to disagree with others and have others disagree with you.

IN CLASS: Offer to help students form study groups. On the basis of their grades so far, arrange the groups so that stronger students and those who need help are distributed throughout each group.

or health centers that can provide resources to help you deal with whatever might be causing stress in your daily life.

8. **Collaborate with others.** One of the most effective ways to study is in a group with other students. In your first year of college, gather a group of students who study together. Study groups can meet throughout the term or can review for midterm or final exams.

This exercise asks students to make tough choices related to behavior changes that will lead to more efficient studying and more success in college.

How You CONCENTRATE Matters

Truly comprehending new material takes a lot of effort on your part. Concentration is the key. If you are unable to focus on what you hear or read, there is very little chance that this information will enter your long-term memory—it won't just magically happen! If you are willing to make a few changes in behavior, you will be able to concentrate better, remember longer, and most likely need fewer hours to study because you will use your time more efficiently.

What are you willing to do in order to make this happen? Are you willing—yes or no—to make the following tough sacrifices if it means you will do better on tests and have more productive study time?

Tough Choices	Your Answer Yes or No
Are you willing to collaborate with others to form study groups or partners?	
Are you willing to find a place on campus (not your home) for quiet study?	
Are you willing to turn off your cell phone for a few moments of uninterrupted reading time?	
Are you willing to turn off disruptive music or TV while you are studying?	
Are you willing to study for tests four or five days before?	
Are you willing to do assigned readings before you come to class?	
Are you willing to position yourself in class so that you can see and hear better?	
Are you willing to reduce stress through exercise, sleep, or meditation?	
Are you willing to go over your notes after class to clean them up or rewrite them?	
Are you willing to take a few minutes on the weekend to organize the week ahead?	

Making these changes in behavior now will save you a lot of headaches in the future. Attending college is a huge responsibility, one that should not be taken lightly. As a mature adult learner, you need to be flexible and change your old patterns to create successful new habits. Making tough choices isn't easy, but it will directly impact your ability to remember and retain the information you will be required to learn in the months and years ahead.

How Memory Works

Everyone has "blanked out" on a test before. Have you ever wondered why this happens? What area of memory might be your weakest? What is your strongest?

Kenneth Higbee describes two different processes involved in memory (see Table 8.1). The first is **short-term memory**, defined as how many items you are able to perceive at one time. Higbee found that information stored in short-term memory is forgotten in less than 30 seconds (and sometimes much faster) unless you take action to either keep that information in short-term memory or move it to long-term memory.[1]

[1]K. Higbee, *Your Memory: How It Works and How to Improve It* (New York: Marlowet, 1996).

short-term memory How many items you are able to perceive at one time. Memory that disappears in less than 30 seconds (sometimes faster) unless the items are moved to long-term memory.

TABLE 8.1 Short-Term and Long-Term Memory

Short-Term Memory	Long-Term Memory
Stores information for about 30 seconds	Procedural: remembering how to do something
Can contain from five to nine chunks of information at one time	Semantic: remembering facts and meanings
Information either forgotten or moved to long-term memory	Episodic: remembering the time and place of events

IN CLASS: Ask students why they think the authors included material in this book about memory. Is memory related to learning and academic success? Why or why not? Can memory be improved? If so, how?

long-term memory The type of memory that is used to retain information and can be described in three ways: procedural, semantic, and episodic.

Although short-term memory is significantly limited, it has a number of uses. It serves as an immediate but temporary holding tank for information, some of which might not be needed for long. It helps you maintain a reasonable attention span so that you can keep track of topics mentioned in conversation, and it enables you to stay on task with the goals you are pursuing at any moment. But even these simple functions of short-term memory fail on occasion. If the telephone rings, if someone asks you a question, or if you're interrupted in any way, you might find that your attention suffers and that you essentially have to start over in reconstructing short-term memory.

The second memory process is **long-term memory**, and this is the type of memory that you will need to improve so that you will remember what you're learning in college. Long-term memory can be described in three ways. *Procedural memory* is knowing how to do something, such as solving a mathematical problem or playing a musical instrument. *Semantic memory* involves facts and meanings without regard to where and when you learned those things. *Episodic memory* deals with particular events, their time, and their place.[2]

You are using your procedural memory when you get on a bicycle you haven't ridden in years, when you can recall the first piece you learned to play on the piano, when you effortlessly type a letter or class report, and when you drive a car. Your semantic memory is used continuously to recall word meanings or important dates, such as your mother's birthday. Episodic memory allows you to remember events in your life—a vacation, your first day in school, the moment you opened your college acceptance letter. Some people can recall not only the event but also the very date and time the event happened. For others, although the event stands out, the dates and times are harder to remember immediately.

CONNECTING MEMORY TO DEEP LEARNING

It can be easy to blame a poor memory on the way we live; multitasking has become the norm for college students and instructors. Admittedly, it's hard to focus on anything for very long if your life is full of daily distractions and competing responsibilities or if you're not getting the sleep you need. Have you ever had the experience of walking into a room with a particular task in mind and immediately forgetting what that task was? You were probably interrupted either by your own thoughts or by someone or something else. Or

[2]W. F. Brewer and J. R. Pani, "The Structure of Human Memory," in *The Psychology of Learning and Motivation: Advances in Research and Theory*, ed. G. H. Bower, vol. 17 (New York: Academic Press, 1983), 1–38.

have you ever felt the panic that comes from blanking on a test, even though you studied hard and thought you knew the material? You might have pulled an all-nighter, and studying and exhaustion raised your stress level, causing your mind to go blank. Such experiences happen to everyone at one time or another. But obviously, to do well in college—and in life—it's important that you improve your ability to remember what you read, hear, and experience. As one writer put it, "there is no learning without memory."[3] On the other hand, not all memory involves real learning.

Is a good memory all you need to do well in college? Most memory strategies tend to focus on helping you remember names, dates, numbers, vocabulary, graphic materials, formulas—the bits and pieces of knowledge. However, if you know the date the Civil War began and the fort where the first shots were fired but you don't really know why the Civil War was fought, you're missing the point of a college education. College is about **deep learning**, understanding the "why" and "how" behind the details. So don't forget that while recall of specific facts is certainly necessary, it isn't sufficient. To do well in college courses, you will need to understand major themes and ideas, and you will also need to hone your ability to think critically about what you're learning. Critical thinking is discussed in depth in Chapter 5 of this book.

MYTHS ABOUT MEMORY

Although scientific knowledge about how our brains function is increasing all the time, Kenneth Higbee suggests that you might have heard some myths about memory (and maybe you even believe them). Here are five of these memory myths, and what experts say about them:

1. **Myth:** Some people are stuck with bad memories.

   Reality: Although there are probably some differences among people in innate memory (the memory ability a person is born with), what really gives you the edge are memory skills that you can learn and use. Virtually anyone can improve the ability to remember and recall.

2. **Myth:** Some people have photographic memories.

   Reality: Although a few individuals have truly exceptional memories, most research has found that these abilities result more often from learned strategies, interest, and practice than from some innate ability. Even though you might not have what psychologists would classify as an exceptional memory, applying the memory strategies presented later in this chapter can help you improve it.

3. **Myth:** Memory benefits from long hours of practice.

   Reality: Practicing memorizing can help improve memory. If you have ever been a server in a restaurant, you might have been required to memorize the menu. You might even have surprised yourself at your ability to memorize not only the main entrees, but also sauces and side dishes. Experts acknowledge that practice often improves memory, but they argue that the way you practice, such as using special creative strategies, is more important than how long you practice.

deep learning Understanding the "why" and "how" behind the details.

IN CLASS: Remind students of the difference between memorization and learning. Explain that once they have mastered important concepts, using memory techniques will be an easy way to file facts for future use.

IN CLASS: Assign groups of students to read and discuss the myths about memory. Which of these myths do most students believe are true? Why?

[3]Harry Lorayne, *Super Memory, Super Student: How to Raise Your Grades in 30 Days* (Boston: Little, Brown and Company, 1990).

4. **Myth:** Remembering too much can clutter your mind.

   Reality: For all practical purposes, the storage capacity of your memory is unlimited. In fact, the more you learn about a particular topic, the easier it is to learn even more. How you organize the information is more important than the quantity.

5. **Myth:** People only use 10 percent of their brain power.

   Reality: No scientific research is available to accurately measure how much of our brain we actually use. However, most psychologists and learning specialists believe that we all have far more mental ability than we actually tap.

This exercise lays out the best ways to remember information and asks students how much they recall from their most recent lecture, which may be eye-opening for many.

EXERCISE 8.2

How You STUDY Matters

If you've ever "gone blank" on a test, it might mean that the information you just read or the notes you took in class never made it into your long-term memory. Reviewing your notes, just once after class, will create a kind of "file folder" in your brain, organizing the information for the test.

A study done at the University of Texas[4] found that MOST people remember

- 10 percent of what they read;
- 20 percent of what they hear;
- 30 percent of what they see;
- 50 percent of what they see and hear;
- 70 percent of what they say; and
- 90 percent of what they do and say

If this is true, then reviewing your notes out loud and rewriting them in your own words are some of the best ways to embed the information in your long-term memory! Let's see if you retain what you hear in a typical lecture. Think back to your most recent lecture class (Was it this morning? Yesterday?), and write a summary in your own words about what you learned.

My class: _____

When it was (date and time): _____

This is what I remember learning:

_____

_____

_____

_____

Then share this paragraph with someone in class, out loud. In doing so, you'll have read it, heard it, seen it, *and* said it, and we just learned that most people remember 70 percent of what they say!

If you cannot recall anything from your last lecture class, this is valuable feedback that your concentration may not be strong enough to allow for deep learning. Practice makes perfect. Take a moment after your next lecture class to review your notes, or at the very least, clean them up. Doing so improves your chances to get the information filed into your long-term memory!

[4]T. Metcalf, "Listening to Your Clients," *Life Association News* 92, no. 7 (1997): 16–18.

Improving Your Memory

What techniques have you used in the past to help you recall information for tests and exams? What strategies discussed in this chapter might you consider adopting as your own?

Throughout history, human memory has been a topic of great interest and fascination for scientists and the general public. Although severe problems with memory are extremely rare, you're in good company if you find that your memory occasionally lets you down, especially if you're nervous or stressed or when grades depend on immediate recall of what you have read, heard, or written.

So how can you improve your ability to store information in your brain for future use? Psychologists and learning specialists have conducted research on memory and have developed a number of strategies that you can use as part of a study-skills regimen. Some of these strategies might be new to you, but others will be simple commonsense ways to maximize your learning—ideas that you've heard before, though perhaps not in the context of improving your memory.

The benefits of having a good memory are obvious. In college, your memory will help you retain information and ace tests. After college, the ability to recall names, procedures, presentations, and appointments will save you energy and time and will prevent a lot of embarrassment.

"Is this the memory seminar?"

An Elephant (Almost) Never Forgets

While elephants apparently do have pretty good memories, they're like the rest of us in that they occasionally forget. Work to develop your memory by using the specific strategies in this chapter. One of the most important strategies you can use is understanding the big-picture context behind bits and pieces of information.

There are many ways to go about remembering. Have you ever had to memorize a speech or lines from a play? How you approach committing the lines to memory might depend on your learning style. If you're an aural learner, you might choose to record your lines as well as lines of other characters and listen to them on tape. If you're a visual learner, you might remember best by visualizing where your lines appear on the page in the script. If you learn best by reading, you might simply read the script over and over. If you're a kinesthetic learner, you might need to walk or move across an imaginary stage as you read the script.

Although knowing specific words will help, remembering concepts and ideas can be much more important. To embed such ideas in your mind, ask yourself these questions as you review your notes and books:

1. What is the essence of the idea?
2. Why does the idea make sense? What is the logic behind it?
3. How does this idea connect to other ideas in the material?
4. What are some possible arguments against the idea?

MNEMONICS

Mnemonics (pronounced "ne MON iks") are various methods or tricks to aid the memory. Mnemonics tend to fall into four basic categories:

1. **Acronyms.** New words created from the first letters of several words can be helpful in remembering. The Great Lakes can be more easily recalled by remembering the word "HOMES" for Huron, Ontario, Michigan, Erie, and Superior.
2. **Acrostics.** An acrostic is a verse in which certain letters of each word or line form a message. Many piano students were taught the notes on the treble clef lines (E, G, B, D, F) by remembering the acrostic "Every Good Boy Deserves Fudge."
3. **Rhymes or songs.** Do you remember learning "Thirty days hath September, April, June, and November. All the rest have 31, excepting February alone. It has 28 days time, but in leap years it has 29"? If this is familiar, you were using a mnemonic rhyming technique to remember the days in each month.
4. **Visualization.** You use visualization to associate words, concepts, or stories with visual images. The more ridiculous the image, the more likely you are to remember it. So use your imagination to create mental images when you're studying important words or concepts. For example, as you're driving to campus, choose some landmarks along the way to help you remember material for your history test. The next day, as you pass those landmarks, relate them to something from your class notes or readings. A white picket fence might remind you of the British army's eighteenth-century approach to warfare, with its official uniforms and straight lines of infantry, while a stand of trees of various shapes and sizes might remind you of the Continental army's less organized approach.

Mnemonics work because they make information meaningful through the use of rhymes, patterns, and associations. They impose meaning where meaning might be hard to recognize. Mnemonics provide a way of organizing material, a sort of mental filing system. Mnemonics probably aren't needed if what you are studying is very logical and organized, but they can be quite useful for other types of material.

Although mnemonics are a time-tested way of remembering, the method has some limitations. The first is time. Thinking up rhymes, associations, or visual images can take longer than simply learning the words themselves through repetition. Also, it is often difficult to convert abstract concepts into concrete words or images, and you run the risk of being able to remember an image without recalling the underlying concept. Finally, memory specialists debate whether learning through mnemonics actually helps with long-term knowledge retention and whether this technique helps or interferes with deeper understanding.

IN CLASS: Have students select information taught in one of their courses or textbooks and use a mnemonic to aid their memory of this information. Ask students to demonstrate the mnemonic in class.

USING REVIEW SHEETS, MIND MAPS, AND OTHER TOOLS

To prepare for an exam that will cover large amounts of material, you need to condense the volume of notes and text pages into manageable study units. Review your materials with these questions in mind: Is this one of the key ideas in the chapter or unit? Will I see this on the test? As suggested in Chapter 7, you might prefer to highlight, underline, or annotate the most important ideas or create outlines, lists, or visual maps.

Use your notes to develop review sheets. Make lists of key terms and ideas (from the recall column if you've used the Cornell method) that you need to remember. Also, don't underestimate the value of using your lecture notes to test yourself or others on information presented in class.

A **mind map** is essentially a review sheet with a visual element. Its word and visual patterns provide you with highly charged clues to jog your memory. Because they are visual, mind maps help many students recall information more easily.

mind map A review sheet with words and visual elements that jog the memory to help you recall information more easily.

Figure 8.1 shows what a mind map might look like for a chapter on listening and learning in the classroom. Try to reconstruct the ideas in the chapter by following the connections in the map. Then make a visual mind map for this chapter, and see how much more you can remember after studying it a number of times.

In addition to review sheets and mind maps, you might want to create flash cards. One of the advantages of flash cards is that you can keep them in a pocket of your backpack or jacket and pull them out to study anywhere, even when you might not think that you have enough time to take out your notebook to study. Also, you always know where you left off. Flash cards can help you make good use of time that might otherwise be wasted, such as time spent on the bus or waiting for a friend.

OUTSIDE CLASS: Have students create a mind map of this chapter.

IN CLASS: Have students compare their maps and discuss any differences between them. Are the differences based on different interpretations of the information, or do they indicate errors?

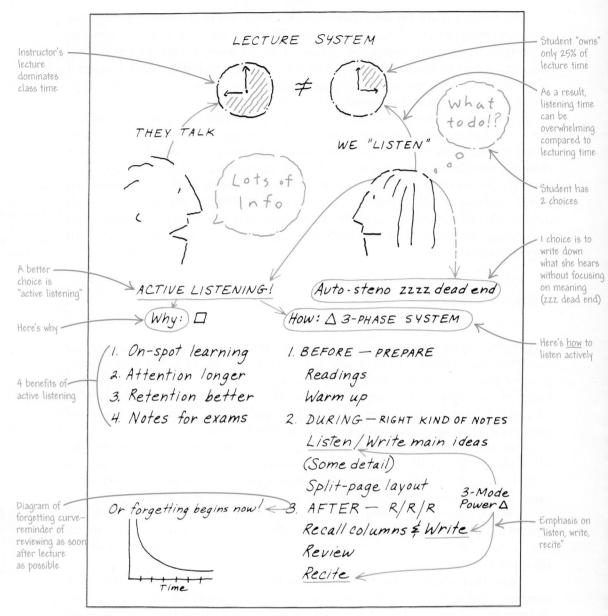

FIGURE 8.1

Sample Mind Map on Listening and Learning in the Classroom

OUTSIDE CLASS: Have students write a summary of this chapter by following the outlined steps on this page. Ask students to discuss the differences between the mind map and the summary. Which was more helpful to them? Why?

SUMMARIES

Writing summaries of class topics can be helpful in preparing for essay and short-answer exams. By condensing the main ideas into a concise written summary, you store information in your long-term memory so you can retrieve it to answer an essay question. Here's how:

1. Predict a test question from your lecture notes or other resources.
2. Read the chapter, supplemental articles, notes, or other resources. Underline or mark main ideas as you go, make notations, or make an outline on a separate sheet of paper.

3. Analyze and abstract. What is the purpose of the material? Does it compare two ideas, define a concept, or prove a theory? What are the main ideas? How would you explain the material to someone else?

4. Make connections between main points and key supporting details. Reread to identify each main point and the supporting evidence. Create an outline to assist you in this process.

5. Select, condense, and order. Review underlined material, and begin putting the ideas into your own words. Number what you underlined or highlighted in a logical order.

6. Write your ideas precisely in a draft. In the first sentence, state the purpose of your summary. Follow this statement with each main point and its supporting ideas. See how much of the draft you can develop from memory without relying on your notes.

7. Review your draft. Read it over, adding missing transitions or insufficient information. Check the logic of your summary. Annotate with the material you used for later reference.

8. Test your memory. Put your draft away, and try to recite the contents of the summary to yourself out loud, or explain it to a study partner who can provide feedback on the information you have omitted.

9. Schedule time to review summaries, and double-check your memory shortly before the test. You might want to do this with a partner, but some students prefer to review alone. Some faculty members also might be willing to assist you in this process and provide feedback on your summaries.

This exercise gets students thinking about the various ways to store information and which method might work best for each of their current classes. It also gets them to commit to following through. Check in with students, and ask them to share their successes in class.

EXERCISE 8.3

How You REVIEW Matters

Take a moment to consider the many ways you can create the big picture of an entire chapter of information: mind maps, summaries, flash cards, time lines, Cornell notes, practice tests. Considering your learning style, which method appeals to you and why?

For some of your classes, a summary or Cornell notes will work best to prepare for an upcoming test. For other classes, the mind map or time line is a better choice. List your classes below, and choose the method that will make it easier to condense and store course information you'll need to recall for the next test. Then—here is the hardest part—actually do it!

Class	Method(s) of Review	Date of Next Test

CHECKLIST FOR SUCCESS

GET THE MOST OUT OF YOUR STUDY TIME

☐ **Make studying a part of your daily routine.** Don't allow days to go by when you don't crack a book or keep up with course assignments.

☐ **Manage your study time wisely.** Create a schedule that will allow you to prepare for exams and complete course assignments on time. Be aware of "crunch times" when you might have several exams or papers due at once. Create some flexibility in your schedule to allow for unexpected distractions.

☐ **Collaborate with others.** One of the most effective ways to study is in a group with other students.

☐ **Be confident that you can improve your memory.** Remind yourself occasionally of things you have learned in the past that you didn't think you could or would remember.

☐ **Choose the memory improvement strategies that best fit your preferred learning styles: aural, visual, reading, kinesthetic.** Identify the courses where you can make the best use of each memory strategy.

☐ **Go beyond simply trying to memorize words and focus on trying to understand and then remember the big concepts and ideas.** Keep asking yourself: What is the main point here? Is there a big idea? Am I getting this?

☐ **Be alert for external distractions.** Choose a place to study where you can concentrate and allow yourself uninterrupted time to focus on the material you are studying.

☐ **Get a tutor.** Tutoring is not just for students who are failing. Often the best students seek assistance to ensure that they understand course material. Most tutors are students, and most campus tutoring services are free.

APPLY IT! What Works for YOU Matters

Think about your current academic situation, and apply some of the suggestions and strategies introduced in this chapter. Select strategies that you think will work best for you, and then write them down in the "Your Response" column. What are YOU planning to do for YOUR college experience?

QUESTIONS	SAMPLE STUDENT ANSWERS	YOUR RESPONSE
	Name: Thomas Sinclair	
Studying to Understand and Remember If you can't remember what you just read or heard in class, you can't expect to do well on the next exam. How can you improve your level of concentration in class? How can you stay more focused while reading?	I'm what you might call a "techie." I love all of my classes that have high-tech modes of learning: PowerPoints, clickers—all that. But straight lecture classes, like my history class, bore me. After reading this chapter, I realize that I can improve my concentration if I can use my laptop to take notes in class and create a time line on my computer while I am reading textbook material. That way I stay engaged.	
How Memory Works Everyone has "blanked out" on a test before. Have you ever wondered why this happens? What area of memory might be your weakest? What is your strongest?	I blank out on essay tests. It just seems overwhelming to me. I don't have problems with lab tests because my procedural memory is pretty strong, but semantic memory (facts and figures) can be difficult. I have learned from this chapter to connect information, like dates in history class, with a story or movie that I can see on film. This way I will remember the material more in depth and then be able to write a stronger essay.	
Improving Your Memory What techniques have you used in the past to help you recall information for tests and exams? What strategies discussed in this chapter might you consider adopting as your own?	Visualization is key for me. I like to be able to see it in order to remember it. When I am studying for any class, especially classes I don't particularly like, I have to put extra effort into remembering details like facts and figures. Making mind maps on my computer helps, and also reviewing my notes with a study partner makes it more "real" for me.	

BUILD YOUR EXPERIENCE

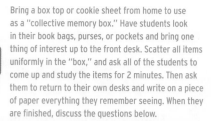

Bring a box top or cookie sheet from home to use as a "collective memory box." Have students look in their book bags, purses, or pockets and bring one thing of interest up to the front desk. Scatter all items uniformly in the "box," and ask all of the students to come up and study the items for 2 minutes. Then ask them to return to their own desks and write on a piece of paper everything they remember seeing. When they are finished, discuss the questions below.

1 COLLABORATIVE ACTIVITY

Take something out of your book bag, purse, or pocket to contribute to a "collective memory box." Bring this item to the front of the room. Don't worry—you'll get it back at the end of class! When everyone has contributed an item or two, your instructor will ask your class to come up and study the collection of items for 2 minutes. Go back to your seat, and quickly write down as many items as you can remember seeing.

How many items did you recall? _____ Was there a pattern or method that you used to recall certain items? For example, did you color-code, make up a story, or mentally break up the items in small areas and memorize them? Did you use mnemonics or acronyms, a rhyme or song? _____

What are some methods that you heard another student use that you might consider useful?

_____

_____

How can this be helpful in learning large amounts of information in an academic class?

_____

_____

If class time remains, try this experiment again, using a different strategy in helping you to remember. How many items did you recall this time? _____ Can you see how using a strategy and making more effort in learning something might help you retain the information?

2 BUILDING YOUR PORTFOLIO

Takes Me Back Is there a song that reminds you, every time you hear it, of a certain time in your life or even the exact moment when something happened? Or maybe you have a photo that you take out every so often for a trip down memory lane? Our senses often trigger memories.

1. Recall a photo, song, or object that prompts you to remember a life event or time period. Create a new document in your word processing software, and describe just what it is about the photo, song, or object that reminds you of something else.

2. Describe your memory in as much detail as possible.

3. Describe how this memory makes you feel.

4. Describe how you might use photos or drawings, songs, or mnemonics to remember ideas or concepts in one of the classes you are currently taking.

5. Save these musings in your portfolio. If possible, save the photos or music files that you described along with your document.

ONE-MINUTE PAPER

Doing well on exams is important, but being able to study, comprehend, and remember what you learn has bigger implications for your life. After reading this chapter, do you find yourself thinking about these concepts in a different way? If so, how? What kinds of questions would you ask your instructor about this chapter?

_____

_____

_____

_____

_____

_____

_____

_____

_____

_____

_____

_____

_____

_____

_____

_____

No matter how well prepared you are in your teaching, what a student hears and understands might not always be what you think you have said. The one-minute paper is a quick and easy assessment tool that will help alert you when students don't understand what was said or discussed in class. The one-minute paper will also give timid students an opportunity to ask questions and seek clarification. Ideally, you should ask for such a paper several minutes before the end of a class. The paper will also help you begin your next class by clarifying points your students seem to be unsure of.

For more on this topic watch
French Fries Are Not Vegetables and Other College Lessons

WHERE TO GO FOR HELP . . .

ON CAMPUS

Your campus probably has a study skills center or learning center that can help you develop effective memory strategies. Other students and faculty members can also give you tips on how they remember course material. And your college library will have many books on the topic of memory. Some were written by researchers for the research community, but others were written for people like you who are trying to improve their memory.

BOOKS

> Buzan, Tony. *Use Your Perfect Memory*, 3rd rev. ed. New York: Penguin Books, 1991.

> Higbee, Kenneth L., *Your Memory: How It Works and How to Improve It*, 2nd rev. ed. New York: Marlowe, 2001.

> Lorayne, Harry. *Super Memory, Super Student: How to Raise Your Grades in 30 Days*. Boston: Little, Brown, 1990.

ONLINE

> Memorization techniques: **http://www.alamo .edu/memory.** This excellent Web site is maintained by the Alamo Community College District.

MY INSTITUTION'S RESOURCES

_____

_____

_____

_____

_____

_____

_____

Improving Your Performance on Exams and Tests

You can prepare for exams in many ways, and certain methods are more effective than others, depending on the subject matter, your preferred learning style, and the type of test you'll be taking. Sometimes you'll need to be able to recall names, dates, and other specific bits of information, especially if you are taking a multiple-choice or short-answer exam. Many instructors, especially in humanities and social science courses such as literature, history, and political science, will expect you to go beyond names and dates and have a good conceptual understanding of the subject matter. They often prefer essay exams that require you to use higher-level critical-thinking skills, such as *analysis, synthesis,* and *evaluation.*

Instructors also expect you to be able to provide the reasons, arguments, and assumptions on which a given position is based, and the evidence that you believe confirms or discounts it. They want you to be able to support your opinions so they can see how you think. They are not looking for answers that merely prove you can memorize the material presented in lecture and the text. Even in math and science courses, your instructors want you not only to remember the correct theory, formula, or equation but also to understand and apply what you have learned.

Knowing your preferred learning style will also help you decide the best ways for you to study, no matter what kind of text or exam you are facing. Remember your VARK score, and review the material in Chapter 4 that helps you link your learning style to strategies for exam preparation.

■ RETENTION STRATEGY: Many of us tell our students that "learning is more important than grades"; however, we should acknowledge that grades do matter. First-year students who have earned A's and B's in high school may be shocked to see their first C, D, or worse. The material in this chapter will help students do their best to earn good grades, but make sure that you also encourage students not to give up on college because they received a disappointing grade on a test or exam.

IN CLASS: Ask students what they know about midterm and final exam periods. Why do colleges set these times aside for examinations?

IN CLASS: Have your students check their schedules and make sure that they have written down all their exam dates for each of their classes.

IN CLASS: Most college instructors would agree that essay exams measure learning far better than objective tests do. Explain why so many objective tests are given (e.g., large classes, easier to grade). Why do students need to alter their study methods according to the type of exam?

Getting Prepared for Tests and Exams

By now you have probably received tests back from a few instructors. Most college students expect to get the same grades in college as they did in high school. Unfortunately, this is not always the case. How can you set yourself up for a greater chance of success as you prepare for an upcoming exam—especially in a difficult course?

Believe it or not, you actually begin preparing for a test on the first day of the term. All of your lecture notes, assigned readings, and homework are part of that preparation. As the test day nears, you should know how much additional time you will need for review, what material the test will cover, and what format the test will take. It is very important to double-check the exam dates on your syllabi, as in Figure 9.1, and to incorporate these dates into your overall plans for time management—for example, in your daily and weekly to-do lists.

Here are some specific suggestions to help you prepare well for any exam:

1. **Ask your instructor.** Find out the purpose, types of questions, conditions (how much time you will have to complete the exam), and content to be covered on the exam. Talk with your instructor to clarify any misunderstandings you might have about your reading or lecture notes. Some instructors might let you see copies of old exams so you can see the types of questions they use. Never miss the last class before an exam, because your instructor might summarize valuable information.

2. **Manage your preparation time wisely.** Create a schedule that will give you time to review effectively for the exam without waiting until the night before. Make sure your schedule has some flexibility to allow for unexpected distractions. If you are able to spread your study sessions over several days, your mind will continue to process the information between study sessions, which will help you during the test. Also, let your friends and family know when you have important exams coming up and how that will affect your time with them.

3. **Focus your study.** Figure out what you can effectively review that is likely to be on the exam. Collaborate with other students to share information, and try to attend all test or exam review sessions offered by your instructor.

PREPARE PHYSICALLY

Maintain your regular sleep routine. To do well on exams, you will need to be alert so that you can think clearly. And you are more likely to be alert when you are well rested. Last-minute, late-night cramming that robs you of sufficient sleep isn't an effective study strategy.

Follow your regular exercise program. Another way to prepare physically for exams is by walking, jogging, or engaging in other kinds of physical activity. Exercise is a positive way to relieve stress and to give yourself a needed break from long hours of studying.

◤ ASSESSING YOUR STRENGTHS

Tests and exams are an unavoidable component of college life. Good students will practice strategies to improve their exam scores. Now that you have read the first section of this chapter, list specific examples of your strengths in preparing for and taking different kinds of exams.

_____

_____

_____

_____

◤ SETTING GOALS

What are _your_ most important objectives in learning the material in this chapter? Do you need to improve your abilities as a test-taker, or do you need to deal with test anxiety that prevents you from doing your best? List three goals in this area (e.g., I will not wait until the last minute to study for my next exam; I will begin studying at least one week before the exam date).

1. _____

_____

2. _____

_____

3. _____

_____

Eat right. Eat a light breakfast before a morning exam, and avoid greasy or acidic foods that might upset your stomach. Limit the amount of caffeinated beverages you drink on exam day, because caffeine can make you jittery. Choose fruits, vegetables, and other foods that are high in energy-rich complex carbohydrates. Avoid eating sweets before an exam. The immediate energy boost they create can be quickly followed by a loss of energy and alertness. Ask the instructor whether you may bring a bottle of water with you to the exam.

PREPARE EMOTIONALLY

Know your material. If you have given yourself adequate time to review, you will enter the classroom confident that you are in control. Study by testing yourself or quizzing others in a study group or learning community so that you will be sure you really know the material.

Practice relaxing. Some students experience upset stomachs, sweaty palms, racing hearts, or other unpleasant physical symptoms of test anxiety. Consult your counseling center about relaxation techniques. Some campus learning centers also provide workshops on reducing test anxiety. If this is a problem you experience, read the section on test anxiety later in this chapter.

IN CLASS: Have your students fill out an anonymous survey that asks (a) how many hours of sleep they get each night, (b) how much exercise they get every day, and (c) what kinds of foods they are most likely to eat each day. Compile and discuss the results. A staff member from the health and wellness center can be invited to class for this discussion.

FIGURE 9.1

**Exam Schedule
from Sample
Course Syllabus**

**History 111, US History to 1865
Spring 2013**

Examinations
Note: In this course, all of your exams will be on Fridays,
except for the final. This is to give you a full week to study
for the exam and permit me to grade them over the weekend
and return the exams to you on Monday. I believe in using a
variety of types of measurements. In addition to those
scheduled below, I reserve the right to give you unan-
nounced quizzes on daily reading assignments. Also, current
events are fair game on any exam! Midterm and final exams
will be cumulative (on all material since beginning of the
course). Other exams cover all classroom material and all
readings covered since the prior exam. The schedule is as
follows:

Friday, 1/25: Objective type

Friday, 2/8: Essay type

Friday, 3/8: Midterm: essay and objective

Friday, 3/22: Objective

Friday, 4/12: Essay

Tuesday, 4/30: Final exam: essay and objective

Use positive self-talk. Instead of telling yourself, "I never do well on
math tests" or "I'll never be able to learn all the information for my
history essay exam," make positive statements, such as "I have
attended all the lectures, done my homework, and passed the quizzes.
Now I'm ready to do well on the test!"

PREPARE FOR TEST TAKING

Find out about the test. Ask your instructor what format the test will
have, such as essay, multiple-choice, true/false, fill-in-the-blank,
short-answer, or something else. Ask how long the test will last and how it
will be graded. Ask whether all questions will have the same point value.

Design an exam plan. Use the information about the test as you design
a plan for preparing. Build that preparation into a schedule of review

dates. Develop a to-do list of the major steps you need to take to be ready. Be sure you have read and learned all the material by one week before the exam. That way, you will be able to use the final week to review and prepare for the exam. The week before the exam, set aside a schedule of 1-hour blocks of time for review, and make notes on specifically what you plan to accomplish during each hour.

Join a study group. You have seen the suggestion to join or form a study group in other chapters because this is one of the most effective strategies for doing well in college, especially in preparing for exams. You can benefit from different views of your instructors' goals, objectives, and emphasis; have your study partners quiz you on facts and concepts; and gain the support and friendship of others to help sustain your motivation.

Some instructors will provide time in class for the formation of study groups. Otherwise, ask your teacher, adviser, or campus tutoring or learning center to help you identify interested students and decide on guidelines for the group. Study groups can meet throughout the term, or they can just review for midterms or final exams. Group members should complete their assignments before the group meets and prepare study questions or points of discussion ahead of time. If your study group decides to meet just before exams, allow enough time to share notes and ideas.

Get a tutor. Most campus tutoring services offer their services for free. Ask your academic adviser or counselor or campus learning center about arranging for tutoring. Many learning centers employ student tutors who have done well in the same courses you are taking. These students might have some good advice on how to prepare for tests given by particular instructors. Learning centers often have computer tutorials that can help you refresh basic skills.

PREPARE FOR MATH AND SCIENCE EXAMS

Math and science exams often require additional preparation techniques. Here are some suggestions for doing well on these exams:

1. Do your homework regularly, even if it is not graded, and do all the assigned problems. As you do your homework, write out your work as carefully and clearly as you will be expected to do on your tests. This practice will allow you to use your homework as a review for the test.

2. Attend each class, and always be on time. Many instructors use the time at the beginning of class to review homework.

3. Create a review guide throughout the term. As you begin your homework each day, write out a random problem from each homework section in a notebook that you have set up for reviewing material for that course. As you review later, you will be able to come back to these problems to make sure you have a representative problem from each section you've studied.

4. Throughout the term, keep a list of definitions or important formulas. (These are great to put on flash cards.) Review one or two of these as part of every study session. Another technique is to post the formulas and definitions in prominent areas in your living space (e.g., on the bathroom wall, around your computer work area, or on the door of the microwave). Seeing this information frequently will help embed it in your mind.

This exercise prompts students to prepare properly by planning the five days prior to their next test.

How You PREPARE Matters

Preparing to take a test sometimes requires you to think *backwards*. In other words, you should plan for a test *ahead of time*—at least five days before the actual test.

Study the following chart to give you an idea of what this means.

Example: Psychology Test on Friday Covering Chapters 6–8

Sunday	Monday	Tuesday	Wednesday	Thursday	Friday
Read Ch 6 & make notes and flash cards Meet with study group	Read Ch 7 & make notes Review notes from Ch 6	Read Ch 8 & make notes Review notes from Ch 7	Review notes from Ch 8 Ask professor about test Design a mock exam Do online practice tests	Meet with study group Go over answers to mock exam Read review notes Get SLEEP!	Take test and then . . . RELAX!

Now it is your turn. Take a moment to think, and ask yourself the following questions: *"When is my next test?"* and *"What chapters does it cover?"*

Subject: _____

Chapters: _____

Date of Exam: _____

Now, map out the five days prior to the day of the test:

Taking Tests and Exams

Tests come in a variety of formats that require different methods of study. What types of tests do you prefer? What tests give you the most trouble? What new method of review would you consider trying?

Throughout your college career you will take tests in many different formats, in many subject areas, and with many different types of questions. The box on page 193 offers test-taking tips that apply to any test situation.

TIPS FOR SUCCESSFUL TEST TAKING

1. Write your name on the test (unless you are directed not to) and on the answer sheet.

2. Analyze, ask, and stay calm. Before you start the test, take a long, deep breath and slowly exhale. Carefully read all the directions before beginning the test so that you understand what to do. Ask the instructor or exam monitor for clarification if you don't understand something. Be confident. Don't panic. Answer one question at a time.

3. Make the best use of your time. Quickly survey the entire test and decide how much time you will spend on each section. Be aware of the point values of different sections of the test. If some questions are worth more points than others, they deserve more of your time.

4. Jot down idea-starters before the test. Before you even look at the test questions, turn the test paper over and take a moment to write down the formulas, definitions, and major ideas that you have been studying. (Check with your instructor ahead of time to be sure that this is okay.) This will help you go into the test with a feeling of confidence and knowledge, and it will provide quick access to the information while you are taking the test.

5. Answer the easy questions first. Expect that you'll be puzzled by some questions. Make a note to come back to them later. If different sections consist of different types of questions (such as multiple-choice, short-answer, and essay questions), complete the types of questions you are most comfortable with first. Be sure to leave enough time for any essays.

6. If you feel yourself starting to panic or go blank, stop whatever you are doing. Take a long, deep breath and slowly exhale. Remind yourself you will be okay and that you do know the material and can do well on this test. Then take another deep breath. If necessary, go to another section of the test and come back later to the item that triggered your anxiety.

7. If you finish early, don't leave. Stay and check your work for errors. Reread the directions one last time. If you are using a Scantron answer sheet, make sure that all bubbles are filled in accurately and completely.

ESSAY QUESTIONS

Many college instructors have a strong preference for essay exams for a simple reason: Essay exams promote higher-order critical thinking, whereas other types of exams tend to be exercises in memorization. Generally, advanced courses are more likely to include essay exams. To be successful on essay exams, follow these guidelines:

1. **Budget your exam time.** Quickly survey the entire exam, and note the questions that are the easiest for you, along with their point values. Take a moment to weigh their values, estimate the approximate time you should allot to each question, and write the time beside each item number. Be sure you know whether you must answer all the questions or choose among questions. Remember, writing profusely on easy questions that have low value can be a costly error because it takes up precious time you might need for more important questions. Wear a watch so you can monitor your time, and include time at the end for a quick review.

2. **Develop a very brief outline of your answer before you begin to write.** Start working on the questions that are easiest for you, and jot down a few

ideas before you begin to write. First, make sure that your outline responds to all parts of the question. Then use your first paragraph to introduce the main points and subsequent paragraphs to describe each point in more depth. If you begin to lose your concentration, you will be glad to have the outline to help you regain your focus. If you find that you are running out of time and cannot complete an essay, provide an outline of key ideas at the very least. Instructors usually assign points on the basis of your coverage of the main topics from the material. Thus you will usually earn more points by responding briefly to all parts of the question than by addressing just one aspect of the question in detail. An outline will often earn you partial credit even if you leave the essay unfinished.

3. **Write concise, organized answers.** Many well-prepared students write good answers to questions that were not asked because they did not read a question carefully or didn't respond to all parts of the question. Other students hastily write down everything they know on a topic. Instructors will give lower grades for answers that are vague and tend to ramble or for articulate answers that don't address the actual question.

4. **Know the key task words in essay questions.** Being familiar with the key task word in an essay question will help you answer it more specifically. The key task words in Table 9.1 appear frequently on essay tests. Take time to learn them so that you can answer essay questions as accurately and precisely as possible.

MULTIPLE-CHOICE QUESTIONS

Preparing for multiple-choice tests requires you to actively review all of the material that has been covered in the course. Reciting from flash cards, summary sheets, mind maps, or the recall column in your lecture notes is a good way to review large amounts of material.

Take advantage of the many cues that multiple-choice questions contain. Careful reading of each item might uncover the correct answer. Always question choices that use absolute words such as *always*, *never*, and *only*. These choices are often (but not always) incorrect. Also, read carefully for terms such as *not*, *except*, and *but*, which are introduced before the choices. Often, the answer that is the most inclusive is correct. Generally, options that do not agree grammatically with the first part of the item are incorrect. For instance, what answer could you rule out in the example in Figure 9.2?

Some students are easily confused by multiple-choice answers that sound alike. The best way to respond to a multiple-choice question is to read the first part of the item and then predict your own answer before reading the options. Choose the letter that corresponds to the option that best matches your prediction.

If you are totally confused by a question, place a check mark in the margin, leave it, and come back later, but always double-check that you are filling in the answer for the right question. Sometimes another question will provide a clue for a question you are unsure about. If you have absolutely no idea, look for an answer that at least contains some shred of information. If there is no penalty for guessing, fill in an answer for every question, even if it is just a guess. If there is a penalty for guessing, don't just choose an answer at random; leaving the answer blank might be a wiser choice.

IN CLASS: If you test your students in this course, expose them to all types of test items: essay, multiple-choice, true/false, and matching. Consider telling them that you will deliberately attempt to mislead them on the multiple-choice and true/false questions so that they will learn how to take such tests successfully in other classes.

IN CLASS: Provide a tip on taking multiple-choice tests: The first answer that comes to your mind is usually the correct one. Generally, students should try not to second-guess themselves.

IN CLASS: Ask the class how often they have crammed in a last review of their notes just before a test is to begin. Tell the class that last-minute cramming usually will not improve a test score. It is better to prepare early and try to relax before the test starts.

TABLE 9.1   Key Task Words

Analyze	Divide something into its parts in order to understand it better; show how the parts work together to produce the overall pattern.
Compare	Look at the characteristics or qualities of several things, and identify their similarities or differences. Don't just describe the traits; define how the things are alike and how they are different.
Contrast	Identify the differences between things.
Criticize/ Critique	Analyze and judge something. Criticism can be positive, negative, or both. A criticism should generally contain your own judgments (supported by evidence) and those of authorities who can support your point.
Define	Give the meaning of a word or expression. Giving an example sometimes helps to clarify a definition, but an example by itself is not a definition.
Describe	Give a general verbal sketch of something in narrative or other form.
Discuss	Examine or analyze something in a broad and detailed way. Discussion often includes identifying the important questions related to an issue and attempting to answer these questions. A good discussion explores all relevant evidence and information.
Evaluate	Discuss the strengths and weaknesses of something. Evaluation is similar to criticism, but the word *evaluate* stresses the idea of how well something meets a certain standard or fulfills some specific purpose.
Explain	Clarify something. Explanations generally focus on why or how something has come about.
Interpret	Explain the meaning of something. In science you might explain what an experiment shows and what conclusions can be drawn from it. In a literature course you might explain—or interpret—what a poem means beyond the literal meaning of the words.
Justify	Argue in support of some decision or conclusion by showing sufficient evidence or reasons in its favor. Try to support your argument with both logical and concrete examples.
Narrate	Relate a series of events in the order in which they occurred. Generally, you will also be asked to explain something about the events you are narrating.
Outline	Present a series of main points in an appropriate order. Some instructors want an outline with Roman numerals for main points followed by letters for supporting details. If you are in doubt, ask the instructor whether he or she wants a formal outline.
Prove	Give a convincing logical argument and evidence in support of some statement.
Review	Summarize and comment on the main parts of a problem or a series of statements. A review question usually also asks you to evaluate or criticize.
Summarize	Give information in brief form, omitting examples and details. A summary is short but covers all important points.
Trace	Narrate a course of events. Whenever possible, you should show connections from one event to the next.

IN CLASS: Divide the class into groups of four to five. Ask each group to prepare several potential essay questions from their notes, using the key task words you have assigned to them.

IN CLASS: Use overheads or a *PowerPoint* presentation to show some typical college essay questions. Incorporate key task words in your examples. Show how essay items generally require conceptual thinking rather than memorization of specifics, although both skills will be useful in writing the answers.

FIGURE 9.2

Example of a Multiple-Choice Question

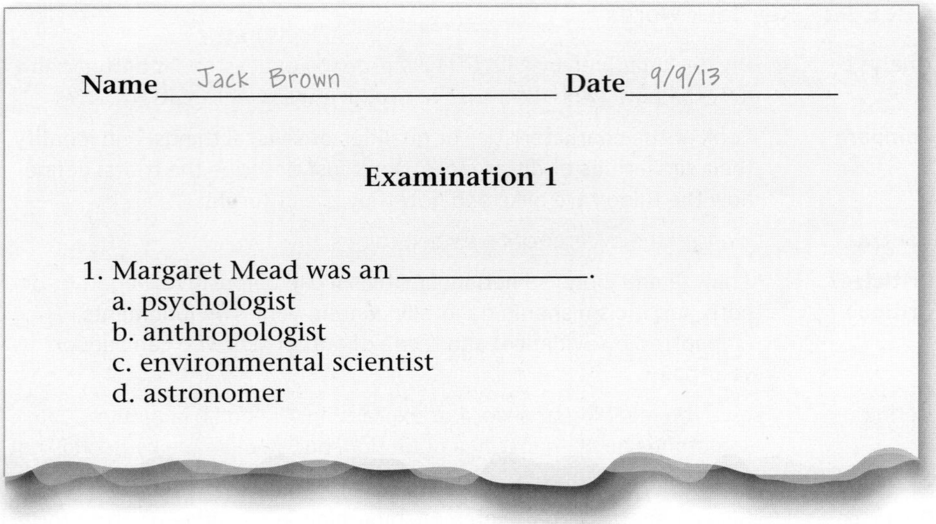

Name ___Jack Brown_____   Date ___9/9/13_____

Examination 1

1. Margaret Mead was an _____.
   a. psychologist
   b. anthropologist
   c. environmental scientist
   d. astronomer

FILL-IN-THE-BLANK QUESTIONS

In many ways preparing for fill-in-the-blank questions is similar to getting ready for multiple-choice items, but fill-in-the-blank questions can be harder because you do not have a choice of possible answers right in front of you. Not all fill-in-the-blank questions are constructed the same way. Some teachers will provide a series of blanks to give you a clue about the number of words in the answer, but if just one long blank is provided, you can't assume that the answer is just one word. If possible, ask the teacher whether the answer is supposed to be a single word per blank or can be a longer phrase.

TRUE/FALSE QUESTIONS

Remember that for a statement to be true, every detail of the sentence must be true. Questions containing words such as *always*, *never*, and *only* tend to be false, whereas less definite terms such as *often* and *frequently* suggest the statement might be true. Read through the entire exam to see whether information in one question will help you answer another. Do not begin to second-guess what you know or doubt your answers just because a sequence of questions appears to be all true or all false.

MATCHING QUESTIONS

The matching question is the hardest type of question to answer by guessing. In one column you will find the terms, and in the other you will find their descriptions. Before answering any question, review all of the terms and descriptions. Then match the terms you are sure of. As you do so, cross out both the term and its description, and use the process of elimination to assist you in answering the remaining items. To prepare for matching questions, try using flash cards and lists that you create from the recall column in your notes.

This exercise asks students to honestly evaluate whether they put themselves in a position to succeed when taking a test.

EXERCISE 9.2

How You PERFORM Matters

It's time for a self-check. What do you do to position yourself for success in a testing situation?

Look below at the tips suggested in Chapter 9, and make an honest evaluation as to whether you typically perform in this way. If not, why not? What would it take for you to make small changes in behavior that would ensure your success on an exam?

When taking a test, do you . . .	Yes or No?	If no, then why not?
Read the directions and survey the test before beginning?		
Write down any formulas, mnemonics, or other major ideas before beginning?		
Double-check to be sure that your answers are logical and make sense? For instance, you can't have a fraction of a person or an animal.		
Wear a watch or have a clock so that you can budget your time accurately?		
Answer the easy questions first?		
Make a brief plan or outline before you begin to answer an essay question?		
Read each question very carefully and make sure that you're responding to each part of it?		
Place a check mark beside a difficult question and come back, knowing that another question might provide a clue?		
Ask the instructor for clarification if a question seems confusing?		
Take the time to recheck your work for errors if you finish early?		

Types of Tests

In addition to using many formats, tests also encompass various difficulty levels, depending on the instructor's expectations. As you think about the tests in your current classes, do some require problem solving or lab work? What about open-book or take-home tests? Which type of test is usually harder for you—tests that demand accuracy or critical thinking? Why?

IN CLASS: Remind students that most testing errors occur when a student does not read or follow directions. This is particularly important in taking problem-solving tests. Ask students whether they have had any experiences with tests when they did not follow the directions. How does test anxiety relate to reading and following directions?

While you are in college, you will encounter many types of tests. Some tend to be used in particular disciplines; others can be used in any class you might take.

PROBLEM-SOLVING TESTS

In the physical and biological sciences, mathematics, engineering, statistics, and symbolic logic, some tests will require you to solve problems showing all steps. Even if you know a shortcut, it is important to document how you got from step A to step B. On other tests, all that will matter will be whether you have the correct solution to the problem, but doing all the steps will still help ensure that you get the right answer. For these tests, you must also be very careful that you have made no errors in your scientific notation. A misplaced sign, parenthesis, bracket, or exponent can make all the difference.

If you are allowed to use a calculator during the exam, it is important to check that your input is accurate. The calculator does what you tell it to, and if you miss a zero or a negative sign, the calculator will not give you the correct answer to the problem.

Be sure that you read all directions carefully. Are you required to reduce the answer to simplest terms? Are you supposed to graph the solution? Be careful when canceling terms, cross-multiplying, distributing terms, and combining fractions. Whenever possible, after you complete the problem, work it in reverse to check your solution, or plug your solution back into the equation and make sure it adds up. Also check to be sure that your solution makes sense. You can't have negative bushels of apples, for example, or a fraction of a person, or a correlation less than negative 1 or greater than 1. Write out each step clearly, with everything lined up as the instructor has indicated in class (lining up the equal signs with each other, for example).

Ace the Test

You have almost certainly taken machine-scored tests in high school. One of the simplest and most important steps you can take to do well on these tests is to make sure you align the questions with your answer sheet. But you must also read each question carefully so that you have the best chance of selecting the right answer.

MACHINE-SCORED TESTS

It is important that you carefully follow the directions for machine-scored tests. In addition to your name, be sure to provide all the necessary information on the answer sheet, such as the instructor's name, the number for the class section, or your student ID number. Each time you fill in an answer, make sure that the number on the answer sheet corresponds to the number of the item on the test. If you have questions that you want to come back to (if you are allowed to do so), mark them on the test rather than on the answer sheet.

Although scoring machines have become more sophisticated over time, stray marks on your answer sheet can still be misread and throw off the scoring. When a machine-scored test is returned to you, check your answer sheet against the scoring key, if one is provided, to make sure that you receive credit for all the questions you answered correctly.

COMPUTERIZED TESTS

Your comfort with taking computerized tests might depend on how computer literate you are in general for objective tests as well as your keyboarding skills for essay exams. If your instructor provides the opportunity for practice tests, be sure to take advantage of this chance to get a better sense of how the tests will be structured. There can be significant variations depending on the kind of test, the academic subject, and whether the test was constructed by the teacher, a textbook company, or by another source.

For multiple-choice and other objective forms of computerized tests, you might be allowed to scroll down and back through the entire test, but this is not always the case. Sometimes you are allowed to see only one question at a time, and after you complete that question, you might not be allowed to go back to it. In this situation you cannot skip questions that are hard and come back to them later, so be sure that you try to answer every question.

For computerized tests in math and other subjects that require you to solve each problem, record an answer and then move to the next problem. Be sure to check each answer before you submit it. Also, know in advance what materials you are allowed to have on hand, including a calculator and scratch paper for working the problems.

LABORATORY TESTS

In many science courses and in some other academic disciplines, you will be required to take lab tests during which you rotate from one lab station to the next and solve problems, identify parts of models or specimens, explain chemical reactions, and complete other tasks similar to those that you have been performing in lab. At some colleges and universities, lab tests are now administered at computer terminals via simulations. To prepare for lab tests, always attend lab; take good notes, including diagrams and other visual representations as necessary; and be sure to study your lab notebook carefully before the test. If possible, create your own diagrams or models, and then see whether you can label them without looking at your book.

You might also have lab tests in foreign language courses. These tests can include both oral and written components. Work with a partner or study group to prepare for oral exams. Ask each other questions that require using key vocabulary words. Try recording your answers to work on your pronunciation. You might also have computerized lab tests that require you to identify syllables or words and indicate the order and direction of the strokes required to create them, particularly in a foreign language that uses a different symbol system, such as Chinese. The best way to prepare for these tests is to learn the meanings and parts of the symbols and regularly practice writing them.

OPEN-BOOK AND OPEN-NOTE TESTS

If you never had open-book or open-note tests in high school, you might be tempted to study less thoroughly, thinking that you will have access to all the information you need during the test. This is a common misjudgment on the part of first-year students. Open-book and open-note tests are usually harder than other exams, not easier.

Most students don't really have time to spend looking things up during an open-book exam. The best way to prepare is to begin the same way you would study for a test in which you cannot refer to your notes or text. As you do so, develop a list of topics and the page numbers where they are covered in your text. You might want to use the same strategy in organizing your lecture notes. Number the pages in your notebook. Later, type a three-column grid (or use an *Excel* spreadsheet) with your list of topics in alphabetical order in the first column and corresponding pages from your textbook and notebook in the second and third columns so that you can refer to them quickly if necessary. Or you might want to stick colored tabs onto your textbook or notebook pages for different topics. But whatever you do, study as completely as you would for any other test, and do not be fooled into thinking that you don't need to know the material thoroughly.

During the test, monitor your time carefully. Don't waste time unnecessarily looking up information in your text or notes to double-check yourself if you are reasonably confident of your answers. Instead, wait until you have finished the test, and then, if you have extra time, go back and look up answers and make any necessary changes. But if you have really studied, you probably will not find this necessary.

Sometimes the only reason a teacher allows open books or open notes is for students to properly reference their sources when responding to essay or short-answer tests. Make sure to clarify whether you are expected to document your answers and provide a reference or Works Cited list.

TAKE-HOME TESTS

Like open-book and open-note tests, take-home tests are usually more difficult than in-class tests. Many take-home tests are essay tests, though some teachers will give take-home objective tests. Be sure to allow plenty of time to complete a take-home test. Read the directions and questions as soon as you receive the test to help you gauge how much time you will need. If the test is all essays, consider how much time you might allocate to writing several papers of the same length. Remember that your teacher will expect your essay answers to look more like assigned out-of-class papers than like the essays you would write during an in-class test.

Unfortunately, issues of academic honesty can arise for take-home tests. If you are accustomed to working with a study group or in a learning community for the course, check with the teacher in advance to determine the extent to which collaboration is allowed on the test. One thing that can be very confusing for students is to be encouraged to work together throughout the academic term and then to be told that there should be no communication outside of class about a take-home test.

TECH TIP FEAR NOT THE ONLINE TEST

1 ▸ THE PROBLEM

You don't know how to take an online test.

2 ▸ THE FIX

Learn to dodge rookie errors that can trip you up.

3 ▸ HOW TO DO IT

Here, our top ten strategies:

1. Don't wait until the last minute to study. Whether this online test is part of a self-paced online course or a face-to-face course, start a study group (either in person or online) as far in advance as possible.

2. Get organized. An open-book quiz can take longer than a normal test if you're not sure where to locate the information you need. Note: Having a solid grasp of the material going in is key; your notes and books should be for occasional reference only.

3. Resist the temptation to surf the Web for answers. The answer you pick might not be what your instructor is looking for. It's much better to check your notes to see what you were taught in class.

4. If your instructor doesn't forbid collaboration on tests, open up an instant message window with a fellow student. Take the test together and early.

5. Don't get distracted. When you're taking a cyber exam, it's easy to fall prey to real-life diversions like Facebook, iTunes, or a sudden urge to rearrange your closet. Whatever you do, take the test seriously. Go somewhere quiet where you can concentrate—not Starbucks. A quiet, remote spot in the library is ideal. You get bonus points if you wear noise-canceling headphones!

6. While taking the test, budget your time. Keep an eye on the clock so you'll be sure to finish the whole test.

7. Tackle easy questions first. Once you get those out of the way, you can revisit the harder ones.

8. Find out in advance if there's any penalty for wrong answers. If not, bluffing is allowed, so you want to be sure to fill in all the blanks.

9. Beware: There's always the risk of losing your Internet connection mid-test. To be on the safe side, type all of your answers and essays into a *Word* document. Then leave time at the end to cut and paste them into the test itself.

10. Finish early? Take a few minutes to obsessively check your answers and spelling. (That's good advice for traditional tests, too.)

PERSONAL BEST

What additional challenges might present themselves during an online test? List three challenges and some strategies for working through them:

1. _____

_____

_____

_____

2. _____

_____

_____

_____

3. _____

_____

_____

_____

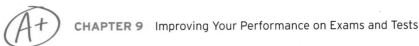

This exercise asks students to analyze their opinions about and strategies for taking different types of tests.

What You ANTICIPATE Matters

Everyone has strengths and weaknesses when it comes to taking tests. For example, some people love essay questions, while others think that essay questions are the most difficult.

What types of tests do you prefer and why? _____

What types of tests do you find difficult and why? _____

Types of Tests	Pros (the benefits)	Cons (the disadvantages)	Suggestions for Success (according to textbook)
Problem-Solving			
Machine-Scored			
Computerized			
Laboratory			
Open-Book/Open-Note			
Take-Home			

Overcoming Test Anxiety

Test anxiety is usually related to the subject, the test format, or expectations of significant others or maybe even yourself. Have you ever experienced test anxiety, even mildly? What happened? Describe your symptoms.

Test anxiety takes many different forms. Part of combating test anxiety is understanding its sources and identifying its symptoms. Whatever the source, be assured that test anxiety is common.

Test anxiety has many sources. It can be the result of the pressure that students put on themselves to succeed. Without any pressure, students would not be motivated to study; some stress connected with taking exams is natural and can enhance performance. However, when students put too much pressure on themselves or set unrealistic goals, the result is stress that is no longer motivating, only debilitating.

IN CLASS: Ask students to share their experiences with test anxiety. Discuss the underlying roots of test anxiety.

The expectations of parents, a spouse, friends, and other people who are close to you can also induce test anxiety. Sometimes, for example, students who are the first in their families to attend college bear the weight of generations before them who have not had this opportunity. The pressure can be overwhelming!

Finally, some test anxiety is caused by lack of preparation—by not keeping up with assigned reading, homework, and other academic commitments leading up to the test. Procrastination can begin a downward spiral because after you do poorly on the first test in a course, there is even more pressure to do well on subsequent tests to pull up your course grade. This situation becomes even more dire if the units of the course build on one another, as in math and foreign languages, or if the final exam is cumulative. While you are having to master the new material after the test, you are still trying to catch up on the old material as well.

Some test anxiety comes from a negative prior experience. Transcending the memory of negative past experiences can be a challenge. But remember that the past is not the present. Perhaps there are good reasons why you performed poorly in the past. You might not have prepared for the test, you might not have read the questions carefully, or you might not have studied with other students or sought prior assistance from your professor or a tutor. If you carefully follow the strategies in this chapter, you are very likely to do well on all your tests. Remember that a little anxiety is okay. But if you find that anxiety is getting in the way of your performance on tests and exams, be sure to seek help from your campus counseling center.

IN CLASS: Invite to class a student development counselor or other staff member who has experience helping students with test anxiety. Ask this person to share his or her expertise and provide practical ways to control or overcome test anxiety.

TYPES OF TEST ANXIETY

Students who experience test anxiety under some circumstances don't necessarily feel it in all testing situations. For example, you might do fine on classroom tests but feel anxious during standardized examinations such as the SAT and ACT. One reason standardized tests are so anxiety provoking is the notion that they determine your future. Believing that the stakes are so high can create unbearable pressure. One way of dealing with this type of test anxiety is to ask yourself: What is the worst that can happen? Remember that no matter what the result, it is not the end of the world. How you do on standardized tests might limit some of your options, but going into these tests with a negative attitude will certainly not improve your chances. Attending preparation workshops and taking practice exams not only can better prepare you for standardized tests but also can assist you in overcoming your anxiety. And remember that many standardized tests can be taken again at a later time, giving you the opportunity to prepare better and pull up your score.

Some students are anxious only about some types of classroom tests. Practice always helps in overcoming test anxiety; if you fear essay exams, try predicting exam questions and writing sample essays as a means of reducing your anxiety.

Some students have difficulty taking tests at a computer terminal. Some of this anxiety might be related to lack of computer experience. On the other hand, not all computerized tests are user-friendly. You might be allowed to see only one item at a time. Often, you do not have the option of going back and checking over all your answers before submitting them. In preparation for computerized tests, ask the instructor questions about how the test will be structured. Also, make sure you take any opportunities to take practice tests at a learning center or lab.

Test anxiety can often be subject-specific. For example, some students have math test anxiety. It is important to distinguish between anxiety that arises from the subject matter itself and more generalized test anxiety. Perhaps subject-specific test anxiety relates to old beliefs about yourself, such as "I'm no good at math" or "I can't write well." Now is the time to try some positive self-talk and realize that by preparing well, you can be successful even in your hardest courses. If the problem persists, talk to someone in your campus counseling center to develop strategies to overcome irrational fears that can prevent you from doing your best.

SYMPTOMS OF TEST ANXIETY

Test anxiety can manifest itself in many ways. Some students feel it on the very first day of class. Other students begin showing symptoms of test anxiety when it's time to start studying for a test. Others do not get nervous until the night before the test or the morning of an exam day. And some students experience symptoms only while they are actually taking a test.

Symptoms of test anxiety can include butterflies in the stomach, queasiness or nausea, severe headaches, a faster heartbeat, hyperventilating, shaking, sweating, or muscle cramps. During the exam itself, students who are overcome with test anxiety can experience the sensation of "going blank," that is, being unable to remember what they actually know. At this point, students can undermine both their emotional and academic preparation for the test and convince themselves that they cannot succeed.

Test anxiety can impede the success of any college student, no matter how intelligent, motivated, and prepared. That is why it is critical to seek help from your college's or university's counseling service or another professional if you think that you have significant test anxiety. If you are not sure where to go for help, ask your adviser, but seek help promptly! If your symptoms are so severe that you become physically ill (with migraine headaches, hyperventilating, or vomiting), you should also consult your physician or campus health service.

STRATEGIES FOR COMBATING TEST ANXIETY

In addition to studying, eating right, and getting plenty of sleep, there are a number of simple strategies you can use to overcome the physical and emotional impact of test anxiety. First, any time that you begin to feel nervous or upset, take a long, deep breath and slowly exhale to restore your breathing to a normal level. This is the quickest and easiest relaxation device, and no one even needs to know that you are doing it.

Before you go into the test room, especially before a multiple-hour final exam or before sitting through several exams on the same day, it can help to stretch your muscles just as you would when preparing to exercise. Stretch your calf and hamstring muscles, and roll your ankles. Stretch your arms, and

IN CLASS: Share your personal experiences with test anxiety. What memories do you have, particularly with high-stakes tests such as the SAT or ACT?

OUTSIDE CLASS: Assign students to do an Internet search on test anxiety. Claude Steele, a professor at Stanford University, conducted interesting research on student performance on high-stakes exams. His research deals with the theory of stereotype threat, which is the idea that individuals sometimes underperform in a manner consistent with the way they are stereotyped. A team of students who are interested can research Steele's work.

IN CLASS: Have the group make a class presentation on what they learned from their Internet research on test anxiety.

IN CLASS: Ask students how breathing, meditation, and exercise can reduce test anxiety. If you feel comfortable doing so, lead the class in a short breathing and relaxation exercise, or invite a physical education or health instructor to come to class. Students can practice outside class. You might already have students in class who meditate regularly. If so, ask them whether they would be willing to show their classmates how it's done.

roll your shoulders. Tilt your head to the right, front, and left to stretch your neck muscles.

When you sit down to take the test, pay attention to the way you are sitting. Sit with your shoulders back and relaxed, rather than shrugged forward, and put your feet flat on the floor. Smooth out your facial muscles rather than wrinkling your forehead or frowning. Resist the temptation to clutch your pencil or pen tightly in your fist; take a break and stretch your fingers now and then.

Anxiety-reducing techniques that might be available through your campus counseling center include systematic desensitization, progressive muscle relaxation, and visualization. One of the most popular techniques is creating your own peaceful scene and mentally taking yourself there when you need to relax. Try to use all five senses to re-create your peaceful scene in your mind: What would you see, hear, feel, taste, or smell?

These strategies can assist you in relaxing physically, but meanwhile, you must also pay attention to the mental messages that you are sending yourself. Focus on the positive! If you are telling yourself that you are not smart enough, that you did not study the right material, or that you are going to fail, you need to turn those messages around with a technique called **cognitive restructuring**. We all talk to ourselves, so make sure that your messages are encouraging rather than stress provoking. When you are studying, practice sending yourself positive messages: I really know this stuff. I am going to ace this test!

Similarly, do not allow others, including classmates, your spouse, parents, or friends, to undermine your confidence. If you belong to a study group, discuss the need to stay positive. Sometimes, getting to the test room early will expose you to other students who are asking questions or making comments that are only going to make you nervous. Get to the building early, but wait until just a few minutes before the exam begins to approach the classroom itself. If at any point during a test you begin to feel like you cannot think clearly, or you have trouble remembering or you come to a question you cannot answer, stop for a brief moment, and take another long, deep breath and slowly exhale. Then remind yourself of the positive self-messages you have been practicing.

GETTING THE TEST BACK

Students react differently when they receive their test grades and papers. For some students the thought of seeing the actual graded test produces high levels of anxiety. But unless you look at the instructor's comments and your answers (the correct and incorrect ones), you will have no way to evaluate your own knowledge and test-taking strengths. You might also find that the instructor made an error in the grade that might have cost you a point or two. Be sure to let the instructor know if you find an error.

It is important that you review your graded test. You might find that your mistakes were caused by failing to follow directions, being careless with words or numbers, or overanalyzing a multiple-choice question. If you have any questions about your grade, be sure to talk to the instructor. You might be able to negotiate a few points in your favor, but in any case, you will let your instructor know that you are concerned and want to learn how to do better on graded tests and examinations.

OUTSIDE CLASS: Encourage your students to attend a workshop offered by the campus counseling or health center on anxiety-reducing techniques.

IN CLASS: Have students report back and share tips they plan to use.

■ RETENTION STRATEGY: While extreme test anxiety is rare, it does happen and can cause some students to leave college. Encourage any student who suffers from a high level of anxiety when being tested in certain subjects to see you for a referral to a counselor. Anxiety management is a skill that can be both taught and learned in college.

cognitive restructuring
A technique of applying positive thinking and giving oneself encouraging messages rather than self-defeating negative ones.

This exercise gives students a chance to evaluate their own test anxiety.

What You EXPERIENCE Matters

TEST ANXIETY QUIZ

Do these statements apply to you? Check the box for the statement if it applies the day before an exam, hours before, or during the exam itself!

Mental

☐ Do you have trouble concentrating and find that your mind easily wanders while studying the material or during the test itself?
☐ During the test, does every noise bother you—sounds from outside the classroom or sounds from other people?
☐ Do you often "blank out" when you see the test?
☐ Do you remember answers to questions only after the test is over?

Physical

☐ Do you get the feeling of butterflies, nausea, or pain in your stomach?
☐ Do you develop headaches before or during the test?
☐ Do you feel like your heart is racing, that you have trouble breathing, or that your pulse is erratic?
☐ Do you have difficulty sitting still, are you antsy, or are you unable to get comfortable?

Emotional

☐ Are you more sensitive and more likely to lose patience with a roommate or friend before the test?
☐ Do you feel pressured to succeed from either yourself or from your family or friends?
☐ Do you toss and turn the night before the test?
☐ Do you fear the worst—that you will fail the class or flunk out of college because of the test?

Personal Habits

☐ Do you often stay up late studying the night before a test?
☐ Do you have a personal history of failure for taking certain types of tests (essay, math)?
☐ Do you drink too much caffeine or forget to eat breakfast before a test?
☐ Do you avoid studying until right before a test, choosing to do other activities that are less important because you don't want to "think about it"?

See below for your Test Anxiety Reflection Score.

TEST ANXIETY REFLECTION SCORE

You may experience test anxiety if you checked . . .

13–16 Severe: You may want to see if your campus counseling center offers individual sessions to provide strategies to combat test anxiety. Your student fees have already paid for this service, so take advantage of it now before it is too late. Learn to be *proactive*!

9–12 Moderate: You may want to see if your campus will be offering a seminar on anxiety-prevention strategies. Such seminars are usually offered around midterm or just before final exams. Take the opportunity to do something valuable for yourself!

5–8 Mild: Be aware of what situations might cause anxiety and disrupt your academic success—things like certain types of classes or particular test formats. If you discover a weakness, address it now before it is too late.

1–4 Slight: Almost everyone has some form of anxiety before tests, and it actually can be beneficial! In small doses, stress can improve your performance, so consider yourself lucky.

Academic Honesty and Misconduct

Integrity is a strongly held value. Taking someone else's ideas, work, or material is not only forbidden, it has dire consequences. Has someone ever used your ideas and presented them as his or her own? How can you prevent this from happening in the future?

Imagine what our world would be like if researchers reported fraudulent results that were then used to develop new machines or medical treatments or to build bridges, airplanes, or subway systems. Integrity is a cornerstone of higher education, and activities that compromise that integrity damage everyone: your country, your community, your college or university, your classmates, and yourself.

CHEATING

Institutions vary widely in how they define broad terms such as *lying* or *cheating*. One university defines cheating as "intentionally using or attempting to use unauthorized materials, information, notes, study aids, or other devices . . . [including] unauthorized communication of information during an academic exercise." This would apply to looking over a classmate's shoulder for an answer, using a calculator when it is not authorized, obtaining or discussing an exam (or individual questions from an exam) without permission, copying someone else's lab notes, purchasing term papers over the Internet, watching the video instead of reading the book, and duplicating computer files.

IN CLASS: Academic honesty is a serious issue. Review the types of misconduct, and discuss the impact of the Internet on academic honesty. Bring in your campus's academic honesty policy for the class to discuss.

PLAGIARISM

Plagiarism, or taking another person's ideas or work and presenting them as your own, is especially intolerable in academic culture. Just as taking someone else's property constitutes physical theft, taking credit for someone else's ideas constitutes intellectual theft.

plagiarism The act of taking another person's ideas or work and presenting it as your own. This gross academic misconduct can result in suspension or expulsion, and even the revocation of the violator's college degree.

Stop! Thief!

When students are seated close to each other while taking a test, they may be tempted to let their eyes wander to someone else's answers. But don't let this happen to you. Cheating is equivalent to stealing. Also, don't make it easy for other students to copy your work. Reduce that temptation by covering your answer sheet.

On most tests, you don't have to credit specific sources. (But some instructors do require this. When in doubt, ask!) In written reports and papers, however, you must give credit any time you use (a) another person's actual words, (b) another person's ideas or theories—even if you don't quote them directly, or (c) any other information that is not considered common knowledge.

Many schools prohibit certain activities in addition to lying, cheating, unauthorized assistance, and plagiarism. Some examples of prohibited behaviors are intentionally inventing information or results, earning credit more than once for the same piece of academic work without permission, giving your work or exam answers to another student to copy during the actual exam or before that exam is given to another section, and bribing in exchange for any kind of academic advantage. Most schools also outlaw helping or attempting to help another student commit a dishonest act.

CONSEQUENCES OF CHEATING AND PLAGIARISM

Although you might see some students who seem to be getting away with cheating or plagiarizing, the consequences of such behaviors can be severe and life-changing. Recent cases of cheating on examinations and plagiarizing major papers have caused some college students to be suspended or expelled and even to have their college degrees revoked. Writers and journalists whose plagiarism has been discovered, such as Jayson Blair, formerly of the *New York Times*, and Stephen Glass, formerly of the *New Republic*, have lost their jobs and their journalistic careers. Even college presidents have occasionally been found guilty of "borrowing" the words of others and using them as their own in speeches and written documents. Such discoveries result not only in embarrassment and shame, but also in lawsuits and criminal actions.

> ### DID YOU KNOW?
>
> Despite serious consequences, 42% of students witness academic dishonesty or cheating in their first year.

Because plagiarism can be a problem on college campuses, faculty members are now using electronic systems such as **www.turnitin.com** to identify passages in student papers that have been plagiarized. Many instructors routinely check their students' papers to make sure that the writing is original. So even though the temptation to cheat or plagiarize might be strong, the chance of possibly getting a better grade isn't worth misrepresenting yourself or your knowledge and suffering the potential consequences.

OUTSIDE CLASS: Ask the class to submit a written summary of their thoughts on this section, Reducing the Likelihood of Academic Dishonesty. What experiences have students had with these issues?

REDUCING THE LIKELIHOOD OF ACADEMIC DISHONESTY

To avoid becoming intentionally or unintentionally involved in academic misconduct, consider the reasons why it could happen:

- **Ignorance.** In a survey at the University of South Carolina, 20 percent of students incorrectly thought that buying a term paper wasn't cheating. Forty percent thought using a test file (a collection of actual tests from previous terms) was fair behavior. Sixty percent thought it was acceptable to get answers from someone who had taken the exam earlier in the same or in a prior term. What do you think?

GUIDELINES FOR ACADEMIC HONESTY

1. Know the rules. Learn the academic code for your college by going to its Web site. Also learn about any department guidelines on cheating or plagiarism. Study course syllabi. If a teacher does not clarify standards and expectations, ask exactly what they are.

2. Set clear boundaries. Refuse when others ask you to help them cheat. This might be hard to do, but you must say no. In test settings, keep your answers covered and your eyes down, and put all extraneous materials away, including cell phones. Because cell phones enable text messaging, instructors are rightfully suspicious when they see students looking at their cell phones during an exam.

3. Improve time management. Be well prepared for all quizzes, exams, projects, and papers. This might mean unlearning habits such as procrastination (see Chapter 2, Managing Your Time).

4. Seek help. Find out where you can obtain assistance with study skills, time management, and test taking. If your methods are in good shape but the content of the course is too difficult, consult your instructor, join a study group, or visit your campus learning center or tutorial service.

5. Withdraw from the course. Your institution has a policy about dropping courses and a deadline to drop without penalty. You might decide to drop only the course that's giving you

trouble. Some students choose to withdraw from all classes and take time off before returning to school if they find themselves in over their heads or if a long illness, a family crisis, or some other unexpected occurrence has caused them to fall behind. Before withdrawing, you should ask about campus policies as well as ramifications in terms of federal financial aid and other scholarship programs. See your adviser or counselor.

6. Reexamine goals. Stick to your own realistic goals instead of giving in to pressure from family members or friends to achieve impossibly high standards. You might also feel pressure to enter a particular career or profession that is of little or no interest to you. If that happens, sit down with counseling or career services professionals or your academic adviser and explore alternatives.

- **Cultural and campus differences.** In other countries and on some U.S. campuses, students are encouraged to review past exams as practice exercises. Some student government associations maintain test files for use by students. Some campuses permit sharing answers and information for homework and other assignments with friends. Make sure you know the policy on your specific campus.

- **Different policies among instructors.** Because there is no universal code that dictates such behaviors, ask your instructors for clarification. When a student is caught violating the academic code of a particular school or instructor, pleading ignorance of the rules is a weak defense.

- **A belief that grades are all that matter.** This might reflect our society's competitive atmosphere. It also might be the result of pressure from parents, peers, or teachers. In truth, grades are nothing if one has cheated to earn them. Even if your grades help you get a job, it is what you have actually learned that will help you keep the job and be promoted. If you haven't learned what you need to know, you won't be ready to work in your chosen field.

- **Lack of preparation or inability to manage time and activities.** If you are tempted to cheat because you are unprepared, ask an instructor to extend a deadline so that a project can be done well.

The box above outlines some steps you can take to reduce the likelihood of problems.

This exercise provides scenarios for individual reflection and also for group discussion about academic honesty.

EXERCISE 9.5

Your INTEGRITY Matters

CASE STUDIES

- Marjorie had been really sick with the flu for months. She had missed a lot of class and had to do some catching up at the end of the term. She borrowed her study partner's notes for the last few weeks of class just so she could pass the final exam. Was this dishonest? Why or why not?

- Keith had a huge paper to write on a subject that was full of technical words and theory. For the most part, he had to use ideas from other authors just to understand the material. He gave credit if he used direct quotes, but if he paraphrased the ideas in his own words, Keith figured that they were his own. Was this plagiarism? Why or why not?

- Samuel was taking a class from an instructor who was notoriously hard. He needed all the help he could get to pass the class. When Samuel found out that his fraternity brother had taken the class last year, he borrowed his old tests. After taking the first test, he was surprised to see that it was almost identical to the test he had borrowed. Samuel didn't mention this to the instructor or anyone else in class. Was this dishonest or not?

- This was Karen's last semester in college. She had fulfilled all of her requirements and completed all her classes and internships, except one. She had found the "perfect" full-time job and didn't have time to actually attend the internship designed by her major adviser. Instead, she created a fictional internship, which she wrote about in her journal using actual examples of situations from her real job. The school's judicial board decided to make her retake the entire term and not let her graduate. Was this a fair consequence?

CHECKLIST FOR SUCCESS

DOING YOUR BEST ON EXAMS AND TESTS

☐ **Learn as much as you can about the type of test you will be taking.** You will study differently for an essay exam than you will for a multiple-choice test.

☐ **Start preparing for test taking the very first day of the course.** Classes early in the term are the most important ones NOT to miss.

☐ **Prepare yourself physically through proper sleep, diet, and exercise.** These behaviors are as important as studying the actual material. You may not control what

is on the exams, but you can control your physical readiness to do your best.

☐ **Prepare yourself emotionally by being relaxed and confident.** Confidence comes from the knowledge that you have prepared well and know the material.

☐ **If you experience severe test anxiety, seek help from your counseling center.** There are professionals who understand how to help you deal with this problem.

☐ **Develop a systematic plan of preparation for every test.** Be specific about when you are going to study, how long, and what material you will cover.

☐ **Join a study group and participate conscientiously and regularly.** Students who join study groups perform better on tests. It's a habit you should practice.

☐ **Never cheat or plagiarize.** Experience the satisfaction that comes from learning and doing your own work and from knowing you don't have to worry about getting caught or using material that may be incorrect.

☐ **Make sure you understand what constitutes cheating and plagiarism on your campus so you don't inadvertently do either.** If you are not clear, ask your instructors or the professionals in your campus learning center or writing center.

APPLY IT! What Works for YOU Matters

Think about your current academic situation, and apply some of the suggestions and strategies introduced in this chapter. Select strategies that you think will work best for you, and then write them down in the "Your Response" column. What are YOU planning to do for YOUR college experience?

QUESTIONS	SAMPLE STUDENT ANSWERS	YOUR RESPONSE
Getting Prepared for Tests and Exams By now you have probably received tests back from a few instructors. Most college students expect to get the same grades in college as they did in high school. Unfortunately, this is not always the case. How can you set yourself up for a greater chance of success as you prepare for an upcoming exam—especially in a difficult course?	**Name: Bernardo Castillo** High school was easy for me. I made straight A's, and a few B's. So when I took college Algebra and made a C on my first test, I was shocked. Now I realize that I could have done a better job preparing. I could have attended study sessions and gone to the tutoring lab. I also could have asked the professor about the test format, because I didn't know it was going to be on the computer—completely unexpected.	
Taking Tests and Exams Tests come in a variety of formats that require different methods of study. What types of tests do you prefer? What tests give you the most trouble? What new method of review would you consider trying?	I prefer objective tests like multiple-choice. I am a good guesser. But the computer test for math was hard because I couldn't go back and change an answer. I also hadn't used the test's computer program before.	
Types of Tests In addition to using many formats, tests also encompass various difficulty levels, depending on the instructor's expectations. As you think about the tests in your current classes, do some require problem solving or lab work? What about open-book or take-home tests? Which type of test is usually harder for you—tests that demand accuracy or critical thinking? Why?	My math instructor is a perfectionist. Every step has to be shown, every parenthesis is important. I guess that makes sense, but I am a big picture kind of person. Details really frustrate me. I prefer essay tests, because I can show all of my knowledge and embellish a little here and there. Most of the time I can at least get part credit. I will need to take my time and go over my math test more carefully before I turn it in next time.	
Overcoming Test Anxiety Test anxiety is usually related to the subject, the test format, or expectations of significant others or maybe even yourself. Have you ever experienced test anxiety, even mildly? What happened? Describe your symptoms.	Math tests make me nervous. I get a stomach-ache before I go in the room, and sometimes I forget to breathe during the test. I just learned some relaxation strategies to try out for my next math test. Also, the more I practice taking math tests, the less nervous I will be.	
Academic Honesty and Misconduct Integrity is a strongly held value. Taking someone else's ideas, work, or material is not only forbidden, it has dire consequences. Has someone ever used your ideas and presented them as his or her own? How can you prevent this from happening in the future?	It really bothers me when I see someone peeking over my shoulder to look at my answers. First of all, how do they know I am right? Honestly, I can't believe they would want my math answers! But more than that, I worked really hard, why don't they? I mean it takes just as much effort to cheat as it does just to study, so why not just learn it the right way the first time?	

211

BUILD YOUR EXPERIENCE

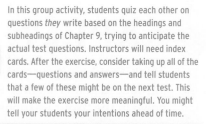

In this group activity, students quiz each other on questions *they* write based on the headings and subheadings of Chapter 9, trying to anticipate the actual test questions. Instructors will need index cards. After the exercise, consider taking up all of the cards—questions and answers—and tell students that a few of these might be on the next test. This will make the exercise more meaningful. You might tell your students your intentions ahead of time.

1 COLLABORATIVE ACTIVITY

One of the best ways to predict test questions is to pay attention to headings and subheadings in the textbook. In small groups, make educated guesses about what questions might be on the next test. Then take an index card and create a set of five potential test questions: multiple-choice and true/false. On a second card, write the answers to these five questions.

When groups are finished creating questions, they should switch the question cards with another group and see if they can answer their questions, and vice versa. Use your textbook if you must to finalize your decisions. When you think your group has the correct answers, ask for the answer card to confirm. How did you do? Did your partner group manage to answer all of your group's questions?

2 BUILDING YOUR PORTFOLIO

A High Price to Pay Academic integrity is a supreme value on college and university campuses. Faculty members, staff, and students are held to a strict code of academic integrity, and the consequences of breaking that code can be severe and life-changing. Create a *Word* document to record your responses to the following activity.

1. Imagine that your college or university has hired you to conduct a monthlong academic integrity awareness campaign so that students will learn about and take seriously your campus's guidelines for academic integrity. To prepare for your "new job":

   a. Visit your institution's Web site and use the search feature to find the academic integrity code or policy. Take the time to read through the code, violations, and sanctions.

   b. Visit the judicial affairs office on your campus to learn more about the way your institution deals with violations of academic integrity policies.

   c. Research online resources from other campuses, such as information from the Center for Academic Integrity, hosted by Clemson University (**http://www.academicintegrity.org/**).

   d. Check out several other college and university academic integrity policies and/or honor codes. How do they compare to your institution's code or policy?

2. Outline your monthlong awareness campaign. Here are a few ideas to get you started:

   - Plan a new theme every week. Don't forget Internet-related violations.
   - Develop eye-catching posters to display around campus. (Check out the posters designed by students at Elizabethtown College in Pennsylvania, found at **http://www.rubberpaw .com/integrity**.)
   - Consider guest speakers, debates, skits, or other presentations.
   - Come up with catchy slogans or phrases.
   - Send students a postcard highlighting your institution's policies or honor code.
   - Consider the most effective ways to communicate your message to different groups on campus.

3. Save your work in your portfolio.

As you were reading the tips for improving your performance on exams and tests, were you surprised to see different tips for different subjects, such as math and science, and for different kinds of tests, such as multiple-choice and essay? What did you find to be the most useful information in this chapter? What material was unclear to you?

_____

_____

_____

_____

_____

_____

_____

_____

_____

_____

_____

_____

_____

_____

_____

No matter how well prepared you are in your teaching, what a student hears and understands might not always be what you think you have said. The one-minute paper is a quick and easy assessment tool that will help alert you when students don't understand what was said or discussed in class. The one-minute paper will also give timid students an opportunity to ask questions and seek clarification. Ideally, you should ask for such a paper several minutes before the end of a class. The paper will also help you begin your next class by clarifying points your students seem to be unsure of.

For more on this topic watch
French Fries Are Not Vegetables and Other College Lessons

WHERE TO GO FOR HELP . . .

ON CAMPUS

> **Learning Assistance Support Center** Almost every campus has one of these, and studying for tests is one of its specialties. The best students, good students who want to be the best students, and students with academic difficulties use learning centers and tutoring services. These services are offered by both full-time professionals and highly skilled student tutors and usually are free.

> **Counseling Services** College and university counseling centers offer a wide array of services, often including workshops and individual or group counseling for test anxiety. Sometimes these services are also offered by the campus health center.

> **Fellow College Students** Often the best help we can get is the closest to us. Keep an eye out in your classes, residence hall, and extracurricular activities for the best students, those who appear to be the most serious, purposeful, and directed. Find a tutor. Join a study group. Students who do these things are much more likely to be successful.

ONLINE

> Florida Atlantic University's Center for Learning and Student Success (CLASS) offers a list of tips to help you prepare for exams: **www.fau.edu/CLASS /Success/keys_to_success.php.**

> Learning Centre of the University of New South Wales in Sydney, Australia: **http://www.lc.unsw .edu.au/onlib/exam.html.** Includes the popular SQ3R method.

MY INSTITUTION'S RESOURCES

_____

_____

_____

_____

_____

_____

_____

_____

CHAPTER 10

Writing and Speaking Effectively

Writing and speaking are the two basic forms of communication. The ability to write well and speak well makes a tremendous difference in how the rest of the world perceives you and how well you will be able to communicate throughout your life. But you will find that you often need to communicate differently depending on who is reading or listening to your words. Each time you speak or write, you are addressing an audience. The audience might be one person—a friend, family member, professor, or a potential employer—or your audience might be a group, such as your classmates in college. Some audiences might be unknown to you. For instance, if you're writing a book or an article for publication, a blog entry, or something on your Facebook page, you never know who might read your words.

To communicate effectively, it's important to think about your audience, what they will understand and expect, and how they will react to what you are saying or writing. It's generally okay to use informal language with your friends, family, and other college students, for example, but your instructors and potential employers will expect more formal writing and speaking.

Experts suggest that there's no single, universally accepted standard for how to speak or write American English. Even so, school systems, professional communicators, and businesses all have standards, and, not surprisingly, the rules do not vary dramatically from place to place. If they did, we would have a hard time understanding one another. Our purpose in this chapter is not to teach you grammar and punctuation (we'll save that for your English classes), but to get you to think of writing and speaking as processes (how you get there) as well as products (the final paper or script) and to help you overcome those writer's and speaker's blocks we all encounter from time to time.

IN CLASS: Have students freewrite anonymously for 10 minutes in response to the following questions: What is keeping me from being a better writer? What are the major problems I have when I want to begin writing? Collect the papers, read some aloud, and ask students to identify common themes and problems.

OUTSIDE CLASS: Ask students to look in the *Wall Street Journal* or *New York Times* to find descriptions of professional jobs in which they might be interested after they graduate. Have them bring the descriptions to class.

IN CLASS: Ask why writing is such an important skill in all their job choices (ability to write letters, reports, proposals, etc.). Stress that the ability to write well is a major criterion for almost any job.

IN CLASS: Ask students to discuss how writing and speaking are both processes and products. Consider brainstorming on the board, first listing how writing and speaking are processes and then creating a second list of how they are products. Discuss the topic further with your students.

IN CLASS: Have students share their thoughts on writing and speaking blocks. Have any students had bad experiences with blocks? Were they able to turn their experiences into something positive? If so, how?

You might wonder: Why can't more people express themselves effectively? The answers vary, but all come back to the same theme: Most people do not think of writing and speaking as processes to be mastered step-by-step. Instead, they view writing and speaking as products; you knock them out and you're done. Nothing could be further from the truth.

Whatever career you choose, you will be expected to think, create, communicate, manage, and lead. According to Plain Language.gov, most of the nation's largest employers say that employees must have good communication skills to get ahead. This means you will have to be able to write and speak well. You will have to write reports about your work and the performance of others, e-mails to describe problems and propose solutions, and position papers to explain and justify to your superiors why the organization must make certain changes.

As you lead and manage others, you also will need strong speaking skills in order to explain, report, motivate, direct, encourage, and inspire. You might have to give presentations in meetings to your superiors and their subordinates and then follow up with a written report or e-mail. So as you prepare yourself for a career, you need to start thinking of yourself as a person who is both a good thinker and an outstanding communicator.

WRITING

William Zinsser, author of several books on writing, claims, "The act of writing gives the teacher a window into the mind of the student."[1] In other words, your writing provides tangible evidence of how well you think and how well you understand concepts related to the courses you are taking. Your writing might also reveal a good sense of humor, a compassion for the less fortunate, a respect for family, and many other things. Zinsser reminds us that writing is not merely something that writers do; it is a basic skill for getting through life. He claims that far too many Americans cannot perform useful work because they never learned to express themselves.

Using Freewriting to Discover What You Want to Say

When faced with writing a paper, have you ever felt like you just can't seem to get started? Have you ever tried freewriting?

Writing expert Peter Elbow asserts that it's impossible to write effectively if you simultaneously try to organize, check grammar and spelling, and offer intelligent thoughts to your readers.[2] He argues that it can't all be done at once,

---

[1]William Zinsser, *On Writing Well* (New York: Harper, 2001).
[2]Peter Elbow, *Writing without Teachers* (New York: Oxford University Press, 1973).

◤ ■ ASSESSING YOUR STRENGTHS ■

Writing and speaking are essential skills for college and for life. Success in your career will depend on your ability to communicate your ideas clearly to others. Now that you have read the first section of this chapter, list specific examples of your strengths as a writer or speaker.

_____

_____

_____

_____

◤ ■ SETTING GOALS ■

What are *your* most important objectives in learning the material in this chapter? Do you need to improve your abilities as a writer or speaker? List three goals in this area (e.g., I will visit the writing center before submitting my next paper so that I can get some feedback on my writing).

1. _____

_____

2. _____

_____

3. _____

_____

■ RETENTION STRATEGY: Students who are focused on a career after college are more likely to be retained, and virtually all careers require good skills in writing. Help your students see the importance of writing to their future careers.

mainly because you use the right—or creative—side of your brain to create thoughts, whereas you use the left—or logical—side for grammar, spelling, organization, and so forth.

Elbow argues that we can free up our writing and bring more energy and voice into it by writing more like the way we speak and trying to avoid the heavy overlay of editing in our initial efforts to write. This preliminary step in the writing process is called "freewriting." By freewriting, Elbow simply means writing that is temporarily unencumbered by mechanical processes, such as punctuation, grammar, spelling, and context. Freewriting is also a way to break the habit of trying to write and edit at the same time.

The freewriting process can be difficult at first because it goes against the grain of how we are accustomed to writing. We normally edit as we write, pausing to collect our thoughts, to recollect the correct spelling of a word, to cross out a sentence that does not belong, to reject a paragraph that doesn't fit with the argument that we are making, or to mentally outline a structure of the argument that we are trying to make. Once you get the hang of it, though, it can become second nature.

IN CLASS: Practice freewriting in class. Have fun with this; tell students they can freewrite on any humorous topic, picture, or sound. Ask students why focus is important (as in the Robert Pirsig example on the next page).

NARROWING YOUR TOPIC

In *Zen and the Art of Motorcycle Maintenance*,[3] Robert Pirsig tells a story about a first-year English class he had taught. Each week he assigned students a 500-word essay to write. One week, a student failed to submit her paper about the town where the college was located, explaining that she had "thought and thought, but couldn't think of anything to write about." Pirsig gave her an additional weekend to complete the assignment. As he said this, an idea flashed through his mind. "I want you to write a 500-word paper just about Main Street, not the whole town," he said. She gasped and stared at him angrily. How was she to narrow her thinking to just one street when she couldn't think of a thing to write about the entire town? On Monday she arrived in tears. "I'll never learn to write," she said. Pirsig's answer: "Write a paper about one building on Main Street. The opera house. And start with the first brick on the lower left side. I want it next class."

The student's eyes opened wide. She walked into the next class with a 5,000-word paper on the opera house. In writing this paper, she had been freewriting but hadn't realized it. "I don't know what happened," she exclaimed. "I sat across the street and wrote about the first brick, then the second, and all of a sudden I couldn't stop." What had Pirsig done for this person? He had helped her find a focus and a place to begin. Getting started is what blocks most students from approaching writing properly. Faced with an ultimatum, the student probably began to see the beauty of the opera house for the first time and had gone on to describe it, to find out more about it in the library, to ask others about it, and to comment on its setting among the other buildings on the block.

Very few writers—even professionally published ones—say what they want to say on their first try. And the sad fact is that really good writers are in the minority. But through practice, an understanding of the writing process, and dedication, more people can improve their writing skills. And good writers can make good money.

EXPLORATORY WRITING

Another way to think about writing is to distinguish between exploratory writing and explanatory writing. Those terms practically define themselves, but here are some clearer definitions: **Exploratory writing**, like freewriting, helps you discover what you want to say; **explanatory writing** then allows you to transmit those ideas to others. Explanatory writing is "published," meaning you have chosen to allow others to read it (your teacher, your friends, other students, or the public at large), but it is important that most or all of your exploratory writing be private, to be read only by you as a series of steps toward your published work. Keeping your early drafts private frees you to say what you mean and mean what you say. Later, you will come back and make adjustments, and each revision will strengthen your message.

Some writers say they gather their best thoughts through exploratory writing: by researching their topic, writing down ideas from their research,

exploratory writing
Writing that helps you first discover what you want to say. It is private and is used only as a series of steps toward a published work.

explanatory writing
Writing that is "published," meaning that others can read it.

---

[3]Robert Pirsig, *Zen and the Art of Motorcycle Maintenance* (New York: Bantam Books, 1984).

TECH TIP BLOG FOR BRILLIANCE

1 THE PROBLEM

You need to improve your writing skills.

2 THE FIX

Express yourself. Keeping a diary, either on paper or onscreen in a blog, is a great way to get in some writing practice.

3 HOW TO DO IT

We know: Inside your head, you're the world's most articulate person. But trying to get your thoughts down on paper is another story, so it makes sense to flex those muscles. Any type of writing exercise is helpful simply because it gets you accustomed to organizing your thoughts, presenting a persuasive argument, and speaking in the language of the written word. It doesn't matter what you write about: politics, sports, your cat, ancient civilizations, whatever. Just start thinking and typing. Later on, when you sit down to write a masterpiece for an actual grade, you'll have valuable experience under your belt.

Remember, if you write about something related to your major or the kind of career that interests you—and you put some time into making your blog shine—you can always use it on your résumé or grad school application.

THE PROCESS:

To set up your own free blog:

1. Open your Web browser and go to **Blogger.com** or **Wordpress.com**. Click on the "Get Started" or "Sign Up Now" button.

2. Follow the prompts to create a blogger account and choose a display name. (Feel free to use your own name or an ingenious nom de plume.)

3. Name your blog, too: It needs a title and an address that people can use to visit it.

4. Follow the prompts to select a template. Once that's in place, you can start posting. Bonus: You can use plug-ins to make your blog more fun and functional.

5. Finished blogging for the day? Click the sign-out button at the top of the screen.

and adding their questions and reactions to what they have gathered. As they write, their minds begin to make connections between ideas. At this stage, they don't attempt to organize, to find exactly the right words, or to think about structure. But when they move from exploratory writing to explanatory writing, their preparation will help them form crystal clear sentences, spell correctly, and have their thoughts organized so that their material flows naturally from one point to the next.

This exercise gives students a chance to freewrite and makes a connection to the content on MBTI in Chapter 4.

EXERCISE 10.1

What You WRITE Matters

The concept of "freewriting" sounds appealing—writing without the constraints of grammar, spelling, syntax, etc. But it can also be uncomfortable if you are not used to it, so let's try it out here.

As with the example from *Zen and the Art of Motorcycle Maintenance*, freewrite as you answer the following question: "Where did you grow up?" Start with a narrow focus—your bedroom, your house, your street, your city, your state, and finally your country. Use descriptive language, and aim for about 75 words. If you do not go beyond describing your bedroom, that is okay.

_____

_____

_____

_____

_____

How does this exercise compare to explanatory writing, when writing needs to be perfected for publication so that others can read it? Was it easier or more difficult for you? What kind of learner do you think would enjoy freewriting best?

Thinking back to your MBTI results (Chapter 4), what kind of preference would freewriting appeal to more, a Judger (J) or a Perceiver (P)? _____

A Sensor (S) or an Intuitive (N)? _____

The Writing Process

Writing is an organized process, not a last-minute task. When trying to tackle a major paper, what blocks you from starting it?

One of the more popular ways of thinking about the writing process includes the following steps:

1. **Prewriting or rehearsing (freewriting).** This step includes preparing to write by filling your mind with information from other sources. It is generally considered the first stage of exploratory writing.

2. **Writing or drafting.** This step is converting exploratory writing so that it becomes a rough explanatory draft.

3. **Rewriting or revision.** This step is polishing your work until it clearly explains what you want to communicate and is ready for your audience.

Many students turn in poorly written papers because they skip the first and last steps and make do with the middle one. Perhaps they don't have time because they have overloaded their schedule or they put off things until the night before the paper is due. Whatever the reason, the result is often a poorly written assignment, since the best writing is usually done over an extended period of time, not as a last-minute task. Most professional writers and speakers would never start preparing an assignment only a day or hours before it

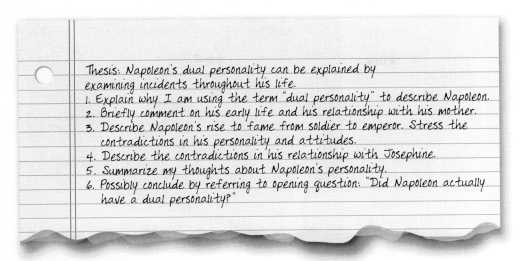

FIGURE 10.1

Example of a Thesis Statement

IN CLASS: Share your online resources for research and writing. Students might know of other sources that they can share with their classmates. One helpful and free tool is available at www.answers.com. Download "1-Click Answers" to be able to "alt-click" on any word in any program on your computer to get instant definitions and facts. The information will appear as a bubble on your screen. With this resource, there is no excuse for not looking up any word you don't understand.

has to be delivered. For one thing, the mere anxiety such a situation creates would be more than enough to shut down any manner of intelligent thinking. Worrying about your grammar and spelling as you write what might be your only draft can lead to a low grade or a rejection from a career inquiry.

PREWRITING: THE IDEA STAGE

Many writing experts, such as Donald Murray,[4] believe that of all the steps, **prewriting** (or freewriting) should take the longest. During freewriting you might question things that seem illogical. You might recall what you've heard other people say. This should lead you to write more, to ask yourself whether your views are more reliable than those of others, whether the topic might be too broad or too narrow, and so forth.

> **prewriting** The first stage of the writing process. It may include planning, research, and outlining.

What constitutes an appropriate topic or thesis? When is it neither too broad nor too narrow? Test your topic by writing, "The purpose of this paper is to convince my readers that . . ." (but don't use that stilted line in your eventual paper). Pay attention to the assignment. Know the limits of your knowledge, the limitations on your time, and your ability to do the necessary research.

WRITING: THE BEGINNING OF ORGANIZATION

Once you have completed your research and feel you have exhausted the information sources and ideas, it's time to move to the writing, or drafting, stage. It might be a good idea to begin with a **thesis statement** and an outline so that you can put things where they logically belong. A thesis statement is a short statement that clearly defines the purpose of the paper (see Figure 10.1).

> **thesis statement** A short statement that clearly defines the purpose of the paper.

[4]Donald Murray, *Learning by Teaching: Selected Articles on Writing and Teaching* (Portsmouth, NH: Boynton/Cook, 1982).

Write. Revise. Repeat.

Good writers spend more time editing and revising their written work than they spend writing the original version, and computers have made this task much easier than it used to be. Never turn in your first draft; spend the necessary time to reread and improve your work.

Once you have a workable outline and thesis, you can begin paying attention to the flow of ideas from one sentence to the next and from one paragraph to the next, including subheadings where needed. If you have chosen the thesis carefully, it will help you check to see that each sentence relates to your main idea. When you have completed this stage, you will have the first draft of your paper in hand.

REWRITING: THE POLISHING STAGE

Are you finished? Not by a long shot. Next comes the stage at which you take a good piece of writing and do your best to make it great. The essence of good writing is rewriting. You read. You correct. You add smoother transitions. You slash through wordy sentences and paragraphs, removing anything that is repetitive or adds nothing of value to your paper. You substitute stronger words for weaker ones. You double-check spelling and grammar. It also might help to share your paper with one or more of your classmates to get their feedback. This is typically called "peer review." Once you have talked with your reviewers about their suggested changes, you can either accept or reject them. At this point, you are ready to finalize your writing and "publish" (turn in) your paper.

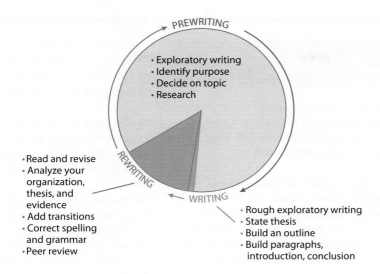

FIGURE 10.2
The Writing Process

ALLOCATING TIME

When Donald Murray was asked how long a writer should spend on each of the three stages, he suggested the following:

> Prewriting: 85 percent (including research and rumination)
>
> Writing: 1 percent (the first draft)
>
> Rewriting: 14 percent (revising until it's suitable for "publication")

When readers offer meaningful feedback, you might want to begin the process again, returning to prewriting, then writing, then rewriting (Figure 10.2).

If Murray's figures surprise you, here's a true story about a writer who was assigned to create a brochure. He had other jobs to do and kept avoiding that one. But the other work he was doing had a direct bearing on the brochure he was asked to write. So as he was putting this assignment off, he was also "researching" material for it.

After nearly three months, he finally decided it was time to move forward on the brochure. He sat at his computer and dashed the words off in just under 30 minutes. The more he wrote, the faster the ideas popped into his head. He actually was afraid to stop until he had finished. He read his words, made revisions, sent the result around the office for peer review, incorporated some suggestions, and the brochure was published.

He had spent a long time prewriting (working with related information without trying to write the brochure). He went through the writing stage quickly because his mind was primed for the task. As a result, he had time to polish his work before the first draft.

You can use a similar process. Begin writing the day you get the assignment, even if it's only for 10 or 15 minutes. That way, you won't be confronting a blank screen or piece of paper later. Write something on the assignment every day; the more you write, the better you'll write. Dig for ideas. *Reject nothing* at first, and then revise later. Read good writing; it will help you find your own writing style. Above all, know that becoming a better thinker and writer takes hard work, but practice can make it nearly perfect.

IN CLASS: Professional writer Donald Murray says that 1 percent of a writer's time should be spent on the writing stage. This seems so short. Ask students why Murray would make such a statement.

AVOIDING PLAGIARISM

The trouble with plagiarism is that a lot of students don't completely understand what it is. *Plagiarism* **is a fancy word that simply means taking someone else's work or ideas and passing them off as your own. Fun fact: The word** *plagiarism* **comes from the Latin word for kidnapping. You probably get the picture.**

It's hard to believe that anybody really thinks it's okay to cut and paste whole sentences from the Internet into their essays. But given that some people don't think twice about downloading copyrighted music tracks and videos, maybe the concept of "borrowing" isn't as clear as it used to be. The fact remains that copying or paraphrasing anything off the Internet, or from any other source, and using it without citing the source is cheating.

Plagiarizing with intent is one thing. But many college students get convicted of plagiarism simply because they forget to define which parts of an essay are their own and which parts belong to another author.

How Not to Cheat: 8 Essential Tips

1. Don't procrastinate. Here's the deal: If you want to write a thorough and honest essay, you need to start early. College papers aren't like movie reviews. You're required to do lots of outside research on your topic. Then you have to weed through it all to figure out what's valuable. Next, you have to incorporate the highlights into an outline, a first draft, and, ultimately, an original work that's all your own. All of that takes time. If you leave things too late, you'll be more tempted to cheat.

2. Don't muddle your notes. It's vital that you keep your own writing separate from the material you've gathered from other sources. Why? Because it's surprisingly easy to mistake someone else's words for your own, especially after you get 2 hours into writing and your brain turns numb. So document everything. Be obsessive about this.

3. Be a stickler for footnotes. It happens all the time: At the end of an essay, a student provides a full bibliography listing all the works he or she has cited. But in the paper itself, there are no references to be found. Without footnotes, you've made it impossible for your instructor to tell the difference between your writing and your references.

4. Familiarize yourself with the proper formatting for a research paper. The MLA style is pretty much standard. If your instructor requires a different style, he or she will let you know. If you need to learn the basic guidelines and rules for citations, *The Owl* at Purdue University is a great source—well written and user-friendly (visit **http://owl.english.purdue.edu/**). You might also want to speak to a reference librarian. Reference librarians have a graduate degree in gathering research, and they

can be some of your biggest allies in college. Alternately, pay a visit to the writing center on campus, or talk to your instructor for advice.

5. Be sure to list all of your research sources in your bibliography. They should run alphabetically, in proper MLA format.

6. Master the art of paraphrasing. Paraphrasing means to restate someone else's ideas or observations in your own words. You don't have to put the text in quotation marks, but a citation acknowledging the original source is still essential.

7. If you need help, seek it early. This sounds painfully obvious, but it's important to go to the writing center or the librarian *well before your paper is actually due.* Proofreading takes time, and chances are, your paper will need more than a few tweaks.

8. If you hand something in and then realize that you used material without giving credit to the source, alert your instructor to your mistake immediately. Don't just hope it will slip through. Better to risk half a grade point on one essay than your whole college career.

In this exercise, students are asked to consider which step of the writing process is the most difficult for them.

EXERCISE 10.2

How You PLAN TO WRITE Matters

Of the three steps listed for the writing process—prewriting, drafting, and rewriting—which do you find is the easiest step? _____

Why?_____

_____

Which step gives you the most difficulty? _____

Is this because you don't use this step very often when writing? _____

What strategy could you use to overcome this mental block? For example, if you have trouble prewriting, could you plan out and then write down the various steps involved before you begin researching? Remember to consider your deadlines.

_____

_____

Choosing the Best Way to Communicate with Your Audience

Have you ever misinterpreted an e-mail or text from a friend, thinking the friend was angry or upset with you, when in fact he or she was just kidding? How can you avoid this problem?

Before you came to college, you probably spent much more time writing informally than writing formally. Think about all the time you've spent writing e-mails, Facebook and blog comments, text messages, and "tweets." Now think about all the time you've spent writing papers for school or work. Typically, writing for wired communications is informal. This can be a detriment to your writing skills. The grammar and structure of e-mail and other types of electronic communication resemble a conversation instead of a formal piece of writing. Additionally, communications via text messaging often use spelling and grammar conventions all their own. As a shortcut, people often condense text messages by using abbreviations such as "brb," "lol," "y?," and "ttyl." They are abbreviated for good reason—imagine how long it would take to type this sentence into a text message. The downside of these shortcuts is that they have gradually crept into our writing habits and caused many of us to become careless in our formal writing. It is important to be aware of when it's okay to be sloppy and when you have to be meticulous.

Electronic communication does not convey emotions as well as face-to-face or even telephone conversations do. Electronic communication lacks vocal inflection, visible gestures, and a shared environment. Your correspondent might have difficulty telling whether you are serious or kidding,

IN CLASS: Ask students to share examples of text messages—ones they have either sent or received. Discuss the ways texting has changed the way we write and communicate.

IN CLASS: Discuss with students the implications of different audiences when sending e-mail. Ask how they would send an e-mail to a friend versus sending one to a professor. Discuss the difference between formal and informal e-mailing.

happy or sad, frustrated or euphoric. Sarcasm is particularly dangerous to use in electronic messages. Therefore your electronic compositions will be different from both your paper compositions and your speech.

Being aware of the differences between formal writing and informal writing will help you build appropriate writing skills for college work. How would you write an e-mail to friends telling them about the volunteer work you did this past weekend? How would you write that same e-mail to a potential employer who might hire you for your first job after college? Another way to improve your writing is to consider the reader's point of view. For the next week, before sending any Facebook messages, e-mails, or text messages, reread them and consider how the people who will receive them will perceive your tone. What kind of mood will they think you are in? Will they feel that you are happy to have them as a friend? In how many different ways might your message be interpreted?

Writing for class projects might be a challenge at first. Visit your institution's writing center when you are starting to work on your paper. Professional staff and trained peer consultants who work in writing centers are available to help students express their ideas clearly through writing. Ask your instructor for examples of papers that have received good grades. You might also ask your instructor to help you review your writing after you have worked with the writing center. Most important, you can practice by using a correct writing style when text messaging. You'll find that your friends won't fault you for it. (Have you ever seen a text asking you to "pls stop using proper grammar"?) Since you spend more time with online forms of communication, it's a great way to get real-world practice in the art of academic writing.

This exercise gives students a chance to consider the difference between appropriate and inappropriate electronic communication.

EXERCISE 10.3

How You COMMUNICATE Matters

The idea of using technology to communicate with friends and family seems reasonable. We all know people who talk too much on the phone, and a quick text or e-mail can be more efficient. But sometimes we receive (and send) electronic communications that are misinterpreted or unprofessional. Most of our friends can be forgiving, but what about your boss or professor or another authority figure?

Scenario: Below, draft an UNPROFESSIONAL e-mail to your professor telling her that you will not be in class today because you are sick.

_____

_____

Now, redo the e-mail, making it sound like you are the intelligent, capable student she knows you to be!

_____

_____

SPEAKING

The advice about writing also applies to speaking in public. The major difference, of course, is that you not only have to write the speech, you also have to present it to an audience. Because many people believe that fear of public speaking ranks up there with the fear of death, you might be thinking: What if I plan, organize, prepare, and rehearse, but calamity strikes anyway? What if my mind goes completely blank, I drop my note cards, or I say something totally embarrassing? Remember that people in your audience have been in your position and will understand your anxiety. Just accentuate the positive, rely on your wit, and keep speaking. Your recovery is what they are most likely to recognize; your success is what they are most likely to remember. The guidelines in this chapter can help you improve your speaking skills significantly, including losing your fear of speaking publicly.

Preparing a Speech

It has been said that public speaking is the number-two fear in the world (right behind death!). Do you suffer from this fear? What resources on your campus might help you in this area?

Successful speaking involves six fundamental steps:

Step 1. Clarify your objective.

Step 2. Analyze your audience.

Step 3. Collect and organize your information.

Step 4. Choose your visual aids.

Step 5. Prepare your notes.

Step 6. Practice your delivery.

STEP 1. CLARIFY YOUR OBJECTIVE

Begin by identifying what you want to accomplish. Do you want to persuade your listeners that your campus needs additional student parking? Inform your listeners about the student government's accomplishments? What do you want your listeners to know, believe, or do when you are finished?

STEP 2. ANALYZE YOUR AUDIENCE

You need to understand the people you'll be talking to. Ask yourself:

- **What do they already know about my topic?** If you're going to give a presentation on the health risks of fast food, you'll want to find out how much your listeners already know about fast food so you don't risk boring them or wasting their time.
- **What do they want or need to know?** If your presentation will be about fast food and health, how much interest do your classmates have in nutrition? Would they be more interested in some other aspect of college life?

IN CLASS: Review college core requirements to determine whether a communications or speech course is mandated. If it is, show the students the course description, and discuss why speech and communication skills are important as students become successful professionals.

IN CLASS: If you asked your students to bring in professional job descriptions to discuss the importance of writing, ask them to review the job descriptions again and see how many of them also require strong speaking and communication skills. Ask students why these jobs require such skills. Remind students that they will need both types of skills when they apply for a job. Well-written résumés will help win them an interview, and good communication will help win them the job.

IN CLASS: Ask students whether they have ever attended a bad presentation. Ask them to describe the negative characteristics of those presentations. Write these characteristics on the board. Follow up by having students brainstorm solutions that could have improved the presentations. This should give you a lead-in to discussing the six steps to successful speaking.

■ RETENTION STRATEGY: For some students, formal public speaking is a terrifying activity, and they will do everything they can to avoid giving a class presentation. Give students the opportunity to practice in front of you or in front of the class, and help them understand the link between developing these skills and getting and keeping a job.

- **Who are my listeners?** What do the members of your audience have in common with you? How are they different from you?
- **What are their attitudes toward me, my ideas, and my topic?** How are they likely to feel about the ideas you are planning to present? For instance, what are your classmates' attitudes about fast food?

STEP 3. COLLECT AND ORGANIZE YOUR INFORMATION

Now comes the most critical part of the process: building your presentation by selecting and arranging blocks of information. One useful analogy is to think of yourself as guiding your listeners through the maze of ideas they already have to the new knowledge, attitudes, and beliefs you would like them to have. You can apply the suggestions from earlier in the chapter for creating an outline for writing to actually composing an outline for a speech.

STEP 4. CHOOSE YOUR VISUAL AIDS

Research has shown that when visual aids are added to presentations, listeners can absorb 35 percent more information and over time they can recall 55 percent more. You might choose to prepare a chart, show a video clip, write on the board, or distribute handouts. You might also use your computer to prepare overhead transparencies or dynamic *PowerPoint* presentations. As you select and use your visual aids, consider these rules of thumb:

- Make visuals easy to follow. Use readable lettering, and don't overload your audience by trying to cover too much on one slide.
- Explain each visual clearly.
- Allow your listeners enough time to process visuals.
- Proofread carefully. Misspelled words hurt your credibility as a speaker.
- Maintain eye contact with your listeners while you discuss the visuals. Don't turn around and address the screen.

A fancy *PowerPoint* slideshow can't make up for inadequate preparation or poor delivery skills, but using clear, attractive visual aids can help you organize your material and help your listeners understand what they're hearing. The quality of your visual aids and your skill in using them can contribute to making your presentation effective (see Figure 10.3).

STEP 5. PREPARE YOUR NOTES

If you are like most speakers, having an entire written copy of your speech in front of you might tempt you to read much of your presentation. Even if you can resist that temptation, your presentation could sound canned. On the other hand, your memory might fail you, so speaking without any material at all could be risky. A better strategy is to memorize only the introduction and conclusion of your speech so that you can maintain eye contact during the rest of your speech and thus build rapport with your listeners.

FIGURE 10.3
Examples of Good and Bad Presentation Slides

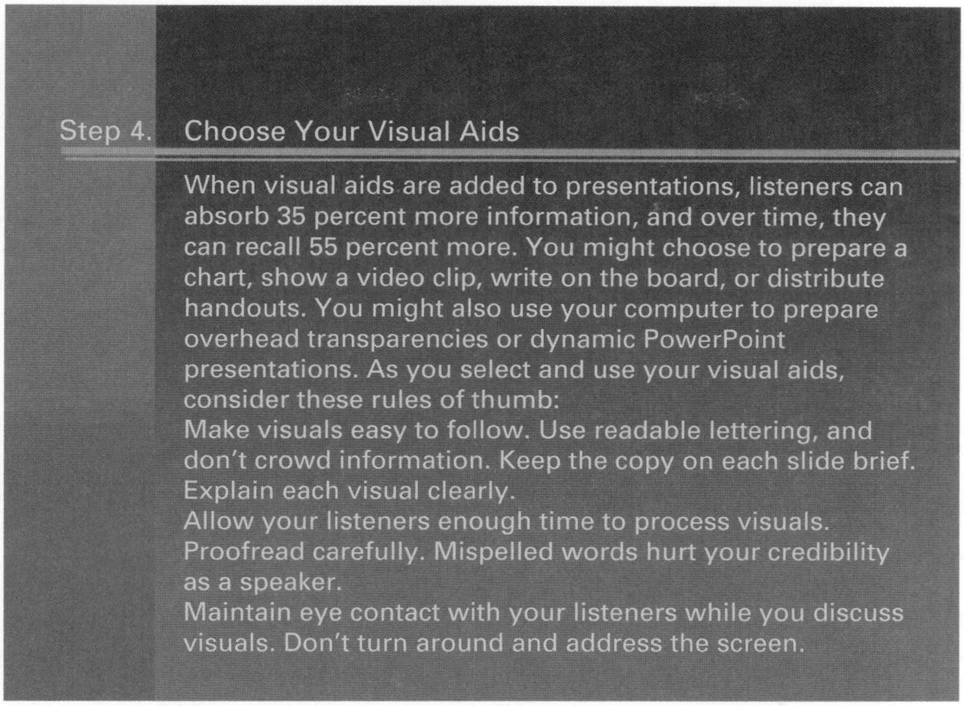

Example of bad presentation slide

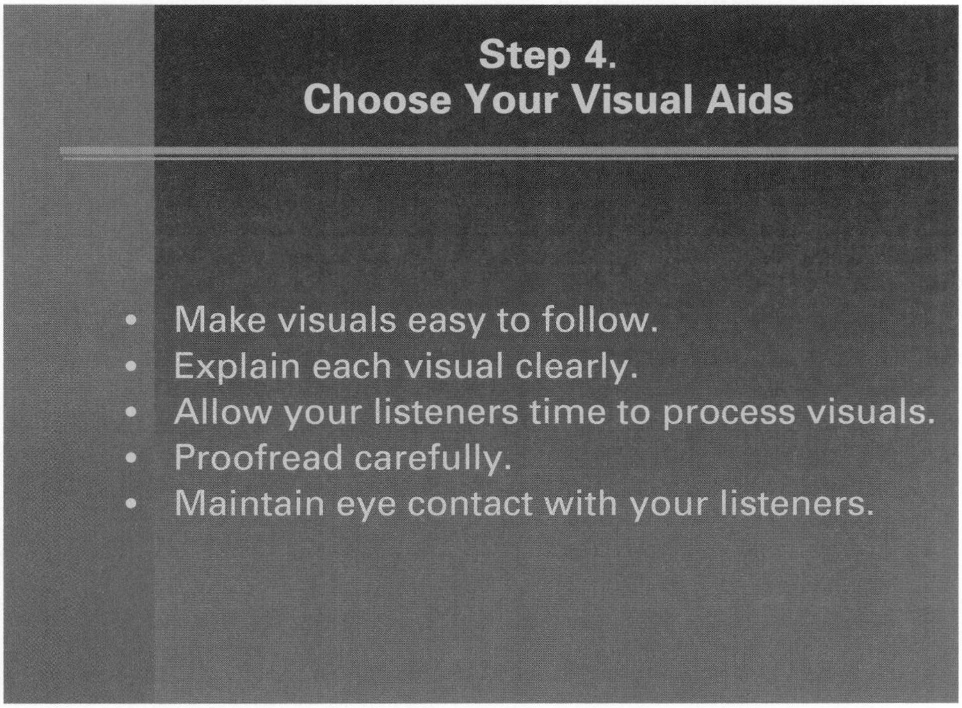

Example of good presentation slide

The best speaking aid is a minimal outline, carefully prepared, from which you can speak extemporaneously. Rehearse thoroughly in advance, and you'll be better prepared for how and when you want to present your points. Because you are speaking from brief notes, your words will be slightly different each time you give your presentation. That's okay; you'll sound prepared but natural. You might want to use some unobtrusive note cards. If so, it's not a bad idea to number them, just in case you accidentally drop the stack; this has happened to the best of speakers! When you become more comfortable with speaking, you might decide to let your visuals serve as notes. A paper copy of the *PowerPoint* slides can also serve as your basic outline. Eventually, you might find that you no longer need notes.

STEP 6. PRACTICE YOUR DELIVERY

As you rehearse, form a mental image of success rather than one of failure. Practice your presentation aloud several times beforehand to harness that energy-producing anxiety.

Begin a few days before your target date, and continue until you're about to present it. Rehearse aloud. Talking through your speech can help you much more than thinking through your speech. Practice before an audience—your roommate, a friend, your dog, even the mirror. Talking to something or someone helps simulate the distraction that listeners cause. Consider recording or videotaping yourself to help you pinpoint your own mistakes and to reinforce your strengths. If you ask your practice audience to critique you, you'll have some idea of what changes it might be helpful to make.

OUTSIDE CLASS: Assign students to groups, and have each group select a topic and prepare a short (5-minute) speech that one member of the group will deliver. Ask the students to follow the six steps to successful speaking and document the process.

IN CLASS: Have group members present their short speech, and have the students share results of the process.

During the week or two leading up to this topic discussion, ask students to keep their eyes open in all their classes for specific examples of ineffective *PowerPoint* presentations.

EXERCISE 10.4

How You USE VISUALS Matters

PowerPoint can be an effective tool for speakers and is especially good for visual learners. However, some *PowerPoint* presentations can overpower your audience. Describe some characteristics of an <u>ineffective</u> *PowerPoint* presentation:

1.

2.

3.

4.

5.

Considering some of the challenges of using *PowerPoint,* what do you think about using *PowerPoint* presentations in your classroom speeches?

_____

_____

_____

Using Your Voice and Body Language

People communicate in two ways: verbally (with their voice, tone, rate of speech) and nonverbally (hand gestures, stance, facial expressions). Have you ever encountered speakers whose verbals or nonverbals distracted from their message? What are some examples?

OUTSIDE CLASS: Ask students either to attend a speech on campus or to watch a speech on TV and to observe and comment on voice and body language.

Let your hands hang comfortably at your sides, reserving them for natural, spontaneous gestures. Unless you must stay close to a fixed microphone, plan to move comfortably and casually around the room. Some experts suggest that you change positions between major points to punctuate your presentation, signaling to your audience, "I've finished with that point; let's shift topics."

Following are some other tips for using your voice and body language:

- Make eye contact with as many listeners as you can. This helps you to read their reactions, demonstrate confidence, and establish command.
- A smile helps to warm up your listeners, although you should avoid smiling excessively or inappropriately. Smiling through a presentation on world hunger would send your listeners a mixed message.

Body Language

Your posture and body language can add to or distract from the effectiveness of your oral presentations. Be sure to stand up straight. Unlike this student, don't lean on the podium, and keep your hands at your side or use them to emphasize the points you are making. Eye contact with listeners is extremely important in U.S. culture and will let your audience know that you are confident and in control.

- As you practice your speech, pay attention to the pitch of your voice, your rate of speaking, and your volume. Project confidence and enthusiasm by varying your pitch. Speak at a rate that mirrors normal conversation—not too fast and not too slow. Consider varying your volume for the same reasons you vary pitch and rate: to engage your listeners and to emphasize important points.

- Pronunciation and word choice are important. A poorly articulated word (such as *gonna* for *going to*), a mispronounced word (such as *nuculer* for *nuclear*), or a misused word (such as *anecdote* for *antidote*) can quickly erode your credibility. Check meanings and pronunciations in a dictionary if you're not sure, and use a thesaurus for word variety. Fillers such as *um*, *uh*, *like*, and *you know* are distracting, too.

- Consider your appearance. Convey a look of competence, preparedness, and success by dressing professionally.

In this exercise, students describe what speakers do with body language and voice that interferes with their message and then think about how they might respond to overcome these distractions.

EXERCISE 10.5

How You SPEAK Matters

Many times we are unaware of how our body language or the way we use our voice controls our message. You have probably listened to speeches, sermons, or lectures in which the way the speaker stood, moved, or spoke was so distracting that it interfered with the message.

What bothers you the most? In other words, what types of verbal or nonverbal messages distract you from comprehending what you hear? And, most importantly, what can you do about this?

Verbal	Your Response	Nonverbal	Your Response
Speaker talks too quickly	Ask questions to slow down the pace	Speaker claps hands after each point	Position yourself toward the back to allow sound to be less distracting

The GUIDE Checklist

> Think back to a time when you heard a wonderful speech, sermon, or lecture. Did the speaker appear to use most of the GUIDE techniques? Which are most important to you as a listener?

Imagine you've been selected as a campus tour guide for next year's prospective first-year students and their families who are visiting your campus. Picture yourself in front of the administration building with a group of people assembled around you. You want to get and keep their attention in order to achieve your objective: increasing their interest in your school. Using the GUIDE method shown in Figure 10.4, you would do the following:

G: GET YOUR AUDIENCE'S ATTENTION

You can relate the topic to your listeners: "Let me tell you what to expect during your college years here—at the best school in the state." Or you can state the significance of the topic: "Deciding which college to attend is one of the most important decisions you'll ever make." Or you can arouse their curiosity: "Do you know the three most important factors that students and their families consider when choosing a college?"

IN CLASS: Show a tape of a speech in class. Have students critique the speech using the GUIDE checklist (Figure 10.4). Follow up with a discussion.

FIGURE 10.4
The GUIDE Checklist

THE GUIDE CHECKLIST

G Get your audience's attention

U "You" – don't forget yourself

I Ideas, ideas, ideas!

D Develop an organizational structure

E Exit gracefully and memorably

You can also tell a joke (but only if it relates to your topic and isn't offensive or in questionable taste), startle the audience, tell a story, or ask a rhetorical question (a question that is asked to produce an effect, especially to make an assertion, rather than to elicit a reply). Regardless of which method you select, remember that a well-designed introduction must not only gain the attention of your listeners, but also develop rapport with them, motivate them to continue listening, and preview what you are going to say during the rest of your speech.

U: "YOU"—DON'T FORGET YOURSELF

In preparing any speech, don't exclude the most important source of your presentation: you. Even in a formal presentation, you will be most successful if you develop a comfortable style that's easy to listen to. Don't play a role. Instead, be yourself at your best, letting your wit and personality shine through.

I: IDEAS, IDEAS, IDEAS!

Create a list of all the possible points you could make. Then write them out as conclusions you want your listeners to accept. For example, imagine that on your campus tour for prospective new students and their parents, you want to make the following points:

Tuition is reasonable.	The campus is attractive.
The faculty is composed of good teachers.	The library has great resources.
The school is committed to student success.	The campus is safe.
College can prepare you to get a good job.	Faculty members conduct prestigious research.
Student life is awesome.	This college is the best choice.

For a typical presentation, most listeners can process no more than five main points. After considering your list for some time, you decide that the following five points are crucial:

- Tuition is reasonable.
- The faculty is composed of good teachers.
- The school is committed to student success.
- The campus is attractive.
- The campus is safe.

Try to generate more ideas than you think you'll need so that you can select the best ones. As with writing, don't judge your ideas at first; rather, think up as many possibilities as you can. Then use critical thinking to decide which are most relevant to your objectives.

As you formulate your main ideas, keep these guidelines in mind:

- **Main points should be parallel if possible.** Each main point should be a full sentence with a construction similar to that of the others. A poor, *nonparallel* structure might look like this:

1. Student life is awesome. (a full-sentence main point)

2. Tuition (a one-word main point that doesn't parallel the first point)

For a *parallel* second point, try instead:

2. Tuition is low. (a full-sentence main point)

- **Each main point should include a single idea.** Don't crowd main points with multiple messages, as in the following:

  1. Tuition is reasonable, and the campus is safe.

  2. Faculty members are good teachers and researchers.

Ideas rarely stand on their own merit. To ensure that your main ideas work, use a variety of supporting materials. The three most widely used forms of supporting materials are examples, statistics, and testimony.

- **Examples** include stories and illustrations, hypothetical events, and specific cases. They can be compelling ways to dramatize and clarify main ideas, but make sure they're relevant, representative, and reasonable.

- **Statistics** are widely used as evidence in speeches. Of course, numbers can be manipulated, and unscrupulous speakers sometimes mislead with statistics. If you use statistics, make sure they are clear, concise, accurate, and easy to understand.

- **Testimony** includes quoting outside experts, paraphrasing reliable sources, and emphasizing the quality of individuals who agree with your main points. When you use testimony, make sure that it is accurate, expert, and credible.

Finally, because each person in your audience is unique, you can best add interest, clarity, and credibility to your presentation by varying and combining the types of support you provide.

D: DEVELOP AN ORGANIZATIONAL STRUCTURE

For example, you might decide to use a chronological narrative approach, discussing the history of the college from its early years to the present. Or you might decide on a problem-solution format in which you describe a problem (such as choosing a school), present the pros and cons of several solutions (the strengths and weaknesses of several schools), and finally identify the best solution (your school).

Begin with your most important ideas. Writing an outline can be the most useful way to begin organizing. List each main point and subpoint separately on a note card. Spread the cards out on a large surface (such as the floor), and arrange, rearrange, add, and delete cards until you find the most effective arrangement. Then simply number the cards, pick them up, and use them to prepare your final outline.

As you organize your presentation, remember that your overall purpose is to guide your listeners. This means you must not neglect transitions between your main points. For example:

"Now that we've looked at the library, let's move on to the gymnasium."

"The first half of my presentation has identified our recreational facilities. Now let's look at the academic hubs on campus."

"So much for the academic buildings on campus. What about the campus social scene?"

In speaking, as in writing, transitions make the difference between keeping your audience with you and losing them at an important juncture.

E: EXIT GRACEFULLY AND MEMORABLY

Plan your ending carefully, realizing that most of the suggestions for introductions also apply to conclusions.

Whatever else you do, go out with style, impact, and dignity. Don't leave your listeners asking, "So that's it?" Subtly signal that the end is in sight (without the overused "So in conclusion . . ."), briefly summarize your major points, and then conclude confidently.

Students are asked to apply the GUIDE checklist to the task of generating ideas to make a class presentation more interesting.

EXERCISE 10.6

How You GUIDE Matters

The textbook offers the example of using the GUIDE method in giving a tour of the campus. In this exercise, you can practice using the GUIDE method yourself by applying it to the topic of **enriching a lecture presentation**. Concentrate on the "I" or "**ideas**" strategy in the GUIDE checklist. For each of five ideas, name and describe a piece of supporting material. As described in the textbook, the three most widely used forms of supporting materials are examples, statistics, and testimony.

To enrich lecture presentations, do the following:

IDEA	TYPE OF SUPPORTING MATERIAL/DESCRIPTION
Listen to classroom podcasts out of class	*Example/My history professor podcasts "stories" about WW II, and I enjoy hearing them again when I work out.*
1. _____	_____
2. _____	_____
3. _____	_____
4. _____	_____
5. _____	_____

Speaking on the Spot

> When asked to speak on the spot, can you recall facts quickly and give your point of view confidently, or do you get flustered? If you do have trouble defending your position, is it because of the audience or your preparation?

Most of the speaking you will do in college and afterward will be on the spot. When you must give an immediate opinion or position on an issue, it helps to use a framework that allows you to sound organized and competent. Suppose your instructor asks, "Do you think the world's governments are working together effectively to ensure a healthy environment?" One of the most popular ways to arrange your thoughts is through the PREP formula.[5] Short for "preparation," this plan requires the following:

IN CLASS: Have students practice impromptu speeches. Write the PREP formula on the board, and provide a list of common topics. List them in a question format—for example, "Do you think that bars should be smoke-free?" Ask some students to volunteer to stand up and answer the question using the PREP formula. Do not allow the impromptu speeches to turn into a debate. The purpose of this activity is to follow a process in communicating on the spot.

P: **Point of view** Provide an overview—a clear, direct statement or generalization: "After listening to yesterday's lecture, yes, I do."

R: **Reasons** Broadly state why you hold this point of view: "I was surprised by the efforts of the United Nations General Assembly to focus on the environment."

E: **Evidence or examples** Present specific facts or data supporting your point of view: "For example, the industrialized nations had set stringent goals on air pollution and greenhouse gases for the year 2012."

P: **Point of view, restated** To make sure you are understood clearly, end with a restatement of your position: "So, yes, the world's governments seem to be concerned and working to improve the situation."

This exercise gets students to apply the PREP formula and links it to the MBTI content in Chapter 4.

EXERCISE 10.7

How You THINK QUICKLY Matters

Have you ever had to think quickly and come up with an answer on the spot? Has a teacher ever asked you a question you couldn't answer, and you had to come up with something—anything—as a response? Just for fun, try PREP on the issue below, which you might know nothing about. Convince someone you are a subject-matter expert in the area. You can make up data to sound convincing.

Issue: Alcoholism and Nature versus Nurture

With a partner, debate the issue of whether alcoholism is a disease with a genetic predisposition or is solely the result of environmental influence. Don't take time to plan or think this through; the point is to make your position clear in a short period of time.

PREP FRAMEWORK	YOU	YOUR PARTNER
P—Point of View	*Genetic Predisposition* (Nature)	*Environment* (Nurture)
	I think that . . .	I believe that . . .
R—Reasons		
E—Evidence		
P—Restate Your Point		

Do you feel like you're in a courtroom or debate class? How did the PREP formula work for you? Are you comfortable speaking on the spot, or do you need time to plan and think through what to say? ______________

____

How are your thoughts about speaking on the spot related to your learning style, specifically your MBTI preference? ____

Do you think that an Extravert (E) or an Introvert (I) would have an easier time with this exercise?

____

What about a Judger (J) or a Perceiver (P)? ______________________________

[5]Kenneth Wydro, *Think on Your Feet* (Englewood Cliffs, NJ: Prentice-Hall, 1981).

CHECKLIST FOR SUCCESS

COMMUNICATE CLEARLY

☐ **Take the time and effort to develop your writing and speaking skills.** Effective writing and speaking are skills for success in college and in life after college. They are skills that employers desire for all employees.

☐ **Understand the differences between formal and informal communication.** When you are in doubt about what's appropriate, use a more formal writing style.

☐ **Learn and practice the distinct stages of writing:** prewriting, drafting, revising, and polishing. Going through each step will improve the finished product.

☐ **Learn and practice the six fundamental steps of effective speaking:** clarify your objective, analyze your audience, organize your presentation, choose appropriate visual aids, prepare your notes, and practice delivery.

☐ **Ask for feedback from others on your writing and speaking.** You will improve if you accept both positive and negative feedback.

☐ **Before making a formal presentation, practice before a friend or the mirror.** Use eye contact, smile, vary your pitch and rate of speaking, pay attention to word choice and pronunciation, and when you are presenting formally, dress appropriately.

APPLY IT! What Works for YOU Matters

Think about your current academic situation, and apply some of the suggestions and strategies introduced in this chapter. Select strategies that you think will work best for you, and then write them down in the "Your Response" column. What are YOU planning to do for YOUR college experience?

QUESTIONS	SAMPLE STUDENT ANSWERS	YOUR RESPONSE
	Name: Betty Givens	
Using Freewriting to Discover What You Want to Say When faced with writing a paper, have you ever felt like you just can't seem to get started? Have you ever tried freewriting?	As a nontraditional student, I am having a hard time with this freewriting thing. I was taught growing up to pay attention to grammar and spelling when writing. But I tried freewriting the other day in my English class and I have to say, it was liberating! I was able to start my paper earlier, but was worried then about whether or not my topic was adequate.	
The Writing Process Writing is an organized process, not a last-minute task. When trying to tackle a major paper, what blocks you from starting it?	I don't usually have problems getting started on my papers, but many things in my life (kids, husband) keep me from continuing my progress. I find that other things distract me and I lose my focus. After looking at the writing process, I realized that if I break it into stages, I can progress forward, taking breaks with my family if needed.	

Choosing the Best Way to Communicate with Your Audience
Have you ever misinterpreted an e-mail or text from a friend, thinking the friend was angry or upset with you, when in fact he or she was just kidding? How can you avoid this problem?

I just started getting e-mails from friends a few years ago. It used to be that we called each other with news, but now we just e-mail. The other day I thought my friend was really sarcastic, but it turns out she was just kidding. I think I should have picked up the phone and checked with her, rather than get upset and assume the worst.

Preparing a Speech
It has been said that public speaking is the number-two fear in the world (right behind death!). Do you suffer from this fear? What resources on your campus might help you in this area?

I absolutely hate speaking in front of an audience. I would rather eat worms! I was telling this to another student who said our counseling center on campus did seminars on public speaking and also helped individuals if needed with one-on-one practice. I was relieved! Our student fees pay for this so I think I will take advantage of this service.

Using Your Voice and Body Language
People communicate in two ways: verbally (with their voice, tone, rate of speech) and nonverbally (hand gestures, stance, facial expressions). Have you ever encountered speakers whose verbals or nonverbals distracted from their message? What are some examples?

My history professor talks really quickly. I try to take notes, but I can never keep up with him. One idea that I read about was asking a question or two. It gives me time to finish writing and helps me organize my thoughts. Plus, it also gives me a participation grade in class. My math professor is distracting for another reason. She wears these glasses that look like something from outer space. I have learned not to look up, just listen, so that I won't get off topic when she lectures.

The GUIDE Checklist
Think back to a time when you heard a wonderful speech, sermon, or lecture. Did the speaker appear to use most of the GUIDE techniques? Which are most important to you as a listener?

My favorite speaker was my high school psychology teacher. She made everything come to life—even the boring theories seemed exciting. She really understood GUIDE—especially with the exit strategy. I never left her class without laughing.

Speaking on the Spot
When asked to speak on the spot, can you recall facts quickly and give your point of view confidently, or do you get flustered? If you do have trouble defending your position, is it because of the audience or your preparation?

The very idea of speaking on the spot makes me queasy. Public speaking isn't for me, and neither is defending my position or point of view without a lot of prior notice. I guess it is because I am an introvert and judger on the MBTI. I like to think before I speak and plan ahead for every contingency. I need more practice in this area, especially if I want to go to graduate school some day.

BUILD YOUR EXPERIENCE

In this exercise, students learn from watching each other role-play—selling themselves to score an interview for the job of their dreams.

1 COLLABORATIVE ACTIVITY

When looking for a job, it can be difficult to come up with the perfect thing to say at the perfect time to a potential employer. Practice helps! Think of all the techniques you learned in this chapter about speaking effectively (PREP, GUIDE, body language, and analyzing your audience), read the scenario below, and then go for it!

SCENARIO: THE ELEVATOR PITCH

The CEO of XYZ Company, the company you *really* want to work for, is standing alone in the elevator, apparently going to his office on the fifteenth floor. You walk into the elevator and punch the button for the door to close, and then you have about 30 seconds to score an interview for the job of your dreams! What can you say to this person to let him know who you are, to describe your skills and talents, and to express that you really want to work for XYZ Company?

After you finish, let someone else give it a try. Pay attention to what your classmates do and say.

Who had good eye contact? Did anyone shake hands? Did anyone ask the CEO a question, or did they just talk about themselves? What did other students say that you didn't but wish that you did? _____

_____

What would you say or do differently next time? _____

_____

On a scale of 1–10 (with 10 being the best), how would you rate your Elevator Pitch? _____

2 BUILDING YOUR PORTFOLIO

In the Public Eye The media provide ample opportunities for celebrities and public figures to show off their public speaking skills. As you have probably noticed, some celebrities are much better speakers than others. However, being a good public speaker is not important just for those who are "in the public eye." Whether you want to be a movie star or a marine biologist, potential employers tend to put excellent communication skills at the top of their "must have" list.

1. Identify a public figure who, in your opinion, is a good public speaker.

2. In a *Word* document, explain why it is important for that person to speak well. List the specific qualities (e.g., humor, eye contact) that you think make that person a good public speaker. For an example, go to the book's Web site at **bedfordstmartins.com/ycestudyskills.**

3. Save your responses in your portfolio. The next time you make a presentation, revisit the chart and spend extra time preparing in the areas in which you rated yourself less than "good."

ONE-MINUTE PAPER

This chapter has information that you can use to improve your writing and speaking skills. Which strategies struck you as methods that you could or should put into practice? If your instructor could cover one area in more depth, what would you want it to be?

_____

_____

_____

_____

_____

_____

_____

_____

_____

_____

_____

_____

_____

_____

_____

No matter how well prepared you are in your teaching, what a student hears and understands might not always be what you think you have said. The one-minute paper is a quick and easy assessment tool that will help alert you when students don't understand what was said or discussed in class. The one-minute paper will also give timid students an opportunity to ask questions and seek clarification. Ideally, you should ask for such a paper several minutes before the end of a class. The paper will also help you begin your next class by clarifying points your students seem to be unsure of.

For more on this topic watch
French Fries Are Not Vegetables and Other College Lessons

WHERE TO GO FOR HELP . . .

ON CAMPUS

> **Writing Center** Most campuses have one. Frequently, it is found within the English department.

> **Learning Assistance Center** In addition to help on many other topics, these centers offer help on writing.

> **Departments of Speech, Theater, and Communications** These offer both resources and specific courses to help you develop your speaking skills.

> **Student Activities** One of the best ways to learn and practice speaking skills is to become active in student organizations, especially those like the Student Government Association and the Debate Club.

ONLINE

> Writing tips: **http://clas.uiowa.edu/history /teaching-and-writing.center.** The University of Iowa's History Department offers help on common writing mistakes.

> **Plain Language** Have you ever been confused by government gobbledygook? Here's a guide to writing user-friendly documents for federal employees: **http://www.plainlanguage.gov/howto /guidelines/FederalPLGuidelines/index.cfm.**

> Toastmasters International offers public speaking tips at **http://www.toastmasters.org/tips.asp.**

MY INSTITUTION'S RESOURCES

_____

_____

_____

_____

_____

_____

_____

_____

CHAPTER 11

Developing Library, Research, and Information Literacy Skills

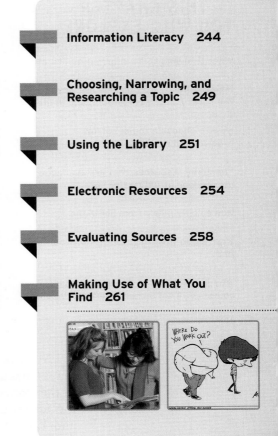

hich airline or travel service offers the cheapest air-fare? Is it true that certain professors always ask true/false questions? What species of poisonous serpent bit the patient, and which antivenom will work? Which is likely to be more reliable, a Subaru or a Toyota? What are the relationships between social class and mental illness? At what stress levels will bridge cables snap? How has William Faulkner's fiction influenced contemporary filmmaking? Who steals more from a chain store: customers or employees? What is the best way to shave time from the manufacture and delivery of tractors?

These questions all have something in common. Although some are academic inquiries and others are questions you might ask as part of your job or daily life, they share one important characteristic: The answers to each can be found through research. A doctor would need instant answers for the question about snakebites because a life hangs in the balance. Other situations might not be as critical, but without the ability to find and evaluate information quickly, the world as we know it would eventually fall apart. Research produces discoveries that improve our quality of life.

Developing the skills to locate, analyze, and use information will significantly enhance your ability to keep up with what is going on in the world; to participate in activities that interest you; and to succeed in college, career, and community. The research skills you learn and use as a student will serve you well as a successful professional. That holds true for whatever career path you choose. Whether you're a student of biology, engineering, business, or public relations, your task in college is to manage information for projects and presentations, both oral and written. In a few years, as a lab technician, a project coordinator, a loss prevention specialist, or a campaign manager for a gubernatorial candidate, your task will be the same: to manage and present

IN THIS CHAPTER YOU WILL EXPLORE

What it means to be information literate

How to employ information literacy in the library, in the classroom, and in life

How to choose a topic, narrow it down, and research it

The many resources that are available at a college or university library

How to obtain help from librarians

What to do with the information you find

Why plagiarism can doom a paper, a course, or a career—and how to avoid it

information for your employers and clients. All colleges and many companies provide libraries for this purpose. But finding and using information involve more than operating a computer or wandering the stacks. To make sense of the vast amount of information at your fingertips in a reasonable amount of time, you'll need to develop a few key research and information literacy skills.

Information Literacy

> We get information every day in many ways: television, radio, computer, texting, the Internet, Twitter, e-mail, and so many more. Is there such a thing as too much information? Are we in an age of information overload?

During the Agricultural Age, most people farmed. Now only a tiny fraction of us work the land, yet edible goods continue to fill our silos and dairy transfer stations and feedlots. During the Industrial Age, we made things. We still do, of course, but automation has made it possible for more goods to be produced by fewer people. Now we live in the Information Age, a name that was created to signify the importance of information in today's economy and our lives.

Most of the global workforce is employed in one way or another in creating, managing, or transferring information. The gross national product (GNP) of the United States is substantially information based. Library science is one of the fastest-growing career opportunities around. Companies such as Google and Yahoo! have earned billions of dollars by simply offering, organizing, and selling information. Put another way, information has value: You can determine its benefits in dollars, and you can compute the cost of not having it.

The challenge is managing it all. There is more information than ever before, and it doubles at rapidly shortening intervals. Because abundance and electronic access combine to produce enormous amounts of retrievable information, people need highly developed **sorting** skills to cope. Information literacy is the premier survival skill for the modern world.

sorting The process of sifting through available information and selecting what is most relevant.

What is information literacy? Simply put, it's the ability to find, interpret, and use information to meet your needs. Information literacy has many facets, among them the following:

IN CLASS: Ask students what it means to be information literate. How does critical thinking relate to information? Can we believe everything we read? If not, why not?

- **Computer literacy:** Facility with electronic tools, both for conducting inquiries and for presenting to others what you have found and analyzed.

- **Media literacy:** The ability to think critically about material distributed to a wide audience through television, film, advertising, radio, magazines, books, and the Internet.

- **Cultural literacy:** Knowing what has gone on and is going on around you. You have to understand the difference between the Civil War and the Revolutionary War, U2 and

DID YOU KNOW?

27% of first-year college students report frequently exploring topics on their own (even if not required for a class) in their first year.

◣ ASSESSING YOUR STRENGTHS ▮

Information literacy is one of the most important skills you will learn in college. There is so much available information that you will also use your critical-thinking skills to determine what's really valid and important. Now that you have read the first section of this chapter, list your experiences in finding and using information successfully.

_____

_____

_____

_____

◣ SETTING GOALS ▮

What are your most important objectives in learning the material in this chapter? Do you need to improve your information literacy skills? List three goals in this area (e.g., I will visit the library and learn about the resources that relate to my classes).

1. _____

_____

2. _____

_____

3. _____

_____

■ RETENTION STRATEGY: Information literacy is an essential skill for employment. Being able to find and use information will help students discover a career path and the majors that prepare them for that path. Students who are committed to a career goal are more likely to be retained.

YouTube, Eminem and M&Ms, or you will not understand everyday conversation.

Information matters. It helps empower people to make good choices. The choices people make often determine their success in business, their happiness as friends and family members, and their well-being as citizens on this planet.

LEARNING TO BE INFORMATION LITERATE

People marvel at the information explosion, paper inflation, and the Internet. Many confuse mounds of information with knowledge and conclude that they are informed or can easily become informed. But most of us are unprepared for the huge number of available sources and the unsorted, unevaluated mass of information that pours over us at the press of a button. What, then, is the antidote for information overload? To become an informed and successful user of information, keep three basic goals in mind:

1. **Know how to find the information you need.** If you are sick, you need to know whose help to seek. If you lose your scholarship, you need to know where to get financial assistance. If you want to win a lawsuit, you

need to know how to find the outcomes of similar cases. Once you have determined where to look for information, you'll need to ask good questions and to make educated searches of information systems, such as the Internet, libraries, and databases. You'll also want to cultivate relationships with information professionals, such as librarians, who can help you frame questions, broaden and narrow searches, and retrieve the information you need.

2. **Learn how to interpret the information you find.** It is very important to retrieve information. It is even more important to make sense of that information. What does the information mean? Have you selected a source you can understand? Is the information accurate? Is the source reliable?

3. **Have a purpose.** Even the best information won't do much good if you don't know what to do with it. True, sometimes you'll hunt down a fact simply for your own satisfaction. More often, you'll communicate what you've learned to someone else. You should know not only what form that communication will take—a research paper for a class, a proposal for your boss, a presentation at a hearing—but also what you want to accomplish. Will you use the information to make a decision, develop a new solution to a problem, influence a course of action, prove a point, or something else?

We'll be spending most of this chapter exploring ways to pursue each of these goals.

WHAT'S RESEARCH—AND WHAT'S NOT?

To discover good information that you can use for a given purpose, you'll have to conduct research. You might be working on a college research paper right now— or anxious about one that's ahead of you. As you contemplate these projects, be sure you understand what research involves.

In the past, you might have completed assignments that asked you to demonstrate how to use a library's electronic book catalog, periodical index, e-mail delivery system, government documents collection, map depository, and interlibrary loan service. Or you might have been given a subject, such as ethics, and assigned to find a definition or a related book, journal article, or Web page. If so, what you accomplished was retrieval. And while retrieving information is an essential element of research, it's not an end in itself.

Nor is research a matter of copying passages or finding a handful of sources and patching together bits and pieces without commentary. In fact, such behavior could easily slip into the category of **plagiarism**, a serious misstep that could result in a failing grade or worse (see page 263). At the very least, repeating information or ideas without interpreting them puts you at risk of careless use of sources that might be new or old, useful or dangerously in error, reliable or shaky, research based or anecdotal, or objective or biased beyond credibility.

Good research, by contrast, is information literacy in action. Let's take up the ethics topic again. If you were assigned to select and report on an ethics issue, you might pick ethics in politics, accumulate a dozen sources, evaluate

plagiarism The act of taking another person's ideas or work and presenting it as your own. This gross academic misconduct can result in suspension or expulsion, and even the revocation of the violator's college degree.

them, interpret them, select a few and discard a few, organize the keepers into a coherent arrangement, extract portions that hang together, write a paper or presentation that cites your sources, compose an introduction that explains what you have done, draw some conclusions of your own, and submit the results. That's research. And if you learn to do it well, you'll experience the rush that comes with discovery and the pleasure that accompanies making a statement or taking a stand. The conclusion that you compose on the basis of your research is new information!

EMPLOYING INFORMATION LITERACY SKILLS

By the time you graduate, you should have attained a level of information literacy that will carry you through your professional life. The Association of College and Research Libraries has developed the following best practices for the information-literate student. Learn how to apply them, and you'll do well no matter where your educational and career paths take you.

- **Determine the nature and extent of the information needed.** In general, this involves first defining and articulating what information you need, then identifying a variety of potential sources.
- **Access information effectively and efficiently.** Select the most appropriate research methods, use well-designed search strategies, refine those strategies along the way, and keep organized notes on what you find and where you find it.
- **Evaluate information and its sources critically.** As an information-literate person, you'll be able to apply criteria for judging the usefulness and reliability of both information and its sources. You'll also become skilled at summarizing the main ideas presented by others and comparing new information with what you already know.
- **Incorporate information into your knowledge base and value system.** To do this, you'll determine what information is new, unique, or contradictory and consider whether it has an impact on what's important to you. You'll also validate, understand, or interpret the information through talking with other people. Finally, you'll combine elements of different ideas to construct new concepts of your own making.
- **Use information effectively to accomplish a specific purpose.** You'll apply information to planning and creating a particular product or performance, revising the development process as necessary, and communicating the results to others.
- **Access and use information ethically and legally.** There are economic, legal, and social issues surrounding the retrieval and use of information. You'll need to understand and follow laws, regulations, institutional policies, and etiquette related to copyright and intellectual property. Most important, you should acknowledge the use of information from sources in everything you write, record, or broadcast.[1]

[1]Adapted from *Information Literacy Competency Standards for Higher Education* (2000), http://www.ala.org/ala/acrl/acrlstandards/standards.pdf.

Many of your students will equate finding information with winning the battle. They might have had instructors who instructed them to "find a book about Abraham Lincoln" or to "locate a magazine article on the future of government in Cuba," and they even might have been told, "Try looking on your own before you ask the librarians for help." These instructors have confused retrieval for research and might have unintentionally deprived students of the opportunity to get help and counsel from information professionals. You know that while locating information is an essential step, how students evaluate, analyze, and use retrieved information will determine whether they have benefited from the experience.

IN CLASS: Information literacy is a skill that is acquired through practice, so the most helpful step a teacher can take at this point is to provide a practice opportunity. Most first-year students have at least one class in which they have to write a research paper. Why not help them get started? Ask a librarian to speak to your class. If students don't have a topic yet, ask the librarian to show them the Library of Congress Subject Headings, the *New York Times* Index, or Facts on File.

This exercise asks students to work through a scenario by employing information literacy skills and helps them see how good research skills can be applied to nonacademic questions that they will need to answer in their lives.

How You USE INFORMATION Matters

Not all research is for academic assignments. In everyday life, adults do research for basic life tasks: what stocks to invest in, what doctor to choose for surgery, what school or child-care facility to use for their children. The skills utilized for your collegiate library research can also be used for these everyday types of tasks.

Let's tackle an issue you may encounter soon: What type of summer employment would be the best choice for you? Work through the following scenario:

Scenario: You are a junior majoring in Public Relations. You have had little to no experience in this career field, and because of the economy, there are no jobs available in PR for summer employment in your hometown.

Your Dilemma: You can return to the job you had last summer—waiting tables at a local steak house, or you can work at a new job and begin by applying for a marketing internship at a summer beach resort 3 hours from home.

What do you need to know to make an informed decision about summer employment? Let's follow the guidelines from your book, employing information literacy skills:

Determine the nature and extent of the information you need to make this decision.	List three questions you need to ask and who you will ask: 1. 2. 3.
Access this information effectively and efficiently.	For the three questions you identified, how will you find out the answers? On the Internet? By phone? 1. 2. 3.

Critically evaluate the information and your sources. Is the compensation enough? Are your sources—friends, the Internet, the potential employer—trustworthy, and are there any hidden agendas to consider?

Incorporate the information into your own personal knowledge base and value system. What other issues in your life might prevent you from taking on such a dramatic change? What else do you need to consider as you compare your old job (a known situation) with your potential new job (an unknown)?

Use the information to accomplish a purpose. If you don't really need the information, you may not have the motivation to continue the process of researching. You may encounter a few brick walls. In our scenario, what would happen if the job were already filled? How would you improvise or revise your search?

Access and use the information ethically and legally. In our scenario, what might be an unethical situation you face as you conduct research for a new job?

(continued)

Having worked through this scenario, can you think of a situation confronting you now that you need to research? How can you use this chart as a guideline to make the research easier?

_____

_____

Choosing, Narrowing, and Researching a Topic

In Chapter 10, we read that prewriting is the stage that takes the longest. What is the danger of not getting a good overview of a topic before selecting a focus?

Assignments that require the use of library materials can take many forms and will come in many of your classes. There are numerous ways to search for information to complete an assignment, and we'll consider some of those later in the chapter. Before you start searching, however, you need to have an idea of what you're looking for.

Choosing a topic is often the most difficult part of a research project. Even if an instructor assigns a general topic, you'll need to narrow it down to a particular aspect that interests you enough to make worthwhile the time and energy you'll spend pursuing it. Imagine, for example, that you have been assigned to write a research paper on the topic of political ethics. What steps should you take?

Your first job is to get an overview of your topic. You can begin by looking at general and specific dictionaries and encyclopedias. To learn something about political ethics, for example, you might consult a political dictionary and the *Encyclopedia of American Political History*. Similar broad sources are available for just about any subject area, from marketing to sports psychology to colonial American literature. Check your library's reference area or consult with a librarian for leads.

Once you've acquired some basic information to guide you toward an understanding of the nature of your topic, you have a decision to make: What aspects of the subject will you pursue? Even if you launch the most general of inquiries, you will discover very quickly that your topic is vast and includes many related subtopics. If you look up "political ethics" in the Library of Congress Subject Headings or your library's online catalog, for instance, you will discover some choices:

Civil service, ethics	Judicial ethics
Conflict of interests	Justice
Corporations—corrupt practices	Legislative ethics
	Political corruption
Environmental ethics	Political ethics
Ethics, modern	Social ethics
Fairness	
Gifts to politicians	

Because the topic is broad, every one of these headings leads to books and articles on political ethics. What you want are a dozen or so focused, highly relevant hits on an aspect of the topic that you can fashion into a coherent, well-organized essay. Begin by assessing what you already know and asking what you would like to learn more about. Perhaps you know a little about the efforts of lobbyists and political action committees to influence legislation, and you're curious about recent efforts to limit what gifts politicians may accept; in that case you might decide on a three-pronged topic: gifts to politicians, political corruption, and lobbyists.

You can follow these steps to focus any topic. By simply consulting a few general sources, you'll find that you can narrow a broad topic to something that interests you and is a manageable size. From reference works and a quick search of a library catalog, periodicals database, or the Internet you will find definitions, introductory materials, some current and historical examples of your topic in action, and related information. You are now ready to launch a purposeful search.

OUTSIDE CLASS: Create an assignment that shows students how important it is to narrow the topic. They can also practice key word searches as described later in the chapter.

This exercise is directly related to the chapter's Tech Tip and helps students understand how online search results differ greatly depending on the database they use.

EXERCISE 11.2

How You USE INFORMATION LITERACY Matters

Narrowing a topic makes writing a paper more manageable. Broad topic searches result in too many articles to review. For instance, searching for "goal setting" in an academic database like Academic Search Complete results in 18,145 articles, and a Google (nonacademic) search results in more than 25,000,000!

Let's narrow your search: Use an *academic database*, and request only "Peer Reviewed Articles," using asterisks to mean exact phrases *Goal Setting* and *College Students*. This results in 90 articles on goal setting—a far more manageable number. Practice narrowing a topic. Fill in the chart below to see how many articles pop up when you search for the key words "time management" and "college students." Compare and contrast the search results using different databases. (Refer to the Tech Tip feature on page 257.)

Key Word Combinations (using Boolean operators and *)	Number of Articles Found with Academic Database (I used _____)	Number of Articles Found with Nonacademic Database (I used _____)
Time Management		
Time Management AND College Students		
Time Management OR College Students		
Time Management NOT College Students		
Time Management in College		

Using the Library

This textbook states that the most important but least used resource in the library is the librarian. Have you had contact with your college librarian? Describe your experience.

Whenever you have research to do—whether for a class, your job, or your personal life—visit a library. We can't stress this enough. Although the Internet is loaded with billions of pages of information, don't be fooled into thinking it will serve all of your needs. For one thing, you'll have to sort through a lot of junk to find your way to good-quality sources online. More important, if you limit yourself to the Web, you'll miss out on some of the best materials. Although we often think that everything is electronic and can be found through a computer, a great deal of valuable information is still stored in traditional formats and is most easily accessed through a library.

Every library has books and journals as well as a great number of items in electronic databases that aren't available on public Web sites. Most libraries also have several other types of collections, such as government documents, microfilm, rare books, manuscripts, dissertations, fine art, photographs, historical documents, maps, and music and films, including archival and documentary productions. Remember that information has been recorded and stored in many forms over the centuries. Libraries maintain materials in whatever form they were first produced and provide access to these materials for free.

OUTSIDE CLASS: Many librarians are responsible for user education and will be glad to host a visit from you and your class. Tell the librarian what you want your students to do so that he or she will know how to conduct the lesson. Provide a copy of your assignment, and the librarian will talk your students through retrieval processes, explaining how to narrow searches, how to select the terms that will deliver hits, how to find general and specific sources, when electronic and print sources are best used, how to recognize and deal with opinion and bias, how to construct good research logic, how to distinguish between database and Internet sources, and how to ask questions.

Get Thee to a Library

How often do you go to your campus library? Beyond having a library tour, have you explored this important academic resource? Although information is available from many sources, the most reliable resource will be a professional librarian, who can guide you to relevant books, articles, and online information.

TAKING ADVANTAGE OF EVERYTHING YOUR LIBRARY HAS TO OFFER

Books and periodicals are essential, but a college or university library is far more than a document warehouse. For starters, most campus libraries have Web sites that offer lots of help for students. Some provide guidelines on writing research papers, conducting online searches, or navigating the stacks. And all of them provide invaluable services to students and faculty members, including virtual spaces for accessing library holdings and the Web, physical spaces where you can study in quiet or meet with other students, and perhaps even social and entertainment programs.

Of course, no one library can possibly own everything you might need, so groups of libraries share their holdings with each other. If your library does not have a journal or book that looks promising for your project, the interlibrary loan department will be happy to borrow the materials for you. In most cases you can expect to receive the materials in as little as a few days, but it's always a good idea to identify and request what you might need from other libraries as far in advance as possible, in case the material is in high demand.

Are you a commuter or distance education student who cannot easily visit your college library in person? Most libraries provide proxy access to their electronic materials to students off campus. Usually, the library's home page serves as an electronic gateway to its services, which may include the following:

- A searchable catalog of the library's physical holdings
- Electronic databases, some of which let you access the full text of newspaper, magazine, and journal articles from your computer

Where Do You Work Out?

Look for ways to balance your life so that you give your body a workout in the gym and your brain a workout in the library.

- Interlibrary loan requests
- Course reserve readings
- Downloadable e-books
- Indexes of Web sites that have been carefully screened for reliability and relevance to particular subject areas
- Online chats with librarians who can help you in real time

To learn more, poke around your library's Web site, or e-mail or phone the reference desk.

Libraries also have a wide variety of physical spaces for students and faculty members to use. From individual study tables to private group rooms to comfortable chairs tucked in quiet corners, you should be able to find a study area that suits you and your needs. You might also discover places to eat, socialize, take in a movie or an art exhibit, check your e-mail and social networking page, search the Web, type your papers, make photocopies, edit videos, give presentations, hold meetings, or take a much-needed nap.

Be sure to use the handouts and guides that are available at the reference desk or online. You will also find tutorials and virtual tours that will help you to become familiar with the collections, services, and spaces available at your library.

IN CLASS: Share information with your students on what is available in your campus library.

ASKING A LIBRARIAN

Of all the resources available in a library, the most useful—and often the least used—are the people who staff it. Librarians thrive on helping you. If you're not sure how to start a search, if you're not successful in your first attempts at retrieving information, or if you just need some ideas about what you might try as you pursue a research project, ask a librarian. Librarians are information experts who are trained to assist and guide you to the resources you need. The librarians who work in the reference area or supervise the computer stations might look busy. But they are busy helping people with projects much like yours. You are not interrupting when you ask for assistance, and with rare exceptions, any librarian will be delighted to help you.

You can contact a reference librarian in several ways. E-mail a query, and you are likely to receive a quick reply. Or call the reference desk to ask a question, such as "Do you have a copy of the report *Problems with the Presidential Gifts System*?" You can have a "live chat" online with a library staffer in real time. And of course, you can visit the reference desk in person or make an appointment for a tutorial or consultation. (Hint: You will be most successful if you bring a copy of your assignment and any written instructions you have to your meeting. Tell the librarian what you have tried—if anything.) Remember that there are no silly questions. A good librarian will treat your inquiries with respect.

The information professionals at your library are authorities on how to find information. Most important, they not only know where to find it, but also have the wonderful ability to help you use information to meet your needs, solve problems, provide explanations, open up new possibilities, and ultimately create new knowledge.

IN CLASS: Have your students select a method to contact a librarian and ask a question. Either assign each student a question or have students develop their own. Follow up with a short discussion about their experiences in contacting a librarian.

This exercise encourages students to visit their library to overcome any apprehension they have in using it.

EXERCISE 11.3

KNOWING YOUR LIBRARY Matters

Why does the idea of going to the library seem so daunting to many students? Is it that many students don't like to ask complete strangers for help when doing their papers? Or is it that the library can be so quiet?

Here is your challenge: Go on a reconnaissance mission! You can do this in person or on the Web.

Answer the following questions about your own campus library. If you visit the facility, you may be surprised how pleasant the experience can be.

Questions about Your Campus Library	Your Answer
What are the days and hours of operation?	
Does the library have private group meeting rooms? Where and how are these reserved?	
Where is the best place to study for complete quiet? How about for semi-quiet?	
Are laptops available for students? What is the return policy?	
How much are photocopies? Printing costs?	
Do students have to make an appointment with a reference librarian or are walk-ins okay? Is there a way to contact a librarian online?	
Is it okay to nap in the library between classes?	
How about talking with friends?	
Can students check out movies for free? What is the return policy?	

Electronic Resources

Literally hundreds of databases contain thousands of electronic journals and other periodicals that are at your disposal. How can you narrow down all of these choices for a particular class?

Online catalogs, periodical databases, and the World Wide Web allow you to quickly and easily locate materials in the vast universe of information. Learning how to use these resources efficiently will save you time and improve your odds of finding the information that best suits your needs.

LIBRARY CATALOGS

The card catalogs that were once common in libraries have been replaced by OPAC (online public access catalogs). These electronic catalogs tell you what books, magazines, newspapers, videos, and other materials are available in a particular library. They might also provide abstracts of the information presented in those materials, tables of contents for individual entries, and related search terms. Typically, they'll provide an identifying number that tells you where in the stacks to locate a particular document. A catalog might also inform you whether an item is already checked out and, if so, when it's due back. The catalog will also allow you to put the material on hold or give you the option of requesting it through interlibrary loan.

You can search the catalogs through terminals at the library or from your home computer or a laptop. The simplest way to search a catalog is by key word (see the guidelines for conducting an effective search on pages 256–58). You might also search by subject, author, title, date, or a combination of these elements. Be sure to spend a few minutes on the catalog's help or FAQ page, which will guide you through the options and demonstrate ways to customize your search terms. Each system has its own preferences.

PERIODICAL DATABASES

A library catalog helps you search for books and the titles of magazines and journals owned by a particular library. By contrast, periodical databases let you hunt down articles published in hundreds (even thousands) of newspapers, magazines, and scholarly journals. Some databases might provide a full-text copy of the article as part of the record returned from your search; other times you'll have to use the information in the record to find a physical copy in your library or request it through interlibrary loan.

Subscription services such as EBSCOHost, LexisNexis, and Gale Research compile and maintain electronic periodical databases. These are not free to the general public and must be accessed through a library. (Ask at the circulation desk for a barcode number and PIN, which will allow you to access your library's databases from remote terminals.) Most libraries subscribe to multiple databases and subdivide them by broad general categories such as Humanities, Social Sciences, Science and Technology, Business, Health and Medicine, Government Information, or by major. Under "Social Sciences," for example, you might find International Political Science Abstracts (PAIS), America: History and Life, and over twenty other databases. There are also multidisciplinary databases, such as Academic Search Premier, InfoTrac, and Reader's Guide to Periodical Literature, that provide excellent material on most topics you will encounter during your first year of college.

Databases have their own specialties and different strengths, so you'll want to select the best ones for your particular subject or topic. Check your library's subscription list for an overview of what's available, and don't hesitate to ask a librarian to make recommendations about which databases are most relevant to your needs.

Information in a database is usually stored in a single location or on a server that is owned by the subscription service company. Human beings, not computers, do the indexing, so you can be fairly sure the information in a database meets certain criteria for inclusion, such as accuracy, timeliness, and authoritativeness. And because most of the material indexed in a database originally appeared in print, you can be fairly certain that it was reviewed for quality by other scholars or an editorial staff.

IN CLASS: Students need to understand that knowing where to look for specific information is important. Use an analogy to illustrate that there are different tools (or databases) for different resources. For example, you wouldn't go to the grocery store to buy lumber. Not everything is available in the same location. This is why it's important that students ask their professor or a librarian where to look. Also point out that many libraries have database lists based on subject. It is helpful for students to look not only for their topics but also for subjects under which their topics might fall.

THE WORLD WIDE WEB

Searching the Web is a totally different story. The material retrieved by Googling is an aggregation of information, opinion, and sales pitches from the vast universe of servers around the globe. Anybody can put up a Web site, which means you can't be sure of the Web site owner's credibility and reliability. The sources you find on the Web might be written by anyone—a fifth grader, a distinguished professor, a professional society, or a biased advocate.

A recent Google search on the subject "political corruption," for instance, generated over 10 million hits. The first page yielded some interesting results:

> A collection of links on politics and political corruption
>
> A Libertarian Party legislative program on political corruption
>
> Two Amazon.com ads
>
> A site that offers "research" on gambling and political corruption
>
> A university site offering research on political corruption in Illinois

These varied results demonstrate that one must be alert when examining Internet sources. Mixed in with credible scholarship on this topic are sales promotions, some arguments against gambling, and useful links to other sources. It isn't always easy to evaluate the quality of Internet sources. Check pages 258–61 in this chapter for some helpful strategies you can use to determine whether a source is credible and authentic.

GUIDELINES FOR EFFECTIVE SEARCHES

Most searches of catalogs and databases are done by using key words. A key word is a single word that would appear in a discussion of the topic you are investigating. Other systems permit searching of phrases. A few databases and Web search engines allow a natural language search, in which you can ask a question or type in a sentence that describes what you are looking for. Some databases, such as the *New York Times* Index and ERIC (Education Resources Information Center), have their own approved lists of subject terms that you should consult before searching. Be careful to choose search terms that are relevant to your investigation; this will help you retrieve material you can use. And don't forget that a librarian can help you with this.

To become a successful and savvy user of electronic resources, follow these guidelines:

- **Consult the Help or FAQs link** the first time you use any catalog, database, or search engine to learn specific searching techniques. You will get the best results if you use the tips and strategies suggested by the database provider.

- **Write out your topic or problem as a statement or question.** "Is it right for politicians to take gifts from lobbyists?" Or "The influence of lobbyists or PACs has dramatically changed American political ethics." Doing so will help you identify potentially useful key words.

- **Write down several terms or synonyms for your topic** so that if one search does not yield any useful hits, you have some backup terms on hand. It's also a good idea to search more than one database or engine; different ones might pull up dramatically different sources.

IN CLASS: Most of your students have probably conducted a search on the Web. You can ask the class to share what kinds of searches they do. Discuss their thoughts on how valuable the Web is for serious research.

TECH TIP CHECK YOUR ENGINE

1 ▶ THE PROBLEM

You understand the basics of online research but don't know how to apply it to an academic setting.

2 ▶ THE FIX

Learn what research passes scholarly muster: peer-reviewed academic journals (e.g., the *Harvard Business Review*), government Web sites (which usually end in .gov), or newspaper Web sites (like the *New York Times* or the *Washington Post*).

3 ▶ HOW TO DO IT

Unlike the examples above, much of the information you find online isn't objective or factual; it's a digital free-for-all out there. When digging for academic research, you need to be fanatically picky and filter out all the garbage. That's called critical thinking, and it's what college is all about.

Your college library offers free access to a wealth of academic databases, LexisNexis, e-journals, etc. If you have questions about how to use them (and about what kinds of materials qualify as academic research in general), make an appointment with a reference librarian. In 30 minutes you'll probably be smarter than anyone else in your class. Go online to **http://libguides.bgsu.edu/library_basics** and visit the library at Bowling Green State University to find helpful "getting started" guides to online research.

- **Hone your online research skills.** Make sure you understand Boolean operators. The most common Boolean operators are the words AND, OR, and NOT, and how you use them affects your search results.

- **Key words separated** by the word AND yield results that contain both of the required words, in any order. According to the Bowling Green Web site, "A search for rock AND roll will locate all records containing both the word *rock* and the word *roll*. It will locate items about rock and roll music. It might also locate records that contain both words in a different context."

- **Key words separated** by the word OR yield results that contain one word or the other. "A search for rock OR roll will locate all records containing either the word *rock* or the word *roll*—not necessarily both. It will retrieve items about bakery rolls, tumbling, rocks, music, gemstones, etc."

- **Key words separated** by the word NOT yield results that feature the first word and exclude the second. "A search for rock NOT roll will locate records containing the word *rock* but NOT the word *roll*. It will retrieve items about rocks, gemstones, diamonds, etc."*

- **Other tips:** Frame key words with asterisks to yield results that include the exact phrase within the asterisks. Or if you get too few hits, omit a search term. Add an asterisk to a key word for a wildcard search that yields results that include any word that starts with the key word.

*http://libguides.bgsu.edu/library_basics.

GOOD TO KNOW

Learn the quirks of the databases or search engines you use often. Whether you use AltaVista, Bing, Google, or Google Scholar, learn tricks to refine your search. Some engines yield better results from Boolean operators (e.g., "politicians AND lobbyists"); others are more attuned to natural language searches (e.g., "ethics in politics" or "gifts to politicians").

PERSONAL BEST

Avoid Internet plagiarism. You cannot cut and paste whole sentences from the Internet into your essays. Instructors can easily catch you and the penalties are stiff.

KEY TIPS

1. **Don't procrastinate.** If you leave a big paper till the last minute, you'll be more tempted to cut and paste, and less scrupulous about footnotes.

2. **Avoid *unintentional* cheating.** Whenever you copy online research into your notes, be sure to add a URL in brackets at the end. While you're at it, place quotation marks around all cited materials, or highlight them in a bright color. It's surprisingly easy to forget which words are your own and which words came from another author.

3. **When in doubt, footnote.** Paraphrasing anything off the Internet, or from any other source, and using it without attribution is cheating. Most colleges have a zero-tolerance policy on the subject.

- **Limit your search.** You can often limit a search by date, language, journal name, full text, or word(s) in title. If you still get too many hits, add more search terms.
- **Check your library's electronic resources page** to see what else is available online. Most libraries have links to other commonly used electronic reference tools. These include online encyclopedias, dictionaries, almanacs, style guides, biographical and statistical resources, and news sources.

EXERCISE 11.4

How You RESEARCH Matters

Now that you are familiar with the services of your campus library, take one more step and get familiar with its electronic resources. Take the initiative to visit your library Web site. (Every library system is different, but it is beneficial to get familiar with your library as soon as possible.) Look for your library's catalog, which helps you search for books, magazines, and journals that are available in your campus library. In addition to those resources *within* your library, your facility has access to online databases from all over the world that provide electronic journal articles.

How many databases (such as EBSCO*host*, ProQuest) does your library subscribe to? _____

Under each category of study, the library also lists databases. If you are an education major, for example, you will utilize ERIC quite a bit.

What is your intended major? _____

Under this area, how many databases does your library contain? _____

Evaluating Sources

Not all sources are created equal. When researching a topic, occasionally a word choice or a simple misspelling may yield completely inappropriate source results. Has this ever happened to you?

It's easy to assume that huge amounts of available information automatically provide knowledge. Some students might at first be excited about receiving 20,800,000 hits from a Google search on political ethics, but shock takes hold when they realize their discovery is utterly unsorted. They might respond by using only the first several hits, irrespective of quality. A more productive approach is to think critically about the usefulness of potential sources by measuring them against three important criteria: relevance, authority, and bias.

RELEVANCE

The first thing to consider in looking at a possible source is how well it fits your needs. That, in turn, will be affected by the nature of your research project and the kind of information you are seeking.

- **Is it introductory?** Introductory information is very basic and elementary. It neither assumes nor requires prior knowledge about the topic.

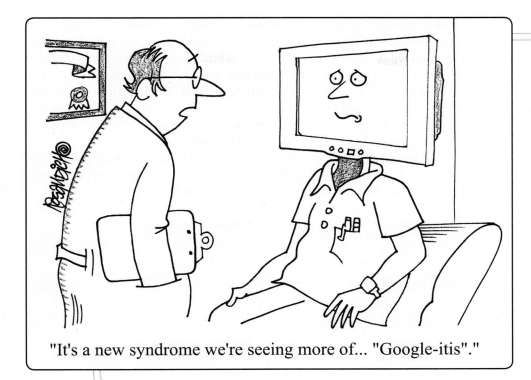

"It's a new syndrome we're seeing more of... "Google-itis"."

Google-itis

Search engines such as Google have made finding immediate answers to any question easier than ever before. But be careful: Although some Google hits may be authentic and valuable, others may take you to advertisements or biased reports that don't give you exactly THE answer you were looking for.

Introductory sources can be useful when you're first learning about a subject. They are less useful when you're drawing conclusions about a particular aspect of the subject.

- **Is it definitional?** Definitional information provides some descriptive details about a subject. It might help you introduce a topic to others or clarify the focus of your investigation.

- **Is it analytical?** Analytical information supplies and interprets data about origins, behaviors, differences, and uses. In most cases it's the kind of information you want.

- **Is it comprehensive?** The more detail, the better. Avoid unsubstantiated opinions, and look instead for sources that consider the topic in depth and offer plenty of evidence to support their conclusions.

- **Is it current?** You should usually give preference to recent sources, although older ones can sometimes be useful (for instance, if your subject is historical or the source is still cited by others in a field).

- **Can you conclude anything from it?** Use the "so what?" test: How important is this information? Why does it matter to my project?

AUTHORITY

Once you have determined that a source is relevant to your project, check that it was created by somebody who has the qualifications to write or speak on the subject. This, too, will depend on your subject and the nature of your inquiry (a fifth grader's opinion might be exactly what you're looking for), but in most cases you'll want expert conclusions based on rigorous evidence.

Make sure you can identify the author and be ready to explain why that author is a reliable source. Good qualifications might include academic degrees, institutional affiliations, an established record of researching and publishing on a topic, or personal experience with a subject. Be wary, on the other hand, of anonymous or commercial sources or those written by someone whose credibility is questionable.

Understand, as well, whether your project calls for scholarly publications, popular magazines, or both. Do you know the difference?

You don't necessarily have to dismiss popular magazines. Many journalists and columnists are extremely well qualified, and their work might well be appropriate for your needs. But as a rule scholarly sources will be more credible.

Scholarly Journals	Popular Magazines
Long articles	Shorter articles
In-depth information on topic	Broad overview of topic
Written by academic experts	Written by journalists or reporters
Graphs, tables, and charts	Photos of people and events
Articles "refereed" or reviewed	Articles not rigidly evaluated
Formally documented	Sources credited informally

BIAS

When you are searching for sources, you should realize that there can be a heavy dose of bias or point of view in some of them. Although nothing is inherently wrong with someone's having a particular point of view, it is dangerous for a reader not to know that the bias is there. A great source for keeping you informed about potential bias is *Magazines for Libraries*,[2] which will tell you about a periodical's editorial and political leanings. *The Nation*, for instance, is generally considered liberal, while *National Review* is conservative.

Some signs of bias indicate that you should avoid using a source. If you detect overly positive or overly harsh language, hints of an agenda, or a stubborn refusal to consider other points of view, think carefully about how well you can trust the information in a document.

A NOTE ON INTERNET SOURCES

IN CLASS: Lead the class in a discussion of bias and point of view in articles. How can students determine whether the author is biased? What is the role of analytical thinking? You might bring in an opinion article to show students an example.

Be especially cautious of material you find online. It is often difficult to tell where something on the Internet came from or who wrote it. The lack of this information can make it very difficult to judge the credibility of the source. And while an editorial board reviews most print matter (books, articles, and so forth) for accuracy and overall quality, it's frequently difficult to confirm that the same is true for information on a Web site—with some exceptions. If you are searching through an online database such as the Human Genome Database or Eldis: The Gateway to Development Information (a poverty database), it is highly likely that documents in these collections have been reviewed. Online versions of print magazines and journals, likewise, have

[2]Cheryl LaGuardia, Bill Katz, and Linda S. Katz, *Magazines for Libraries*, 13th ed. (New Providence, NJ: RR Bowker LC, 2004).

usually been checked out by editors. And information from academic and government Web sites (those whose URLs end in .edu or .gov, respectively) is generally—but not always—trustworthy.

Exercise 11.5 prompts students to think critically about Wikipedia. Consider presenting your own views of Wikipedia.

EXERCISE 11.5

How You THINK CRITICALLY Matters

Most of us are familiar, at least to some degree, with Wikipedia. It is a collaborative written reference on the Web maintained by volunteers, not professionals in the field. It can be edited by anyone at any time and thus is not scholarly or "peer reviewed" but is reviewed by people.

Many professors do not approve of the use of Wikipedia as a reference for a paper. What do you think? Is this Web site worthy of being used as a reference, or is it just light reading?

_____

_____

_____

_____

Do you think that Wikipedia has merit because so many people can review it for errors, or do you think it is biased because nonprofessionals can post their opinions, rather than facts?

_____

_____

_____

_____

_____

Making Use of What You Find

> The quote "Knowledge is power" is mentioned in this chapter in conjunction with giving proper credit to others' ideas. NOT giving proper credit is like stealing. Has someone ever taken something from you that you cherished? How does this feel?

IN CLASS: Ask students to brainstorm ways to check the reliability of an Internet source. Suggest that they always include references from other media, such as books, periodicals (both popular and scholarly), and specialized databases, in their research.

You have probably heard the saying "Knowledge is power." While knowledge can certainly contribute to power, this is true only if that knowledge is put to use. When you retrieve, sort, interpret, analyze, and synthesize sources from an information center, whether it is the library, a computer database, or the Web, you can produce a product that has power.

But first, you have to decide what form that product will take and what kind of power you want it to hold. Whom are you going to tell about your discoveries, and how? What do you hope to accomplish by sharing your conclusions? Remember that a major goal of information literacy is to use information effectively to accomplish a specific purpose (pages 245–46). Make it a point to *do* something with the results of your research. Otherwise, why bother?

SYNTHESIZING INFORMATION AND IDEAS

Ultimately, the point of conducting research is that the process contributes to the development of new knowledge. As a researcher, you sought the answer to a question. Now is the time to formulate that answer and share it.

Many students satisfy themselves with a straightforward report that merely summarizes what they found. Sometimes, that's enough. More often, however, you'll want to apply the information to ideas of your own. To do that, first consider all of the information you found and how your sources relate to each other. What do they have in common, and where do they disagree? What conclusions can you draw from those similarities and differences? What new ideas did they spark? How can you use the information you have on hand to support your conclusions? (Refer to Chapter 5 for tips on drawing conclusions from different points of view and using evidence to construct an argument.)

Essentially, what you're doing at this stage of any research project is processing information, an activity known as **synthesis**. By accepting some ideas, rejecting others, combining related concepts, assessing the implications, and pulling it all together, you'll create new information and ideas that other people can use.

synthesis The process of combining separate information and ideas to formulate a more complete understanding.

CITING YOUR SOURCES

At some point you'll present your findings. Whether they take the form of an essay, a formal research paper, a script for a presentation or broadcast, a page for a Web site, or something else entirely, you must give credit to your sources.

Citing your sources serves many purposes. For one thing, acknowledging the information and ideas you've borrowed from other writers shows respect for their contributions; it also distinguishes between other writers' ideas and your own. Source citations demonstrate to your audience that you have based your conclusions on thoughtful consideration of good, reliable evidence. Source citations also provide a starting place for anyone who would like more information or is curious about how you reached your conclusions. Most important, citing your sources is the simplest way to avoid plagiarism.

The particular requirements of source citation can get complicated, but it all boils down to two basic rules. As you write, just remember:

- If you use somebody else's exact words, you must give that person credit.
- If you use somebody else's ideas, even if you use your own words to express those ideas, you must give that person credit.

Your instructors will indicate their preferred method for citation: footnotes, references in parentheses included in the text of your paper, or endnotes. If you're not provided with guidelines or if you simply want to be sure that you do it right, consult a handbook or writing style manual, such as those prepared by the Modern Language Association (*MLA Handbook for Writers of Research Papers*), the American Psychological Association (*Publication Manual of the American Psychological Association*), the University of Chicago Press (*The Chicago Manual of Style*), or the Council of Science Editors (*Scientific Style and Format: The CSE Manual for Authors, Editors, and Publishers*).

ABOUT PLAGIARISM

Several years ago, a serious candidate for the American presidency was forced to withdraw from the race when opponents discovered he had failed to give proper credit to a source he used in one of his speeches. A reporter at a top newspaper was fired for deliberately faking his sources, and a famous historian lost her peers' respect (and a portion of her royalties) when another writer noticed that the historian had included passages from her work in a book without citation.

All three writers were accused of plagiarism, but notice that only the reporter plagiarized on purpose. The political candidate and the historian were probably more guilty of poor note taking than of outright fraud, yet the consequences were just as dire. When information or ideas are put on paper, film, screen, or tape, they become intellectual property. Using those ideas without saying where you got them—even if you do this by mistake—is a form of theft and can cost you a grade, a course, a degree, maybe even a career.

It should go without saying (but we'll say it anyway) that deliberate cheating is a bad idea on many levels. Submitting a paper you purchased from an Internet source or from an individual will cause you to miss out on the discovery and skill development that research assignments are meant to teach. Intentional plagiarism is easily detected and will almost certainly earn you a failing grade, even expulsion.

Although most cases of plagiarism are the result of misunderstanding or carelessness, be aware that "I didn't know" is not a valid excuse. Although your instructors might acknowledge that plagiarism can be an "oops!" thing, they will still expect you to avoid errors, and they will call you on it if you don't. Luckily, plagiarism is relatively easy to avoid. Most important, always cite your sources. Keep careful notes as you conduct your research, so that later on you don't inadvertently mistake someone else's words or ideas for your own. Finally, be sure to check out your own campus's definition of what constitutes plagiarism, which you will find in the student handbook or in first-year English course materials. And if you have any questions or doubts about what is and isn't acceptable, ask.

> ■ RETENTION STRATEGY: For some students, plagiarism is an innocent mistake; for others it is intentional cheating. The penalties for cheating may include academic failure or suspension. Either penalty reduces a student's likelihood of remaining on campus in good standing.
>
> IN CLASS: Students often do not understand the complexities of plagiarism. Begin a discussion by brainstorming the meaning of plagiarism, especially as it relates to Internet sources.
>
> IN CLASS: Some of your students will know about plagiarism; some will have only foggy impressions about what it is and why they should avoid it. Some students will have practiced it, thinking that they were doing nothing wrong. Others might come from a culture in which ideas, once expressed, become the free property of all who want to use them. Get your academic institution's statement about plagiarism, and discuss it with your students. Enforce the stated rules. You will be doing your students, and scholarship, a great favor.

Students are asked to discuss their thoughts about plagiarism.

EXERCISE 11.6

YOUR STANDARDS Matter

What do you think about cheating? How do you view plagiarism? _____

_____

The textbook discusses issues of cheating and plagiarism, using examples of professionals in the field who have made mistakes. How do these examples make you feel? Relieved? Angry? Indifferent? _____

_____

Should professional speech writers, reporters, or authors be held to a higher ethical standard than, say, a high school student writing an English paper? Why or why not? _____

_____

(continued)

Conversely, should the idea of plagiarism be taught earlier, maybe even during middle school, so that by the time students reach college they are very familiar with how to avoid this problem? How would you explain this concept to a sixth grader? Plagiarism is like _____

_____

_____

You don't have to answer whether you have ever plagiarized. Most of us have, maybe even unintentionally, because it is difficult to write a completely original idea. But now, having read this chapter and realizing the importance of this topic, would you agree that citing your sources and/or ideas would prevent theft of "intellectual property"? _____

Look in your **Student Handbook** for a definition of what constitutes plagiarism at your institution. What is the "official" definition?

Plagiarism is defined at _____ *College/University as* _____

_____

_____

_____

Cite your source! Where did you find this definition? _____

CHECKLIST FOR SUCCESS

DEVELOPING RESEARCH SKILLS

☐ **Work to learn "information literacy" skills** because you will be working in the information economy, which uses and produces information. Most professions that you could prepare for in college require that you be able to find, evaluate, and use information.

☐ **Become comfortable in your campus library.** Use it as a place to read, relax, study, or just be by yourself.

☐ **Accept that research projects and papers are part of college life.** Learn how to do them well. This will teach you how to "research" the information you need in life after college. After all, modern professional life is one big term paper after another!

☐ **Get to know your college librarians.** They are anxious to help you find the information you need. Ask them for help even if they look busy. If possible, get to know one as your personal "library consultant."

☐ **Take courses early in college that require you to do research and use your library skills.** Yes, they will demand more of you, especially in writing, but you will be thankful for them later. Go ahead—bite the bullet.

☐ **Learn as many new electronic sources as possible.** You must be able to do research and seek the new information you need now and after college by doing more than using Google or Wikipedia.

☐ **When you use the ideas of others, it is important to give them credit and then create your own unique synthesis and conclusions.** Someday you will create what we call "intellectual property," and you will want others to give you credit for your ideas.

☐ **Consider becoming an information professional (librarian).** The world as we know it is going to need more and more of them. Explore this potential occupation in your campus's career center. If your campus is a university with a school of library and information science, drop by and see what you can learn.

APPLY IT! What Works for YOU Matters

Think about your current academic situation, and apply some of the suggestions and strategies introduced in this chapter. Select strategies that you think will work best for you, and then write them down in the "Your Response" column. What are YOU planning to do for YOUR college experience?

QUESTIONS	SAMPLE STUDENT ANSWERS	YOUR RESPONSE
	Name: Candace Lee	
Information Literacy We get information every day in many ways: television, radio, computer, texting, the Internet, Twitter, e-mail, and so many more. Is there such a thing as too much information? Are we in an age of information overload?	I love using technology to communicate. I know everything about my friends and even celebrities who use Twitter. But I wonder if I am overdoing the social dates because I can't remember my history dates at all.	
Choosing, Narrowing, and Researching a Topic In Chapter 10, we read that prewriting is the stage that takes the longest. What is the danger of not getting a good overview of a topic before selecting a focus?	I thought I had a good grasp on my topic: seat belt laws and child safety. But I forgot the new toddler car seat rule, and my instructor took off points. I spent too little time on research just trying to do it quickly.	
Using the Library This textbook states that the most important but least used resource in the library is the librarian. Have you had contact with your college librarian? Describe your experience.	I have to say my college library is nothing like my high school library. I went to campus the other day, and after visiting with the reference librarian, I had all my resources in 20 minutes! I will never avoid librarians again.	
Electronic Resources Literally hundreds of databases contain thousands of electronic journals and other periodicals that are at your disposal. How can you narrow down all of these choices for a particular class?	I discovered that if I search under my major, Early Childhood Education, there are a few huge databases. I have chosen ERIC and use it to find journal articles. Using Boolean operators limits my search even more!	
Evaluating Sources Not all sources are created equal. When researching a topic, occasionally a word choice or a simple misspelling may yield completely inappropriate source results. Has this ever happened to you?	One time I was trying to book a cruise. I went on what I thought was the cruise Web site, but because I didn't put in the exact Web address, it sent me to the fraudulent site where they were trying to scam me! I guess you just have to be so careful nowadays!	
Making Use of What You Find The quote "Knowledge is power" is mentioned in this chapter in conjunction with giving proper credit to others' ideas. NOT giving proper credit is like stealing. Has someone ever taken something from you that you cherished? How does this feel?	When someone steals something from me, I just get furious! I can see, having really struggled writing some of my papers, that if someone took my ideas, I would be so angry. Now that I know how important it is not to plagiarize, I cite everything.	

BUILD YOUR EXPERIENCE ▪▪▪

Students work together to gather the items on this scavenger hunt. Encourage students to use the staff at the library so they can develop a positive relationship with them.

1 COLLABORATIVE ACTIVITY

LIBRARY SCAVENGER HUNT

Find the following information with your team or partner. Each question is worth 5 points. Some of the answers can be found on the library Web site, but others will necessitate a visit!

1. Get a signature from a reference librarian: _____

2. Get a signature at the circulation desk: _____

3. What are the hours of operation on Sunday afternoon? _____

4. Can you bring coffee into the library? _____

5. What is the number of days a student can check out a book before it is due back? _____ Can you renew a book online? _____

6. Does your library have an interlibrary loan program? _____

7. How many electronic journals are in the Academic Search Premier database? _____

How many points did you and your team or partner get right? _____/35

What did you learn about your library that was unexpected or surprising to you? _____

2 BUILDING YOUR PORTFOLIO

In the Know   Reviewing multiple sources of information can help you to get the whole story. While the Internet is becoming a primary source of worldwide news, there is no quality control system for information posted on the Internet.

1. Choose a national current event. Carefully read about it in two places:
   a. On your favorite news Web site (e.g., **www.cnn.com**).
   b. In a traditional national newspaper (e.g., the *New York Times, Wall Street Journal, Christian Science Monitor,* or *USA Today*). Find them in a library or online.

2. In a *Word* document, compare and contrast how the two sources portray the event.
   - Are the authors' names or another source provided?
   - Describe any clues that the authors are taking a biased stand in reporting.
   - Were the facts presented the same way by both the Internet source and the print source? Explain your answer.
   - Were the writers' information sources listed? If so, what were those sources?

3. Save your responses in your portfolio. Use this process as a tool to make sure you use valid resources the next time you are doing research for a project or paper.

Did the material in this chapter make you think about libraries and research in a new light? What did you find to be the most useful information in this chapter? What would you like to learn more about?

_____

_____

_____

_____

_____

_____

_____

_____

_____

_____

_____

_____

_____

_____

No matter how well prepared you are in your teaching, what a student hears and understands might not always be what you think you have said. The one-minute paper is a quick and easy assessment tool that will help alert you when students don't understand what was said or discussed in class. The one-minute paper will also give timid students an opportunity to ask questions and seek clarification. Ideally, you should ask for such a paper several minutes before the end of a class. The paper will also help you begin your next class by clarifying points your students seem to be unsure of.

For more on this topic watch
French Fries Are Not Vegetables and Other College Lessons

WHERE TO GO FOR HELP . . .

ON CAMPUS

> **Your Instructor** Be sure to ask your instructor for help with your information search, especially if you need to narrow your topic.

> **Library** Libraries offer a variety of forms of help, including library orientation sessions, workshops, and, on some campuses, credit-bearing courses to develop your library search and retrieval skills.

> **Specialized Libraries/Collections** At a large university, it is very common to find multiple libraries that are part of separate schools or colleges. For example, if you are a business administration major at such a university, there will probably be a separate business library that you will need to learn to use in addition to the central library. This is true for many majors.

> **Technology Support Centers** Many campuses have units staffed by personnel who are responsible for the institution's entire technology infrastructure. These units frequently offer noncredit workshops and help sessions. In addition, many of the departments in larger universities will have their own separate technology labs and centers where you can work and get assistance. It won't surprise you to find that much of the help provided to students comes from fellow students, who are often ahead of their faculty in these skills. Some campuses also provide such assistance in residence halls, where there might even be a "computing assistant" in addition to the resident assistant.

> **Discipline-Based Courses** Many academic majors will include specialized courses in discipline-based research methods. You will find these listed in your campus catalog or bulletin. Students don't usually take these courses in their first year, but check them out. If you are interested in credit courses dealing with technology, check out the courses in computer science.

ONLINE

> Research and documenting sources: **http://owl .english.purdue.edu/owl/resource/584/02.** Purdue University has an excellent resource on documenting sources, both print and electronic.

MY INSTITUTION'S RESOURCES

_____

_____

_____

_____

_____

_____

_____

_____

EPILOGUE

Maintaining Your Momentum as a Successful Student

The great baseball player Yogi Berra is often quoted as having said, "It ain't over 'til it's over!" This course is over—or is it? One thing is for sure: College isn't over for you, and what you learned in this course isn't over. But finishing this course has to feel good. It is something you have accomplished early in college.

Because there has been so much research done on students like you, we can confidently tell you that successful completion of this course is a good predictor for overall success in college. In this last chapter we are going to provide you with some concrete action steps that you can put in place for next term and next year.

When you finish any of your courses in college, take some time to step back, reflect, and ask yourself some thoughtful questions:

- What did I learn in this course?
- Can I apply what I learned to other courses?
- How will I use what I learned both in and out of class?
- What did I learn that I am most likely to remember?
- Do I want to stay in touch with this instructor?
- Did I improve my basic skills?
- How do I feel about what I accomplished?
- Did I do better than I thought I would?
- What did I do that helped me progress, and how can I repeat those kinds of successful efforts in other courses?
- What challenges do I still face?

Whether you are finishing this course at the end of your first term in college or at the end of your first year in college, you have learned many success strategies that will continue to help you as you move through the rest of your college experience.

Unfortunately, many students, and many college educators too, think that when you finish the first year of college and, hopefully, have achieved sophomore status, you are over the hump. The rest is downhill because the most difficult part is behind you. Well, there is some truth to those beliefs. For many students the first year is by far the most challenging, especially in terms of adjustment to college life. But there are still many decisions you will have to make and many opportunities that await you. We know that you will need a set of strategies to succeed beyond the first year.

TAKING THE NEXT STEPS TO SUCCESS

You are still at the beginning of your college journey. Here are some suggestions for next steps you can take as you make your way toward graduation.

Keep in Touch with Your Instructors. We suggest that you consider keeping in touch with the instructor of this course. Educators who volunteer to teach a college success course or first-year seminar really do care about students and enjoy staying in touch with them over time and noting their progress. You will also want to stay in touch with your other instructors. Later in college you may need to ask them to write letters of reference for you as you seek employment or admission to graduate school. When an instructor becomes part of your larger support group, this is a form of networking.

In particular, discuss with the instructor of this course what your options might be for staying in touch. If you have enjoyed this class and would like to take another course from your instructor, find out what other courses he or she teaches. Choosing courses by selecting excellent instructors is a very important success strategy for the entire college experience.

Stay in Touch with Your Fellow Students. If you developed some good friendships in this class and discovered one or more students with whom you really connected, stay in touch with them. As we have explained in this book, the people with whom you choose to associate in college really matter.

Use Campus Resources. Continue using the campus's services and resources that you learned about in this course, such as the learning center or career center. Remember, these services are most heavily used by the best students, and you want to be one of those. Successful students continue to seek help. It's a lifelong behavioral pattern of successful people.

Practice Study Strategies in All Your Courses. It's important to continue practicing the success strategies that were presented in this book. Usually, you don't learn these in just one term or even one year. And if you don't keep practicing them, you'll get rusty. But we also realize that you may not have been ready to attempt some of the strategies we endorsed in this book. The next term or the next year may be a better time to revisit some of these ideas.

Hang on to This Book. There will probably be times ahead when this book will come in handy for dealing with special challenges in some of your future courses. You may need to revisit how to study, take notes, or prepare for different types of exams.

We know that students like to resell their books. If you do resell them, perhaps you could get library copies at some point in the future. But your books could be valuable resources when you might need to revisit course topics.

Consider Maintaining Your Momentum in Summer School. You may have learned in high school that summer school was usually for students who slacked off during the year. In college, nothing could be further from the truth. We now know from national research on college students' progress that continuous enrollment is a good thing; it keeps students in the swing of things, they don't fall out of practice, and they are more likely to graduate on time. If you really need a break from campus, you could shake things up by studying abroad over the summer.

Consider an Internship.   An alternative to summer school is to find work that is connected to your education or sponsored by your college, like an internship or practicum. Continuing your learning by working in the summer maintains your fast pace of uninterrupted development and doesn't allow you to backtrack and get out of practice. Also, students who have held summer jobs or internships are often more attractive to future employers.

Start Planning Your Remaining Time in College.   As you end this course, we suggest that you plan for the rest of your college career. First, think seriously about your major. That decision is important because eventually you have to get a degree in something, and you want to feel confident and comfortable about the major you select. If you're not happy with your choice of major, don't worry. Unlike in the rest of the world, U.S. colleges and universities give students the opportunity to change majors. So this is something we encourage you to revisit now. This course may have given you some new insights into yourself and what might really motivate you now and in the future. Whether you continue with or change your major, you will want to create a tentative plan for the courses you are going to take for the balance of your undergraduate career. If your college has degree-audit software for long-term course planning, use it. You also need a plan for how you are going to finance college. And you need to think about what will be the best living arrangement in the future: on campus, off campus, at home, with old friends, with new friends, and so on.

Reassess Your Relationship with Your Academic Adviser.   Now is also a good time to ask yourself about your academic adviser. Are you getting what you need from this important relationship? If not, don't hesitate to request a change.

Use Your Institution's Career Center.   It's possible that you haven't used the career center yet, even though you learned about it in this course. Now would be a great time to visit the career center to learn about possible internships, summer employment, and additional help with decisions about selecting a major. When you visit the career center, use its career library and career guidance software to give you more insight into your fit for certain occupations.

Reassess Your Most Important Relationships.   Many students come to college with good friends from high school. Some come with a boyfriend or girlfriend. Are these relationships serving you well? Do they still meet your needs, or is it time to move on? College success is achieved in and through relationships with others. They really matter to your sense of well-being and overall success.

Reassess the Merits of Your College Choice.   Now that you have been in college for at least a term, what are your thoughts about the wisdom of your college choice? Does this institution seem to be a good "fit" for your interests, needs, and values? Do you feel at home here yet? If you are getting pressure from family or a significant other to transfer, have you given yourself a chance at the place where you started? Changing colleges is not easy. Is this the best time to move on? Or do you need to hunker down and make the most of your initial choice?

Take Stock.   Ending a course like this is a good time to take stock of your accomplishments this term. By all means, you should pat yourself on the back. But you also may want to take a hard look at those things that didn't go so well. Learn from your mistakes and apply what you learn to future decisions.

Think about Your Purpose and Goals for Being in College.   Let's circle back to the concept of purpose. Here at the end of the term, do you feel that this particular institution is helping you find your sense of purpose and meet your goals? Of course, your goals may change during the college years. What may have felt like a good fit when you began college may no longer be appropriate for you. Practice the goal-setting strategies we have tried to teach you in this book.

Think Commitment.   When you think about it, nobody can be successful without commitment. Whether we are talking about the president of the United States, a great athlete, or a great musician or actor, anybody who is really good at anything has commitment. You may feel you are not ready for a high level of commitment yet because there are still too many things that are uncertain about your major and your future life. That's perfectly natural. But at the very least, we urge you, we invite you, to make a commitment to returning to college next term and next year to get as much as you can out of this often unpredictable but life-changing experience.

Consider Giving Us Some Feedback.   We love to hear from our student readers as well as our teaching colleagues, such as the instructor of this course. You can write Betsy at **barefoot@jngi.org** or John at **gardner@jngi.org**.

In conclusion, we wrote this book to help students like you. Much of what we know about what students need to be successful we learned from our students. Thanks for giving us the chance to help you as you began *Your College Experience*. You've already come a long way from where you started, and there are many great college experiences ahead. So practice the strategies we tried to teach you in this book, and remember, if millions of students before you have made it, you can too. All you have to do is make the necessary commitment and the rest will fall into place.

Sincerely,

John N. Gardner
Betsy O. Barefoot

GLOSSARY

abstract A paragraph-length summary of the methods and major findings of an article in a scholarly journal.

abstract conceptualization A learner's ability to integrate observations into logically sound theories; one of the four stages of the Kolb Inventory of Learning Styles.

academic freedom The virtually unlimited freedom of speech and inquiry granted to professors to further the advancement of knowledge, as long as human lives, rights, and privacy are not violated.

accommodators Individuals who prefer hands-on learning. They are skilled at making things happen, rely on their intuition, and might use trial and error, rather than logic, to solve problems. Accommodators often major in business. One of the learner groups of the Kolb Inventory of Learning Styles.

active experimentation A learner's ability to make decisions, solve problems, and test what he or she has learned in new situations; one of the four stages of the Kolb Inventory of Learning Styles.

active learning Learning by participation, such as listening critically, discussing what you are learning, and writing about it.

adaptability The ability to adjust your thinking and behavior when faced with new or unexpected situations.

annotate To add critical or explanatory margin notes on the page as you read.

argument Reason and evidence brought together in logical support of a claim.

assimilators Individuals who like to develop theories and think about abstract concepts. Assimilators often major in math, physics, or chemistry. One of the learner groups of the Kolb Inventory of Learning Styles.

aural learner A person who prefers to learn by listening to information. One of the preferences described by the VARK Learning Styles Inventory.

autonomy Self-direction or independence. College students usually have more autonomy than they did in high school.

biorhythms The internal mechanisms that drive our daily patterns of physical, emotional, and mental activity.

Boolean operators The words "AND," "OR," and "NOT." They are added to specific terms when searching in databases and search engines to help yield more relevant matches.

budget A spending plan that tracks all sources of income and expenses during a specific period of time.

chunking A previewing method that involves making a list of terms and definitions from the reading and then dividing the terms into smaller clusters of five, seven, or nine to more effectively learn the material.

citation A source or author of certain material. When browsing the Internet for sources, use only material that has citations crediting the author, where it came from, and who posted it.

cognitive restructuring A technique of applying positive thinking and giving oneself encouraging messages rather than self-defeating negative ones.

concrete experience Abilities that allow learners to be receptive to others and open to their feelings and specific experiences; one of the four stages of the Kolb Inventory of Learning Styles.

content skills Cognitive, intellectual, or "hard" skills, acquired as one gains mastery in an academic field. These include writing proficiency, computer literacy, and foreign language skills.

convergers People who enjoy the world of ideas and theories, and are good at thinking about how to apply those theories to real-world, practical situations. Convergers tend to choose health-related and engineering majors. One of the learner groups of the Kolb Inventory of Learning Styles.

Cornell format A method for organizing notes in which one side of the notebook page is designated for note taking during class, and the other as a "recall" column where main ideas and important details for tests are jotted down as soon after class as is feasible.

credit score A numerical representation of your level of fiscal responsibility, derived from a credit report that contains information about all accounts in your name. This score can determine your loan qualification, interest rates, insurance rates, and sometimes employability.

critical thinking Thoughtful consideration of the information, ideas, observations, and arguments that you encounter; in essence, a search for truth.

deep learning Understanding the "why" and "how" behind the details.

discipline An area of academic study, such as sociology, anthropology, or engineering.

discrimination The act of treating people differently because of their race, ethnicity, gender, socioeconomic class, or other identifying characteristics, rather than on their merits.

divergers Individuals who are adept at reflecting on situations from many viewpoints. They excel at brainstorming and are imaginative and people-oriented, but sometimes have difficulty making decisions. Divergers tend to major in the humanities or social sciences. One of the learner groups of the Kolb Inventory of Learning Styles.

dyslexia A widespread developmental learning disorder that can affect the ability to read, spell, or write.

emotional intelligence (EI) The ability to recognize, understand, use, and manage moods, feelings, and attitudes.

empathy Recognition and understanding of another person's feelings, situation, or point of view.

examples Stories, illustrations, hypothetical events, and specific cases that give support to an idea.

explanatory writing Writing that is "published," meaning that others can read it.

exploratory writing Writing that helps you first discover what you want to say. It is private and is used only as a series of steps toward a published work.

extraverts Individuals who are outgoing, gregarious, and talkative. They are good communicators who are quick to act and lead. One of the personality preferences described by the Myers-Briggs Type Indicator.

feeling types Individuals who are warm, empathetic, compassionate, and interested in the happiness of others as well as themselves. They need and value harmony and kindness. One of the personality preferences described by the Myers-Briggs Type Indicator.

financial aid   Monetary sources to help pay for college. Financial aid can come in the form of scholarships, grants, loans, work-study, and cooperative education.

freewriting   Writing that is temporarily unencumbered by mechanical processes, such as punctuation, grammar, spelling, context, and so forth.

grade point average (GPA)   A student's average grade, calculated by dividing the grades received by the number of credits earned. The GPA represents the level of academic success attained while in college.

Information Age   Our current times, characterized by the primary role of information in our economy and our lives, the need for information retrieval and information management skills, and the explosion of available information.

information literacy   The ability to find, interpret, and use information to meet your needs.

interdisciplinary   Linking two or more academic fields of study, such as history and religion. Encouraging an interdisciplinary approach to teaching can offer a better understanding of modern society.

interpersonal   Relating to the interaction between yourself and other individuals. Friendships, professional networks, and family connections are interpersonal relationships that can be mutually beneficial.

intrapersonal   Relating to how well you know and like yourself, as well as how effectively you can do the things you need to do to stay happy. Knowing yourself is necessary in order to understand others.

introverts   Individuals who like quiet and privacy and who tend to think a lot and reflect carefully about a problem before taking action. One of the personality preferences described by the Myers-Briggs Type Indicator.

intuitive types   Individuals who are fascinated by possibilities, the meaning behind the facts, and the connections between concepts. They are often original, creative, and nontraditional. One of the personality preferences described by the Myers-Briggs Type Indicator.

judging types   Individuals who approach the world in a planned, orderly, and organized way. They strive for order and control, making decisions relatively quickly and easily so they can create and implement plans. One of the personality preferences described by the Myers-Briggs Type Indicator.

keyword   A method of searching a topic by using a word related to the topic.

kinesthetic learner   A person who prefers to learn something through experience and practice, rather than by listening or reading about it. One of the preferences described by the VARK Learning Styles Inventory.

learning disabilities   Disorders, such as dyslexia, that affect people's ability either to interpret what they see and hear or to connect information across different areas of the brain.

learning styles   Particular ways of learning, unique to each individual. For example, one person prefers reading to understand how something works, while another prefers being "hands-on."

long-term memory   The type of memory that is used to retain information and can be described in three ways: procedural, semantic, and episodic.

mapping   A preview strategy of drawing a wheel or branching structure to show relationships between main ideas and secondary ideas and how different concepts and terms fit together and help you make connections to what you already know about the subject.

marking   An active reading strategy of making marks in the text by underlining, highlighting, and writing margin notes or annotations.

mind map   A review sheet with words and visual elements that jog the memory to help you recall information more easily.

mnemonics   Various methods or tricks to aid memory, including acronyms, acrostics, rhymes or songs, and visualization.

outsource   To contract out jobs to an external organization in order to lower costs.

perceiving types   Individuals who are flexible and can comfortably adapt to change. They tend to delay decisions to keep their options open to gather more information. One of the personality preferences described by the Myers-Briggs Type Indicator.

plagiarism   The act of taking another person's ideas or work and presenting it as your own. This gross academic misconduct can result in suspension or expulsion, and even the revocation of the violator's college degree.

prejudice   A preconceived judgment or opinion of someone based not on facts or knowledge, such as prejudging someone based entirely on his or her skin color.

prewriting   The first stage of the writing process. It may include planning, research, and outlining.

primary sources   The original research or documentation on a topic, usually referenced at either the end of a chapter or the back of the book.

procrastination   Putting off doing a task or an assignment.

racism   Prejudice directed at a racial group, which often stems from one group's fear of losing power and privilege to another.

read/write learner   A person who prefers to learn information displayed as words. One of the preferences described by the VARK Learning Styles Inventory.

reflective observation   A learner's ability to reflect on his or her experiences from many perspectives; one of the four stages of the Kolb Inventory of Learning Styles.

sensing types   Individuals who are practical, factual, realistic, and down-to-earth. Relatively traditional and conventional, they can be very precise, steady, patient, and effective with routine and details. One of the personality preferences described by the Myers-Briggs Type Indicator.

service learning   Unpaid volunteer service that is embedded in courses across the curriculum.

short-term memory   How many items you are able to perceive at one time. Memory that disappears in less than 30 seconds (sometimes faster) unless the items are moved to long-term memory.

social responsibility   The establishment of a personal link with a group or community and cooperation with other members toward shared goals.

sorting   The process of sifting through available information and selecting what is most relevant.

statistics   Numerical data used to support ideas in a speech or written work.

Supplemental Instruction (SI)   Classes that provide further opportunity to discuss the information presented in lectures.

syllabus   A formal statement of course requirements and procedures or a course outline provided by instructors to all students on the first day of class.

synthesis   The process of combining separate information and ideas to formulate a more complete understanding.

thesis statement   A short statement that clearly defines the purpose of the paper.

thinking types   Individuals who are logical, rational, and analytical. They reason well and tend to be critical and objective without being swayed by their own or other people's feelings. One of the personality preferences described by the Myers-Briggs Type Indicator.

transferable skills   General skills that apply to or transfer to a variety of settings. Examples include solid oral and listening abilities, leadership skills, critical thinking, and problem solving.

visual learner   A person who prefers to learn by reading words on a printed page or by looking at pictures, charts, graphs, symbols, video, and other visual means. One of the preferences described by the VARK Learning Styles Inventory.

CREDITS

INDEX

Note: Boxes, illustrations, and tables are indicated by (*b*), (*i*), and (*t*) following page numbers.